SUN S·P·A·C·E·S

NEW VISTAS FOR LIVING AND GROWING

PETER CLEGG
AND
DERRY WATKINS

A GARDEN WAY PUBLISHING BOOK

STOREY COMMUNICATIONS, INC.
POWNAL, VERMONT 05261

PHOTO CREDITS

The National Trust Photographic Library, Pg. 19 (1.1)
Courtesy of Bicton Park Trust Co. (Charitable Trust), Pg. 22 (1.6)
Greater London History Library, Corporation of London, Pg. 23 (1.7)
Pilkington Brothers, St. Helens, England, Pg. 23 (1.8)
Historic American Buildings Survey, Pg. 24 (1.10)
Mark Twain Memorial, Hartford, CT, Pg. 25 (1.11)
Courtesy of Mark Twain Memorial, Pg. 26 (1.12)
Courtesy of Alton Towers Leisure Park, North Staffordshire, England, Pg. 30 (2.1)
Photographer, Robin Jacques; Architect, Jacques & Adams, Pg. 32 (2.4)
Photographer, Alastair Hunter; Architect, Troughton McAslan, Pg. 33 (2.5 & 2.6)
Simon Doling, Pg. 34 (2.10 & 2.12)
Courtesy of Boston Shutter and Door, Inc., Pg. 78 (4.5)
One Design Inc., Pg. 82 (4.11)
Courtesy of Pella Windows and Doors, Pg. 89 (4.17)
Barbara Norfleet, Pg. 95
Kent Bloomer, Pg. 111

Unless otherwise noted, photographs by the authors
Cover design by Leslie Morris Noyes/Graphic Design
Edited by Sarah May Clarkson and Gwen W. Steege
Production by Nancy M. Lamb and Wanda Harper
Text design by Leslie Morris Noyes/Graphic Design
Front cover photograph by Simon Doling
Back cover photograph, left, courtesy of Lord & Burnham
Drawings in Chapters 6 and 7 by Judy Eliason; all others by Peter Clegg
Typesetting by Rawlston Type & Design
Printed in the United States by The Alpine Press

The following publisher has generously given permission to use an illustration. Permission is gratefully acknowledged for use of bio-climatic chart, Figure 2.16 originally appeared in Victor Olgyay, with Aladar Olgyay, *Design with Climate: Bioclimatic Approach to Architectural Regionalism.* Copyright ©1963 by Princeton University Press. Reprinted by permission of Princeton University Press.

The name Garden Way Publishing is licensed to Storey Communications, Inc., by Garden Way, Inc.

First printing September 1987

Library of Congress Catalog Card Number: 86-45974

International Standard Book Number: 0-88266-453-0 (paperback)
0-88266-452-2 (hardcover)

Library of Congress Cataloging-in-Publication Data
Clegg, Peter.
Sunspaces: new vistas for living and growing.

"A Garden Way Publishing book."
Bibliography: p. 202.
Includes index.
1. Greenhouses. 2. Garden rooms. 3. Greenhouse gardening.
I. Watkins, Derry, 1947- II. Title.
SB415.C527 1987 728'.9 86-45974
ISBN 0-88266-452-2
ISBN 0-88266-453-0 (pbk.)

SUN S·P·A·C·E·S

NEW VISTAS FOR LIVING AND GROWING

PREFACE

The history of architecture is
the history of the struggle for the window.

LE CORBUSIER

In 1981 we built a sunspace onto our old, Cotswold stone house. We had already written a book about greenhouses and read everything we could find about sunspaces/solar greenhouses/conservatories, but we were still surprised by the actuality of having a greenhouse attached to the house. No one had prepared us for the change it would make in the quality of life inside the house or above all for the changes it would bring to the course of Derry's life. A common theme throughout the interviews in this book is that the plants in a sunspace will absorb as much time as you are prepared to give them. Derry joyfully let our conservatory absorb virtually all her time and then had to look around for some way to make it support her addiction. So she began selling plants—cuttings, seedlings, offsets of everything she grew. First to friends and neighbors, then at a local market, now at several markets, and occasionally through the plant sales of a famous garden nearby. Our sunspace has provided her with a nearly full-time job.

Perhaps there is no way you can tell beforehand what effect building a sunspace will have on your life. But by offering a close look at other people's experiences of living with a sunspace on their house, we hope to map out some of the possibilities. This book is therefore retrospective—a look back at what it has been like for twenty-odd people. We talked to people all over the United States, and several in England, people of different ages, backgrounds, sexes, city dwellers and country dwellers. We included sunspaces of different sizes, from almost too small to turn around in to big enough to contain a small house, sunspaces built for different purposes, and on vastly different budgets.

We wanted to find out how having a sunspace affected people's lives; what problems they encountered, both in building and in using it, what changes they made, and what turned out to be the real benefits.

We are also fascinated by the theoretical underpinnings of how a sunspace works, how plants grow, how heat moves. A thorough understanding of this should help you to design and maintain, much more efficiently, a sunspace that will work the way you want it to.

We hope this is a book of ideas, inspiration, motivation, and human interest, full of details to try to include and details to avoid. With its help we hope you will get the sunspace you want and will enjoy it to the hilt. Let the sun shine in! ■

INTRODUCTION

Sunspace, solarium, attached greenhouse, glazed porch, conservatory—many terms for one thing, evidence of the different roles a mostly-glass room can take on. Whether for growing plants, collecting heat, or providing a pleasant place to relax, "sunspace" to us means any room that is enclosed primarily in glass. Usually, but not necessarily, it is on the south side of the house and can be shut off from the rest of the house, often with sliding glass doors which continue the impression of an all-glass room.

Why do people want to build glassed-in spaces on their houses? In the eighteenth century, glass conservatories were places to grow tender plants that could not be grown out of doors. By the nineteenth century they were often attached to the house, partly so the beauty and fragrance of the flowers could be easily admired, but even more to provide an exotic ambiance, a luxuriant tropical background for Victorian social life. After the First World War they fell out of fashion. Traditional conservatories are very expensive to heat and maintain and many were pulled down between the wars. In the fifties picture windows and sunporches took their place. Sunspaces are a relatively new feature in American houses. First, in the energy crisis of the seventies, people built them as solar collectors. Interest in self-sufficiency, energy conservation, organic gardening, and getting back in touch with nature all came together in the solar greenhouse movement. Soon, people found solar greenhouses attractive as living spaces, too, and in the more self-indulgent eighties, water barrels and vegetables have tended to disappear in favor of hot tubs and lounge chairs. Sunspaces are often built now primarily as attractive living spaces. The Victorian desire for an elegant ambiance, the image of a leisured life, the creature comforts of lying snoozing in the sun, exert a strong call.

Sunspaces are fairly flexible, they can be adapted to different purposes. But one designed specifically for solar collection can be converted to a comfortable year-round living space only at considerable effort and expense. In particular, the needs of plants for maximum light and ventilation should be designed in at the beginning; it is harder to add such features later than it is to remove those you don't need.

Everyone wants a sunspace that will heat their home, overflow with beautiful plants, and be the most comfortable and attractive room in the house. A sunspace can do any one of these things splendidly, but not all of them equally well at the same time. By compromising, the three functions can coexist, but the sunspace will then be a less than perfect heat collector, a less than perfect greenhouse, and a less than perfect living room. To avoid disappointment, it is usually best to choose a primary function and try to fit the other functions around it. At least one aspect of the sunspace will then work to your satisfaction, and some added benefit can usually be gained from squeezing in a few plants or chairs or venting some hot air to the house on sunny days.

There will be days when your sunspace serves all three functions well, but don't expect it to do so all the time. Some days it entices you out for a sunny breakfast, warms your whole house by midday, and seems to burst with healthy greenery. Other days it is too damp and chilly ever to open the doors to it, the plants seem to be pining, and you wonder why you ever built it. On still other days, when the thermometer tops 100°F. in the sunspace, both you and your plants would like to tear all the glass out and let the breezes in.

It is easier to make a sunspace successfully serve two functions than three. Extra living space is particularly easy to achieve in a sunspace designed for another purpose: just add more floor area and be prepared to heat it or cool it when necessary—an expensive but simple solution. Growing plants and collecting heat are less compatible, unless you provide for very high rates of heat transfer (see Chapter 4) and your house can handle high humidity.

The conflicts between the different functions a sunspace can serve often go unrecognized until the building stage is over and the sunspace comes into use. Then day by day, hour by hour, choices must be made. Shall I open the vents and let out the heat I will be needing tonight so that I can sit here comfortably? Or shall I let it get up to 100° while I cower indoors and the plants shrivel? Shall I wet the floor to add more humidity so the plants grow better and risk mildew on the north windows of the house? Shall I throw this plant out in order to make room for another chair or some more heat-storage materials?

Even more distressing once the sunspace is built, is the conflict between reality and the image you were hoping for. Whether you were imagining an elegant filigree of white wrought iron with cane furniture and palm trees, or a sleek sophisticated modern look, all smoked glass and tubular steel, the reality may be surprisingly clumsy. It may leak, it may be by turns too hot or too cold, it is likely to be too bright at times. It may prove too small, or be more expensive than you had planned.

The most important decision in designing a sunspace, and indeed in deciding whether to build one at all, should be made right at the beginning. What do you want it *for?* What do you hope to get out of it? Make a list of priorities, being as specific as possible about what time of day and what time of year you are likely to want to use it for what purposes. How much space will those activities occupy? What conditions need to be fulfilled to make them successful?

To help you think seriously about what you want from a sunspace, we have devised the following questionnaire. The italicized pros are followed in each case by the cons. Weight the importance of each factor on a scale from 1 to 10. Add up the pros and subtract the cons for each section. You may decide not to choose the option with the most points but at least the exercise will give you a framework for thinking in detail about what you want and help you to understand how important different factors are for different members of the family.

SUNSPACE AS LIVING SPACE

■ *Adds cheap, but attractive and elegant, additional living space*
Likely to be useful only sporadically, certain times of the day or certain times of the year only, unless heavily modified

■ *Delightful for basking in the sun even in winter*
May require additional heat for nighttime use in winter; or may be too hot in sun even when temperature is moderate

■ *May make rest of house seem brighter and larger*
May block light from rest of house and make house feel smaller

■ *Provides direct connection with outdoors—unobstructed view of woods, stars, and space*
Condensation between layers of glazing may be unsightly and/or impede view out

■ *Sunny, relaxing space, good for eating in, playing in, giving parties in*
Very large areas of glass to keep clean

■ *A potential workspace, exercise area, meditation room, music room, hot tub enclosure*
May lack privacy; glare may be too bright for comfort

■ *When used as living space only, automatic climate controls not necessary*
Hand-operated movable insulation and/or movable shading devices may be cumbersome

SUNSPACE AS GROWING SPACE

■ *Varieties of plants that do not grow well in house or garden thrive in controlled environment of greenhouse*
Plants can easily grow too big for space

■ *Can grow out-of-season, expensive, or difficult-to-find vegetables that are instantly available, fresh, and guaranteed organically grown*
Insects thrive, and diseases are quite common

■ *Useful for starting plants or overwintering tender plants for outdoor garden*
Trays of seedlings and other work in progress may be unsightly

■ *Can grow unusual flowers for house*
Plants generate dirt, dead leaves, and other debris

■ *Individual plants as well as massed groupings add beauty and fragrance to the house*
Pesticides and fertilizers add less desirable smells

■ *Looking after plants provides relaxation and pleasure*
The amount of time spent in caretaking can be considerable; it's hard to leave for more than a few days without a plant sitter

■ *Provides connection with earth and growing things even in winter*
May be too dark and/or too hot to use in summer

■ *Adds oxygen-rich, moist air to house*
Excess humidity, condensation, and mold may become problems in the house as well as in the sunspace

■ *Automatic controls can be timesavers*
Automatic controls break down and add to costs

■ *Overhead glazing will collect a lot of heat on sunny days to help warm the house*
Overhead glazing loses heat faster at night, may cause overheating in the day, and is more likely to leak

■ *Plants may be used for shading*
Plants themselves may need to be shaded in summer

■ *Plants tolerate cooler temperatures than do people*
May need auxiliary heat to keep plants from freezing, or, on the other hand, excess heat may need to be vented even in cold weather; large vent areas are prone to leakage

■ *Sunspace or greenhouse use may require less luxurious finishing, therefore may be less expensive to build*
All surfaces must be waterproof and easy to clean

SUNSPACE AS SOLAR HEATER

■ *Free heat once built*
Heat collection dependent on weather conditions and local climate

■ *Comfortable heat—no forced air, no reduced oxygen*
May need to overheat sunspace on winter days to store enough heat for night; may provide too much heat, especially in fall and spring

■ *Even heat distribution; no drafts, if reasonably well designed*
May provide more heat for upstairs than for downstairs of house

■ *May be able to use single-glazing, which is cheaper, if acceptable for temperature to plummet at night*
Allowing temperature to drop at night may make space unsuitable for plants and people

■ *Massive amounts of heat-storage material can be used to reduce extremes of hot and cold*
Heat storage materials most effective if placed in full sun, will compete with plants and people for space, may be unattractive, and, if intended to hold liquid, may leak

■ *Controls can be automated*
Automatic controls break down and can be expensive; fans can be noisy and/or drafty

■ *With no reliance on fossil fuels or other resources, satisfies one's ecological conscience*
Heat gained is unlikely to repay building investment for many years

■ *Possible state or local tax credits*
Tax credits apply only to parts of sunspace that are designed exclusively for solar heating

The questions that follow should help you get a clearer view of what sort of sunspace you want and also direct you to those parts of the book that are pertinent to your particular needs.

When you are clear about exactly what your needs are, it is much easier to achieve a space that will give you what you want. In the following chapters, after a brief history of sunspaces, we take a close look at what is needed in order for a sunspace to be a successful living space, a successful greenhouse, or a successful solar collector. Each chapter deals with one of these functions by first presenting basic principles, as well as current scientific research and the accumulated experience of everyone we talked to, and then by considering in detail how a sunspace should be designed best to fulfill that role. A selection of interviews follows. Looking at real life successes and failures grounds the theory, making it easier to grasp and to apply. We have tried to include interviews with a wide variety of people, living in different climates and wanting different things from their sunspace. Finally, we offer some detailed horticultural advice for the plant enthusiast.

Living with a sunspace on your house is quite different from living with solar collectors on the roof or a greenhouse in the garden. Unexpected problems as well as unexpected pleasures crop up. The sunspace is right there with you—it affects the rest of the house at all times. Everyone we interviewed had gone through at least two years of living with their sunspace. Almost all of them would want a sunspace on any house they owned, but many would modify the next one in the light of their experience. In this book, they give you the opportunity of sharing that experience so you can avoid the pitfalls and maximize the pleasures of living with your own sunspace.

HOW TO DESIGN YOUR SUNSPACE

The following checklist serves a dual purpose. It both takes you through most of the basic questions involved in designing a sunspace and acts as a subject index to the rest of the book. As you go through the questions, jot down those answers that seem obvious. Concentrate on the unanswered questions as you read the rest of the book. When more information is wanted, you are guided to the most relevant interviews in Part II and sections of text.

■ *If you want a sunspace primarily for people, read all of Chapter 2, and ask yourself:*

What will I use it for? Eating, sitting, working, playing, exercising, chatting?

Is privacy going to be a problem?

How can I moderate the glare? (See pages 38-39.)

How can I control the temperature? (See pages 37-38 and 77-84.)

How can I prevent fabrics from fading? (See page 40.)

■ *If you want a sunspace primarily for plants, read all of Chapter 3, and ask yourself:*

What kind of plants do I want to grow? Tropical, halfhardy, or hardy? Edible or ornamental? (See pages 50-51 and 149.)

Do I want to grow in pots or in ground beds? (See pages 64-66.)

How can I maximize winter sunlight? (See pages 46-48 and 72-73.)

How can I control humidity? (See pages 54-55.)

How can I control the temperature? (See pages 49-53 and 77-84.)

■ *If you want a sunspace primarily for solar gain, read all of Chapter 4, and ask yourself:*

How can I get the most heat? (See pages 69-77.)

How can I distribute the heat? (See pages 84-87.)

How can I keep the heat in at night? (See pages 77-79.)

How can I store the heat for later use? (See pages 80-84.)

How can I prevent overheating? (See pages 87-90.)

■ *How should the sunspace relate to the rest of the house?*

How will it relate to the other rooms? (See pages 32-33.)

1. Part of a larger room, such as kitchen, dining room, living room? (Osterberg, Thompson)
2. A separate room with an identity of its own? (Engel, Horner)
3. A circulation space—entrance porch or passageway? (Keil, Kenin)
4. A decorative space for other rooms to look into, but not much used by people? (Champion, Downey, Lycett-Green)

HOW WILL THE SUNSPACE JOIN ONTO THE HOUSE?

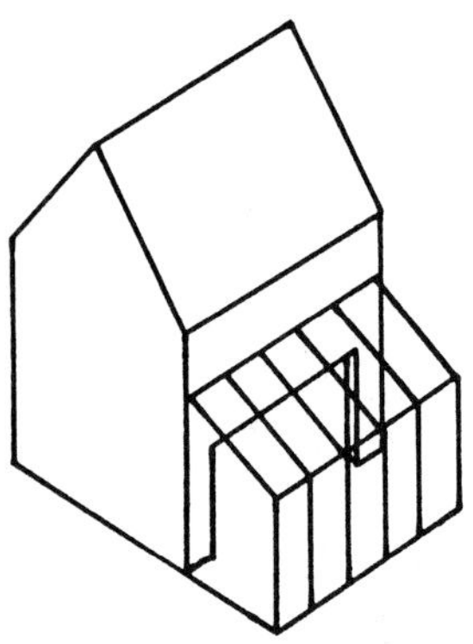

Completely open to adjacent room.

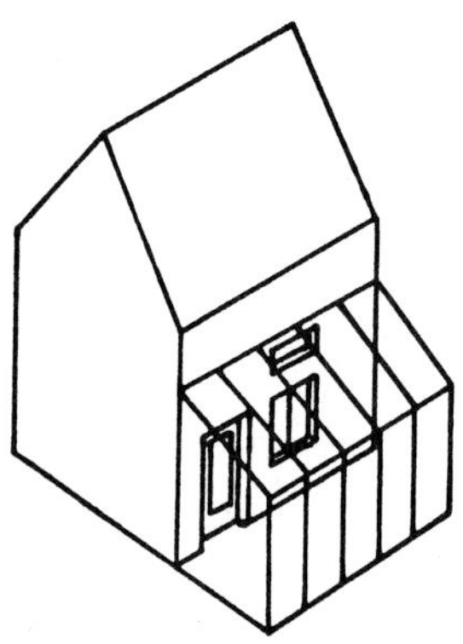

Partly divided.

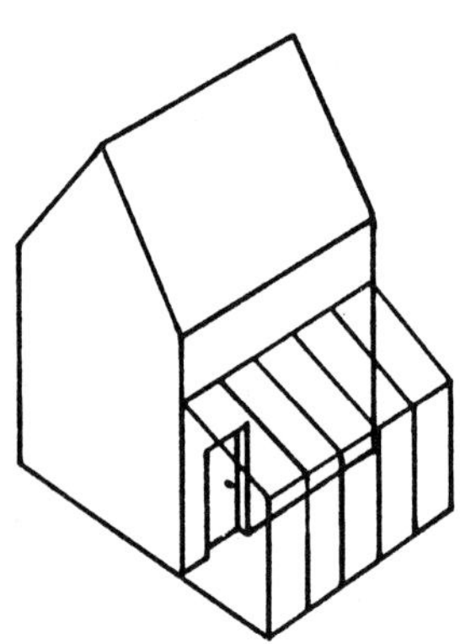

Solid Wall between.

5. A central room around which the whole house is organized? (Balcomb, Chalom)

How will the sunspace join onto the house? (See page 85.)

1. Completely open to adjacent room? Will extremes of temperature be difficult to control? (Deye, Orr, Osterberg, Thompson)
2. Partly divided? (Kelbaugh)
3. Compromise?
4. Solid wall between (which is better for solar heating and horticulture)?

- should the wall be mostly glazed? (Downey)
- should just the door be glazed? (Watkins)
- should there be windows into the sunspace? (Champion)
- should there be no visual connection? (Langer, Nakosteen)

How will the sunspace relate to the outside of the house? (See page 34.)

1. Blend in or contrast? (See pages 32-36.)
2. What about color?

- texture?
- roof angle?
- roofscape—pattern of forms?
- scale of house and sunspace?
- scale of materials?
- style?
- type of glazing and glazing bars?

How will the sunspace relate to its outdoor surroundings? (See page 30.)

1. Substitute for garden? (Champion, Keil, Reason)
2. Transition into garden? (Engel)
3. Transition into house—welcoming visitors? (Keil)
4. Outdoors but protected from the weather? (Keil, Nakosteen, Thompson)
5. What about doors to outside?
6. Should paving or walling materials from the sunspace extend into garden?
7. Should sunspace plants echo outside leaf shapes and plant forms?

■ *What should the sunspace look like?*

How many walls should it share with the house? (See page 32.)

1. One wall shared, with a projecting sunspace? (Huenink, Kelbaugh, Lycett-Green) With the sunspace wrapping around a corner of the house? (Spicer)

- provides maximum light and maximum heat loss
- hardest shape to integrate

2. Two walls shared, with the sunspace fitting into a corner of the house? (Chalom, Horner)
3. Three walls shared, with the sunspace embedded in the house? (Balcomb, Champion, Thompson)

- provides maximum insulation and maximum heat-transfer potential
- house walls will shade some part of sunspace at most times of day

HOW WILL THE SUNSPACE RELATE TO ITS OUTDOOR SURROUNDINGS?

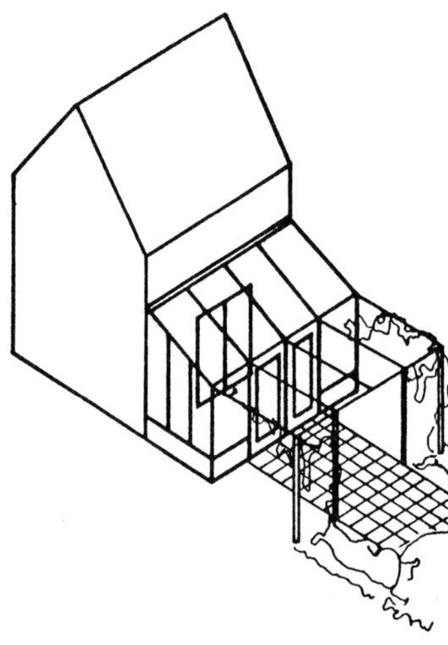

Transition into the garden.

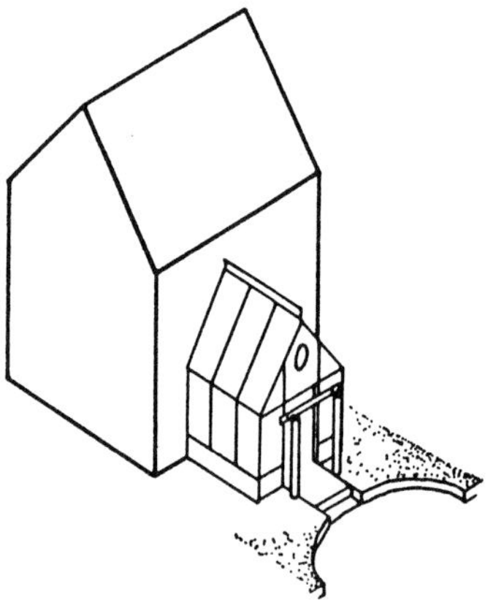

Transition into the house.

HOW MANY WALLS SHOULD IT SHARE WITH THE HOUSE?

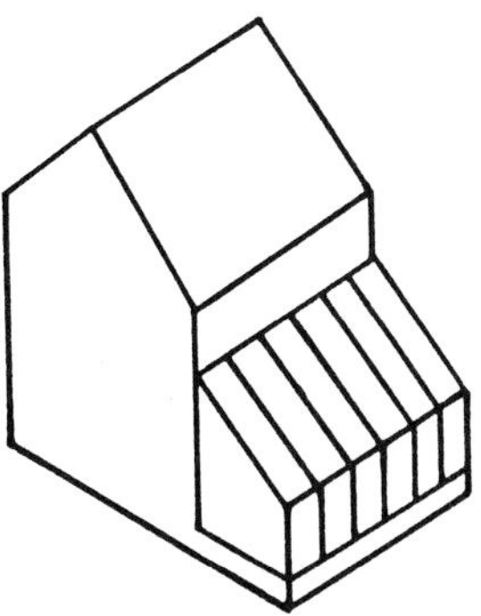

One wall shared.

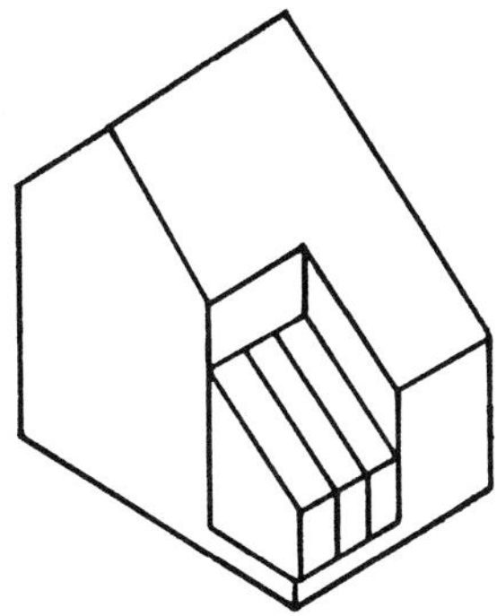

Two walls shared—sunspace fits into corner of house.

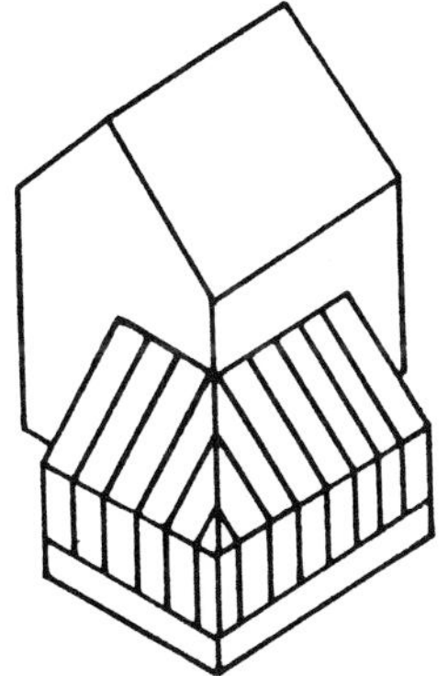

Two walls shared—sunspace wraps around the house

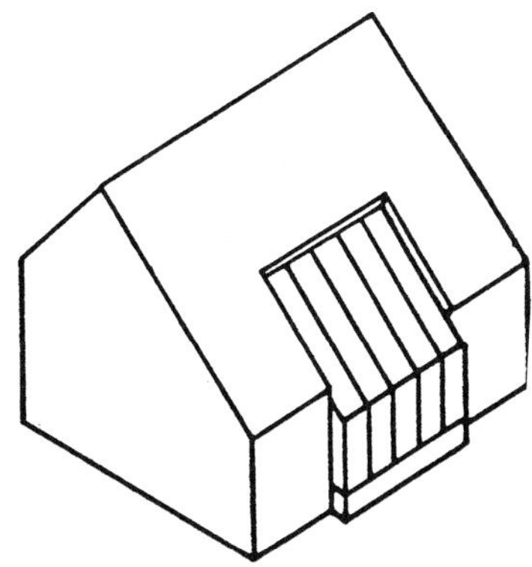

Three walls shared.

How big should it be?

1. How much space do I need? (Engel, Reason, Watkins)
2. How much space will the house allow?
- __ will it reduce light and ventilation in other rooms?
- __ will its height be adequate if limited by necessity to fit under eaves of house?
- __ how big can it be without visually overpowering the house?
- __ what are the local zoning ordinances, setbacks, etc.?

3. How much space can I afford?
- __ there is a direct cost-per-square-foot relationship, though the bigger, the more economical

How tall should it be?

1. One-story sunspace on one-story house? (Kenin)
- __ check eaves height, which will limit not only height of sunspace but depth as well, in order to keep glazing angle more than 15°

2. One-story sunspace on two-story house? (Kelbaugh, Watkins)
- __ check sill height of upstairs windows, as with eaves height
- __ consider enclosing upstairs windows to give better air circulation and heat transfer (See page 85.)

3. Two- or three-story sunspace? (Balcomb, Chalom, Engel)
- __ can link bedrooms and living rooms
- __ allows balconies and possible second staircase
- __ improves thermal performance, convection, etc.
- __ gives better light for growing, and allows much larger plants, even trees
- __ gives less floor area for each dollar spent
- __ is unusual in kit form

How much roof glazing should there be? (See pages 72-73.)

1. Totally glazed roof? (Jones, Kelbaugh, Watkins)
- __ maximum heat gain and heat loss
- __ maximum light for growing
- __ will probably need shading in summer
- __ problems with leaks and condensation fairly common
- __ must be strong enough to bear weight of accumulated snow

2. Part glazed roof? (Engel, Horner, Osterberg)
- __ shades back wall in summer; allows sun in winter
- __ good light for growing at front
- __ good compromise between reducing heat loss and maximizing light

3. Solid roof, vertical glazing only? (Nakosteen, Sparn)
- __ insufficient light for growing most plants in summer
- __ insufficient light for many plants in cloudy climates in winter
- __ good for winter heat collection
- __ little summer overheating
- __ fewer problems with leaks and condensation
- __ easier to build
- __ narrow growing area at front
- __ double height space improves light levels

4. Glazing angle as steep as possible? (See pages 47 and 73.)
- __ improves thermal performance
- __ reduces problems with leaks
- __ reduces snow loads

HOW TALL SHOULD IT BE?

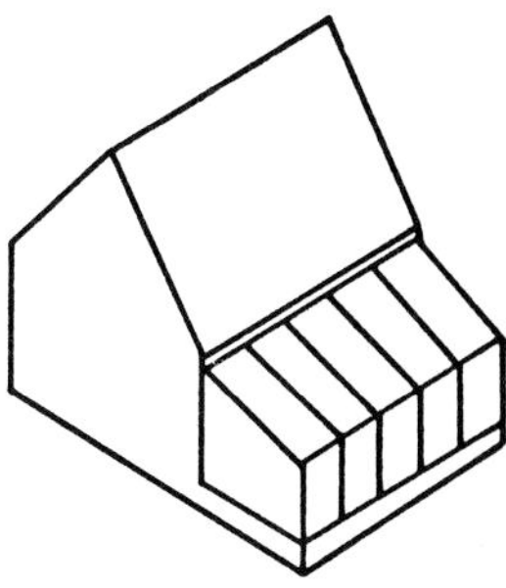

One story sunspace—one story house.

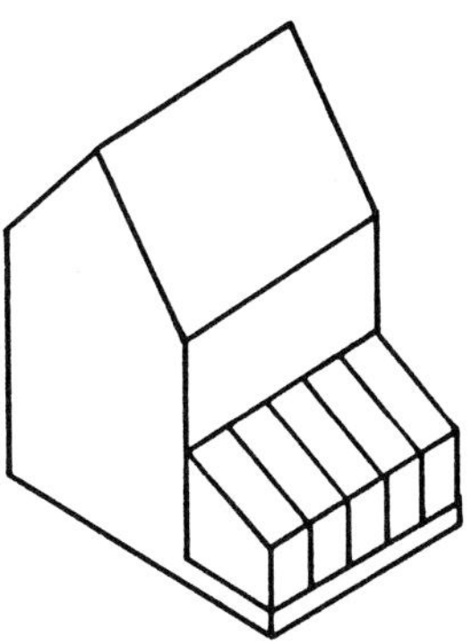

One story sunspace—two story house.

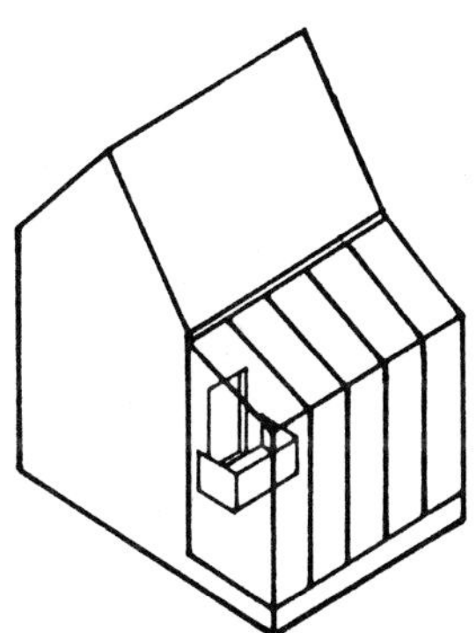

Two story sunspace—two story house.

HOW MUCH ROOF GLAZING SHOULD THERE BE?

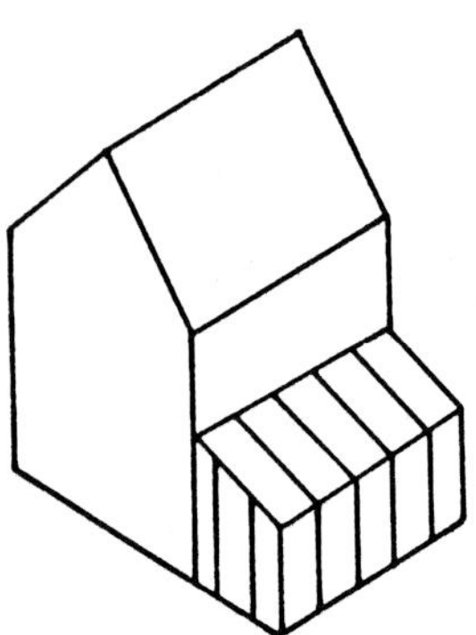

Totally glazed roof.

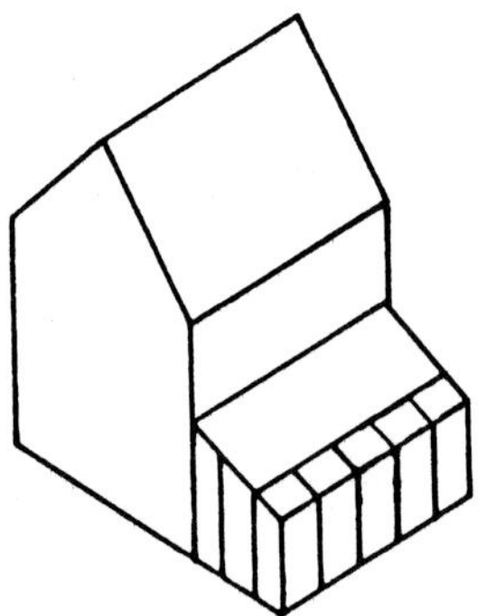

Part glazed roof.

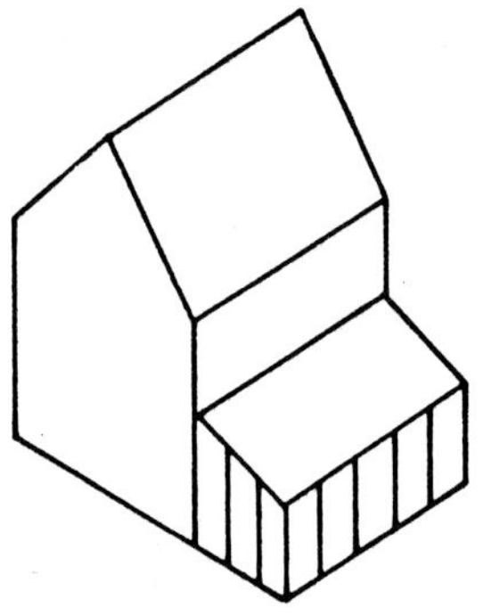

Opaque roof.

How much wall glazing should there be? (See pages 72-73.)

1. More glazing means more overheating and more heat loss; design to deal with both
2. Consider solid knee walls and/or solid end walls (especially on west side)

At what level should the sunspace be?

1. Below ground (pit greenhouse); floor dug out (Watkins)
- maximum growing space for amount of structure
- ground-level beds at convenient working height
- surrounding earth must be well-drained
- beware of undermining foundations of house

2. Ground level
- most convenient for access

3. Upper story (Deye, Reason)
- tricky to build; check that structure can bear weight
- can reduce shading problems
- have to carry all soil and other materials upstairs

■ *What direction should it face? (See pages 47 and 73.)*

South for solar collection and plants?

West, increasing overheating dramatically?

North, losing heat, but pleasant light for people?

East, good for people, acceptable for plants? (Spicer)

Do I wish a view out? view in? shading from nearby trees and buildings? (See pages 47-48 and 73.)

What position would best fit in with the rest of the house? (See pages 32-35.)

■ *Who should design it?*

Should it be designed and built especially for me? (Downey, Orr, Osterberg, Sparn, and others)

1. Important to find a local architect and builder with considerable experience of sunspaces.
2. Risk of design and construction failures (particularly leaks)
3. Relatively more expensive unless I build it myself
4. Usually takes longer to build
5. Easier to integrate architecturally
6. Shading and ventilation can be difficult unless carefully considered at the beginning
7. Can recycle old materials more easily (Huenink)

Should it be a standard kit adapted for my situation? (Deye, Watkins)

1. Manufacturer may help with design
2. Look for systems that provide maximum flexibility

Should it be a standard kit sunspace? (Kelbaugh, Kenin)

1. Quickest to construct
2. Relatively cheap, but consider additional cost of foundations, floor, opening to house, etc.
3. Look for ease of construction (ask for installation manual as guide)

HOW MUCH WALL GLAZING SHOULD THERE BE?

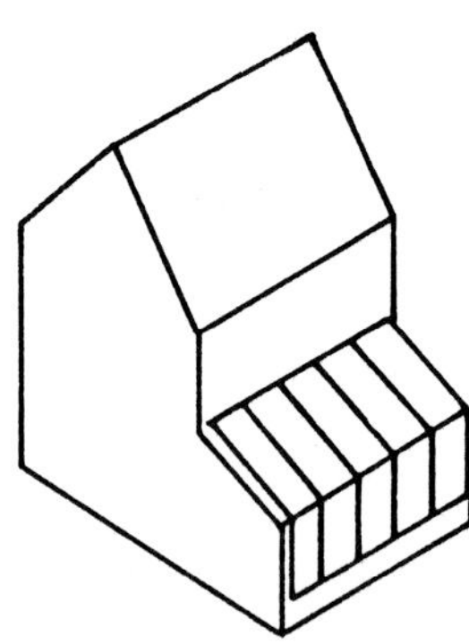

Opaque knee walls and end wall.

AT WHAT LEVEL SHOULD THE SUNSPACE BE?

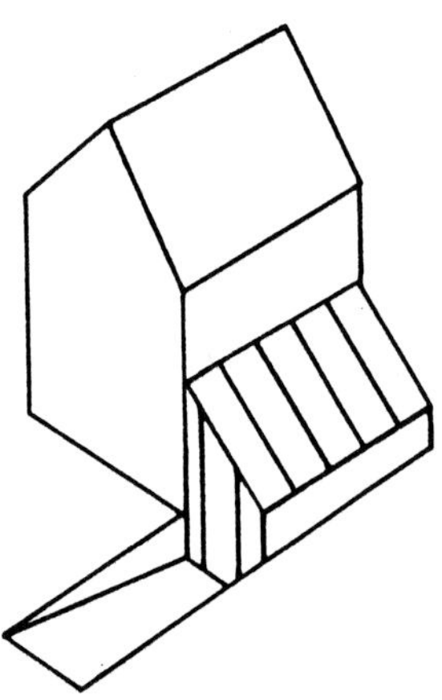

Below ground—pit greenhouse.

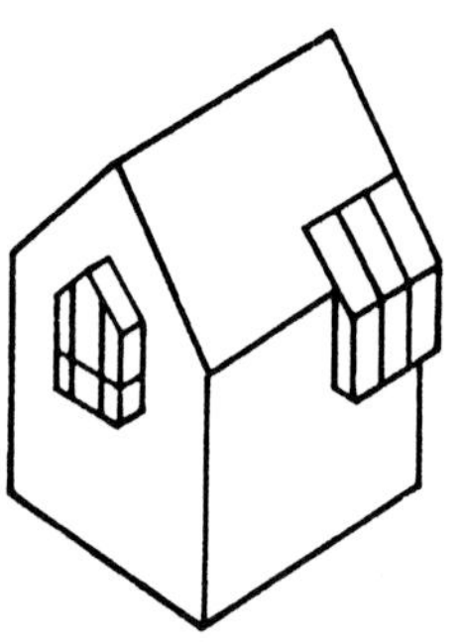

Upper story sunspaces.

4. Helpfulness of manufacturer or dealer is important; ask around
5. Guaranteed leakproof
6. More difficult to integrate aesthetically
7. Manufacturers stock and design for shading, ventilation, etc., but adequate ventilation for growing may not be included on standard model
8. Curved eave designs common in kit form, hard to build otherwise

■ *What should it be made of?*

Do I want it to blend in with or contrast with the house?

1. Consider color, style, scale, materials, roof pitch

Should it have an aluminum frame? (Deye, Kelbaugh, Watkins)

1. Thinner sections, therefore more light
2. Maintenance free if properly coated
3. Easier to guarantee sealed roof glazing
4. Difficult to adapt and attach
5. Hard to fit in aesthetically with most houses
6. Thermally more conductive; look for thermal break in glazing bar

Should it have a wooden frame? (Keil, Orr, Yanda)

1. Thicker sections, therefore less light
2. Annual maintenance required
3. Roof glazing requires very careful detailing to avoid leaks
4. Easy to adapt and attach
5. More easily integrated aesthetically with most houses
6. Thermally less conductive
7. Less harsh look

What kind of glazing should it have?

1. Consider longevity, safety, beauty, cost, handling ease
2. Glass? (See pages 74-75.) Single, double, or low-E coated?
3. Polycarbonate or acrylic? (See page 75.) (Jones)
4. Fiberglass? (See pages 75-76.)
5. Plastic film? (See pages 76-77.) (Kenin)

■ *Who is going to build it?*

Me? (Huenink, Orr)

1. It will take longer to build; is that acceptable?
2. Have I the time to do the work?
3. Have I the skill for all parts of the operation?
4. Can I organize all the necessary materials?
5. I will have no recourse in case of problems

Me, with some help from local contractors? (Engel)

1. Can I do
— excavation and foundation concrete work?
— external framed walls/masonry?
— glazing framework?
— roofing and insulation?
— glazing?
— internal drywall finishes?
— internal floor finishes?
— electricity?
— plumbing?
— decoration?
— external finishing?
— supervision/ordering and collecting materials?
2. Contract out those jobs I feel least confident about

A local contractor? (Deye)

1. Are they reliable? recommended?
2. Have they done this type of work before?
3. Will they come when promised and finish on time?
4. Will they come back and sort out problems that arise later?

Manufacturer to install?

1. Most expensive
2. Most reliable
3. They are definitely responsible for any problems that arise

■ *How much will it cost?*

Estimating the cost

1. Compare prices of different manufacturers, taking into account the cost of supplying the components that are not included, such as foundations, flooring, openings into house, etc.
2. Get estimates from local builders and architects as well
3. Consider phasing the operation by building the external skin one year and doing the internal decorations the following year.
4. Labor costs are often equal to material costs

Is it a good investment?

1. Generally sunspaces with high-quality interior finishes designed to be lived in are more likely to repay their investment on resale
2. Ask local realtors how much a sunspace will add to the value of the house
3. Will it increase my property taxes?

Tax advantages?

1. In certain states opportunities exist to write off against taxes a sunspace designed as a solar collector; check local regulations

■ *What else should I think about?*

Local building codes, fire regulations, and zoning ordinances

How will wind affect the sunspace both structurally and in terms of increasing heat loss?

Will snow fall on the sunspace from a higher roof?
What weight of snow and ice might accumulate? (Orr, Yanda)

Consider foundations, ground-water levels, soil type

Try to use standard size materials; they are usually cheaper, and there is less waste and less labor from cutting things to size

How long will it take to build?

How much will the building work disrupt my house and life? (Deye)

As you read this book, come back to this checklist from time to time to fine-tune your answers and to remind yourself what questions still need to be dealt with. ■

PART I

SUNSPACES FOR PEOPLE, PLANTS, AND HEAT

CHAPTER 1

A SHORT HISTORY OF THE SUNSPACE

Ever since the inhabitants of colder climates discovered the exotic plants of warmer regions there has been an interest in creating artificial environments in which to grow them. Northern European botanists developed the use of glass for horticultural purposes during the sixteenth and seventeenth centuries in their attempt to grow the plants brought back by explorers from all over the world. Glass was also becoming more and more important in other kinds of buildings at that time. The technology of building in stone and glass, developed for the late Perpendicular Gothic churches in England, was put to use in Elizabethan country houses such as Hardwick Hall (Figure 1.1), built in the sixteenth century and renowned as "Hardwick Hall, more glass than wall." It was a tremendous achievement to bring so much light into a building when a piece of glass could be no

1.1 ▲ Hardwick Hall in Derbyshire, built in 1685, by Bess of Hardwick, who was in many ways as strong a character as Queen Elizabeth herself. The phrase "Hardwick Hall, more glass than wall" was coined at the time to describe both its splendor and its difference from all other contemporary buildings.

larger than a few inches square, and the supporting structure was heavy cut stone and cast metal.

Elizabethan bay windows and oriel windows, which are like bay windows raised up in the air, push the glass out beyond the confines of the wall and so can be seen as forerunners of the attached greenhouse. The oriel windows at Montacute (Figure 1.2), which dates from the late sixteenth century, are a masterpiece of craftmanship in masonry, extravagantly detailed and ornately decorated. Their sole purpose is to allow inhabitants to step from the normal rectilinear confines of a room into a space which is more outside than in. The delights of view and sunshine brought a new dimension to the architecture of Northern Europe, which had previously focused on principles of enclosure and fortification.

The seventeenth century saw the development of horticultural science and the collecting of unusual plants in botanical gardens. But it was not until the following century that gardening itself became a popular and respectable pastime for the landed gentry. Fashions in garden design were started in Holland and France, where the formal style typified by Le Notre's garden at Versailles for Louis XIV set a precedent throughout Europe. Orange trees fitted well into the neat and clipped style of gardening practiced at Versailles. They were grown in wooden tubs protected in a heated undercroft to the main palace during the winter. In the summer they formed neatly regimented rows along the avenues of the park.

The orangery at Dyrham Park in England (Figure 1.3) was built by the architect Talman for William Blaythwayt, a politician and European ambassador, in the first decade of the eighteenth century. This was probably one of the first attached greenhouses in England, built onto the side of the main house and entered via one of the ground floor "apartments." It provided an artificially heated shelter for orange trees which, as at Versailles, were grown in large tubs and moved outside in the summer. The orange trees did not need much light in winter and in fact the roof of the orangery was originally of slate, to be replaced with glass in the nineteenth century. But the impressively large, arched sash windows to the east and south obviously delighted visitors to the house. Stephen Switzer in his *Ichnographica Rustica* (1718), one of the first books ever on garden design, gives an eloquent description of the building, explaining how it was used both in winter and summer.

1.3 ▲ The Orangery at Dyrham Park, Avon, England, a property of the National Trust. Designed by William Talman in 1701, it is one of the first examples of a greenhouse attached to a house. The walls are still more stone than glass.

1.2 ▲ One of the oriel windows at Montacute House, built in 1651 in Somerset, England, a property of the National Trust. Each end of the Long Gallery, which runs the length of the top floor of this large Elizabethan house, finishes with a flourish in a large oriel window.

To pass by the Magnificance of the Seat with the greenhouse adjoining it, is, I think, one of the most beautiful and commodious Piles for its Purpose, I ever saw; it is near one hundred Foot in Length and of a proportional Breadth and

Height.... This Green-house in the Winter is replete with all Manner of fine Greens, as Oranges, Lemons, Mirtles, etc. set in the most beautiful order; several Rows of Scaffolds one above another, are erected for this Purpose, on the Topmost whereof are plac'd the most tender, but largest Plants; and the Shrubs, Flowers, etc. below so as to make the Figure of a Slope with Walks between the whole Length, for the gardener to examine into the Health and State of his numerous Vegetables: The Inside of the House, if I mistake not, is cas'd with Bricks which keeps it naturally warm and healthy; there are several Stoves underneath at convenient Distances for Firing whereby a regular Heat is diffus'd over the whole House, and the Outside is so well guarded with Shutters in the Winter as to disdain the Fury of the most penetrating Winds....

[In summer] when most of the hardiest Plants are expos'd Abroad, it is usual here to preserve two or three Rows of Oranges etc. the Length of the House which make most beautiful and fragrant Walks within Doors; and the whole House is whitewash'd, and hung around with the most entertaining Maps, Sculpters etc. And furnish'd with fine Chairs of Cane for the Summer.

This description of the conservatory at Dyrham explains how the delights of a building contrived primarily for looking after plants produced spaces with a particular quality that intrigued the occupants of and visitors to the aristocratic country house. For the rest of the century the attached greenhouse remained an architectural feature composed primarily of masonry, often with elaborate classical decoration. It was basically a room with large windows and a lavish supply of heat for the winter, relying on considerable resources of fuel as well as human energy to care for the exotic plants it housed.

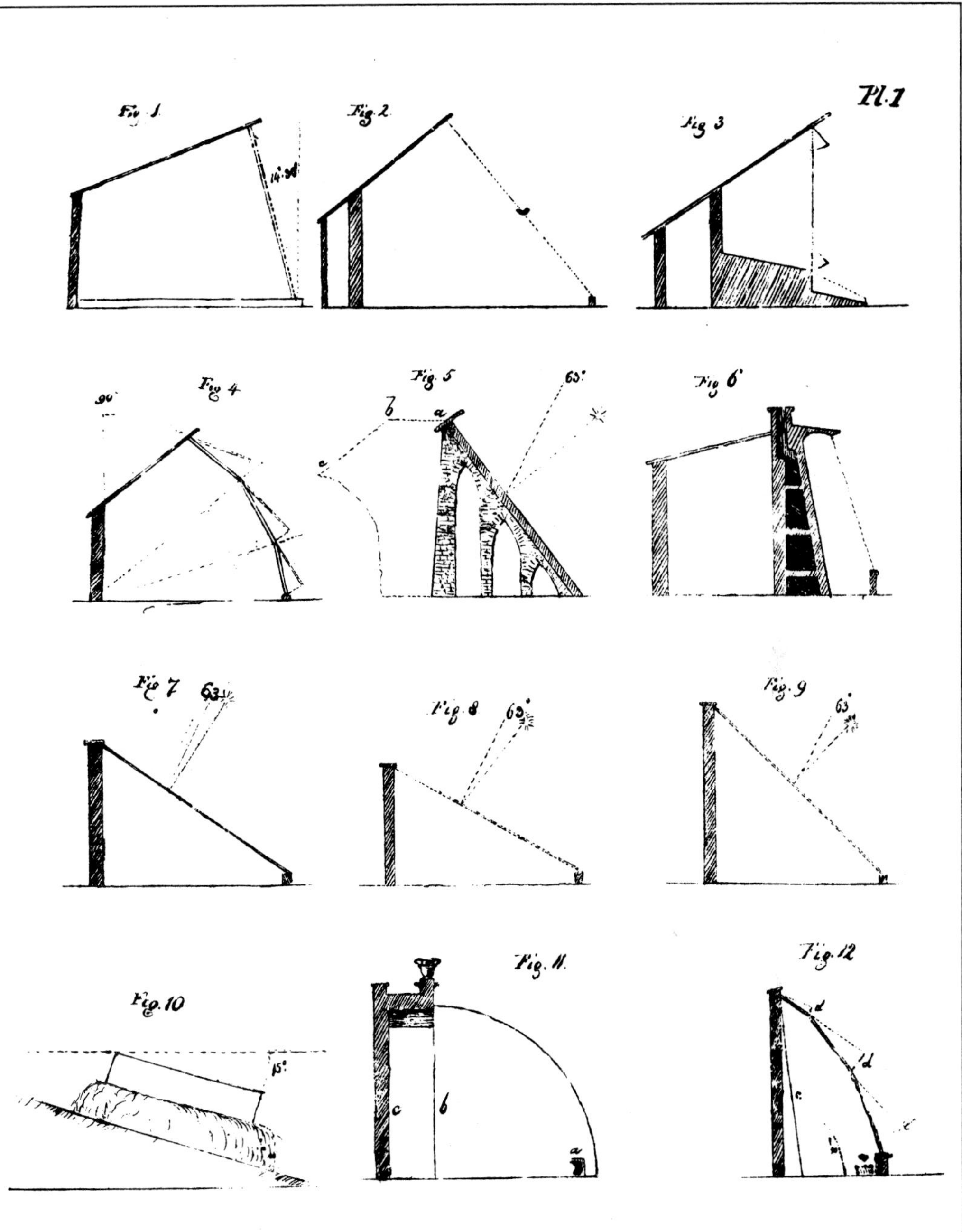

1.4 ▲ Illustrations from J.C. Loudon's *Remarks on the Construction of Hothouses*, published in London in 1817. Note that all his examples have south-facing glazing attached to a solid north wall.

Not until the beginning of the nineteenth century did gardeners and botanists demand more glass and less wall. This began a revolution in building technology that had far-reaching effects on all forms of architecture. The most influential of these horticulturalists was J.C. Loudon, who began the trend toward greenhouses with solid north walls and glazed roofs (Figure 1.4). He was one of the first greenhouse designers to look closely at the effects of different glazing angles capturing the maximum amount of sunlight, and he made a very careful study of the ways in which the framing members could be kept to a minimum in order to block out as little natural light as possible. If not the actual inventor of the ridge-and-furrow glazing system, Loudon was certainly responsible for developing and popularizing it in the early nineteenth century (Figure 1.5). Ridge-and-furrow glazing produced what is in effect a corrugated glass skin with alternate panes facing to the east and west. He believed this

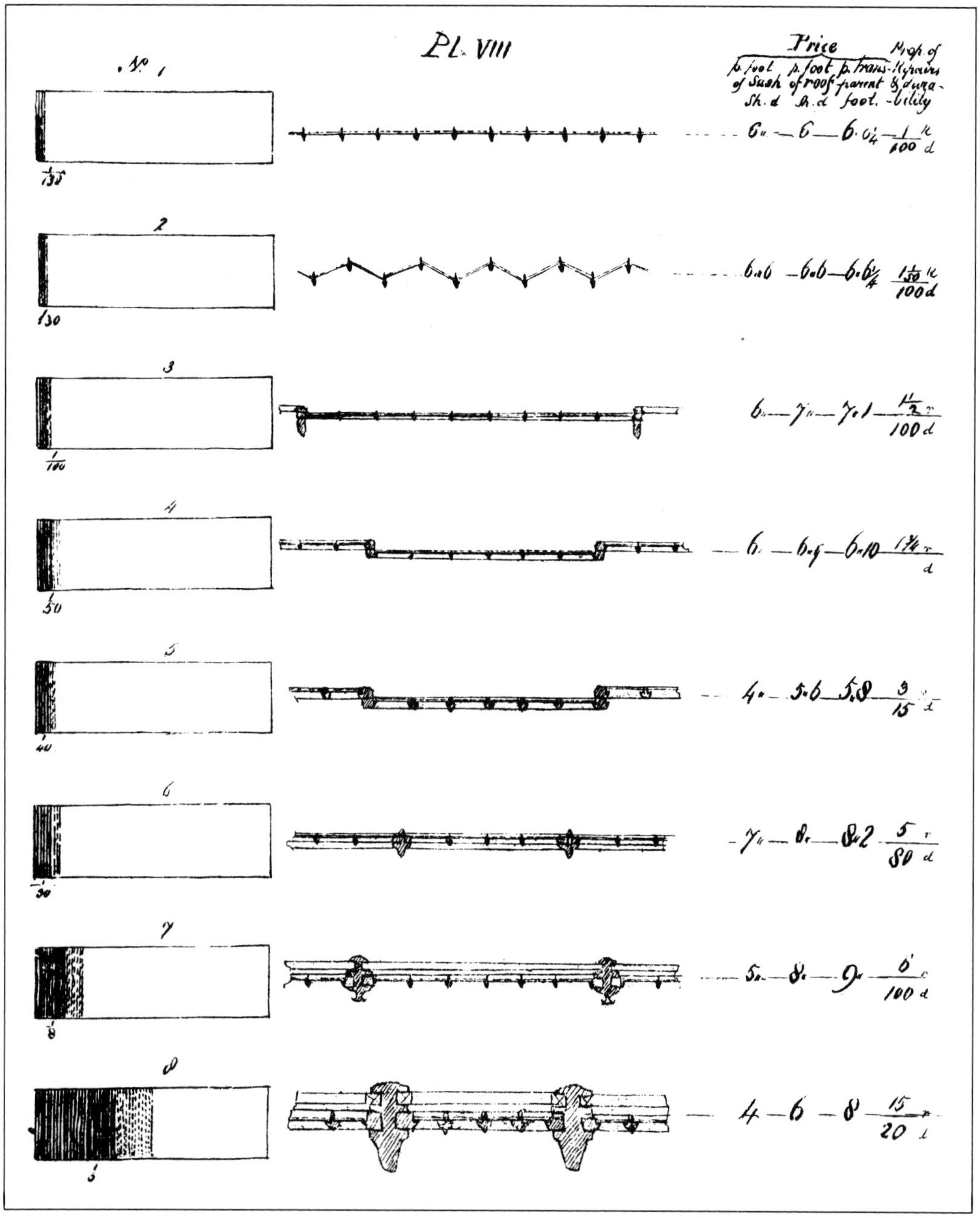

1.5 ▲ J.C. Loudon's comparative analysis of the effects on light levels of increasing the size of glazing bars. Ridge-and-furrow glazing is second from the top.

1.6 ◀ The greenhouse at Bicton Gardens near Exeter, England. The designer and the exact date of construction are not known, but it appears to have been built in the 1820s by the firm of W. and D. Bailey, whose work was based on the designs of J.C. Loudon.

would admit more solar radiation than a flat sheet of glass because the sun's rays were perpendicular to the glass for a longer period. Though this theory has subsequently been disproved, ridge-and-furrow glazing did have hidden structural advantages, in that the ribs formed by the glass itself could span fairly large distances with narrower structural supports.

Loudon also favored the use of hemispherical shapes for greenhouse glazing to provide maximum exposure to the sunlight and sky. Faced with a skeptical audience of architects and their aristocratic clients who preferred stone greenhouse buildings with traditional window openings, he launched an attack on the architectural profession for constructing greenhouses unfit for plants and for not being able to recognize the beauty of the simple functional qualities of glass and iron.

In respect to the principle of design or beauty, the foundation of which we consider, in works of utility at least, to be "fitness for the end in view" they [greenhouses] are no more subject to the rules of civil architecture than is a ship or a fortress; for these forms and combination of forms, and that composition of solids and openings which are very fitting and beautiful in a habitation for man or domestic animals, are by no means fitting and consequently not beautiful in a habitation for plants. Such, however, is the force of habit and professional bias that it is not easy to convince architects of this truth; for structures for plants are considered by them no further beautiful than as displaying not only something of architectural forms, but even of opaque materials. Fitness for end in view, we repeat, is the basis of all beauty in works of use, and, therefore, the taste of architects, so applied, may safely be pronounced as radically wrong.

Loudon's "fitness for the end in view" precisely foreshadows the twentieth century "form follows function." The functionalist modern movement in architecture was also characterized initially by the same delight that Loudon showed in radical new forms and in technology developed through advances in engineering.

Loudon's materials were cast-iron sash bars and thin fish-scale pieces of glass. At that time in England there was a tax on glass by weight, though the glass itself was sold by surface area. It made sense therefore to manufacture the thinnest possible glass, which in turn dictated the use of very small panes. The best surviving example of this type of structure is at Bicton Gardens near Exeter (Figure 1.6). It was most likely built to Loudon's design. The entire structure, rising 35 feet in the air, is a thin, curved skeleton of cast-iron bars no more than one and a half inches thick, covered with glass scales about ten inches long. It is a lean-to structure with a solid masonry north wall, though it was never attached to any other building.

The glass tax was repealed in 1845, and gradually manufacturers started producing larger sizes to meet the growing demand for conservatories and "winter gardens." In 1850 Joseph Paxton, designer of the Crystal Palace, the Great Exhibition Building in Hyde Park, persuaded his glass manufacturers to produce sheets 12 by 49 inches (larger than any that had ever been produced previously) and to produce it in such quantities as to be able to cover the nineteen acres of building in a matter of a few months.

Joseph Paxton began his working life as gardener for the Duke of Devonshire, under whose patronage he produced many splendid glasshouse structures. It was the Great Exhibition Building, opened in 1851 however, that earned him public acclaim and eventually a knighthood (Figure 1.7). Paxton designed it in a matter of weeks and erected it in less than nine months. It was 4,000 feet long and more than 100 feet high, completely covering an avenue of mature lime trees. One of the first great prefabricated structures, it was composed of cast-iron columns, glazing bars, and glass, all to modular dimensions. When the Great Exhibition was over, the Crystal Palace was taken down and re-erected at Sydenham on the other side of London. Paxton not only designed and engineered the building but also the machinery that produced the materials (his patented wooden sash bars) and the glazing trolleys that ran between the structural gutters and allowed the glaziers to keep pace with the carpenters (Figure 1.8). The building was a remarkable product of an age that had supreme confidence in its abilities to stretch the bound-

1.7 ▲ The Crystal Palace under construction. One of the two figures is Sir Joseph Paxton.

1.8 ▲ Workmen pose for a photograph during the reglazing of the Crystal Palace in 1899 after it had been moved to Sydenham.

aries of technology.

The Crystal Palace was undoubtedly very influential in the growing demand for domestic greenhouses in the latter half of the nineteenth century. For the country estate, ranges of greenhouses in the kitchen garden became commonplace, and the design of the greenhouses became very specialized. It was not unusual to have slightly different kinds of enclosures for peaches, grapes, and citrus fruits, as well as for decorative plants such as ferns, alpines, and orchids. It was at this time also that greenhouses attached to the house, conservatories as they were called in England, became popular. To some homeowners, the conservatory was their own miniature Crystal Palace, to some it was an exotic dining room with vines growing overhead so that dinner guests could pluck their own dessert grapes. To some it conveyed an image of Shangri-la, a paradise at their doorstep. To others it was primarily a decoration for the adjoining room, a pleasant view. Many more saw it as a space to sit in, so that the British summer could be lengthened at each end. For whatever reason, the conservatory became a commonplace, if not essential, adjunct to the home of the ever-increasing Victorian middle class (Figure 1.9).

The idea also became fashionable in the United States, particularly in areas such as the Northeast, which were heavily influenced by European fashions. The huge glasshouse for Colonel Merritt at Tarrytown, New York, was 380 feet long, incorporating a 100-foot central tower surmounted by a glass cupola. It was built by the firm of Lord & Burnham in 1870, and has recently been repaired and restored to its original splendor (Figure 1.10).

On a smaller sale, Mark Twain's exotic house in Hartford, Connecticut, de-

1.9 ▲ A Victorian conservatory illustrated in the catalog of Messenger and Co., which prefabricated structures like this and exported them all over the world.

1.10 ▲ The great greenhouse at Lyndhurst near Tarrytown, New York, recently restored.

signed by the New York architect Edward Tuckerman Potter, sported a conservatory which opened up from the library (Figure 1.11). The idea is reputed to have come from Twain's immediate neighbor Harriet Beecher Stowe, who at any rate saw to it that the conservatory was well furnished with plants. Glazed sliding doors separated the space. When opened, they disappeared into the walls on either side, making the two rooms one. A cloth blind could be drawn down to block the view into the conservatory completely.

The relative darkness of the surfaces within the library (most of the woodwork is mahogany, and the walls lined either with books or dark, stencilled wallpaper) threw the conservatory, brightly lit and full of luscious plants, into striking contrast. The entire building has now been restored faithfully to the state it was when Twain and his family lived there. Authentic details such as the Japanese lanterns, the bubbling fountain in the center, and even the type of plants have been used to recreate the conservatory, which also served as backdrop to the plays the Twain children put on for their parents.

1.11 ▲ Looking into the conservatory from the living room at Mark Twain's house near Hartford, Connecticut.

Twain's house is a freestyle extravaganza. With every inch of space cluttered with decoration, it epitomizes the late nineteenth-century, picturesque New England villa (Figure 1.12). The conservatory by contrast is a relatively modest and simple structure: the plants provide the exotic atmosphere.

But this was not true of many late nineteenth-century conservatories. In England, architects developed more and more fanciful decorative themes, and toward the end of the century conservatories in Gothic, Moorish, or even "Anglo-Japanese" styles became popular (Figure 1.13). Eclecticism was rife. Companies competed to produce ever more exotic fashions, and the growing of plants became very much of secondary importance. Throughout the history of attached greenhouses and winter gardens, we find a battle raging between horticultural scientists and style-conscious architects—the latter often coming out on top.

Victorian architecture could more easily accommodate glazed additions than could the earlier neoclassical styles, because buildings were more ornate and detailed, and glass became more significant. The popularity of bay windows and dormers recalled Elizabethan and Tudor precedents, once again extending the room to the sun and daylight outside.

In the period of austerity that followed the First World War, many of the large greenhouses and winter gardens of the nineteenth century were destroyed. Their maintenance costs in terms of both labor and fuel were extremely high. At the same time architectural interest shifted to the modern movement, where buildings constructed of steel, reinforced concrete, and large panes of glass brought a sense of spaciousness and light into the heart of the house. The conservatory, which pushed out beyond the confines of the house to reach the light, was no longer necessary, and the elaborate detailing associated with it was out of fashion. Simultaneously, horticultural interest switched back to outdoor gardens and to indigenous and hardy plants rather than tender exotics.

By the 1950s, the use of large areas of glass unbroken by glazing bars, or mullions, had become a conventional feature of suburban housing. The occupants began to realize, however, that such picture windows collected too much heat during the day and lost too much heat at night, although energy in those days was still cheap. Lack of privacy, overheating, and glare caused by too much glass were additional drawbacks.

1.12 ▲ (Bottom) The outside of Mark Twain's house gives some idea of the elaborate ornamentation inside. Courtesy Mark Twain Memorial.

1.13 ▲ (Top) A fanciful conservatory by E.W. Godwin, from *Artistic Conservatories,* a book of designs for Messenger and Co.

The answer to these problems seemed to be the attached solar greenhouse. It provided a space separate from the main living area of the house, where temperatures could fluctuate above comfort levels on sunny days when it was soaking up heat for the house at night, and below comfort levels at night when it was separated from the main house and acted as a buffer to reduce heat loss to the outside air. But at many times of the year it could also be used as a living space—breakfast room, playroom, or den—somewhere to sit and enjoy the winter sun. In addition it was a place where you could raise seedlings for the garden, winter vegetables, and possibly grow exotic plants all year round. For a while it seemed to be all things to all people. In reality, plants, people, and solar collectors have very different requirements. Balancing the needs of each is now seen to be the most difficult aspect of sunspace design.

The sunspace has come a long way from its ancestor, the nineteenth-century conservatory. Changes in technology, particularly in glazing materials, have altered it so much that it hardly seems to belong to the same species. But human aspirations remain the same. The idea of reaping the benefits of winter sunshine, whether for growing plants, for yourself, or for heating your house, remains fascinating. It all has to do with the magic of glass trapping the light and warmth of the sun for use indoors. ■

CHAPTER 2

THE SUNSPACE AS LIVING SPACE

Almost everything people do can be done in a sunspace. They can be used for everything from napping to exercycling, from raising rabbits or fish for food to giving elegant dinner parties, from drying the laundry to re-creating a lost paradise, from repairing old furniture to playing string quartets, from storing bicycles to wintering-over a garden's worth of plants, from learning to walk to playing dominoes, from dancing to hot-tubbing. No doubt they are as good for arguing in as for making love in.

DESIGNING A SUNSPACE TO SUIT YOU

Before embarking on designing a sunspace, carefully analyze what you want to do there and what else you hope to get out of it. If you want a living space and a good plant growing area but don't mind their being separate, perhaps an ordinary room with a small greenhouse extension would fill your needs better than a large glazed space where you have to sit amid the plants. Or if you want a sitting area decorated with plants, an ordinary room with extra windows and a skylight might serve your purposes better. If you want living space and heat for your house, a traditional room with an all-glass south wall would be cheaper to build and nearly as effective.

Think about the effect the sunspace will have on the rest of the house. Both the light coming from it and the views into and through it are important aesthetic considerations for the adjacent rooms. Try to put the sunspace where it will most benefit the rest of the house. Think about circulation patterns: Where will you most often be coming from when you want to go into the sunspace? Will it turn an otherwise useful room into a passageway? Think about the different ways in which it will add or reduce light in the rest of the house: Will it remove too much light and ventilation from the room it is attached to? Even a mostly glass structure will re-

A WINDOW GREENHOUSE

The most modest sunspace of all is a simple bay window. If it is designed to catch the sun through a full 180° arc and is packed with plants and a space to sit, it could fulfill all your desires without introducing many of the major temperature- and solar-control problems of a conventional sunspace.

2.1 ▲ The principal delight of traditional conservatories often derives from the shadow patterns cast by slender mullions, as in this mid-nineteenth-century conservatory at Alton Towers, near Manchester, England.

duce the light coming in by at least 15 percent. Will it send shafts of light into dark corners or add interesting shadow patterns to dull areas? (Figure 2.1). Will it be visible from sitting areas in the house?

Early on you must decide whether you want the sunspace to be a separate room or an extension of an existing room. If the sunspace is separated by a solid wall and thus functions as an additional room, visually and acoustically private from the rest of the house, you will have more control. You can let the sunspace get too hot or too cold for comfort without worrying about its effect on the rest of the house. You can also provide both thermal storage and increased insulation to the house. Excess humidity and unpleasant smells can be kept out of living areas, and mess can be concealed. On the other hand, if you remove the intervening wall you will add considerably more light to the house itself, enlarge the original room, and form new spatial connections between rooms, as well as a new connection to the out-of-doors.

Having a glazed wall between house and sunspace is a compromise between these options. The house gains in light and spaciousness without necessarily being heated or chilled by the sunspace. By making as many openings, both doors and windows, as possible, you will allow visual connections, but even more important, you will allow for heat transfer when you want it. Throwing open the windows on a sunny winter morning makes one feel that June has arrived out of season.

Wide open doors and windows make the sunspace feel like part of the adjacent room. As at Mark Twain's house (see page 25), the doors can be made to disappear into the walls, or they can open through 180° to fold back against the wall on either side. Sliding glass doors provide more glazing than ordinary doors because the framing members tend to be smaller. But usually one half slides back against the other so a completely open connection is impossible to achieve. A pair of outward opening doors, while more difficult to draft-seal, are often easier to use and give a better sense of unity. Remember that any large expanses of glass, particularly close to the ground, are hazardous if people fall against them, and the glass should be toughened or laminated.

Consider also the effect on the exterior of the house. The sunspace has to fit into your landscaping as well as suit the house. It should form a transition space, with the solid enclosure of the house giving way to a lightweight glazed structure, then perhaps to an open deck or pergola, and finally to the garden itself. The different degrees of enclosure offer increased possibilities for use at different times of year and soften the dividing line between house and garden. Extending the same flooring out of the sunspace onto a terrace or path into the garden will increase the sense of connection between the two. Having a working area in the greenhouse with direct access to the garden is also a great asset.

What image do you hope your sunspace will project? Many people assume a sunspace will achieve the elegance of a traditional Victorian conservatory just because it, too, is mostly glass. But careful attention to detail is necessary to reproduce that effect. The small panes and slender glazing bars that give Victorian greenhouses their crystalline delicacy are usually uneconomical today. Clip-on mullions can be used to break up the large panels of glass normally used, but a sleek modern look may be easier to achieve.

The other image that attracts people to sunspaces is

2.3 ▲ Large plants give this room a dramatic jungle air.

2.2 ◀ The bold use of fluorescent lights and gloss white paint produces the effect of brightness without any windows.

THE INTERIOR DECORATOR'S SUNSPACE

If it is only the image you are interested in, it is possible to achieve this with a more conventional house extension, putting the effort into careful interior design rather than into the exterior skin of the building. Careful design of both natural and artifical lighting combined with the use of highly reflective finishes can reproduce the brightness of a sunspace with much less than the usual amount of glazing. If you are trying to make the most out of a relatively small glazed area, use highly reflective white surfaces (Figure 2.2). They are almost as good at bouncing light around as mirrored surfaces are, but they diffuse the light, reducing glare and harsh reflections.

You can get the feeling of exotic greenery by using a few well-chosen, lush foliage plants like ficuses, scheffleras, monsteras, Boston ferns, and indoor palms (Figure 2.3). If you are not careful, however, you could reproduce the rather impersonal quality of commercial indoor landscapes. Try experimenting with color and a greater variety of plants.

Furniture will add to the effect—bamboo, metal, bentwood, or slatted furniture is so reminiscent of gardens we have known that it will help create a garden feeling indoors. Rough stone walls, wooden trellising, or even wallpaper in rustic patterns can enhance this feeling.

the sensation of being outside but protected from the weather. Surrounded by a starry night or experiencing a thunderstorm from the shelter of a sunspace can be truly exhilarating. The effort to remove the barriers between us and the world of nature became evident in early twentieth century architecture when the use of large expanses of glass gave architects the opportunity to blur the distinction between inside and out. The constraints on the window virtually disappeared. A technology of reinforced concrete, steel, and glass provide new freedom for designers.

Unfortunately, the majority of sunspaces we see today fall somewhere in between the small-scale, exquisitely detailed Victorian conservatory and the enormous sweeps of pure glass evident in modern architecture. On the one hand, the new generation of double-glazing materials, which are far more economical in large sizes, produces an architecture lacking in intricacy and detail. On the other hand, more often than not a sunspace is a small addition that cannot possibly make the bold statement of a modern office building. To take a traditionally built house

2.4 ▲ Robin Jacques designed a large sunspace into the corner of this house in the Orkneys in the north of Scotland.

with all the intricacy of small-scale materials (bricks, weatherboarding, glazing bars, shingles, guttering, downpipes, etc.) and add on to it a relatively small extension made out of large-scale materials often leads to aesthetic disaster.

The currently available range of off-the-shelf greenhouse additions, with curved eaves and glazing bar technology borrowed from larger buildings, has to be handled very carefully if added to a traditional building. The principal advantage of good quality kit-built greenhouses is that they are quick and easy to erect, and the components are carefully designed to avoid the many problems (expansion and contraction, water leakage, and the like) that often occur with custom-designed sunspaces.

If you are building a new house from scratch, or putting on an addition much larger than the sunspace itself, you can more easily integrate the large area of glazing with the house. It is often advantageous to build the sunspace in an internal corner and surround it with more solid parts of the house. Embedding the sunspace in the house allows it to be adjacent to more than one room. And by omitting the glazed end-walls of a conventional sunspace extension that sticks out from the house, the heat loss is reduced without sacrificing much winter solar gain.

The sunspace designed by Robin Jacques for the rigorous climate of the Orkney Islands off the north coast of Scotland is cleverly built into the corner of the house (Figure 2.4). By continuing and connecting both roof planes, and by using sympathetic detailing, the sunspace fits into the traditional building form and settles into the landscape very naturally.

By contrast, in another conservatory built a little further south in Scotland, the architects Troughton and McAslan sought not to integrate the new addition with the house, but to allow it to express its own identity as boldly as possible. The client's principle interest being to maximize the potential of the 180° view, the sunspace was raised to the second floor and juts out into space, making no compromises with the surrounding architecture (Figure 2.5). The sunspace becomes an elevated bubble, a building designed for looking out of rather than looking into (Figure 2.6). Its use of glass and steel obviously owes much to the precedents set by the great nineteenth-century conservatory makers.

These two extreme examples show how, in the hands of a good architect, it is possible to create an extension that succeeds either by achieving a sympathetic or a contrasting relationship with the existing house. Arguably the strong contrasting relationship is more difficult to achieve. Unfortunately, with ready-made designs what emerges is often a watered-down contrast—or misfit.

In our own conservatory (Figure 2.7) we were attracted to the aluminum kit-built product principally on grounds of economy but also because the glazing bar itself was very slender, and we wanted to ensure that as much light as possible came through the tall windows in the thick masonry wall behind. Tilting the glazing bars theoretically produced a glass wall that was more perpendicular to the winter sun and therefore increased our solar collection, but it also helped aesthetically, in that the greenhouse feels more like a lean-to with less identity of its own to compete with the main house. We also wanted to ensure that the greenhouse was as light and transparent as possible, not only for the plants but also in order to retain the solidity and integrity of the stone house behind.

As architects we find quite often that clients come to us with the idea that they might like an attached greenhouse, whereas in fact they have more pressing problems that need solving first to make their houses meet their needs. James Robertson and Alison Pritchard are a case in point. Both are firmly committed to energy conservation in buildings and to harnessing solar energy. She is an avid gardener, and they both work at home. They inherited a house that faced the wrong way for adding a sunspace for solar

2.5 ◀ **This second-floor sunspace in Lanarkshire, Scotland, was built by architects Troughton and McAslan.**

2.7 ▲ **In the author's own conservatory lightweight aluminum glazing bars contrast the thick masonry rubble walls.**

2.6 ▲ **Bright green, steel glazing bars maximize the potential of the view from an elevated, bubble-like sunspace.**

collection, and after several hours of discussion, we concluded that the kitchen, which faced north and was isolated from the other rooms, needed reconstructing to receive an infusion of sunlight and become the true center of the house. The sunspace therefore became part of the kitchen (Figure 2.8).

Because the Robertson/Pritchard sunspace faces southeast and is partially shaded by a projecting wing of the house, solar collection is limited. Horticultural use is compromised in that the space is primarily for human occupation. Both urges are nevertheless somewhat satisfied, and the house itself is a lot more livable. The double-glazed units are argon filled and have a low-emissivity (low-E) coating on the internal layer. This means that together with insulating shades, the family can use the space at night without feeling surrounded by cold, black glass. Triple-glazed rooflights admit more south light into the back of the kitchen and also ensure sufficient ventilation to the space in summer.

Another example where the addition of a conservatory was only part of a solution to reorganizing the house was the extension for Elizabeth Adeline and Peter Reason (Figure 2.9) on the front of a Georgian town house in Bath (see page 136). Here the family required an additional bedroom. The solution was to convert the existing large bathroom into a bedroom, and build an extension with a new bathroom on the second floor. The space below this formed an entrance porch to the house and the space above gave Peter Reason the attached greenhouse he longed for. It also admitted light, solar heat, and a feeling of space into the central stairway of the house.

Jeremy and Carolyn Walsh were faced with a sunless kitchen and a house closed off from the garden. The logical

2.8 ▲ The kitchen sunspace built into the Robertson / Pritchard house near Oxford, England.

2.9 ▶ The third-floor greenhouse on the Reason/Adeline rowhouse in Bath, England, was built above a bathroom extension over the entrance.

2.10 ▲ The sunspace for Jeremy and Caroline Walsh, near Bristol, England, forms a link between a north-facing kitchen and a south-facing garden.

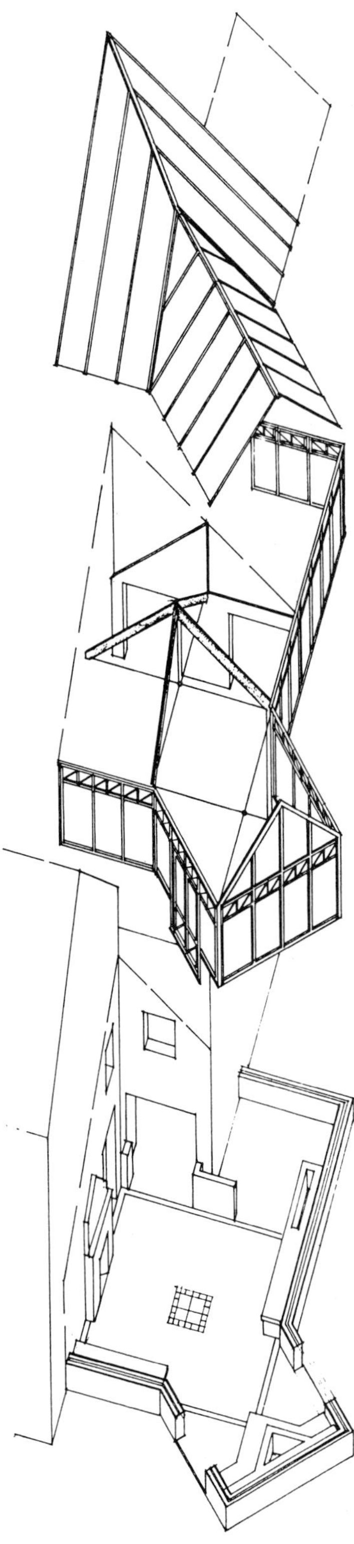

2.11 ▲ The architectural drawing shows how the Walsh sunspace wraps around the corner of the house and projects at 45 ° into the garden.

space for an attached greenhouse was in a northeast-facing corner of the building. By extending out from that corner at 45 degrees to the main house, a new connection was created between house and garden (Figure 2.10), and the greenhouse benefitted from a more southerly aspect. Both the kitchen and the dining room open into the main greenhouse space, which in turn opens onto two different areas of garden (Figure 2.11). The 45-degree geometry is carried through into the tiled work and the planting beds, and helps to form a gently flowing sequence of spaces from inside to out. This greenhouse is also double-glazed and in general uses large panes of glass. Great care was taken, however, with the intricate level of detail, which includes a cornice line of stained-glass panels along the top of the wall (Figure 2.12). The clay floor tiles, brick walls, and stained timber help to tie the new building to the earthy qualities of the main house.

The conservatory for Fran Landsman and her husband (Figure 2.13) is a halfway house between their living room and terrace, both of which have splendid views to the southeast. It was conceived as a simple and relatively cheap additional living space which, when double-glazed with low-E coated glass in the roof, would provide an extra room for more than half the year. It gets morning sun and warms up quickly, yet is protected from too much summer sun by the garage wall to the southwest. It is much more of a living space than a plant house (Figure 2.14) (the owners even have quite a liking for plastic flowers!). Once again the problem was how to bring the scale of the detailing down to the intricacy of the existing house. One solution here was to use an appliqué of trellis work around the eaves of the building, which produces another level of detailing, dap-

2.12 ▲ A cornice line of stained-glass panels ornaments the top of the wall of the Walsh sunspace.

2.13 ▲ Trelliswork applied to the outside of the structure on the Landsman house in Bath, England, breaks up the large expanse of glass into interesting patterns.

2.14 ▶ The Landsman sunspace combines color and comfortable furnishings with a wide-open view to make an ideal spot for good conversation and relaxation.

ples the incoming light, and creates shadow patterns reminiscent of traditional Victorian conservatories.

Many of the sunspaces we visited for this book manage to achieve a sympathetic relationship between a contemporary glazed structure and a traditional house. But architectural skill and judgment are often necessary not only to produce this sympathetic conjunction, but also to analyze carefully what is often a mismatch between the existing house and the occupants' needs. Those needs may be for more space, better facilities, more warmth, a higher real estate value, or healthier plants. An outsider with some experience in building design can look at you, your family, and your house, and help clarify what those needs really are and how the house could best be modified to achieve them. Ideally you should look for both an architect and a builder with experience in the detailing and construction of sunspaces. You can escape plenty of headaches, both on paper and on site, by using the skill and experience of a professional.

GETTING IT COMFORTABLE: SOME PRACTICAL CONSIDERATIONS

A sunspace designed only for living in does not need great

expanses of glazing, and certainly not overhead glazing. There is no need for it to face south; indeed north or east will often give a more pleasing quality of light. There is no need for bare masonry walls and floor. To be comfortable to live in a sunspace, like any other room in the house, must be warm but not hot, bright but not glary, and pleasing to look at. A traditional greenhouse addition will fill those needs only sporadically.

An all-glass Victorian conservatory (Figure 2.15) was beautiful to look at, but nearly always either too hot or too cold to sit in. When the sun shone it was certainly too bright for comfort until the plants grew up to form a jungle canopy. Modern attached-greenhouse kits suffer the same problems without the aesthetic advantages. They are not usually pleasant spaces to live in unless heavily modified. They have their delightful moments, but for human comfort much of the time the temperature needs to be modified and the glare reduced.

2.15 ▲ A typical Victorian conservatory from the late-nineteenth-century catalog of Messenger & Co., Loughborough, England.

MODERATING THE TEMPERATURE SWINGS OF A SUNSPACE

Compared to plants or solar collectors, humans are very intolerant of climatic extremes. We have grown to expect the air temperature in our houses to remain within a few degrees of the thermostat setting, and we are generally prepared to spend money and burn energy to keep it so. We don't expect to have to change our clothes when going from one room in the house to another. Nor do we expect the daily variation in outside temperature to affect the microclimate of our own house.

Most of us are unaware of the other factors affecting thermal comfort besides air temperature. First the surface of our bodies is cooled by air moving over it. This makes it possible to endure higher air temperatures with more air movement or, alternatively, lower air temperatures with less air movement. Second, our bodies respond to the radiant temperature of the surrounding surfaces. We can therefore sit comfortably in a greenhouse in winter with the sun beating down even though the air temperature may be very low. Conversely it takes a much higher air temperature to keep us comfortable when we are sitting in a greenhouse at night, since our bodies are losing a considerable amount of heat by radiation to the cold surface of the glass around us.

Third, the relative humidity of the air affects our rate of perspiration. Perspiring cools us, and our bodies find it more difficult to perspire in a more humid atmosphere. We can therefore cope with hot, dry conditions better than with hot and humid ones. Our only recourse in hot, humid environments is to increase air movement, which speeds up our rate of evaporation. Our skin is also sensitive to very high rates of relative humidity when temperatures are decreasing. This adds to the nighttime chilliness of the greenhouse. Finally, of course, we can adapt to temperature extremes by the use of clothing, although as Western civilization "progresses" it would appear that clothing is becoming more decorative and less functional. What we wear may be less responsive to daily and seasonal changes than it used to be.

All these variables are summarized in Figure 2.16, the "bio-climatic" chart devised by Victor Olgyay, who laid down the basic principles of environmental design in his book *Design with Climate.* It shows the human body's fairly narrow range of tolerance to changes in air temperature and humidity. The boundaries of the comfort zone, however, can be extended considerably, given beneficial variations in radiant temperature and air movement.

However cleverly we may use these climatic factors to balance out one another, the fact remains that, unlike members of the plant kingdom, we do not thrive on large daily variations in temperature. This makes any attempt to get an attached greenhouse for plants to perform equally well as an evening living space a very challenging task.

If you decide on a sunspace with a large glazed area for plants or heat collection, every energy-conserving measure you can afford will increase the time the sunspace is comfortable for people. Radiation temperature is the most significant variable affecting our comfort in a sunspace. The radiant heat of the sun makes us feel too hot during the day, and at night the cold glass drawing radiant heat from us makes us feel too cold. Double glazing increases the internal surface temperature somewhat, but low-emissivity glass maintains a higher internal surface temperature and therefore gives greater thermal comfort. Movable insulation is even more effective at reducing radiant heat loss and is highly recommended for any sunspace used often at night.

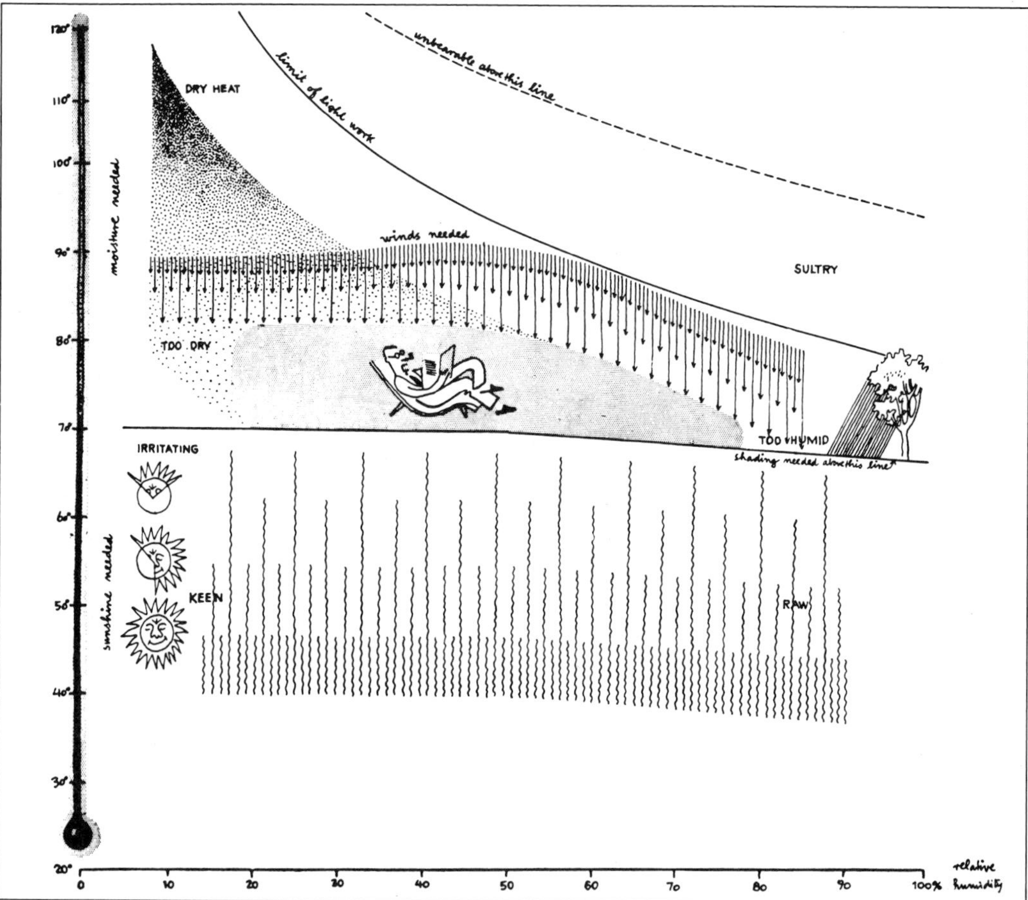

2.16 ▲ Victor Olgyay's bioclimatic chart, showing the human comfort zone on a graph of temperature and humidity.

REDUCING GLARE

Even when a greenhouse looks most inviting, say on a sunny day in March with outside temperatures below freezing, it can be hard to sit in without sunglasses. Snoozing in the sun is fine, but if you want to read or talk or even eat you may soon find yourself squinting or developing a headache. The contrast between dense shade under a solid roof and full sun under the glass is often uncomfortably strong. Anything that can moderate the transition will make the sunspace easier to live with.

Early morning and evening light is usually delightful but at midday some form of shading is generally necessary for human comfort. Anything from a sunhat to a beach umbrella to a canopy of vines will help. In summer, painting the overhead glazing with a shading compound or covering it with shade cloth will reduce both glare and overheating without interfering much with the view. But these are a nuisance to apply, well worth it for a season but not a job you would want to repeat daily. In northerly climates in the middle of winter little shading is needed even for people, and everyone is grateful for whatever sun there is. But in spring and fall, and even in winter with snow on the ground, there are many days when it is too bright for comfort, although you may want to collect all the available heat. A shade you can pull down over a particular area is valuable for making large areas of glazing easier to live with. Those you can adjust to admit different amounts of light are the most useful. But don't forget to open any shade as you leave if you want the plants to grow and the heat to collect.

Shading from plants or from fine trellis work creates a pleasant, dappled light (Figure 2.17). The small panes and numerous glazing bars in traditional conservatories contributed much to the delightful quality of the space inside.

SOLAR PEOPLE

People who live in passive solar houses find that in order to facilitate efficient solar collection they need to put up with greater climatic extremes than people in ordinary houses do. The house must be allowed to swing between 60° and 80°F. if it is to make the best use of the sun's energy. Some people have a distinct psychological preference for such variations in climate. Most find that their houses are quite livable with a greater range of comfort conditions than a conventional heating engineer would regard as acceptable. But for those who insist on a constant 75°F. air temperature, a solar greenhouse is not the best option.

Hanging baskets, vines trained under the roof, and small trees growing in the sunspace all help to break up direct sunlight into pleasing patterns. Vines can also be trained up the outside of a sunspace in summer. If they are annuals, or herbaceous perennials that die back in winter, they will let in all the winter sun. Deciduous vines are a nice compromise, dappling light somewhat even in winter. Translucent water storage tubes also cast a pleasant light, mottling the floor with shifting patterns (Figure 2.18).

Translucent glazing will diffuse the light and cut down the glare somewhat. But it is less beautiful to look at and overheats the space just as easily as clear glazing. It is usually most appropriate for the overhead sections of glazing or situations where you want to avoid view to the outside.

SPACE FOR PEOPLE

In order to be useful as a living area, a sunspace must meet one basic requirement: there must be enough room for people. Plants and heat storage materials will compete for every inch of sunny space. A sensible plan and an iron will are necessary to prevent them from taking over (Figure 2.19). Right at the beginning you should provide space for people, even if only for enough to squeeze in a deckchair for a sunny catnap. If you plan to eat in the sunspace, leave at least 9-feet square free. Four chairs and a small table may take up only 5-feet square, but by the time people are sitting in the chairs, they will need considerably more space to walk by without feeling crowded. Likewise, if you intend to use your sunspace partly as a playroom or workshop, be sure to allow at least 8 or 9 feet clear in each direction.

FLOOR COVERINGS

A sunspace much used by people needs an attractive, comfortable, smooth, easily cleaned floor. Glazed tiles are one of the most successful all-around floorings (Figure 2.20). They are handsome, durable, easy to clean, and relatively even for chair and table legs. Moreover, they store heat well, and they can be extended into the garden to ease the transition between inside and out. Less shiny tiles absorb heat better and are less slippery than highly glazed ones. The two main drawbacks of tiles are their cost (they are expensive both to buy and to install), and their hardness. Toddlers' heads and china plates will both suffer from a fall onto a tile floor.

A carpet will soften the impact and also the looks of the room, but it dramatically reduces the heat storage capacity of the area it covers. As the floor is one of the easiest places to locate masonry heat storage—and one of the best from the point of view of

2.17 ▲ (Top) Rush mats overhead dapple the light and reduce overheating in this California sunspace.

2.18 ▲ (Bottom) Kalwall water storage tubes absorb heat and reduce glare, letting only diffuse light through.

2.19 ▲ (Top) The Engel sunspace in Vermont is devoted to tropical plants, but one corner, defined by the rush matting, has been reserved for people.

2.20 ▲ (Bottom) Handsome, easy-to-clean quarry tiles store heat in this energy-efficient California sunspace.

even heat distribution—covering it wastes a golden opportunity. If for some reason the floor is not made of a heat-storing material, then carpeting is no drawback though obviously inappropriate in a plant space. If you want a floor surface that is not as hard as brick or tile, say for a toddler's play area, then linoleum or vinyl tiles, if well bedded into a concrete floor below, will provide almost as much heat transfer and will also be easy to clean.

Small, washable rugs will not reduce heat storage much and can be used to define sitting areas. Rush matting is cheap and attractive in a garden room, but will rot quickly if allowed to get wet. Rugs and carpets are a particular problem in a working greenhouse. Dirt and water constantly spill on the floor. Even if only the sitting area is carpeted, it is impossible not to carry the dirt there on the soles of your shoes. Concrete, flagstones, bricks, gravel, or tamped earth, often used as floors in horticultural greenhouses, are not very sensible in a sunspace designed for people. Hard, smooth surfaces are much easier to clean.

ELECTRICITY AND WATER SUPPLIES

Every sunspace will need lighting, and a power supply is useful for other appliances. If you plan to grow many plants, all electrical wiring and fittings should be used with a ground fault interrupter (GFI), since the high humidity levels make electrical problems more likely; GFI-equipped outlets cut off the power supply in the event of a short circuit. You should also consider using light fittings designed for exterior use. If you anticipate only normal levels of humidity and do not intend to splash water around, use standard electrical wiring and fittings following local building codes.

Lighting a sunspace requires careful thought. In conventional rooms the background illumination depends on bouncing light off the walls and ceiling, but in a sunspace the glass at night is not at all reflective, and the light will be wasted on the out-of-doors, though it could provide spectacular effects from the garden. Spotlights should point towards smoother and lighter surfaces in the greenhouse if you want to produce a high level of illumination. If you don't want to use directional lights, then use fittings with large translucent diffusers, since they reduce glare. Avoid placing the lights where they will cast a significant shadow during the day. Lighting large plants from below creates really dramatic nighttime effects.

If you are creating a sunspace primarily for plants, a water supply is essential in order to avoid trailing hoses and carrying buckets. Insulate the pipework in the sunspace if you intend to let the temperature drop below freezing in winter. Insulation will also guard against condensation on the pipes in summer, which causes unsightly stains and drips. A deep bowl sink with draining boards and a hot and cold supply would be invaluable for a committed horticulturalist, but a small cold-water sink and drain concealed in a corner would be enough for a parttime devotee.

CHOOSING FURNITURE FOR A SUNSPACE

If you want to live in your sunspace you will probably need furnishings to make it more comfortable (Figure 2.21). Soft, upholstered furniture, unfortunately, is not well suited to either a greenhouse or a heat collector. Many fabrics will fade severely in the bright and continuous light of a sunspace. A greenhouse full of plants will have a humid atmosphere which encourages mold and may eventually cause fabric to rot. Soft materials do not store heat well and stop the heat from reaching areas with a higher heat storage capacity. In a sunspace designed for heat collection they may seem worth the small sacrifice in heat, however, for the gain in comfort.

2.21 ▲ Soft furnishings make a comfortable sunspace for living in.

2.22 ▲ Wood and leather garden chairs are often used in New Mexican sunspaces, where they match the earthy tones of the adobe walls.

Garden furniture is often the most appropriate choice for a sunspace (Figure 2.22). It is designed to withstand both moisture and strong light, and it is usually easy to clean. Folding chairs are very useful where space is limited. You can sit in the aisle while you drink your coffee, then fold up your seat and turn the space back into a passageway when you are finished. Likewise, heat storage materials will be shaded only while you are actually sitting down.

In the nineteenth century the manufacturers who produced the cast-iron structures for greenhouses also made cast-iron furniture to match. It looks good in most sunspaces, is hard-wearing, easy to clean, and casts less shadow than most other types of furniture. But it is not very comfortable for prolonged sitting. Cane furniture can add to the tropical atmosphere of a sunspace but you must choose with care pieces that are both comfortable and easy to clean. You may find that insects treat cane furniture as additional plant material and a good place to hide during the day. If frequently splashed with a hose or allowed to sit in puddles, cane will quickly rot.

A good compromise is to use garden furniture with pillows or foam pads, which you can take into the sunspace when you want to sit for an extended time. If they are left there, expect to replace them fairly frequently. In either case washable covers will prove useful.

One of the most comfortable and entertaining options for furnishing a sunspace is a hammock. It takes up little or no room if one end is unhooked and laid over the other when not in use. It is fun and relaxing and somehow seems to suit the indoor/outdoor style of a sunspace. One drawback is that for energetic swinging you need considerable space or you will find yourself bumping into plants on both sides (Figure 2.23).

WATER FEATURES

Whether hidden from view or featured as a central element in the sunspace, water can make a big aesthetic contribution. Fountains, hot tubs, even swimming pools are becoming more common indoors. With a few basic precautions, a water feature can be installed in a sunspace with no great expense or upkeep.

From the slow drip of water falling on stones to the tinkle of a stream or the rush of a waterfall, the sound of falling water makes the most delightul background music; it adds another dimension of peace and tranquility, reminiscent of mornings sparkling with dew or indolent tropical islands. Many of the most beautiful flowering plants, moreover, grow at the water's edge or even under water. And a hot tub or indoor swimming pool tempts even the most confirmed puritan into self-indulgence.

ORNAMENTAL POOLS AND FOUNTAINS

Anything from half a wooden tub to a full-length swimming pool can be used to contain the water. It can either be sunk into the floor or free-standing. Flexible pool liners made of polyethylene, polyvinyl-chloride (PVC), or butyl rubber are normally used for ornamental pools sunk in the ground. Polyethylene is the cheapest and shortest lived; expect to replace it every two to three years. PVC and butyl rubber can be repaired if torn. PVC should last five to ten years and butyl rubber considerably longer than that. A flexible liner will conform to any shape of pool, with the pressure from the water holding it in place.

Rigid, preformed fiberglass or plastic pool liners are available, but they are more expensive and cannot be altered in shape. Both rigid and flexible liners will need a base molded to the correct shape, smoothed off, and lined with sand or old carpets to prevent punctures.

Precast concrete or stone "patio" pools do not need a preformed base into which to be set, as they are self-supporting, and thus are convenient if you want a free-standing pool. The edge of the pool can often be used as a seat and the water is a convenient height for looking into. But there is not much point in burying a patio pool underground as a much cheaper flexible liner will do the job as well. Likewise, casting a concrete pool in situ is not worth the trouble and expense.

Usually the water for a fountain or pool is recycled through a filter by a pump, and very little fresh water has to be added. A pump can create water currents in a pool, bubble the water up gently, spray it into the air, or raise it through a hidden tube to cascade down in a noisy waterfall or a slow trickle depending on the output of the pump. It also helps to oxygenate the water, thereby keeping plants and fish healthy. Submersible pumps are small, waterproof, and easily camouflaged under the surface of the water. But some system for replacing the water lost by evaporation should be installed to prevent the pump being exposed to the air. Air getting into the pump can create air locks which are difficult to clear. In an enclosed space it is important to choose a pump which is not too noisy. Some are so quiet you cannot hear them above the splashing of the water, but others hum quite loudly.

You can avoid the expense of a pump, by allowing a trickling fountain simply to overflow and supply the water for a ground bed. Care would have to be taken to get the amount of water right, and it would have to be adjustable so it could be much reduced in winter.

ESTABLISHING A POOL FOR PLANTS

A healthy pool should be faintly green but not opaque. Pools in

2.23 ▲ This hammock makes good use of the limited room available.

which the water is not circulated artificially will quickly turn into a thick pea soup of algae and slime unless a balanced ecosystem of plants and fish and snails is established. Plants provide oxygen for fish, which in turn provide nutrients for the plants. Water snails clean up plant debris (avoid snails with pointed shells because they feed on living as well as dead plant matter) and are in turn eaten by fish. Water weeds (underwater oxygenating plants) are particularly important in providing oxygen and in using up mineral salts which would otherwise feed algae. Larger plants shade areas of water, restricting algal growth. Ideally, plant foliage should cover about one-third of the pool, and one bunch of water weeds should be planted for each square foot of surface area to ensure sufficient oxygen.

2.24 ▲ A hot tub or spa adds interest and color, as well as an inviting place to relax away tension and fatigue.

Aquatic plants grow naturally at different depths. The sides of the pool should step down, forming underwater shelves every 5 or 6 inches, to keep the plants at the right level so they don't all slide down to the deepest point. Many plants will grow in shallow water, but fish prefer at least 18 inches of water. In summer a shallow pool will need to be shaded to prevent the water overheating.

Any good garden soil without too much fresh organic matter or fertilizer can be used. Heavy soil with a considerable amount of clay is an advantage. Six to 8 inches of soil can simply be placed on the bottom of the pool and plants will grow well there, but it is much easier to care for them if they are planted in individual containers. This also prevents invasive plants from taking over. Mesh sides on a broad solid base make the best containers. When planting up the containers, fill the top inch with coarse sand or gravel to hold the soil in place and discourage fish from nosing about in it. Leave the pool to settle down and the plants to establish themselves for six to eight weeks before introducing any fish.

2.25 ▲ A tight insulating cover for pools and hot tubs helps avoid problems of condensation in the sunspace.

POOLS FOR PEOPLE

Hot tubs (or "spas" as they are sometimes called) can be small enough to hold only one person at a time or big enough to accommodate a whole party (Figure 2.24). They were traditionally made of wood, but are often now made of preformed acrylic or fiberglass. Usually a seating level about half the depth of the tub is built into the rim.

Unlike a bath tub, a hot tub is designed for pleasure rather than cleanliness. It is a place to soak away your cares, relaxing in the steamy heat, perhaps being pummelled by water jets from the side or tickled by bubbles from below. The water in a hot tub is constantly being filtered and disinfected as in a swimming pool, so both soap and dirt are best not allowed in. Because the water is replaced infrequently there is no great need to connect to the water supply. Fill the tub with a garden hose, which may also be used to syphon the water out occasionally for cleaning. A drain in the bottom is of course more convenient, but considerably more work to install and connect.

All hot tubs need electricity to run the pumping and filtration system, and most use electricity to heat the water (usually 220 volts is required but sometimes 110 volts with a 20 amp plug will do). Some come with their own gas heaters, and some wood stoves can be adapted to heat hot tubs. The sun will pre-heat the water, keeping it over 60° for most of the year if it falls directly on the hot tub. Or in sunny climates, solar panes can be used to provide most of the heat.

A hot tub loses both heat and moisture to the air when it is uncovered, especially if bubblers or waterjets or splashing children are in operation. Plants love the resulting steam bath, but in cold weather the surrounding glazing is almost bound to cloud up with condensation. It is important to cover the tub with a tight-fitting insulating cover as soon as you finish using it (Figure 2.25). The condensation should then clear within a few hours. Brief spells of high humidity should create no problems in either the sunspace or the rest of the house, provided you have followed the rules about constructing vapor barriers on the warm side of any insulation and that you ventilate the excess moisture away quickly. Insulating the sides and bottom of the hot tub will help keep the heat where it is wanted.

The floor nearby will inevitably get wet as people climb in and out. The floor surface should be made waterproof and easy to mop up. And any electrical connections should be kept up out of the way.

2.26 ▲ A heated pool, while a luxury, provides opportunities for exercise and for moderating the whole building's temperature.

Most hot tubs are built in permanently, usually sunk into the floor, though wooden-sided ones can be very attractive freestanding features. Portable hot tubs are also available. They are self-supporting and can be plugged into any ordinary electric outlet. In either case it is very important to make sure the floor of your sunspace can bear the weight of a full hot tub—often several thousand pounds. A wooden floor will usually need reinforcing. Hot tub manufacturers can advise about such problems.

The ideal accompaniment to a hot tub is a cold plunge pool. Climbing lobster-red and steaming out of a hot tub and throwing yourself into a cold pool is an extraordinarily exhilarating shock. In size halfway between a hot tub and a swimming pool, a plunge pool offers all the exercise potential of a full-length swimming pool in less than half the space. A powerful jet at one end creates a current to swim against, making you swim upstream in order to stay in place. On some the current can be adjusted according to the strength of the swimmer. Wonderful for playing in as well as for serious swiming, but usually too shallow for diving. Some manufacturers combine hot tub and plunge pool in a hot "swim spa," ideal for elderly people who need to exercise in warm water.

For those with enough space and money, an indoor, heated swimming pool is the ultimate luxury (Figure 2.26). As with any heated pool it is important to keep it covered when not in use in order to avoid problems with excessive moisture as well as unnecessary heat loss. Swimming pools can be cast in place or assembled from preformed modules. Careful preparation of the foundation is vital to troublefree maintenance, and insulation all round the base will help to conserve the heat.

Whether in a swimming pool or a heat storage barrel, in an ornamental pool or a watering can, in a hot tub or a fountain, water will enhance your pleasure in and improve the performance of your sunspace. ■

CHAPTER 3

THE SUNSPACE AS GREENHOUSE

A sunspace can provide an ideal environment for many plants. But to use it in this way you must design it with the needs of plants in mind. And you must be prepared to spend the time necessary to look after them. Plants in an enclosed space need more attention than plants in a garden. They are utterly dependent on human beings for food and water and temperature regulation. Not a lot of time is required, but you must give it regularly. If you don't think you can rely on your faithful attention, don't go overboard in designing a sunspace for plants. They won't thrive even in a perfectly designed greenhouse without regular care. Better to design your sunspace for living in or for heating and then grow whatever plants will adapt to those conditions.

If growing plants in a sunspace *is* important to you, then careful attention to design will pay off. It is miraculous how quickly plants will reward you when their needs are met. In fact it is quite common to have problems with plants that grow too big too fast.

Plants you may have associated only with expensive florists will suddenly become easy to grow at home. Freesia, jasmine, orange trees, bulbs forced in midwinter—all are a cinch in a cool, well-lit sunspace. More spectacular flowering plants, such as stephanotis, orchids, poinsettias, and gardenias, are not quite as easy, but are quite possible if the sunspace is kept warm enough. You can feed your family fresh, homegrown vegetables all winter long if temperature swings can be moderated. In sunny climates even tomatoes are possible in midwinter.

Most people who like growing plants find looking after them in a sunspace more of a pleasure than a chore. The plants are happy and that is very seductive. Even the most disinterested visitors find themselves drawn toward the sun-speckled greenery of a healthy growing sunspace. The atmosphere is calm and reflective, the air is fresh, and often fragrant. Life slows down a bit and there is time to observe. Spending time with your plants, you learn what they like and what they don't. Your gardening skills fine-tune themelves to the plants you have in the conditions of your particular sunspace. And as a result the plants grow even better.

But watch out! A thriving greenhouse can easily absorb

hours of your time. There is always some little job that needs doing—something to be potted, pinched back, tied in, trained up, cut down. Under your tender care the plants may grow and multiply until there is no room for people and no time for other things in your life. So self-control is essential to a good gardener's survival in the sunspace jungle. Learn to say no to other people's overgrown plants (unless they will fill a definite need) and especially to their ailing plants. The invalids will quite likely revive in a healthier environment, but equally likely they will bring their ailment with them and infect your healthy plants.

For plants to grow well under glass, they need both an attentive gardener and a carefully controlled environment. In order fully to understand what they need both from you and from the sunspace, it helps to understand how they grow. If you understand why plants need light, fresh air, certain temperatures, and the like, you will be less likely to compromise on critical factors.

HOW PLANTS GROW

Photosynthesis is the basis of plant life and growth. It uses the sun's energy to power a complex chemical process. Chlorophyll, a green pigment found in the leaves of almost all plants, uses only one percent of the energy in the sunlight falling on the plant, but this one percent is the energy source which ultimately powers all life forms on earth. With the energy from light, chlorophyll is able to combine two simple, commonly available molecules, carbon dioxide and water, into complex carbohydrate molecules.

During photosynthesis, water is taken from the roots and carbon dioxide (CO_2) is taken from the air through the pores in the leaves. Hydrogen from water, and carbon and oxygen from carbon dioxide combine to form a carbohydrate with the help of energy from the sun. The oxygen in the water is given off as a byproduct. This process allows the plant to store the sun's energy for later use. When the carbohydrate is broken back down into water and carbon dioxide, it releases the energy used to fuse it together. Carbohydrates can be burned for energy, as in respiration, stored for the future as starch, or used as raw materials in the manufacture of leaves, stems, flowers, and so on.

MAKING SUGAR FROM SUNLIGHT

Photosynthesis is a highly complex series of chemical reactions, only some of which require light. The overall process can be summarized as $6CO_2$ + $6H_2O$ + energy from sunlight = $6C_6H_{12}O_6 + 6CO_2$. The product of photosynthesis, $C_6H_{12}O_6$, is a simple sugar. The plant stores excess sugar as starch (long chains of simple sugars wound around themselves). Starch is more compact, easier to store, and relatively insoluble, so it does not interfere with osmosis. When needed the starch can easily be broken back down into simple sugars. Both starch and sugar are forms of carbohydrate.

BURNING SUGAR

Respiration is the opposite of photosynthesis. It breaks down carbohydrates into carbon dioxide and water, giving off energy for the plant to use. $C_6H_{12}O49/6 + 6CO_2 = 6CO_2 + H_2O$ + energy. Respiration, like fire, burns carbohydrates by adding oxygen. In the process, they both release energy, using up oxygen and giving off carbon dioxide. Respiration takes place twenty-four hours a day, producing the energy needed to maintain the life processes of the plant. So plants give off CO_2 all the time, but when the sun is out a plant may use up to thirty times more carbon dioxide in photosynthesis than it is giving off in respiration.

The rate of photosynthesis dictates the rate of carbohydrate formation and therefore the rate of growth. The rate of photosynthesis depends on the amount of light falling on the leaf, its temperature, the carbon dioxide concentration in the air, and the amount of water and nutrients available from the roots. Take for example a plant in a greenhouse. Before dawn there is no light, so no photosynthesis. As the sun rises the light increases, and photosynthesis begins but will be very slow until the temperature rises. As the plant warms up photosynthesis increases until much of the available carbon dioxide in the greenhouse air has been converted into carbohydrate. Then the rate will drop appreciably until a vent is opened and fresh carbon dioxide-rich air rushes in. The rate of photosynthesis will then speed up again until perhaps the plant has used most of the available water in its pot. Then the rate drops again until the gardener arrives with the watering can.

Light, heat, carbon dioxide, water, and nutrients are all interdependent factors affecting the rate of photosynthesis. When one is in short supply, the plant cannot make full use of the others. We will now look more closely at all five factors.

LIGHT

Sunlight is the basic fuel that powers photosynthesis. At midday in summer there is far more light than a plant can use. For three-quarters of the year there is adequate light for good growth. But from November to February, in most of the continental United States, lack of light is the limiting factor preventing faster growth of indoor plants, so every effort should be made to maximize the light falling on the plants at that time.

The more glass or other glazing in the sunspace, the happier most plants will be in winter, so try to reduce solid areas of walls and roof to a minimum if winter growth is important to you. The shade cast by the structure supporting the glass can itself significantly decrease light levels inside. Metal glazing bars are usually thinner than wooden ones (which need to be larger to bear the same amount of weight), so a metal structure is often preferable in a sunspace for plants.

GLAZING MATERIALS

Different glazings transmit different amounts of light (see Chapter 4, pages 74ff). For optimum plant growth when light levels are low it is important to choose a glazing material that transmits as much light as possible. Keeping it clean is important, too, since dirt can easily reduce light transmission by 15 percent.

Translucent materials such as fiberglass may appear to reduce the total amount of solar radiation admitted, but in fact the total amount of light often remains the same. It is just dispersed, which increases the plant's ability to use the light because it falls more evenly over all the leaves. The effect is small but noticeable in low light conditions.

Double glazing cuts available light by about 10 percent, depending on the material. Each additional layer of glazing cuts the light transmission down by a further 10 percent. On the other hand double-glazed plastic units are more rigid structurally than single sheets, and so need fewer supports. The reduction in shading due to the reduced number of supports is sometimes sufficient to compensate for the increase in shading due to double glazing. Also because condensation is reduced on double glazing, light transmission may increase at certain times of the day.

Double glazing is highly desirable in areas with cold but sunny winters. But from the plant's point of view, it should usually be avoided in cloudy, mild areas. Movable insulation that keeps the heat in at night and does not reduce the light during the day is better for most plants where light levels are low.

If the back wall, the floor, the benches, and shelves are all light-colored, they will reflect the light hitting them instead of absorbing it. This increases the light falling on nearby plants, evening out differences in light distribution. Some of the light, however, will pass back out through the glass and the overall temperature gain will be slightly less. Aluminum foil is an even more efficient reflector of direct light, and the improvement in plant growth in front of a shiny reflector is marked when the sun shines. But under cloudy conditions it is negligible.

GLAZING ANGLE

To let in the maximum amount of direct sun the glazing needs to be at right angles to the incoming light. In winter when the sun is low this means the angle of the glazing must be very steep. In northern latitudes vertical glazing is perfectly satisfactory for admitting winter sun. But direct sun is not a very frequent occurrence in many areas during winter. In climates where cloudy days predominate, collecting the maximum amount of diffuse sky radiation is more important than getting 100 percent of the occasional ray of sunshine. In this case the roof of the sunspace is the most important source of light and as much of it as possible should be glazed at a relatively shallow pitch to collect light from the whole sky (Figure 3.1).

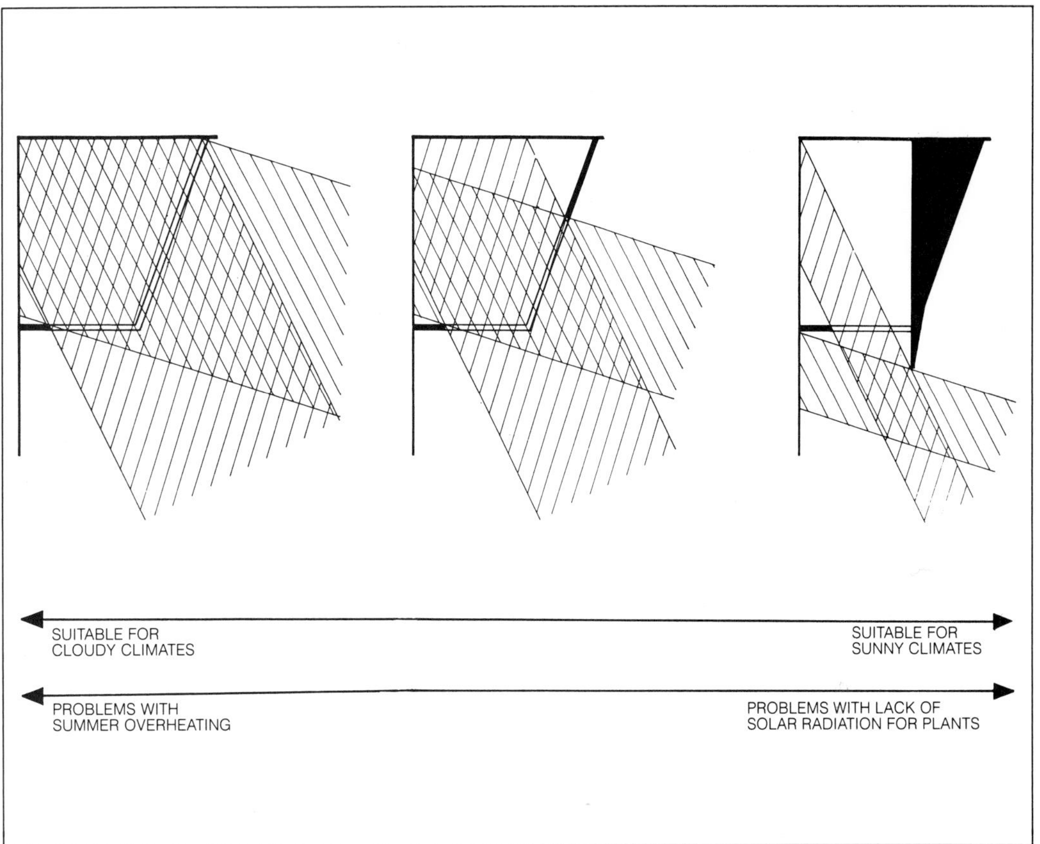

3.1 ▲ Optimum shapes for different climates. Plants need more overhead glazing in overcast conditions.

FOOL'S GOLD

Beware of colored glass, which can cut down light levels and affect plant growth in other ways. In particular, gold-reflecting glass, although it has very good heat retention properties, cuts out the wavelengths necessary to initiate blooming in most plants.

ORIENTATION

Most of the glazing should face reasonably close to due south. Slightly east of south is preferable to west, in order to warm the sunspace earlier in the day and allow photosynthesis to get started. A western exposure often causes problems with overheating in the afternoon. If you want to make one wall solid to reduce heat loss, choose the west wall rather than the east one.

Any shading in the winter is best avoided. Even a tree without leaves can reduce the available light considerably (see page 73 for calculating winter shading). Trees cast a shadow about three times their height in winter, so don't plant trees to the south of the sunspace if their final height will be more than one-third of their distance from the house. Equally important, the plants inside the sunspace should be

THE HIGHER THE BETTER

If the glazing needs to be vertical, make it as high as possible. A 12-foot-high glass wall will let in considerably more diffuse sky light than a 6-foot-high one. Plants respond to the amount of sky they can "see." So all-vertical glazing is more acceptable to plants in a two-story sunspace than in a single story.

WHY LEAVES ARE GREEN

Plants absorb red and blue light selectively. Green light is mostly reflected by the chlorophyll, which makes the leaves look green. Colored leaves—purple, red, brown etc.—have other pigments that mask the characteristic green color. But white and pale yellow areas of variegated leaves have little or no chlorophyll, so the plant's rate of photosynthesis is reduced and it grows more slowly.

spaced well apart in winter so they do not shade each other, even quite early or late in the day.

PHOTOPERIOD

The length of exposure to light can have nearly as important and profound an effect on a plant as the intensity of the light. Many plants are sensitive to the exact number of hours of light and dark they receive, known as the "photoperiod." They will usually grow well but refuse to set flowers or fruit until they experience either the short nights or the long nights they require. Some plants are sensitive to very small deviations from their requirements—as little as 15 minutes can upset them. Chrysanthemums and poinsettias are famous for needing long nights to set flowers, but usually the photoperiod response is a complex interaction of temperature, light intensity, and day length at different stages of growth. A little research into the conditions in which the plant would flower in nature will often pay off when coaxing a reluctant plant to bloom. Very low light intensities are sufficient to trigger photoperiod responses, so an incandescent light in the middle of the living room, which has a negligible effect on photosynthesis, may prevent a poinsettia on the windowsill from blooming, unless the curtains are drawn to keep it in the dark.

LIGHT INTENSITY

The amount of light falling on a plant in a sunspace is usually the main factor determining its rate of growth. Water, food, air, and warmth are all easier to supply than extra light once the sunspace is built. Artificial lights (see below) are expensive and unattractive compared to sunlight. So everything should be done to maximize the light entering the sunspace if plants are an important consideration.

In an existing sunspace it is well worth measuring the light levels in different areas. You may be surprised how little light there is even close to the glass. For perfect accuracy use a light meter that measures photosynthetically active light. But the light meter of any camera will give a good indication of how much light is available.

When light levels are low, spacing the plants well apart will help them to collect all the light they can. Keeping the leaves clean will allow them to use all the light that does fall on them. Wipe the leaves with a cloth wrung out in half skim milk and half soft water (rain water or distilled water are best) every few months. They will shine beautifully and grow faster. Dust on the leaves blocks sunlight. It also encourages burning where waterdrops have fallen on leaves in full sun.

ARTIFICIAL LIGHT

Where light levels are too low for good growth, they can be supplemented with artificial light. Almost all light visible to humans is useful, but the blue

MEASURING LIGHT LEVELS

Set the camera (or the light meter if it is separate) for a film speed of 50 ASA and a shutter speed of 1/125 of a second. Place a sheet of white paper where you want to measure the light (horizontal on a cloudy day or perpendicular to the position of the sun on a sunny day). Hold the camera or light meter one foot away, making sure you don't shade the paper in the process. Read the f-stop indicated by the meter.

At midday on a sunny day, f16 or f22 indicates plenty of available light. Flowering and fruiting plants should do well. At f8 to f11 most plants grow well, but flowers and fruit may be delayed. A reading of f4 or f5.6 is the equivalent of light shade, and most foliage plants will do well. But f2.8 or below is too little light for most plants. Only ferns, ivies, and a few houseplants such as dumb cane (Dieffenbachia), Swiss cheese plants (Monstera deliciosa), and fatsias will do well. Be sure to place your plants where they get the light they need.

The same technique can be used in the house for finding the best places for different houseplants. Just for interest try measuring the light outdoors at the same time. The difference is often greater than you would expect.

and red wavelengths (450nm and 660nm) are the most important for photosynthesis.

Different wavelengths of light have different effects on plants. Red light tends to produce soft growth with longer stems, whereas plants grown in blue light tend to be harder, darker and more compact. A bit of far-red light is needed to control photoperiod responses. In winter, red and far-red wavelengths predominate due to the low angle of the sun in the sky, so blue light is more valuable as an addition to natural winter light. But the difference it makes is small.

When light levels are low any additional light will result in increased growth, but it can be expensive. Young plants respond most strongly to improved light levels, and one light can cover a greater number of small plants, so it makes sense to use supplementary lighting mainly on seedlings and rooted cuttings.

The closer the plants are to the light source, the more effective it will be, provided overheating does not occur. The intensity of the light decreases by the square of the distance, so every inch counts. Fluorescent lights are not very intense so they should be only 3 to 8 inches away from the leaves. They still have a considerable effect at 15 inches, but by 30 inches they are hardly worth having. The light fixture should be on a pulley so it can be readjusted as the plants grow taller. Incandescent light (from ordinary light bulbs) is not much use for photosynthesis, but it does contain the far-red wavelengths which control photoperiod and some flowering responses. Incandescent bulbs produce a lot of heat, so keep them at least 18 inches above the top leaves. Any artificial light source is more effective if used with a reflector so that all the light is directed toward the plants.

One problem with supplementary lighting is that the light fixture itself casts a shadow, reducing the amount of daylight reaching the plant. Fluorescent lights which are the cheapest form of effective lighting for plants, are particularly bad at this. They take up large areas for the amount of light they give off. In an attached greenhouse the lights can be fixed to the wall of the house thus reducing the problem caused by shading and also incidentally encouraging the plants to look toward the house rather than toward the sun.

Professional growers usually use sodium lamps or high-pressure mercury lamps to supplement daylight. These are much more intense sources of light, so they are smaller and can be placed farther apart from each other and farther away from the plants. Designed as street lights, they are very efficient and very long-lasting—up to 20,000 hours of use from one bulb, about twenty times the life of an ordinary light bulb. The initial installation is expensive but in the long run they are the most cost-effective form of supplementary lighting. Although they emit a very narrow range of wavelengths, plant response has been shown to be good. High pressure mercury lights are the cheapest to install, but high pressure sodium lamps (Lucalux) are cheaper to run.

Although low-pressure sodium lamps are the most efficient at converting electricity to light, they have a very narrow waveband indeed (virtually all the energy is in two wavelengths only), which can cause problems unless sufficient daylight or incandescent light is available to balance it out.

Plants can be grown under artificial light alone. Commercial growers often use special highly insulated "grow rooms" to start seeds and young plants. Grow rooms receive no natural light. Temperature, humidity, carbon dioxide, and light levels are all controlled very accurately.

HOW MUCH LIGHT

Comparing light sources can be complicated since they give out different amounts of light for the same wattage (it is the watts you pay for on your electricity bill). As a rough guide, approximately the same amount of light would be given by two 180-watt low-pressure sodium lamps or one 400-watt high-pressure sodium lamp or two 400-watt high-pressure mercury lamps or five 8-foot-long, 125-watt fluorescent tubes.

ELECTRICAL PRECAUTIONS

As with any electrical installation in the presence of high humidity and the possibility of dripping or splashing water, you must use great care. All electrical outlets should be equipped with a ground-fault interrupter so they will cut out if there is a short. Industrial rather than domestic fittings should be used. We advise consulting an electrician about which fittings are most suitable for greenhouse use.

To substitute for natural daylight altogether, use both warm and cool-white fluorescent tubes with a little incandescent light (approximately 100 watts of incandescent for every 400 watts of fluorescent light). A combination of Wide Spectrum and Standard Grow-lux lights is just as satisfactory but more expensive. For good growth of plants liking high light intensity, you need a solid ceiling of fluorescent tubes, but for shade-loving plants and for propagation a tube every few inches will suffice (Figure 3.3). Fluorescent tubes give out progressively less light as they get older, so make sure you have new ones at the beginning of winter when the extra light is most important. If substituting for daylight altogether, replace the tubes every few months in order to maintain adequate light levels.

With a soil-heating cable below, a source of suitable light above, and a piece of plastic draped across the opening, the space under a bench can become an extremely useful propagating area.

Because artificial light rarely reaches the intensity of direct sunlight plants need more hours of it, usually twelve to sixteen. But not twenty-four hours of light. Plants need a rest, too, and most grow better if given a period of darkness. Lettuce is an exception and can be lighted continuously.

TEMPERATURE

Plant growth is the sum of a series of complex chemical processes all of which are dependent on temperature. Below 40°F. almost no growth takes place. In the presence of adequate light, carbon dioxide, water, and food, growth will double for every 18°F. (10°C.) increase in temperature up to an optimum temperature (usually 60°-80°F.), after which it will slow down and eventually stop as the enzymes controlling the process cease to work

3.3 ▲ Artificial lighting does not have to be ugly. The mirror behind directs all the light at the plants, but it also serves to enlarge the apparent size of the room and double the apparent number of plants. Because most of the plants are shade-loving, the fluorescent tubes can be spaced quite far apart.

at higher temperatures.

All plants have an optimum range of temperatures within which they grow best. Many will adjust to a different range but should not be expected to switch back and forth. Extremes of temperature put a lot of stress on the plant. Ideally the day and night temperatures should not be more than 15° or 20°F. apart. Many amateur greenhouses fluctuate by much more than this and the plants manage to survive, but a plant in the full flush of growth will resent a sudden cold night. Likewise a plant that has adjusted to the cold should not be encouraged by a spate of warm days to burst into growth in the middle of February. As much as possible, avoid wide temperature swings.

You will find it well worth buying a maximum/minimum thermometer and keeping track of the temperature in your greenhouse day by day. By resetting the thermometer every day at the same time you can record the maximum and the minimum temperature experienced in the greenhouse during the last twenty-four hours. Experiments have shown that plants respond to the average night temperature rather than to the absolute minimum temperature but the max/min thermometer provides a helpful guideline.

Incorporating heat storage materials (see Chapter 4, page 81) will keep the sunspace warmer at night and cooler in the day—a great benefit for most plants. All the forms of night insulation discussed in Chapter 4 will help to keep the temperature above freezing at night.

PLANTS FOR DIFFERENT TEMPERATURES

The night temperature of your greenhouse in winter will be the strongest factor determining what you can grow there in winter. Growing only those plants suited to the conditions in your greenhouse (see Chapter 5) will greatly improve your chances of success and reduce the time and energy needed to keep them healthy.

A sunspace that is an integral part of the house will obviously experience higher temperatures at night (especially in winter) than one that can be closed off. Warmer night temperatures greatly increase the rate of respiration without necessarily increasing the rate of photosynthesis, unless long, bright days are the rule. If respiration is too high the plant may burn more carbohydrates than it makes by photosynthesis, resulting in a net loss.

Some respiration needs to go on at night but cooler temperatures will slow the rate and conserve the carbohydrates that have been formed during the day. In winter, when low light levels limit the amount of carbohydrate produced by photosynthesis, the plant may produce only as much carbohydrate as it is consuming in respiration. Obviously no growth will occur, and if respiration rises or photosynthesis falls the plant will decline.

Plants for sunspaces open to the home will have to be chosen carefully, because the atmosphere is likely to be warm and dry with low light levels in winter. Many houseplants grow naturally on the floor of tropical or subtropical forests and are well adapted to warm, low-light situations. Unfortunately, most forest-floor plants require high humidity. But there are some tough house plants—ivy, philodendron, Swedish ivy, spider plants, etc.—that will thrive to an almost frightening extent even if the air is quite dry. Plants that like this atmosphere in the low light of winter, however, will resent the bright sun of summer and will have to be brought further into the house. Then brightly colored annuals—short-lived, sun- and heat-loving plants—can fill the sunspace.

If the humidity can be maintained along with the warmth, then a wonderful range of rain forest plants can be grown, limited only by the light available.

Sunspaces physically separated from the house by a wall are likely to be much cooler in winter. If the sunspace can be kept below 55°F. at night and below 70°F. in the day in winter, a wide range of temperate-climate plants can be grown. Some will go dormant for the cool, dark parts of the year, in which condition they will survive much better than if they were in active growth. Others just slow down. A few come into their own, blooming through the dark days of winter.

Almost all food-producing plants require either bright light and warmth (tomatoes, cucumbers, melons) or moderate light and cool (brassicas, spinach, lettuce). For vegetable growers a clear pattern emerges of green leafy vegetables in winter and fruiting vegetables in summer.

Obviously different plants prefer different temperatures, but a considerable range can be grown in the same sunspace by placing the plants in different positions. The back wall is generally warmer than it is closer to the glass. Higher levels are usually warmer than lower ones. Proximity to any heat-storage materials provides extra warmth, too. Making use of the gradation from coolest at floor level close to the glass and warmest near the apex against the back wall allows you to grow plants with different needs. Otherwise you can heat part of the space more than the rest, either by using a thermal curtain (see page 77) to divide the area, or by sectioning off one end with a clear plastic sheet and adding extra heat to it.

AUXILIARY HEATING

If there is no wall dividing it from the house, the sunspace will remain within a few degrees of the house temperature. The simplest way to heat other sunspaces is to open the doors into the house and turn up the furnace or wood stove if necessary. This provides not only heat but dry air relatively rich in carbon dioxide for the plants. On sunny days the reverse situation holds. As the sunspace heats up, open the doors to the house to let the solar heat in and turn the central heating down. The humid, oxygen-rich greenhouse air will be welcome in the house.

But there are times when a door open to an attached sunspace can provide uncomfortably cold drafts, so you should have an auxiliary heater available. Kerosene heaters are the cheapest, but not very practical on a regular basis. The temperature is hard to control, and the risk of fumes from the incomplete combustion of kerosene damaging the plants is considerable. In some towns and municipalities they are illegal for home use, as well. Check your local laws.

An electric heater is the simplest and most reliable form of supplementary heat, provided there is no power failure. But assuming the house has a backup form of heat for such occasions, the open door can always prevent disaster. Any electric equipment in a humid environment should be specially designed for greenhouse use. All outlets should be with a ground fault interrupter to cut off the electricity if anything goes wrong. Obviously, protecting the equipment from drips and splashes will help to prevent anything going wrong in the first place.

A fan heater helps to circulate the air, which both reduces temperature stratification (it can sometimes be 70°F. at the apex and 45°F. on the floor) and produces sturdier plants. It should be placed near one end, blowing along the length of one side of the sunspace. The air will automatically flow back up the other side. When heat is not needed, a fan heater can be used as a fan only, just by turning down the thermostat. This does not require much electricity and the resulting air movement is beneficial. Fan heaters do make a certain amount of noise, which some people find irritating.

Radiant heaters are more economical but they heat only objects in the direct path of the radiation. Since they do not heat the air, plants close to the heater will block plants far away. In fact one side of a plant can overheat while the other side stays chilly.

An extension of the central heating system of the house provides the most reliable heat at no great additional cost once installed. If there is a time switch which simply turns the furnace off for several hours in the middle of the night, it will have to be removed. Ideally the sunspace should be on a separate loop with a thermostat which can be controlled independently of the house thermostat. Putting radiators along the outside walls will give the most even heat, but slightly more will be lost to the outside.

If you decide to heat your greenhouse, there are three times of day when it is most useful. The most important time is probably at dusk when the area has started to cool down. It is wise to open all the vents for ten minutes to exhaust the warm, moist air which has accumulated. This may be very difficult to persuade yourself to do, but plants don't like high humidity during the cool night. Let the air out without giving the objects too much time to cool down, then shut the sunspace up tight and heat it to 10°F. above the minimum temperature you want to maintain. It is not worth venting at sunset on mild, moist days because humidity will not be significantly reduced if the incoming air is not going to be heated much.

This late afternoon heat may be enough to keep the temperature above the desired minimum all night in a well-insulated greenhouse. If not, supplementary heat may be needed in the early hours of the morning. This should be thermostatically controlled so that it goes on only as necessary.

The third time when a small boost of heat is very beneficial is shortly after sunrise. After a cold night the plants cannot begin to photosynthesize until their temperature

HEAT STARVATION

Respiration provides the energy for plant growth, but if it is not balanced by the input of energy from photosynthesis, the plant weakens and eventually dies. It is a chemical process directly dependent on temperature.

HOW HUMID IS IT?

The relative humidity is a measure of the amount of water vapor in the air compared to the maximum possible amount the air could hold at that temperature. That is, at 50 percent relative humidity the air holds half as much water as it would if it were fully saturated. For every 10°F. rise in temperature of a given amount of air, the relative humidity of that air will drop by 20 percent. The cold air from outside, even if it has a relative humidity of 100 percent when it comes in, will be considerably drier after being heated than the greenhouse air was. Assuming at least a 20°F. difference in temperature between indoors and out, the fresh air would have at most 60 percent relative humidity.

reaches 40°F., so when the sun first hits the leaves, a small input of heat can increase the time a plant spends photosynthesizing by half an hour or more, which on a short winter's day is considerable. Ideally this morning heat should be applied to the soil, since the soil takes much longer to warm up than the leaves and stems.

Soil heating is probably the most energy efficient way to add heat to a greenhouse. All the heat goes where you want it, and only a very small amount is required. A soil temperature of 50° to 60°F. is desirable. Above that, little increase in growth occurs. Low root temperatures can reduce photosynthesis by slowing the uptake of water. They can also interfere with the uptake of nutrients (if their roots are below 65°F., tomatoes go blue from lack of potassium). For low crops like lettuce, soil heating has the added benefit of warming the air closest to the soil slightly. Most importantly of all, propagation is much quicker and less risky when soil heating is used.

Like supplementary light, supplementary heat is most cost-effective when applied to young plants. So early spring, when light levels are high enough to justify increased heat and there are many seedlings and rooted cuttings waiting to surge ahead, is the most valuable time for supplementary heating.

DAYTIME TEMPERATURE

Generally an increase in daytime temperature above the minimum needed for photosynthesis (about 45°F.) is valuable only if there is a considerable amount of light. When little light is available, extra heat will only result in pale, spindly, etiolated plants. On heavily overcast days in winter it is best to keep the temperature under 50°F. unless you are growing tropical plants. On sunny days 60° or 65°F. is needed in order to use the extra light efficiently. Nature usually takes care of this difference, as the extra sunlight provides extra heat. By April you can allow the temperature to go as high as 80°F. Because of the extra light available it may well go higher, to the detriment of the plants. In any season too much heat for the amount of light available will result in unhealthy plants.

VENTILATION

When temperatures get too high, venting is the easiest way to get rid of excess heat. Automatic vent openers, set to open with the maximum useful temperature for the time of year, are a vital safety valve to prevent overheating when no one is at home. In winter, of course, the excess heat can benefit the house. In summer, to provide sufficient ventilation allow at least 1 square foot of vent area for every 5 square feet of floor area. Half the vents should be near the apex where hot air collects. The other half should be close to ground level so that cooler air can be drawn in. The greater the difference in height between the openings, the faster the air will flow, increasing the ventilation rate and mixing hot and cold air inside to give an even temperature distribution. Thus, two-story sunspaces vent better than single story ones.

The large vent area needed for adequate ventilation by natural convection creates a large number of cracks where hot air can leak out in winter, so many people prefer to have fewer openings and use a fan for summer ventilation instead (see page 90). The fan should be installed near the apex at one end, with an air inlet low down at the opposite end. Both should be sealed with automatic back flaps when not in use. To calculate the size of the fan, multiply the floor area by three. The result gives the flow rate of the fan in cubic feet per minute. If the fan is the only source of ventilation, it needs to have a wide range of speeds to provide for the very small amounts of ventilation needed in the colder months of the year.

A fan between the house and greenhouse can save a lot of heat that would be wasted on sunny winter days when the glazed area overheats despite natural convection into the house. In those circumstances, without a fan the excess heat would have to be vented to the outside to keep the temperature suitable for plants. A fan between the house and sunspace can also provide just the kind of air movement and relatively dry, carbon dioxide-rich air plants need in the enclosed conditions of a winter greenhouse. Any ventilation to and from the house in winter is usually beneficial. You will have to provide large openings, preferably some near the ceiling and some lower down, if a fan is not used.

FAINTING FROM COLD

Cold roots are unable to take up the water required for photosynthesis. On a sunny morning after a cold night sometimes this is dramatically demonstrated by plants wilting despite adequate water in the soil. As the soil warms up, they recover. Plants in pots are more subject to this since the small amount of soil in a pot gets colder than the large amount of soil in a bed. If the soil is in fact dry, watering with warm water as soon as the sun hits the plants would be very helpful.

SCREENS

Vents can be screened to keep out mosquitoes, flies, and plant-eating pests, but they will also keep out bees and ladybugs and other friendly insects. Most fruiting plants will have to be handpollinated if the sunspace is screened. Screens reduce air flow, so vent areas must then be increased by about one-third. If the glazing will be shaded in the summer, the size of the vent openings can be reduced considerably.

SHADING

The best way to avoid overheating is to prevent the sunshine getting in. Various forms of shading are discussed on page 000.

DAMPING DOWN

Evaporating water uses up a large amount of heat, so wetting the floor and walls on a sunny day will reduce the air temperature dramatically as the hot air absorbs the water. Unfortunately the effect is only short-lived, so the sunspace needs to be hosed down every half hour in hot weather if damping down is to have much impact. Spraying the outside of the glass with water helps a bit, lowering the temperature of the glass itself and slightly reducing the amount of light (and therefore heat) that can get in. Misting the plants is more effective since it removes the heat from the place where it will do the most damage—the leaves. Spraying the plants is not a good idea as large droplets can cause water marking and even burn the leaves, leaving small dead spots on them if they are dusty.

A pad humidifier, also called a "swamp cooler," will lower the temperature very effectively if the air is relatively dry. It blows air across a continually wet pad. As the water evaporates, it absorbs a considerable amount of heat from the air, converting it into latent energy. When the water vapor condenses later on, it will release that energy again, but meanwhile the temperature of the air drops. The extra humidity is usually beneficial with the high rates of ventilation necessary for summer cooling.

CARBON DIOXIDE

The carbon and oxygen in the carbohydrates the plant makes by photosynthesis come from carbon dioxide in the air. The concentration of carbon dioxide in the air is normally well below the optimum level for photosynthesis. Plants grow faster and are sturdier when the level is three times higher than normal. Even at temperatures as low as 40°F., increasing the carbon dioxide level increases the rate of photosynthesis so the plants are able to make better use of whatever light is available.

In an enclosed space, plants quickly use up the available carbon dioxide unless fresh air is constantly brought in to replenish it. On cold, sunny days you face a dilemma, because icy drafts can damage plants and precious heat must be conserved, yet some ventilation is essential to maintain carbon dioxide levels. Owners of attached greenhouses have the ideal solution: they open the door into the house, letting the warm, humid, oxygen-rich air from the greenhouse in and letting the dry, carbon dioxide-rich air from the house out. People, pets, and fires all use up oxygen and give off carbon dioxide. Plants use up carbon dioxide and give off oxygen when they are photosynthesizing, so the exchange is mutually beneficial. Talking to plants may have other benefits, but at the very least it gives them a little boost of carbon dioxide.

At night the concentration of carbon dioxide in an enclosed greenhouse rises considerably as the plants and soil bacteria respire, using oxygen and giving off carbon dioxide. (They respire during the day, too, but the amounts given off are tiny compared to the amount of carbon dioxide used in photosynthesis.) By 10 or 11 A.M. on a sunny day the night's excess of carbon dioxide has been used up and ventilation into the house will prove helpful.

Ventilation will prevent the carbon dioxide level in the sunspace from falling below the normal level, but it is impossible to raise the level any higher while the vents are open. On days when the sunspace is too cold to vent into the house, artificial carbon dioxide enrichment is very beneficial. Even on cloudy days when the temperature in the sunspace is as low as 40°F., extra carbon dioxide will speed up photosynthesis, not only increasing growth, but also improving quality and encouraging more rapid maturity.

Special cylinders of carbon dioxide gas are manufactured for commercial growers. If you have access to these they are a cheap source. Melting dry ice is an expensive but very useful source of carbon dioxide. Because it actually lowers the air temperature in the greenhouse, enrichment can continue for longer on the bright sunny days when it is most useful. When the temperature rises so much that the vents have to be opened, put the dry ice back in the freezer for another day.

Air movement is very important in making the best use of all available carbon dioxide. When the air is still, the layer of air immediately surrounding each leaf quickly becomes depleted, even when the overall level of carbon dioxide has dropped only slightly. As plants transpire (see next section) the air near the leaves also becomes very humid, encouraging fungus diseases. A fan circulating the air in the greenhouse when vents are shut helps to break up this stagnant layer of air. Air movement is also said to reduce problems with insects. Both fresh air and moderate amounts of air movement encourage healthy, sturdy plants.

CARBON DIOXIDE GENERATORS

The bacteria in the soil give off small amounts of carbon dioxide as they digest the organic matter. Compost heaps and organic mulches help to raise the carbon dioxide level as they decay. Chickens, rabbits, guinea pigs, and other small animals all produce a bit of heat and carbon dioxide. But their cages need regular cleaning to prevent their giving off harmful ammonia fumes (your nose will quickly tell you if ammonia is becoming a problem).

CARBON DIOXIDE IN EDEN

Millions of years ago when the first plants were developing, the earth's atmosphere contained .09 percent carbon dioxide. Today the level has been reduced to .03 percent but plants still grow better in the conditions they were originally designed for. That prehistoric .09% carbon dioxide level is perfectly harmless to human beings, but it is only possible in enclosed conditions and is difficult to maintain if any ventilation is used.

WATER

Water and air are the two basic building blocks for plant growth. Water provides the hydrogen needed for the photosynthesis. It is essential to most of the other life processes of the growing plant as well, and it provides structural strength. Plants use more water than any other single substance. One sunflower, for example, can use 200,000 liters of water in a season.

Water enters the plant through the roots by osmosis due to the relatively higher concentration of sugars and salts in the roots than in the soil.

TRANSPIRATION

Water is drawn up through the stems to the leaves by a combination of root pressure (from the constant influx of water to the roots) and transpiration pressure. Water evaporates from the leaves continually, leaving behind a more concentrated sap solution, which then draws more water up to replace what has been lost. This process, called transpiration, pulls water up the stem toward the surface of the leaves by suction.

Transpiration is essential to many aspects of plant growth. It ensures an adequate supply of water to provide the hydrogen needed in the formation of carbohydrates. It carries nutrients absorbed through the roots, to all parts of the plant. It insures sufficient water to maintain turgidity—i.e., cells swollen to their full size pressing outward on the cell walls.

Without turgidity, the cells become flaccid and the plant droops. Turgidity helps to keep the plant erect with its leaves spread out so they catch the sun. It allows the stomata (the pores in the leaf) to open so that carbon dioxide can enter for photosynthesis.

And most important of all, turgidity allows the growth of individual cells. If turgor pressure is not pushing outward on the cell wall as it forms, the cell will be much reduced in size and can never make up the difference, although new cells will grow to full size when turgidity is restored.

Finally, transpiration cools the leaves by evaporation—a very important function in an organism designed to trap energy from light, most of which is then converted to heat. The enzymes that make photosynthesis, respiration, growth, and development possible do not work above certain temperatures, so in full sun cooling is vital.

Water evaporates from the leaf cells into the small openings beneath each stoma. The outside of the leaf (the epidermis) is quite impermeable to water, so when the pores are shut the plant can conserve water efficiently. When the pores are open water vapor diffuses out and carbon dioxide diffuses in (Figure 3.4).

If the air around the leaves is still, then a layer of air saturated with water vapor and deficient in carbon dioxide builds up immediately outside each pore opening. Evaporation will not take place if the air is already completely saturated. Spraying plants and damping down the greenhouse in hot weather can sometimes actually make the leaf surfaces hotter by reducing transpiration if ventilation is restricted and very high levels of humidity build up. But given the high ventilation rates usual in summer, damping down will at least briefly lower the temperature in the sunspace. Misting the plants is even more effective because it cools the leaves, removing the heat from where it could do the most damage. The plant itself begins to act as a pad humidifier.

COPING WITH LOW HUMIDITY

Very low humidity also reduces transpiration, because the pores close to restrict excessive water loss. Ideally plants prefer about 60 percent relative humidity, which is normal out of doors at all times of year. Below 40 percent most plants begin to suffer from dry air. Above 75 to 80 percent most diseases begin to thrive. Above 90 percent, evaporation from the leaves is impeded.

In winter because the air outside is cold, even when the relative humidity is 100 percent the air carries little moisture. On entering the house, the cold air is warmed, increasing its capacity to hold water and so decreasing its relative humidity. The greater the temperature difference between inside and outside, the lower the humidity is likely to be indoors. The air in an average house in winter often has a relative humidity of less than 10 percent. A healthier range for human beings is 30 to 50 percent relative humidity. A greenhouse full of actively transpiring plants is unlikely to suffer from low humidity even in midwinter and can usually contribute some beneficial moisture to the house.

In summer, with high temperatures and full ventilation, too little humidity is likely to be a problem in most sunspaces. Grouping plants together on trays of gravel or capillary matting will help to create a slightly more humid microclimate in a given area (Figure 3.5), but will not do much unless the quantity of plants is very great. Damping down the floor and walls and misting the plants are the traditional solutions. Unfortunately the increase in humidity is not long lasting, and the damping and misting must be repeated as often as

CIRCULATING FANS

According to research at the University of Connecticut, the most efficient position for a circulating fan is about one-quarter of the way across the width of the sunspace and about seven feet above the ground. It will then push the air down one side and back up the other. The fan should be 10 to 12 inches in diameter and have a cfm rating (that is the number of cubic feet of air it can move in one minute) equal to three times the floor area of the sunspace.

OSMOSIS

Nature always tries to equalize the concentration of salts in a solution, so water will pass from a dilute solution to a more concentrated one. This is called osmosis. If the soil contains too many salts due to overfertilizing, the concentration gradient may be reversed and water will not enter the roots. In fact it may even be drawn out of the roots by osmosis, resulting in fertilizer burn. New cuttings and seedlings, which have small, immature roots and have not yet begun to manufacture many sugars, must be fertilized very sparingly if at all, so as not to impair their ability to draw in water.

THIRST LEADS TO HUNGER

The first effect of a water shortage on photosynthesis is not the lack of hydrogen, but the reduction in carbon dioxide due to the closing of the stomata in response to a reduction in water. The stomata begin to close down and conserve water long before the plant shows signs of wilting. This is a major cause of reduced photosynthesis.

WATER-COOLED

Evaporation is an amazingly efficient way to lower temperature. About 540 calories of heat are dissipated for every gram of water evaporated. Approximately 95 percent of the water entering the plant passes out again by evaporation. Only 5 percent remains to be incorporated into plant cells.

once an hour in hot weather. The cooling effect of damping down is even more short-lived.

An electric humidifier will do the job much more efficiently. It can be thermostatically controlled to come on at a certain temperature, or a humidistat can turn it on when the humidity drops below a certain level. Be sure to get one with a large reservoir so its supply of water does not have to be topped up too often. A pad humidifier, or swamp cooler, is even more efficient at lowering the temperature, provided the air is dry to begin with.

COPING WITH HIGH HUMIDITY

Mild overcast spells in spring and fall or mild, damp winter days are the most conducive to high relative humidity. The outside air is high in humidity and not many degrees below the inside temperature, so ventilation will not reduce the relative humidity significantly. Stagnant air encourages disease, and ventilation will provide air movement and extra carbon dioxide so you gain some benefit. But opening vents between the sunspace and the house is much more effective, since the heated air of most houses is quite dry. If temperatures are mild out of doors the sunspace is unlikely to be very cold and will not lower the house temperature much.

Although the excess humidity from a sunspace full of plants will benefit the human occupants of the house, however, it may damage the house itself. In cold weather even quite moderate humidity levels can cause condensation problems on single glazing and on under-insulated walls. Humidity from a sunspace open to the house can not easily be regulated; often the air will be too dry for plants or too damp for the well-being of the house.

Watering in the morning, watering carefully to avoid splashes, and watering only when the soil is quite dry will reduce the water available for the air to pick up. If fungus diseases seem to be getting the upper hand, venting when the sunspace is at its warmest should help some. A small amount of heat applied with only the top vents open will do a lot to dry the atmosphere. The best time for this additional heat is late afternoon to get rid of the warm humid air which has accumulated in the greenhouse.

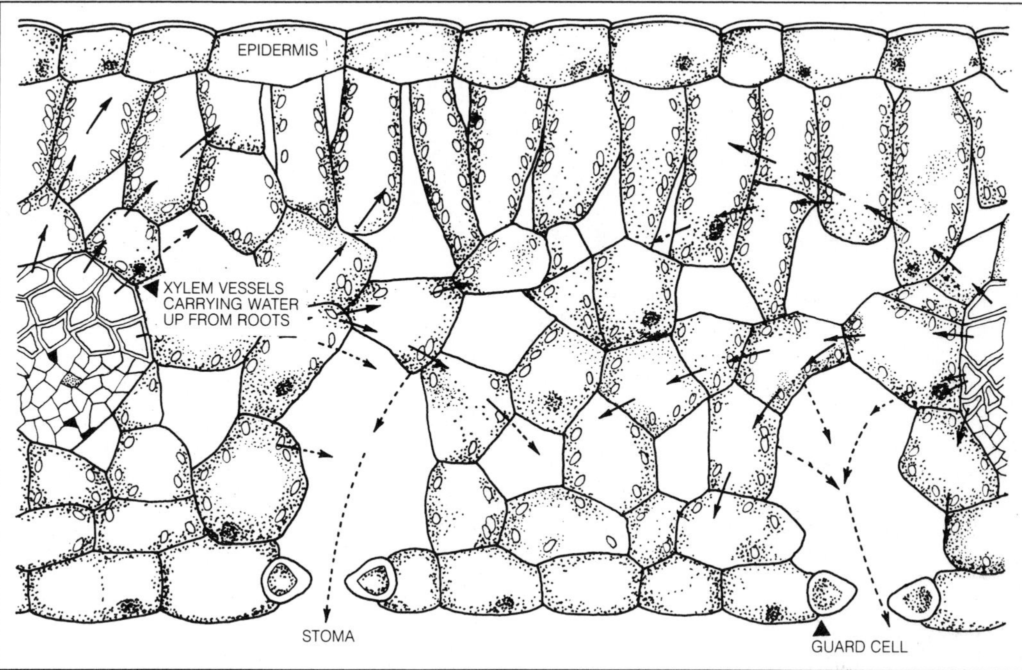

3.4 ▲ The structure of a leaf. The tin waxy epidermis on the top surface of the leaf prevents evaporation. The long cells immediately below are full of chlorophyll and do most of the photosynthesizing. Below them are many air spaces where gases and water vapor can diffuse in and out. The arrows show the flow of the water as it comes up the xylem vessels from the roots and diffuses through the cell walls by osmosis. When the guard cells surrounding each stoma (pore) are full of water, they hold the stoma open so that fresh air diffuses in and water vapor diffuses out. When they are flaccid, the stoma shuts and transpiration is reduced to almost zero.

CONDENSATION

When the relative humidity is high and the temperature begins to fall, some of the water in the air will condense onto any cool surface. Condensation usually occurs first on the glazing. This is harmless, indeed it can even be beneficial in removing excess moisture from the air and reducing radiation heat loss at night by coating the glazing. But if enough condensation occurs to start dripping on the plants, that is harmful, particularly as drips are likely to recur in the same places, encouraging diseases there.

Drips are more of a problem with plastic glazing materials than with glass, because moisture on glass tends to spread out into an even film

3.5 ▲ Large plants grouped together on a gravel tray filled with water to maintain a humid atmosphere.

rather than collecting into droplets as it does on plastic. Sprays (such as Sun-Clear) change the surface-tension properties of plastic and allow the water to spread into a thin film. After spraying, the plastic becomes more transparent when wet, so it admits more light when condensation forms, but for the same reason it allows more heat to radiate out at night.

If the glazing is steep enough, condensation will collect and run down it. It is important that nothing impede this run-off. Sash bars, glazing joints, even dirt encourage drips to form. The sills at the bottom of the glazing should be bevelled to shed the accumulated condensation or it will collect there, encouraging wooden sills to rot and providing a breeding place for algae and fungi.

Condensation does not occur only on the glazing materials, although it occurs there first. As the temperature outside drops, objects in the sunspace begin to radiate heat out. In some circumstances, they can lose heat faster than the air loses heat by conduction and convection. If the air already has a relative humidity of 100 percent and the objects in the greenhouse are colder than the air, condensation will form on the objects. Condensation on the structural elements on the greenhouse is not too serious because they will dry again when the temperature rises next day. But on plant leaves a film of condensation all night long is an open invitation to disease.

Any form of movable insulation (see page 77) that controls radiant heat loss is a big help in reducing humidity problems. Even though it will not reduce the actual level of humidity, insulation makes condensation less likely to occur on the plants.

WATER SOURCE

Any sunspace designed with plants in mind should include a source of water and a drain in the floor. Lugging full watering cans across the house from the nearest sink is no joke. Hot water is a luxury for plants, allowing you to water with warm water on chilly mornings, and a luxury for people, allowing you to scrub pots in comfort, but it is not absolutely necessary. Cold water is.

The source of water should be near the middle of the sunspace for convenience, usually against the back wall. Place the faucet high enough to fit a watering can under easily. If possible get a tap threaded for a tight connection with a hose. If there is room, you will find a sink with ample draining board space either side a blessing when repotting. You can cover the sink when not in use and place plant pots in it. If there will be no sink make some other provision for soaking pots. A large galvanized tin tub under a bench is invaluable for soaking large numbers of pots.

A central floor drain should be installed in any horticultural sunspace. The floor should be smooth and laid to a fall so the dirt goes down the drain when you hose down the floor and walls. Otherwise damping down the sunspace will simply lead to large mud puddles.

WATERING

Different plants growing in different conditions, in different soils, at different phases in their life cycle, need differing amounts of water. There is no hard and fast rule, although once you get to know a plant's rhythm, its need for water does tend to remain quite regular under the same conditions. Many plants show some signs of water stress before they actually begin to wilt. The leaves may change color slightly, hold themselves less erect, or feel slightly flaccid. The soil will look pale and crumbly. Many people feel the weight of the pot, but if you have plants in different sizes and types of containers and perhaps in different soils, weight can confuse the issue. If a clay pot makes a ringing noise when tapped, or the base feels dry, it needs to be watered. Most of the time you should be able to tell by looking if a plant needs water. If uncertain, stick your finger a quarter to half an inch into the soil. The surface may be dry when there is sufficient moisture below, but if it feels dry a quarter-inch down, chances are it needs watering. With ground beds it is best to remove a trowelful of soil and feel it for moisture.

The next big question is how much water to apply. It is important to wet the soil all the way down. If you use too little water, the top layer will be saturated and below that the soil will be dry. Water will not pass through to the lower layers of soil until the upper layer is saturated (assuming of course that there is no open channel for water to pour through without wetting the soil—in which case the plant needs repotting).

To make sure the soil is thoroughly wet, water sufficiently for some water to run out of the bottom of the pot. This helps flush out any excess fertilizer. But don't let the pot sit in a pool of water for long. If it cannot drain away, the water must be tipped out or sponged up.

The soil in most pots should come about half an inch below the rim. Large pots need a proportionately deeper gap. Filling this space with water is a rough guide to the amount of water needed, but experience is the best judge. Ground beds are more difficult to gauge, but in hot weather a gallon per square yard every day would not be too much for actively growing plants. During cloudy weather a gallon per square yard every week might be enough. Check with a trowel a few hours after watering to make sure the water has penetrated 8 to 10 inches down.

In summer it is hard to overwater, assuming the soil is

LOSING WATER TO GAIN WATER

Plants growing in conditions of very high relative humidity, which inhibits evaporation, often force water out of their leaves in droplets (guttation) in order to increase their rate of transpiration.

HOMEMADE HUMIDIFIER

Do-it-yourselfers can rig up a simple misting system to raise humidity and lower temperature. Just set a fine mist nozzle on the end of the hose in front of a fan blowing into the greenhouse.

WATER-RESISTANT PLANTS

If the soil dries out too much between watering it may shrink away from the sides of the pot. When you finally water it, the water will run down the outside without wetting the soil. If this happens, the plant needs to be soaked for a few hours to thoroughly rewet the rootball. If soaking is inconvenient, repeated small doses of water, a trickle from a dripping hose, or a few melting ice cubes can rewet the soil. If the soil becomes parched frequently, probably the plant is in too small a pot or the soil needs more waterholding material added to it.

WINTER FLOODS

Ground beds not in use for a few weeks will benefit from being flooded to leach out excess fertilizer salts. Apply 24 gallons per square yard over a period of a day or so. Leave the bed to drain for ten days before planting.

well aerated and the container well drained. The tricky times come when light and temperature levels are less than optimum and you have to restrict the water you apply to keep the system in balance. In these circumstances, try to apply only enough water to wet the soil without any run off and let the soil dry out more thoroughly between waterings. This not only helps to reduce the relative humidity of the greenhouse but also helps to harden off the plant tissues so they are less vulnerable to cold. Likewise stop fertilizing at the end of summer, except for a bit of potash to help harden the woody growth. Lush, soft, nitrogen-rich growth is very much more vulnerable to frost damage. By drying a plant off in autumn and not letting the temperature get too high on sunny days in winter, you encourage the plant to go a bit dormant and it will survive the long winter better than a plant in active growth. Obviously winter greens and winter-flowering plants will need more fertilizing and watering than semi-dormant plants, but they still need much less than they would get in summer.

It is always better to water in the morning so the leaves get a chance to dry off during the day, and so the humidity given off by the damp soil occurs in the hottest part of the day. Do not water on cloudy days if you can avoid it, because humidity will be higher than usual and the plants will be using less water during the day.

In winter, if the soil is dry, it is well worth watering with warm water early in the morning to warm the cold soil quickly so the plant can make use of every bit of sunlight. If you have no hot water supply in the greenhouse, leave buckets of water out over night to bring them up at least to the greenhouse temperature.

Rainwater is ideal for watering but if you cannot conveniently collect it, tap water will do. Be careful to avoid contamination of stored water. Very hard water causes problems for some plants, but water softeners should not be used because they sometimes contain harmful chemicals. If the water is heavily chlorinated, it is a good idea to leave it standing in a bucket or watering can overnight so the chlorine can evaporate.

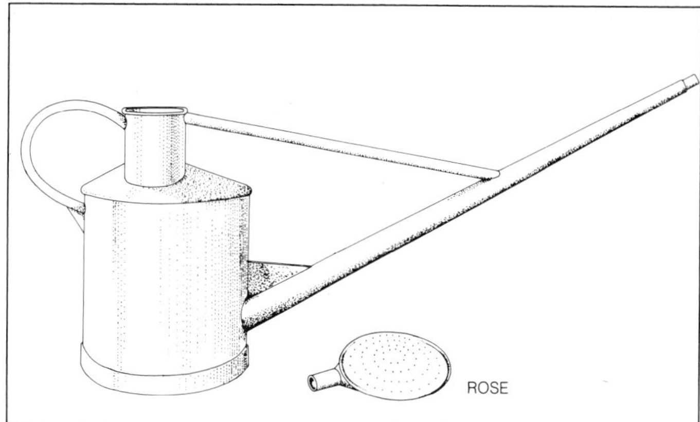

3.6 ▲ A traditional well-balanced greenhouse watering can with a long neck for reaching distant plants and a fine rose for watering seedlings.

WATERING BY HAND

Most owners of attached greenhouses water by hand. A long-necked greenhouse watering can (Figure 3.6) is ideal for reaching among pots and applying the right amount of water to individual plants. Make sure it is well balanced when full. Use a rose with many fine holes where possible to break the force of the water. Turn the rose face up for maximum effect. If you don't want to wet the foliage a narrow nozzle helps to apply the water accurately, but pour slowly so the soil is not compacted.

In summer when splashing is more of an advantage than a problem, and when a tremendous amount of water has to be applied daily, the hose comes into its own. It should be as flexible as possible so it does not knock over plants or pots as you pull it along. Garden hoses are usually too stiff and unnecessarily large in diameter. Charley's Greenhouse Supply Company sells one that coils itself like a spring when not pulled straight and is very convenient to use.

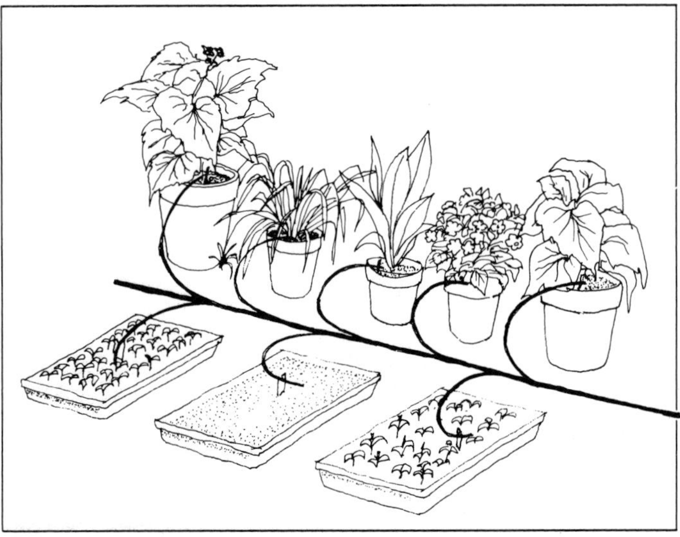

3.7 ▲ **A trickle-feed system with a nozzle for each pot and seed tray.**

ROOTS BREATHE, TOO

Like all living cells, root cells use oxygen and give off carbon dioxide as they respire. Respiration breaks down the carbohydrates formed in photosynthesis, which releases the energy used to power all the life processes of the cell. The harder the cell is working, the more energy it needs, so the more oxygen it must have for respiration.

A hose should be stored neatly coiled with the nozzle off the floor so it doesn't pick up dirt and diseases. Often the best storage place is on a wall where it won't get in the way. If this is in the sun, the water will be warmed automatically.

Various attachments make watering with a hose easier. A pistol grip to turn the water on and off as it comes out reduces the amount of water spilled and gives you time to stop and attend to other problems as you are watering. A Fogg-it nozzle gives a fine spray for misting. A waterbreaker, like the rose on a watering can, breaks up the stream of water into many fine rivulets, reducing problems with compaction. A long, narrow extension wand will help you to reach between plants to deliver the water just where it is needed.

In the summer it takes us half an hour a day to water the greenhouse and wet down the walls and floor with a hose, but once a week we mix up a dilute feed and apply it with a watering can, even though it takes more than twice as long that way. Diluters that can be inserted in the hose line (e.g., Hozon) will apply liquid fertilizer automatically as you water with the hose, but it is very easy to fertilize cuttings, seedlings, or dormant plants unintentionally this way. Also, a fairly high water pressure must be maintained in order to keep the system going and a lot of fertilized water falls on the floor, encouraging the growth of algae and weeds there.

Probably the best way to water pot plants is from below. Set the pot in a tub of water and soak for several hours, keeping the water level about halfway up the pot. When the soil glistens, remove the pot and let it drain for a few hours before setting it back in place, unless a gravel bed or slatted staging allows it to drain in place. Soaking is a messy, time-consuming business, but it insures that both pot and soil are thoroughly saturated.

Newly potted plants—especially those in clay pots—benefit greatly from soaking. Seed flats and cuttings are also best watered from below to disturb the soil as little as possible. Some special plants such as African violets and cyclamen, which are fussy about water on their leaves or on the growing point of the bulb, do better if regularly watered from below. All plants in pots will appreciate being watered from below every few months even if you cannot be bothered to do so every time they need watering. Hanging baskets benefit particularly. The larger the container for soaking, the better. The more you can soak at one time, the more efficient the operation becomes.

AUTOMATIC WATERING

Automatic watering systems can save a considerable amount of time. The simplest consist of a reservoir of water, which has to be topped up regularly (daily in summer unless the reservoir is very large), and some means of getting it to the plant. Trickle feed systems supply water through small nozzles inserted in individual pots (Figure 3.7). Seep hoses, or ooze tubes, let the water ooze out through small holes all along their length and are used for ground beds. Both trickle feeds and seep hoses release water at a constant rate, not in response to the dryness of the soil, so they have to be regulated either by hand or with a time clock. Capillary systems are self-regulating (Figure 3.8). In this method the porous surface is kept constantly wet, so any soil in contact with the wet surface will draw moisture up by capillary action (as a sponge draws water into its pore spaces). Each plant takes up as much moisture as it needs.

All these automatic watering systems can save a considerable amount of time, but none can be left for more than a day or two without risk. Daily checking that all parts of the system are functioning is the key to success.

SOIL

A plant's roots supply water for photosynthesis, transpiration, and structural strength, and transport of nutrients. The roots supply almost all the mineral nutrients the plant needs. They also anchor the plant, bracing it to help it remain upright. Although they are underground, the roots need oxygen in order to function, indeed in order to live. So the plant's soil (even though it may be a "soilless" compost made of peat, we prefer to use the term soil rather than "the growing medium" or "the compost") must serve all these functions. It must be able to retain water and nutrients, be sufficiently dense to support the plant, and contain a good supply of air.

Water enters the roots passively, by osmosis, but the plant has to expend energy to pull nutrients such as nitrogen, potassium, and phosphorus from a solution that is less concentrated—the soil water—to one that is more concentrated—the plant sap. The energy comes from respiration and requires oxygen.

Only highly specialized aquatic plants can use the oxygen in water; most plant cells need oxygen from the air for respiration. Root cells are below ground, but gaseous oxygen diffuses in and carbon dioxide diffuses out at those points where the root is in contact with pockets of air in the soil.

The amount of air and water in the soil are intimately connected. Water is held in small pore spaces by capillary action (see page 53). The smaller the capillary, the more tightly the water is held, so as the soil dries, the larger capillaries empty first, pulling air in to fill the spaces left by the water. But air and water are not necessarily mutually exclusive. A porous, well-aerated soil will hold more water and more air than a compacted soil because there are more pores of every size. Between one-third and one-half of the volume of the soil should be pore spaces, about half of which should be filled with air after the plant has been watered and any excess drained away.

If the soil is waterlogged or compacted, insufficient air spaces are available and respiration is reduced. With an inadequate supply of energy from respiration, the roots cannot take up the nutrients the plant needs. The roots, and soon the whole plant, stop growing and become more vulnerable to disease. Eventually the roots will begin to die because they cannot get enough oxygen for the basic processes of life. Cold soil slows respiration but does not usually cause the roots to die, because all life processes are slowed proportionately.

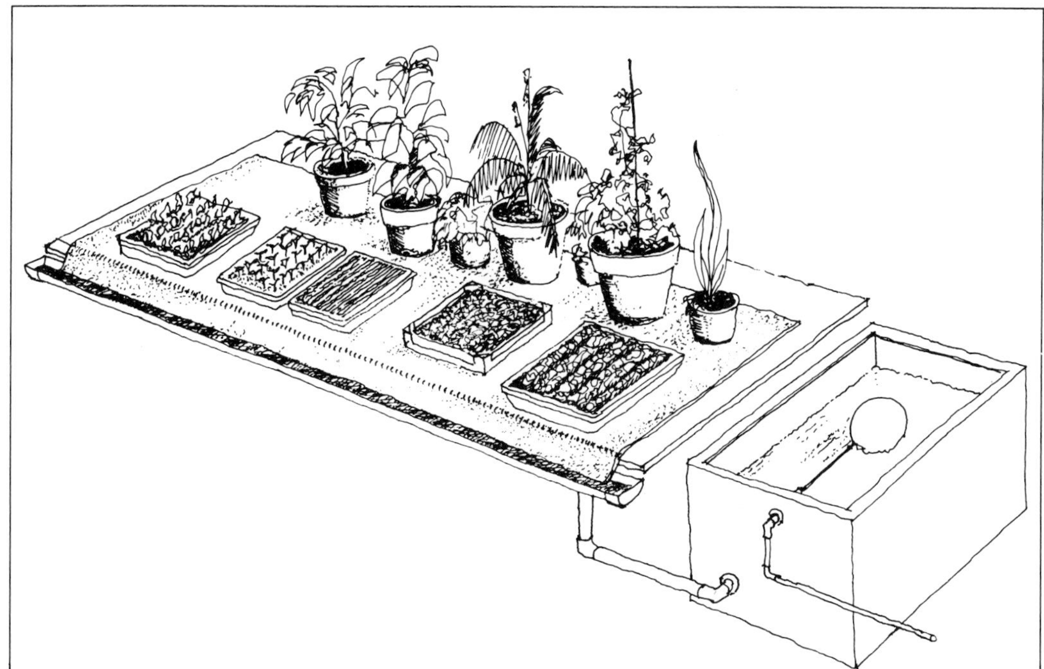

3.8 ▲ Capillary matting in a watertight tray draws water up from the attached gutter, kept full by the ballcock on the reservoir.

Water, nutrients, and air in the soil are crucial to the life processes of the plant. On the other hand, anchoring the plant in the soil is a purely mechanical problem and can be solved in several ways. Almost any soil will provide sufficient support for seedlings. But as plants get larger and heavier, plants in pots become increasingly top-heavy and easy to tip over. The pots can be wedged together or placed in specially made trays to keep them upright. But if the soil has very low density (weight to volume ratio) the plant may not even be able to keep itself upright within the pot or when planted in a bed. It can be staked or supported by twine suspended from the ceiling if necessary.

Very light materials such as perlite and vermiculite have low density and don't provide much support. Likewise they make staking ineffective. On the other hand, heavy soil-based soils make moving large pots or seed pots a tremendous chore. Often you must compromise. You can use many materials successfully for growing plants. In different combinations they serve different functions.

MATERIALS USED IN GREENHOUSE SOILS

Garden soil.

Soil from the garden generally does not hold enough air for successful use in containers. The shallow depth of the containers encourages waterlogging, so greenhouse soil needs more large pore spaces for air.

Garden soil contains pests and diseases that would multiply rapidly in a greenhouse environment. Pasteurization removes these dangers, but it also causes the organic matter in the soil to break down rapidly into ammonia gas, which is toxic to most plants. Adding chopped straw or sawdust—about one part to four parts of soil—reduces ammonia poisoning, because a considerable amount of the nitrogen which would have been converted to ammonia will be grabbed by the bacteria trying to decompose the straw. After pasteurization the soil should be overwatered to leach out any excessive ammonia.

The organic matter in garden soil is usually only 2 to 5 percent of the total volume. In the greenhouse you need much more organic matter to provide sufficient drainage. Paradoxically, organic matter also aids in water retention because of its porous nature. Greenhouse soil usually has between 20 to 50 percent organic matter. Most commercial greenhouse soils are made up of sterile organic matter, usually peat, and an inert aggregate such as sand, perlite, or vermiculite.

WHY SHALLOW CONTAINERS HOLD MORE WATER

The depth of the container affects the amount of water the soil in it will hold. A saturated sponge held flat stops dripping when it is holding the maximum amount of water it can against gravity. If that sponge is held vertically it will begin to drip again because the force of gravity on the relatively taller columns of water inside the vertical sponge is greater and so pulls more water down. A vertical sponge can hold less water than a horizontal sponge of the same size. Likewise deep pots tend to drain better than shallow pots.

SOURCES OF EASILY DECOMPOSED ORGANIC MATTER

Manure, compost, and leafmold.

These are very valuable sources of organic matter for the garden, but less so for the greenhouse. Their main benefit is as soil conditioners, improving aeration and drainage. They also contain a small proportion of nutrients (see page 61). They all decompose easily, releasing their nutrients into the soil and contributing humus as they decay. Unfortunately, because they decompose fast, they are very prone to producing ammonia when pasteurized. And since they may contain large amounts of pests, diseases and weed seeds, pasteurizing is recommended.

Well-made compost that has been turned often and whose internal temperature has reached 150°F. is the best of the three. If you don't mind running a slight risk of virus diseases, some insects, and a fair number of weeds, unpasteurized compost is worth using. Well-made compost is richer nutritionally than manure or leafmold. But don't use neglected compost unless you pasteurize it.

Manure, compost, and leafmold are more suitable for deep beds, which can be dug over and enriched every year, than for pots. Deep beds are almost like outdoor gardens in that they can support a whole range of creatures decomposing materials at different stages. In the extremely limited area of a pot, every bit of soil must be contributing to the plant, not to the lifecycle of some other creature. Earthworms, for example, cause havoc in pots but are quite desirable in deep beds.

Easily decomposed organic matter also makes a valuable mulch on top of a deep bed; it keeps soil cool and moist while gradually contributing nutrients and carbon dioxide as it rots down. But be sure to keep it at least a few inches away from the leaves and stems of your plants or they may begin to rot, too.

SOURCES OF SLOW-TO-DECOMPOSE ORGANIC MATTER

Peat.

Peat is the most widely used source of organic matter in greenhouses. Use only moss peat, from either sphagnum moss or hypnaceous moss, not reed peat. Sphagnum moss is slightly better because it is particularly slow to decompose. Any peat moss is spongy and elastic, which makes it an ideal soil conditioner, holding both air and water in large quantities. It is usually quite acid (pH 3 to 4.5), but this is easy to modify with the addition of ground limestone. It is light, easy to use, and sterile. Another advantage is that peat is widely available, although it is a bit more expensive than the organic materials available as the residue of local industries. Buy horticultural grade peat rather than very fine peat or any with large lumps.

Peat usually comes compressed in a bale, which needs to be broken up and wetted before it is used. It has the most enormous capacity to absorb water but, strangely, it resists wetting at first. You can wet small amounts of peat with boiling water. Large amounts are more easily dealt with by sprinkling with water as the peat is forked and turned over. One bale will take up to ten gallons of water. It should be wet enough so that water will drip from it when you squeeze a handful.

Sawdust.

In some areas sawdust is readily available, often for free if you are willing to collect it. It is almost as effective as peat in improving aeration, drainage, and water retention. It also decomposes slowly so that, like peat, it has a lasting effect on the soil. It is usually less acid than peat (generally between pH 4 and 5) and only slightly affects the pH of the soil it is added to. Avoid sawdust from redwood, cedar, or walnut trees. It will inhibit plant growth, and can actually poison susceptible plants.

The major problem with sawdust is that it locks up nitrogen. Sawdust is rich in carbon but low in nitrogen, so the bacteria that digest the sawdust, slowly breaking it down into its component parts to get carbon and energy, need extra nitrogen for their own growth. These bacteria are more efficient than plants at extracting available nitrogen. Until the process is finished and the bacteria themselves die and decay back into the soil, a considerable amount of nitrogen is locked up, unavailable for plant use.

When using sawdust—or similar and equally useful organic wastes such as ground bark, peanut shells, rice hulls, ground corncobs, chopped straw, or spent hops—always add 1 to 2 percent additional nitrogen by weight. Knowing how much to add is tricky. Too little and plants will be starved of nitrogen; too much and their roots will be burned. Organic sources of nitrogen (see page 62) which decompose slowly will help to reduce the risk of root burning from overfertilization. The organic wastes should be pasteurized first, mixed with the nitrogen source, and then added to the soil. Or they can be pasteurized together with garden soil or with quick-to-decompose organic matter to use up some of the excess nitrogen released by pasteurization.

Fersolin-treated sawdust is a most valuable addition to greenhouse soils. It is very stable, slow to break down, and improves the porosity of the soil like any other sawdust. But it has the special advantage of being a slow-release source of nitrogen itself rather than a nitrogen consumer. It is more expensive, but it is more reliable as well.

SOURCES OF INERT AGGREGATE

Grit.
Some inorganic grit is needed in greenhouse soil to improve drainage and aeration. Grit increases the number of large pore spaces filled with air, giving an "open" compost. Most forms of grit decrease somewhat the amount of water the soil can hold, since they themselves are impervious to water.

Sand.
Sand is the cheapest and most easily available form of grit. It is chemically inert: it supplies and holds no nutrients. It should be well washed and free from silt, clay, or salt residues. Sharp sand is by far the most useful. The large uneven particles (.5 to 2mm in diameter) help to form innumerable air spaces in the soil. When you find a source of sharp sand, rub some between your fingers. You will know why it is called sharp. Builder's sand and sea sand rarely have the necessary grittiness. Sharp sand is wonderful for rooting cuttings because it practically eliminates waterlogging. Except for the University of California recipe for peat-based composts, fine smooth sand is hardly ever used in horticulture.

Sand is relatively heavy compared to other forms of grit. This can be an advantage—providing stability for tall pot plants in lightweight soilless composts—or a disadvantage—making large containers too heavy to move and increasing the labor of mixing.

Some people sterilize sand for added safety. This is easy as the sand cannot be damaged by overheating. But if the sand has been well looked after and not allowed to come in contact with diseases or weeds it should be relatively sterile already.

Perlite and vermiculite.
These are expanded minerals. They have been heated until they pop like popcorn. They are very light, sterile, and rather alkaline (pH 7 to 7.5). Both are good at improving drainage and aeration. And they cost about the same. The major difference is that perlite is chemically inert, does not absorb water, and is very durable. Vermiculite on the other hand is good at absorbing both water and nutrients, helping to buffer plants in soilless composts against temporary overfeeding and watering. Vermiculite breaks down fairly quickly and releases some potassium and magnesium as it does so. It also crushes quite easily, so it should not be used where the soil is cultivated often or where it must last for more than a few months. It is very good for rooting cuttings, however.

Perlite should be damped before using to reduce its dustiness. Some people find its whiteness and tendency to rise to the surface of the soil unattractive, but its long-lasting effect on soil texture and light weight make it valuable for large containers and ground beds.

Other sources of inert aggregate.
All of the following improve aeration and drainage.

Hard cinders from coal furnaces—should be weathered for a year outdoors; absorb water.

Crushed scoria—absorbs water.

Crushed pumice—very lightweight.

Crushed brick—absorbs water; may be alkaline.

Calcined clay—absorbs water and minerals; long-lasting.

Expanded polystyrene particles—long lasting; avoid heat treatment; usually white, which can be unattractive.

Urea formaldehyde foam particles—absorb water; slow-release source of nitrogen; acidic.

Gypsum (for soil-based compost)—improves soil structure by encouraging clay to form crumbs; alkaline.

PLANT NUTRITION

Hydrogen, oxygen, and carbon make up approximately 90 percent of plant tissue. Fortunately, they are provided by the air and water around the plant. Watering, ventilation, and good soil structure should ensure an adequate supply. The remaining elements are usually provided by the gar-

SOIL PASTEURIZATION

Pasteurizing the soil consists of heating damp soil to 160° to 180°F. and keeping it there for thirty minutes. For small amounts the simplest method is to fill a baking tray with damp soil, cover with tin foil, insert a meat thermometer (don't let the end touch the metal) and heat in a 300°F. oven until the thermometer reads 180°F. (or 160°F. if weed seeds are not likely to be a problem). Then turn the oven off and leave for 30 minutes before removing. For larger amounts, you can buy electric soil sterilizers.

DON'T GROW MUSHROOMS BY ACCIDENT

All wood products should be pasteurized to eliminate wood fungi, which will grow rapidly in greenhouse conditions. The fungi won't harm the plants, but the mushrooms they produce can interfere with watering and look unsightly.

dener. These nutrients are taken up through the roots from the soil solution, though small amounts of some can be applied as foliar sprays. They are all equally necessary, but some are needed in much larger quantities. These are called the major elements.

MAJOR ELEMENTS

Nitrogen.
If any one mineral is central to the growth of plants it is nitrogen. The plant cannot live just on the sugar and starch it makes by photosynthesis. Like a growing child it must have protein as well as energy. Protein is made up of carbohydrates combined with nitrogen. So with sufficient light, water, and carbon dioxide for photosynthesis of carbohydrates and sufficient nitrogen to make proteins, the plant will grow rapidly.

Nitrogen is essential for all living protoplasm, but in particular is the main constituent of chlorophyll. With insufficient nitrogen, leaves turn yellow, photosynthesis slows, and the plant stops growing and becomes stunted. Too much nitrogen causes lush soft growth with large, vivid, blue-green leaves and a delay in producing flowers and fruit. It is essential that nitrogen be balanced with the other major elements for healthy growth.

Most nitrogen is absorbed by plants in the form of nitrates. A very small amount of ammonia can be used, but larger amounts of ammonia or nitrites are toxic. Chemical fertilizers usually contain almost pure nitrate. Nitrates are very water-soluble and are easily absorbed, but also easily leached away. Slow-release forms of nitrogen are valuable to avoid erring in either direction. The breakdown of proteins in organic matter is a good slow-release source. Like plants, the bacteria that break down organic matter work best when warm and moist so they tend to produce most nitrogen when the plants are growing fastest. But slow-release chemical fertilizers which dissolve very gradually are of immense benefit for container-grown shrubs and trees that must stay in their pots for several years.

Compost and manure have a higher nitrogen content than most forms of organic matter and are fairly quick to break down, so are good sources of nitrogen to add to the soil, but use only in small amounts unless you want to risk using them unpasteurized (see page 60). Organic wastes like cottonseed meal, leather dust, hoof and horn meal, feather dust, and fish meal are all useful sources of nitrogen to incorporate in the initial soil mix. But check for toxic residues by mixing up a small amount of soil in the proportions you intend to use and germinate some tomato seeds in it. If the tomato seedlings look miserable, don't use it.

The nitrogen content of organic materials is closely related to the protein content, so animal and seed residues usually contain more nitrogen than leaf and fruit residues like spent hops or the pulp from cider mills. High nitrogen materials must be used sparingly for fear of fertilizer burn, even with organic materials.

Blood meal is the most concentrated and fastest acting organic source of nitrogen; it is also usually the most expensive. Rake it into the surface of the soil to supply a temporary deficiency. In an emergency it can be used as a foliar feed or liquid fertilizer, but be very careful not to apply too much. One tablespoon soaked in a quart of boiling water overnight and mixed with three quarts of tepid water next morning will be a strong enough mixture.

Bone meal is hard to overuse. Mixed into the soil it adds a little nitrogen gradually over a long period. Purchase steamed bone meal to avoid any possibility of catching anthrax from it. Steamed bone meal is also slightly faster acting.

Phosphorus.
This mineral is found primarily in the growing points, the tips of roots and shoots, and the seeds. Phosphorus is essential to the storage and release of energy. It encourages a good root system, sturdy growth, and early ripening of flowers and fruits. It helps in the transport of other nutrients around the plant's system. It is vital to photosynthesis, respiration, and the formation of proteins, and it is an essential part of the nucleus of every cell. Only a relatively small amount is needed, but this minimal amount is critical for healthy growth. Phosphorus is used mainly in fast-growing parts of plants. It can move through the plant, so old leaves show signs of deficiency first when they are depleted to supply the young growth. Suspect phosphorus deficiency if the older leaves show an unusual blue-purple color and eventually die. If the deficiency is severe, the plant will be stunted because of poor root growth.

Because most phosphorus is insoluble it cannot move through the soil. It cannot be leached away, but applying it to the surface of the soil is useless. It is best added to the soil when it is initially mixed. Later liquid applications of phosphate are less effective because they remain in the top inch or so. Phosphorus combines easily with clay or other elements in the soil, so a plant may experience a deficiency even if plenty of phosphorus exists, particularly if the soil is very acid or very alkaline (below pH 6 or above pH 7).

Phosphorus, usually applied as superphosphate, is the one nutrient seedlings need as soon as they germinate. It is usually the only nutrient added to seed compost (8 to 10 ounces of superphosphate per bushel). Most of the phosphorus is absorbed in the first month or so of a plant's life. Because it helps with root growth, using a bit extra when transplanting is also beneficial. A plant concentrates a great deal of its available phosphorus in its seeds in order to ensure them a good start in life. Plants that fruit over and over again such as tomatoes generally need more.

Plants can most easily absorb water-soluble phosphate, known as mono-calcium phosphate, but, perversely, this form is most quickly locked up into insoluble combinations with other elements. Di-calcium phosphate is not soluble in water but it is soluble in a weak acid solution such as is usually present in the soil. Though less easily absorbed, it remains available over a much longer period and so is really more useful. The phosphorus in bonemeal is released slowly over a long period. The phosphorus in fishmeal is available much more quickly. Watering transplants with fish emulsion gives them an extra dose when they most need it.

Potassium or potash.
This nutrient is needed for the life processes of the plant. It is not itself a constituent of any cells, but it regulates and catalyzes reactions thorughout the plant. It moves from one part of a plant to another as needed. Because it is water soluble, it easily leaches out of the soil. When there is a deficiency of potash, the plant tends to appear hard and stunted, the edges of the leaves may turn brown, and eventually the whole leaf takes on a bronzed look.

Sufficient potash produces better fruit and flowers. Tomatoes have a particularly high requirement. It also helps to harden woody growth, so feed an extra amount to perennial plants in autumn.

Potassium helps to regulate the metabolism of nitrogen. The two minerals should be applied together in approximately equal amounts so the lush effect of the nitrogen can balance the woody, stunting effect of the potash.

Seaweed meal, wood ashes (from a slow, smoldering fire if possible), greensand (a kind of sandstone), granite dust, and corncobs contain a lot of potassium. Potassium chloride or sulphate of potash can be used to supply potassium chemically.

TRACE ELEMENTS

Sulphur.
A plant needs almost as much sulphur as phosphorus. It is used in protein formation for strong healthy growth. It is not usually in short supply, partly because it occurs in superphosphate. Enough superphosphate to supply the plant's needs for phosphorus will also supply sufficient sulphur. Air pollution, ironically, is another good source of sulphur, as is gypsum. Flowers of sulphur is used as a fungicide in the greenhouse, and it can also be added to the soil to acidify it and will of course increase the supply of sulphur there.

Magnesium.
This is a central element of the chlorophyll molecule, so all green plants need a considerable amount. It also helps transport other elements as needed within the plants. Lack of magnesium leads to yellowing of the leaves from lack of chlorophyll. Because magnesium moves around in the plant to where it is most needed, a deficiency usually shows first as yellowing between the veins of the older leaves (interveinal chlorosis). The yellow areas eventually turn brown and the leaf dies. Yellowing leaves can be a symptom of lack of nitrogen, magnesium, iron, or manganese, so a soil test is sensible to be sure of applying the right nutrient.

Magnesium uptake is easily inhibited by any problem with the soil. If the soil is too cold, too wet, or too dry, magnesium cannot be readily absorbed. Poor soil structure prevents the roots from searching out all the existing magnesium. Any problem with root growth—pests, diseases, or bad conditions—will decrease the amount of magnesium taken up. Too much potassium in the soil also inhibits the absorption of magnesium, although some is needed in order to use the magnesium efficiently.

If you suspect a magnesium deficiency, apply a foliar feed first, as the problem is more likely to be the plant's ability to take magnesium in through its roots than to be an extremely low level of magnesium in the soil. Epsom salts are 10 percent magnesium and are very good for spraying on the leaves or watering the soil to increase the available magnesium. Dolomitic limestone (3 to 12 percent magnesium) is usually used in soil mixes to both raise the pH level and supply magnesium with calcium.

Calcium.
Plants require calcium for both cell division and cell enlargement; therefore, they need calcium in order to grow. But calcium has another effect which in some ways is even more important. It alters the pH of the soil, making it more alkaline. Since most greenhouse soils contain peat moss and the peat is relatively acid, calcium is generally added to bring the pH up close to neutral.

Soil pH.
If the soil is too acid or too alkaline, plant nutrients become "locked up," unavailable to the plant even though present. Alkalinity over pH 7.5 causes problems with the absorption of iron, potassium, nitrogen, and phosphorus. Below pH 5.5, nitrogen, phosphorus, and magnesium deficiencies occur. Most plants grow well with a pH of between 5.8 and 7. Most beneficial bacteria also prefer this pH range. Some plants are especially adapted to grow well in either acid or alkaline conditions, but they are then very sensitive to the reverse. Azaleas, gardenias, and heathers, for example, prefer a pH of 5 to 5.5.

Hard water will cause a gradual increase in soil alkalinity. Using rainwater is preferable in hard water areas, especially for acid-loving plants. In any case do not use water that has been through a chemical water softener, as it is likely to contain harmful residues. A few drops of vinegar in the watering can will help to compensate for the hardness of the water if rainwater is unavailable.

Most chemical fertilizers (e.g., ammonium sulphate and ammonium nitrate) gradually increase the acidity of the soil. This can help counteract the effects of hard water, but pH levels should be checked from time to time. Soil testing kits can measure pH levels easily.

Ground limestone is often added to the initial soil mix to achieve the correct pH. Once the plants are growing, raking wood ashes into the surface will help to raise the pH levels by adding potassium, whch is very alkaline. If the soil is too alkaline, work flowers of sulphur into the surface. This will slowly break down, providing a long-lasting effect. Iron sulphate works faster but does not last as long.

pH

Technically, pH is a logarithm of the reciprocal of the hydrogen ion concentration. Basically it measures acidity or alkalinity, with pH7 being about neutral. Lower numbers are more acid, higher numbers more alkaline.

FERTILIZING

Add liquid fertilizers to the soil to replace those nutrients the plant has used up. Plants recently repotted should need no liquid fertilizer for at least a month. Wait until their roots have filled the pot and used up most of the immediately available nutrients. Slow-growing plants need less fertilizer both initially and later since they use up nutrients more slowly.

A good liquid fertilizer should contain all the major nutrients in approximately the proportions in which they are used by the plant. Any of the solid fertilizers can be raked into the surface of the soil to gradually reduce deficiencies, but for more immediate effect and for greater control, use liquid fertilizers in the growing season. They are particularly valuable in March and April when the soil is too cold for the bacteria to work effectively but light levels are high enough to start plants growing again.

Most plants need no fertilizing in winter because they are not growing fast enough to use up the nutrients already present. Any extra fertilizer is likely to accumulate in the soil and cause problems in the spring when bacteria start working faster to dissolve it. A foliar feed in March and April will help get the plants off to a good start. Then liquid feed fast-growing plants every two weeks. If the greenhouse is in full production in summer, plants may need to be fed as often as once a week, tailing off again as light levels decline in autumn. In the best of all possible worlds, actively growing plants would have a constant supply of very, very dilute fertilizer, but this would be considerably more work. Feeding twice as often at half the recommended dilution would be an improvement if you can be bothered.

One of the best all-around liquid fertilizers is fish emulsion mixed with liquid seaweed (in the ratio of 6:4), but fish emulsion is quite smelly, especially when sprayed. Liquid seaweed is said to have strengthening properties and it supplies many trace elements.

Liquid fertilizers can be watered directly onto the soil or sprayed on the leaves as a foliar feed. Dilute the spray by 50 percent to avoid any risk of burning the leaves.

SPACE FOR PLANTS

Plants require a lot of space, particularly in winter when they need all the light and air circulation they can get. But human beings need space, too, as do heat storage materials. So you must make compromises.

If plants are in pots they can be put on raised benches where they are easier to see and tend. To get the most out of the space the benches can be raised in tiers toward the back wall, so the plants shade each other as little as possible. Tiered benches are very attractive for display purposes as well, but the plants are harder to inspect if you cannot get around behind them. And air circulation is somewhat reduced, particularly if the risers between the different levels are solid.

Most benches are flat and about table height. They should never be wider than you can comfortably reach across, usually about 3 feet, but up to 6 feet if there is a path on each side. They must be solidly built to carry the weight of many pots. A lip along the edge will help to prevent your pushing off plants accidentally. Be sure to leave a gap between the wall and the bench to encourage air circulation.

The surface of the bench can be either slatted or solid. If slatted, like a park bench, then water drips straight through so pots are less likely to pass diseases to one another or to become waterlogged. Air circulation is better with slats, and a certain amount of light will filter through them, allowing ferns and other shade-loving plants to grow underneath. Heavy-duty galvanized wire mesh or 1/4-inch hardware cloth can be used instead of the traditional 2-inch wooden slats spaced one inch apart.

Covering a solid bench with gravel or sand allows the pots to drain well and increases humidity. Or you can install automatic watering with a capillary mat (see page 000). A solid surface is better for summer growing when increasing humidity is a problem. Slats or wire mesh are better in winter when air circulation is all important.

Seedlings, rooted cuttings, and potted plants are usually better off on raised benches where they will get the attention they deserve. But most plants in fact grow better in beds than they do in pots. Vegetables are nearly always grown in beds. Ground beds connected directly with the earth underneath the floor are ideal for large plants, provided the water table is not too high and sufficient drainage can be provided. Such plants get the largest possible root run and the greatest amount of headroom. The temperature and the water content of the soil do not fluctuate as rapidly as they do in smaller containers. Ground beds can be larger than raised beds or benches because you can walk among the plants as you would in a garden (Figure 3.9). Stepping stones will help prevent compacting the soil where you walk.

There are disadvantages to ground beds. First, if a bad soil-borne pest or disease invades the sunspace it is extremely difficult to dig out 18 inches of soil from below floor level, and even when you have done that you can't be certain the problem won't reinfect the new soil from below. A 5-inch layer of gravel or coarse sand between the soil in the bed and the ground below will help improve drainage and prevent reinfection.

Other problems with ground beds include the stooping necessary to work with plants at ground level, the difficulty of inspecting small plants carefully enough, and the possibility of the more vigorous plants shouldering the slower-growing ones out of the way. Air temperatures are coldest at ground level and the soil is likely to stay around 45°F. all winter. If possible the beds should be surrounded by insulation at least 18 inches below ground level. Even so, it

MANURE TEA

Many organic growers swear by manure tea or compost tea. Soak a pint of well-rotted compost or manure in a gallon of water overnight and strain. Use the solids as a mulch.

3.9 ▲ A sunspace laid out like a garden with almost all the plants growing in the earth. The ample paths make working with the plants much easier.

will be colder than a bed higher up in the sunspace unless the air falls to near freezing when the near 40°F. surrounding earth will begin to act as insulation.

To improve drainage and raise soil temperature, the sides of the bed can be built up above ground level. This also helps to keep the soil in place and to discourage both animals and people from stepping in the beds accidentally. If the sides are at least 18 inches high and fairly broad, they form pleasant sitting places until the plants grow to cover them. Where the floor of the sunspace is solid, a raised bed can be made with no connection with the ground below. It must have at least 12 inches of soil and 3 inches of gravel for drainage at the bottom, so must be at least 15 inches deep overall for good growth of plants. Eighteen to 30 inches of soil is better for large or deep-rooted plants such as tomatoes, grapes, and jasmine. Holes for drainage should be provided all around the bottom of the bed.

Wooden sides for the beds are adequate but will not last as long as masonry walls. Cast concrete, concrete blocks, or bricks are all easy to build a low wall with. Cedar, redwood, or cypress will resist rot for longer than other woods. A copper-based preservative such as Cuprinol should be used on any other wood. Let it dry for a few weeks to get rid of any fumes before bringing it into the sunspace. Pressure-treated timber may well contain arsenic or pentachlor phenol so it is not safe to use in contact with the soil.

Line the walls of any bed with polyethylene to avoid leaks and prevent recontamination when changing the soil. It will also increase the life of a wooden structure. The outside of a wooden bed can be painted or stained as desired. Do this only in hot weather when the sunspace can be vented 24 hours a day for

3.10 ▲ The wooden beds are raised several inches off the floor for greater warmth and better drainage. The beds are lined with polyethylene to prolong the life of the timber.

about a week so no harmful fumes will build up. Or paint boards outside and let them dry before bringing them in.

You can also build free-standing raised beds (Figure 3.10). These are usually warmer and better drained than beds built on the ground. Great care must be taken to support the bottom while still allowing sufficient ventilation. Nothing could be worse than coming out one morning and finding the bed collapsed and your plants buried in an avalanche of soil. Heavy-duty, plastic-coated wire mesh laid over 2-inch deep wooden strips placed every 4 inches provides a good base. You can also use wooden slats placed 1 inch apart with 1-inch holes drilled in them every 6 inches, but because wood in the base is almost constantly moist it is very vulnerable to rotting. Place fine nylon mesh over the wood to keep the gravel from falling through the holes.

You can make raised beds at waist height for convenience but often there will not be sufficient head room for tall plants. Consider too what other parts of the sunspace will be shaded when plants in the raised bed are fully grown. If the glazing in the sunspace goes all the way to the ground, a ground bed against the front wall and benches or a raised bed against the back wall will usually make the most effective use of the space.

If the bottom section of the south wall is solid, ground beds are less useful, since they will be shaded most of the time in winter. Plants should be grown at, or just below, the level of the glazing.

Leave paths at least 2 feet wide in beds or between benches; 3 feet for wheelbarrows or wheelchairs. Try out a variety of path layouts on paper to see which gives you the most growing space, the most convenient access, and/or the most attractive display from a sitting area. ■

STERILIZING A GROUND BED

Powerful chemical fumigants can be used to sterilize the soil, but they are as bad for you and for any plants growing in the sunspace as they are for the nasties you are trying to kill. Usually the sunspace must remain empty for several weeks after using a soil fumigant.

CHAPTER 4

THE SUNSPACE AS SOLAR COLLECTOR

Sunshine is energy; lots and lots of energy. The fusion of hydrogen atoms in the center of the sun releases enormous quantities of energy, which travel across space in the form of electromagnetic radiation. The amount of solar energy falling on the earth in one day is almost one hundred times greater than the amount of fossil fuel energy used by all the people on earth in one year. The sun is by far the greatest source of energy on this planet and the ultimate source of all other forms of energy we use. Coal, oil, and gas come from plants that could not have grown without the sun. Wind, waves, tide, the cycle of evaporation, and rainfall that makes the rivers flow, all are ultimately caused by energy from the sun. The sun is the one free, infinitely renewable, nonpolluting source of energy for the earth. The only trouble is that its energy is not evenly distributed throughout the day or throughout the year. We must figure out how to collect and store as much of the sun's energy as possible on winter days. Likewise we must try to avoid collecting it on summer days. To understand how best to use the sun's energy it helps to go back to basics.

SOLAR RADIATION

The sun gives off electromagnetic radiation (see page 71) of every wavelength from very short-wave radiation, which we call X rays and gamma rays, to very long-wave radiation, which we call radio waves. But the vast majority of the sun's energy is given off in the form of visible light and infrared radiation.

About half of the sun's output is relatively short-wave radiation that our eyes are sensitive to: visible light. Visible light ranges in wavelength from the relatively long red band of the spectrum through orange, yellow, green, blue, and purple to violet, the shortest wavelength we can see. Between 40 and 50 percent of the solar energy that strikes the earth is in wavelengths too long to see, infrared, which are below red in the visible spectrum. We feel

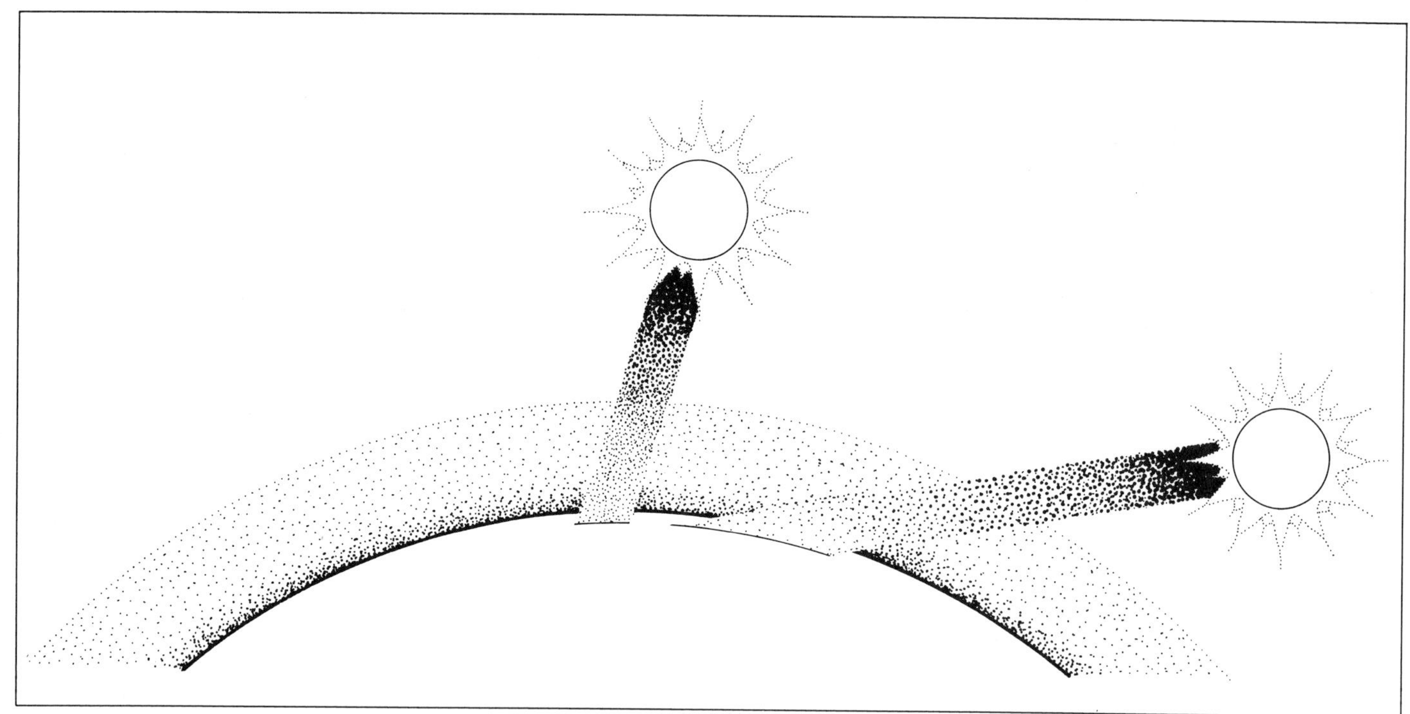

4.1 ▲ The amount of solar radiation reaching the earth is affected by the angle at which the radiation strikes the earth and the distance it has to travel through the atmosphere.

infrared radiation as heat. Wavelengths shorter than those of visible light are called ultraviolet, which are above violet in the visible spectrum. Ultraviolet radiation is harmful to both plants and people. Fortunately the earth's atmosphere screens out most of the ultraviolet radiation (only about 4 percent of the solar energy reaching the earth is ultraviolet).

VARIATIONS IN AVAILABLE SOLAR ENERGY

About 30 percent of the visible and infrared solar radiation is reflected back into space or absorbed by the earth's atmosphere even on a clear day. Clouds will reflect and absorb even more. At dusk, when the sun is nearly on the horizon, the sun's rays have to travel a longer distance through the atmosphere to reach the earth, and so more energy is lost by reflection and absorption than at noon (Figure 4.1). In winter, because of the tilt of the earth, the sun is further away from the perpendicular even at noon; therefore its rays must pass through more of the atmosphere to reach the earth. So the greatest intensity of solar radiation occurs at noon on a clear summer's day.

The intensity of solar radiation landing on the earth decreases as the angle of the sun's rays moves away from the perpendicular for another reason as well. The same amount of sunlight that strikes one square foot of earth when the sun is overhead is spread over a larger area when the sun is at an angle to that patch of earth (see Figure 4.1). These three effects, together with cloud cover, cause daily and seasonal fluctuations in the amount of solar radiation falling on the earth, leading to fluctuations in air temperature and climate.

TRAPPING SOLAR ENERGY

Stepping from shade into sun we feel the warmth caused by the sun's radiation immediately. When solar energy hits a solid object, some is reflected but most is absorbed and converted into heat, causing the molecules of the object to move faster. The solid object in turn begins to radiate as it warms up, but at a much longer wavelength because it is not as hot as the original source of radiation, the sun. The radiation of objects at ordinary temperatures is called thermal radiation or "far infrared" to distinguish it from the sun's relatively shorter wavelength, near infrared.

To trap the energy from the sun we must use a material that lets the solar radiation in but does not let the resulting thermal radiation out. Glass is the traditional material. It is transparent to visible light, so we can see through it, and it is transparent to near-infrared solar radiation, so it lets in almost all of the sun's energy. By a remarkable stroke of luck, glass is not very transparent to far-infrared thermal radiation, because it absorbs energy in those wavelengths and is itself heated. Only about 3 percent of far infrared is actually transmitted directly through the glass. As the glass absorbs the far infrared, it warms up. About half the far-infrared radiation hitting the glass is then re-radiated to the outside. The rest returns to the interior. As solar energy enters a glass structure there is therefore a net build-up of heat and of far-infrared radiation, which is converted to heat whenever it hits a solid object. Both direct and diffuse light cause heat to accumulate under glass.

All greenhouses, whether glass or polyethylene, lose heat by conduction, by convection, and by radiation (from the warmed glass). The rate of heat loss by both conduction and convection increases considerably if it is windy outside or if the air in the greenhouse is very humid.

To maximize the collection of the sun's energy and to minimize its loss is the goal of solar heating.

PRINCIPLES OF SUNSPACE DESIGN

All passive solar design concepts attempt to use the sun's energy to heat buildings in the simplest possible way. To make a sunspace an efficient solar collector it is necessary to consider four primary goals: **1)** to collect as much solar heat as possible during the heating season, **2)** to store the heat for use when it is needed, **3)** to get the heat to where it is needed in the house, and **4)** to prevent overheating.

As with all passive solar systems there is a delicate balance to maintain between the amount of south-facing glazing and the heat storage capacity. If you are collecting heat to significantly reduce fuel bills for the house, then you must allow temperatures in the house to fluctuate somewhat more than usual. If the house is 60°F. when the sun begins to heat it, it can use more of the sun's energy than if it were 70°F. And if indoor temperatures are allowed to reach 75° or even 80°F. during the day, you will need to add less heat at night. The auxiliary heating system must be responsive to irregular inputs of heat so that both sunspace and furnace are not heating the house at the same time. And, as with all passive solar systems, there is a very real problem of overheating, particularly if you are going to use the sunspace as a living area.

Recent research has shown that sunspaces can be quite effective solar heat collectors, but are too expensive to be justified by energy savings alone. Simple south-facing windows are obviously much cheaper to incorporate in a house and perform more efficiently in terms of energy collection. In virtually every case, increasing insulation and draftproofing an existing house will pay for the capital outlay faster than the addition of a sunspace will. Passive solar collection and insulation measures often work against each other. In cloudy climates a low energy house can have a very short and sunless heating season. This is not only because the heating requirement itself is lower, but also because the heating season for a well-insulated house is shorter, and is concentrated in exactly the time of year when there is less sunshine.

A sunspace for passive solar collection, however, is by definition a buffer zone—a largely unheated space occupied only when the climate permits, that protects the inner part of the house from the extremes of the outside climate. There are therefore two ways in which a sunspace reduces the home heating bill. First, it captures solar energy, which can be transferred into the house, and second, it reduces the heat loss from the house by raising the temperature on the other side of the house wall considerably. Since the heat lost through the walls is directly

HOW HEAT MOVES

Heat moves by radiation, conduction, and convection, always from hotter to colder (see Figure 4.2). Conduction and convection are easy to understand. Radiation is a bit less obvious.

Conduction

Conduction is the movement of heat through a solid object or from one solid object to another object touching it. As each molecule heats up, it passes some of its heat on to its neighbors and heats them until gradually the heat is distributed evenly throughout the object.

Convection

Convection is the movement of heat through fluids (both liquids and gases are fluids in this sense). The heated molecules heat their neighbors as in conduction, but they are able to move through the fluid, forming convection currents, mixing and spreading the heat more rapidly than would be possible by conduction alone. The old truism "heat rises" is in fact only true for convection in a fluid. The heated fluid expands, thus becoming lighter and rising, while the colder fluid sinks. Losses by convection are greatly increased if the fluid is moving by the warm object for some other reason as well. When wind blows over heated glass, for instance, the glass loses its heat much faster than it would by natural convection through still air.

Radiation

Radiation does not depend on passing heat from one molecule to the next. It can take place across a vacuum and it travels at the speed of light. Infrared radiation (heat), like visible radiation (light), consists of electromagnetic waves (energy) passing directly from one object to another without affecting anything in between. Everything above absolute zero (-273°F.) radiates some electromagnetic energy all the time. But the amount of radiation depends heavily on the difference in temperature between the object and the surfaces it is radiating energy toward. At 98.6°F. you radiate a small amount of heat to the walls around you. But if you sit next to a single-glazed window on a cold night, you will soon become aware that you are losing considerably more heat in that direction despite the fact that the air is about the same temperature on all sides of you. On the other hand, if you were sitting near a woodstove, you would gain heat from the stove faster than you lose it toward the stove, because the stove is at a relatively higher temperature than you are.

Radiation moves in straight lines, so a radiant heater only heats those objects which it can "see." If you hold a newspaper, or any solid object, between you and the woodstove it will dramatically cut down the heat you feel. Likewise it is cooler in the shade on a sunny day, because the sun cannot "see" you.

proportional to the temperature difference between inside and out, a sunspace covering a substantial area of the outside wall of the house can make quite a contribution.

A further aspect of the thermal buffering effect of a sunspace is that it can preheat any ventilation air required in the house itself. There has been concern recently about houses being so tightly constructed as to be stultifying and unhealthy to the occupants. The minimum recommended ventilation rates are around one-half air change per hour; i.e., the air in the house should be changed completely every two hours. In cold climates the heat lost by ventilation even at this minimal rate may be quite significant, since the outside air can be 40° to 60°F. below the indoor comfort temperature. If this air is introduced via the sunspace, it is preheated, thus reducing the amount of heat required from the home heating system. In the same manner the sunspace can act as an entry airlock. An outside door lets in a lot of cold air when it is opened. If the house door opens into a sunspace, the air rushing in will be considerably warmer than the outside air, thus reducing heat losses.

The many ways in which a sunspace reduces heat loss, in addition to its positive contribution to heat gain, make it difficult to calculate the actual savings in energy. Other methods of saving energy are likely to be more effective in pure energy terms, but unlike any other method, building a sunspace adds extra living area to your home, and so increases its value and provides a delightful setting for both plants and people.

AREA OF GLAZING

For a potential sunspace owner the first question is, how big should it be? Or, more exactly, how big should the glazed area be? Too much glazing can easily overheat the space in daytime and lose an enormous amount of heat at night (even double glazing loses five times as much heat as a standard insulated stud wall). Too little glazing will fail to provide the heat needed by the house while costing almost as much to build. Solid walls cannot let in the sun's energy, but keeping the glazing down to what is strictly necessary for heat collection (or plant growth) will pay off.

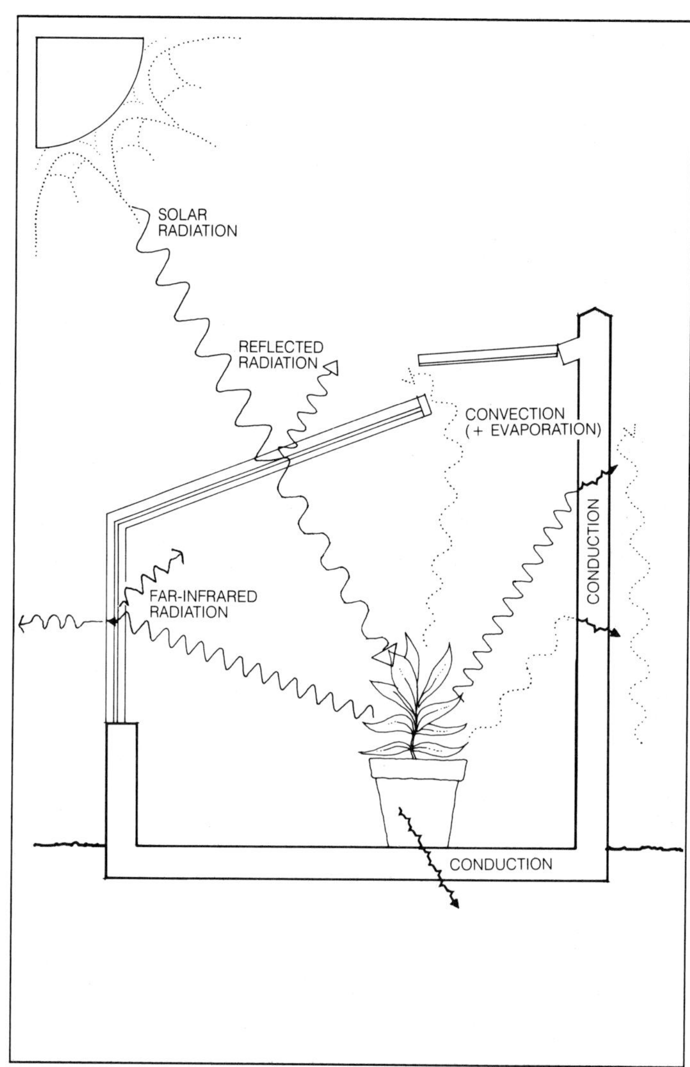

4.2 ▲ How heat moves: plants in a greenhouse are heated by solar radiation; they then give off heat (far-infrared radiation) by convection, conduction, and radiation to the walls and glazing.

Keep overhead glazing and, in particular, east- and west-facing glazing, to a minimum. Overhead glazing loses heat faster than vertical glazing because the night sky is much colder than the surrounding objects. Also, because hot air tends to collect under the roof, overhead glazing will be slightly warmer and will thus radiate somewhat faster than lower-level glazing. In addition overhead glazing collects more unwanted heat from the overhead sun in summer than vertical glazing would. East- and west-facing glazing lose heat as fast as any other vertical glazing without contributing much to winter heat gain, because the winter sun rises and sets quite far south of due east and west. They also collect plenty of unwanted heat in summer as the sun moves around closer to due east and due west in the morning or afternoon.

South-facing glazing is obviously the key to winter heat collection. But too much of a good thing can cause trouble. Seventy passive solar houses, some of them incorporating sunspaces, were carefully monitored from 1981 to 1983 by the Department of Energy and the Solar Energy Research Institute. One of the key findings was that most passive solar houses overheat even in winter because they have too much south-facing glazing.

The recommended ratio of glazed area to floor area of the house has been falling in recent years. Current wisdom suggests that to avoid overheating the area of glazing should not exceed approximately 5 percent of the floor area for a superinsulated house in a warm climate or, at the other extreme, 60 percent for a leaky house in a cold climate. Of course most houses lie between these two extremes. If you have an old leaky house in a cold climate, you should insulate and draftstrip it first, since this will be a much more cost-effective way of saving energy. For most houses the optimum ratio of glazed area to floor area will be between 15 and 30 percent.

There are, however, other factors to take into account. One is whether your house already benefits from south-facing windows. Windows are three times as valuable as sunspace glazing for heating a house, so you should reduce the maximum area of glazing by three times the area of the windows that will remain uncovered by the sunspace. Second, the percentages given above are based on frame houses with drywall construction. If your house has intrinsic thermal mass—e.g., masonry walls or concrete floors, or added thermal mass such as water barrels—then you can increase the area of south-facing glazing substantially. The area of glazing can be as much as doubled on a house with considerable thermal mass. Adding heat storage materials is dealt with more fully later in this chapter (page 81). Third, by judicious use of shading devices you can greatly reduce the problem of overheating, which is the main limitation on the size of sunspace a house can accommodate. Finally, if you intend to use your sunspace primarily for growing, the plants themselves will use up a considerable amount of the available solar energy, primarily in transpiration, and once again you can incorporate more south-facing glazing.

The problem of deciding exactly how much south-facing glazing a particular house needs is so complex and subject to so many variables that it is well worth consulting a local architect or engineer with experience with passive solar design.

ANGLE OF GLAZING

To capture the maximum amount of solar energy, the glazing material must be as nearly perpendicular to the sun's rays as possible. Otherwise some of the incoming radiation will be reflected back. Since the greatest intensity of solar energy occurs at noon, and since heating is wanted mainly in winter, the ideal angle of the glazing for heat collection is perpendicular to the position of the sun at noon in midwinter (Figure 4.3). To achieve this, the angle between the glazing and the horizontal should be about the angle of latitude plus 15°; that is, between 50° and 60° from the horizontal for most of the continental United States. However, changing the angle by up to 15° in either direction affects solar transmission by less than 6°, so the precise angle is not critical. But the transmission decreases rapidly if the angle is more than 25° from the ideal.

In northern latitudes, especially where direct sunshine is the rule in winter, vertical glazing is perfectly adequate and considerably easier to build and maintain, as well as being less prone to overheating in summer. Vertical glazing usually collects 10 to 20 percent less heat than glazing at the optimum angle, but in areas where snow stays on the ground for long periods, reflection off the snow will increase light levels by up to 20 percent if the glazing is near vertical. This at least partially offsets any losses due to a less than ideal angle.

Steep glazing angles maximize the collection of direct sunlight in winter, but they are not very good for collecting diffuse light on overcast days. Most solar energy available on overcast days comes from directly overhead, rather than from the sun's actual position. Diffuse solar radiation is especially important in areas that do not receive much direct sun in winter. It also seems to be vital for healthy growth in many plants, so consider carefully the local climate and the purpose for which you want the sunspace before building only vertical windows.

ORIENTATION OF GLAZING

The closer to due south the glazing faces, the more solar energy it can collect. Slightly east of south will help to warm up the space after a cold night and reduce problems of overheating in the afternoon. But as with the angle of glazing, the exact orientation is not critical. Up to 15° or even 20° from due south still gives good results. Weather patterns should be considered in choosing the best orientation for the glazing. If easterly light is obscured by early morning fogs or immovable obstructions it may be worth angling the glazing to the west of south.

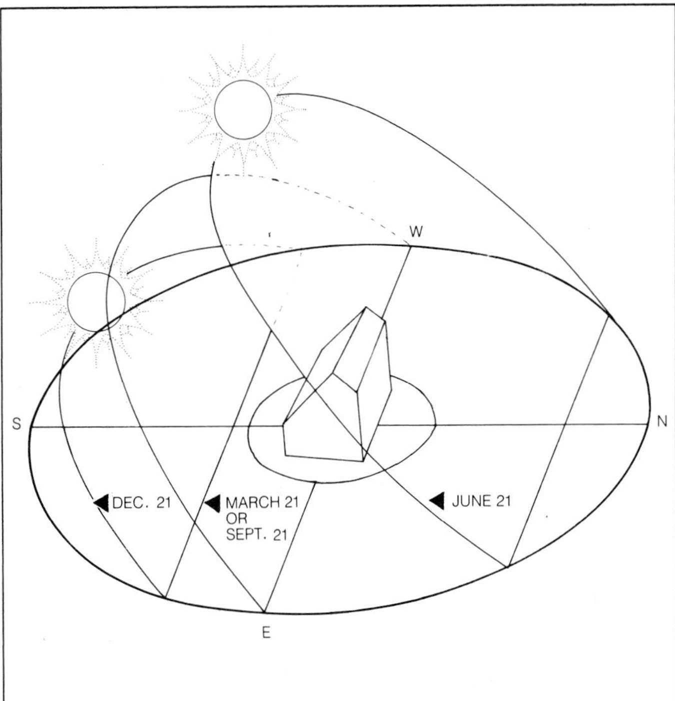

4.3 ▲ The sun is much closer to the horizon at noon in winter than in summer, so vertical glazing will receive much more sunshine in the coldest part of the year than glazing at a shallow slope, which will receive most sunshine in summer. The diagram shows the passage of the sun through the sky at different seasons for latitude 50° N.

SHADING

Any object that stops sunlight from falling on the glazing will obviously reduce the amount of solar energy received. Some shading in summer is desirable, but for maximum heat collection, shading in winter must be minimized. At midsummer it is hard to remember just how long the shadows cast by faraway trees and buildings are on December twenty-first. Even a deciduous tree can cut out up to 50 percent of the available light if the shadows of its bare branches fall on the glazing. It is well worth analyzing the site to see what obstructions will shade the glazing. With a transparent Solar Site Selector, the passage of the sun through the sky is represented on a transparent sheet. Looking through it, you can see what objects will block the sun at different times of day for each month of the year.

GLAZING MATERIALS

It is important to consider both the solar and thermal transmittance of the glazing material you intend to use. Until recently plant greenhouses were always single glazed to admit as much solar radiation as possible. Nighttime temperatures were maintained by using auxiliary heating. But for sunspaces it is usually worth trading off some of solar transmittance for better performance in reducing heat loss. The general wisdom nowadays is that it is not worth building single-glazed sunspaces north of the Mason-Dixon line. Judging by Canadian and Scandinavian experience, where energy efficiency is imperative, there will be a southward flow of *triple* glazing unless the tide is stopped, as it has been in Europe, by the development of low-emissivity, high-performance glass.

New glazing materials are being developed all the time and are likely to have a profound effect on the evolution of passive solar design in the next decade.

GLASS

Glass is the traditional glazing and does an excellent job. A single layer lets in 86 percent of the solar energy hitting it. Most of the solar energy is converted into long-wave thermal radiation when it hits the objects inside. Since glass is relatively opaque to long-wave radiation, much of the heat generated inside is trapped there. Glass is structurally strong, scratch-proof, long-lasting, and easy to clean. Because of its traditional appearance it fits in aesthetically with most buildings. It does not expand or contract with temperature changes as much as most plastics, so it is less prone to leaking. Best of all, it is not very expensive, especially if used in standard sizes.

On the negative side, glass shatters easily. In areas where hail is likely to be a problem toughened, laminated or wired safety glass should be used overhead; and in many areas it is required for all sloped glazing, so check with local building codes. Safety glass should also be used wherever there is any danger of people falling against it or running into it. Glass is heavier than the plastic alternatives, and thus requires a strong support structure that may block additional light. Because it is both breakable and heavy it is awkward to handle, so construction is more difficult. It is not as easily cut to shape as plastic, and it will not bend to form a curved eave. Like all thin materials it conducts heat well, warming the outside air when it heats up, and it does reradiate about half the infrared radiation striking it.

Each additional layer halves the heat lost by radiation, but more important, the air in the gap between the layers conducts heat poorly, as long as there is no air movement. Any gap less than 4 inches discourages air currents so the air will conduct the heat very slowly. At least 1/2 inch should be allowed between the glazing layers in order to get the maximum benefit from the insulating properties of stagnant air. One and a half inches is considered ideal, but gaps between 5/8 of an inch and 4 inches give very similar results. The choice is mainly one of convenience. Commercially available double glazing often uses a 1/4-inch gap to reduce the overall thickness of the unit to fit into slender window mullions, but for a small additional charge they can usually increase the gap to 1/2 inch, which is much more effective.

The most important factor in reducing heat loss by double glazing is getting an airtight fit, so that hot air from inside cannot get between the layers. If air leaks do occur, considerably more heat will escape, and condensation will form between the layers, where it cannot easily be removed.

PLASTICS

All plastic glazings have certain disadvantages compared with glass: they expand and contract more with temperature changes so are harder to seal; their lifetime is somewhat uncertain because they have only been in use for 50 years, whereas 500-year-old glass still works well; they are more flammable and may produce poisonous fumes even when they don't actually catch fire (check local fire regulations for allowable materials); many are vulnerable to damage from ultraviolet light and from scratches; and they are generally less attractive. On the other hand, they are considerably lighter and require less structural support; they are less likely to shatter and less dangerous if they do; they are easier to cut and bond to shape, and are easier generally for the do-it-yourselfer to handle.

Sealed double glazing units avoid problems with condensation. They are readily available and inexpensive in standard sizes, such as for patio doors. Nonstandard sizes can be made to order. Most manufacturers are reluctant to guarantee sealed units used on sloping roofs, so check the guarantee carefully. Thermal expansion and contraction combined with the slipping action of the glass is liable to break the seal, and once this seal goes, moist air can leak in.

Triple glazing, with two 1/2-inch air spaces, loses only 40 percent as much heat as single glazing while transmitting just over 60 percent as much solar energy. Because it lets in 10 percent less solar energy, triple glazing usually collects only 10 to 20 percent more energy than double glazing. It is rarely worth the extra cost unless nighttime comfort in the sunspace is important. In very sunny climates triple glazing can actually reduce the overall heat gain. An additional disadvantage of triple glazing, besides cost, is that the overall thickness of the unit, about 1¾ inches, is difficult to accommodate with conventional glazing bars.

To improve the transmittance of multiple glazings, you can use low-iron glass. The iron in conventional glass (which gives it a green appearance on the edges) absorbs about 4 percent of the solar radiaton striking it. Each layer of low-iron glass lets through slightly more solar energy. In multiple glazings this can add up to 10 to 12 percent more solar energy in the sunspace. In areas where low-iron glass is only slightly more expensive than conventional glass, it may be worth the extra cost.

You can achieve approximately the same effect as triple glazing with a conventional double-glazed unit with a low-emissivity (low-E) coating on the outer face of the inner pane, which reduces the rate of thermal radiation. This not only results in energy savings, but also makes the inner pane considerably warmer, thus increasing the surface radiant temperature within the room so the glass no longer feels as cold when you are standing next to it. It also filters out considerably more ultraviolet light, which reduces fading in fabrics and furnishings. Low-E coatings have been used extensively in Europe and are becoming more popular in the United States.

Most low-E coatings are suitable only for use within a sealed double-glazed unit. The coating itself is soft and easily damaged if left unprotected. A more recent development is the hard-coat low-E glass called pyrolitic glass, where the low-emissivity surface is baked on and becomes as hard as the glass itself. Its thermal properties are not quite as good as those of its soft-coat competitors, but the glass can be cut to shape and handled like ordinary glass. Because it is only marginally effective when used as a single layer, it is best for storm windows and secondary glazing.

Similar low-E coatings can be applied to polyester film. Like the soft coat on glass, the film is very fragile and must be used inside a sealed double-glazed unit. It constitutes an extra layer of glazing with very little additional reduction in solar transmittance. Southwall Corporation and 3M Company both manufacture films with varying degrees of solar transmission and infrared emissivity to suit different climate-control requirements.

The thermal performance of a sealed glazed unit can also be improved by reducing the convection and conduction of heat through the air space itself. The best way is to fill the space between the glazings with a heavy gas, argon or krypton, which reduces convection currents between the outer panes. Argon-filled units have been used extensively for more than ten years in Scandinavia. They reduce the heat loss by about 15 percent for a fractional extra cost and with no reduction in light transmission. Krypton-filled units perform even better and have an added advantage: they can achieve a similar thermal performance with a smaller gap between glass panes.

CLEAR RIGID PLASTICS

Clear rigid plastics—polycarbonate and acrylic—are available as single ⅛-inch or ¼-inch thick sheets similar to glass, or they can be extruded into double- or triple-walled materials characterized by their reeded or ribbed appearance.

As single sheets, polycarbonates such as Lexan, and Tuffak and acrylics such as Plexiglas and Texaglas look like glass when new. They are just as transparent to visible light and absorb infrared in the same way. They are strong, and polycarbonate has especially good impact resistance (in fact it is almost unbreakable) so it is preferred where pets or children are a factor or where hail or vandals pose a problem. The glazing system must allow for their considerable expansion and contraction. They can be used anywhere glass is used, but they are significantly more expensive, so they are normally used only to bend around a curve at the eaves of a building or where impact resistance is needed.

Double-wall extruded polycarbonates and acrylics are generally more useful. Their rigidity and light weight mean they need fewer structural supports, so they often let in as much solar energy as a single layer of the same material would with the additional shading from its increased structure. They both come in 4-foot widths and 8- to 16-foot lengths. Longer lengths are available from some manufacturers. Transmittance of solar and visible light is as good as with two layers of glass. They have been used extensively for roofing of both sunspaces and industrial buildings.

Twin-wall extruded plastics are cheaper than double glass units, but when you add the price of the special glazing bars they require, the difference is often minimal. The reeded effect of the many internal connections between the layers is not very elegant and hard to see through, so it is unsuitable where a view is desired.

Triple-wall polycarbonates have similar properties to triple glazing with glass, but three layers of glass would cost more than twice as much, while letting 10 percent less solar energy through and weighing many times more.

Exposure to ultraviolet light causes twin-wall and triple-wall polycarbonates to become gradually more opaque. They develop a yellowish haze which cuts down the transmission of solar radiation by around 1 percent more every year. Acrylic is more ultraviolet resistant and it is now possible to get acrylic-coated polycarbonate to reduce the yellowing with age.

WORKING WITH FIBERGLASS

Fiberglass is an easy material to work with. It can be cut with a fine-tooth saw or cheap metal cutter. It can be drilled, screwed, and nailed fairly easily. Slightly oversized holes should be drilled, and rubber washers used around the nails or screws to allow for expansion.

FIBERGLASS

Fiberglass is a term used loosely for all forms of glass-reinforced plastic (GRP) and fiber-reinforced plastic (FRP). It is generally translucent; it transmits light, but you cannot actually see through it. Although it appears to let in less light than fully transparent materials, it usually transmits at least as much useful solar radiation as glass does, and sometimes more. It diffuses the light, so the solar energy is more evenly distributed over both plants and heat storage materials, which may be an advantage. It absorbs infrared radiation in the same way as glass, but is relatively shatterproof. The surface can be scratched but this is not very noticeable due to its translucency, and the surface can be refinished periodically to eliminate scratches.

Different grades of fiberglass are available based on the quality and durability of the fiber or glass cloth, which acts as reinforcement, and the resin, which provide rigidity. Flat fiberglass comes in rolls, usually 4 feet wide. There should be no need for horizontal joints because you can cut full length sections off the roll. It is floppy and needs to be supported on all its edges and every few feet along its length, unless it is vertical, when only the edges need support. Corrugated fiberglass is stronger, but not a good idea as its greater surface area increases the heat lost without increasing the solar energy gained. Also it is harder to draftproof and to finish off neatly.

Fiberglass is cheaper than glass or the rigid plastics, but it degrades fairly quickly and loses much of its ability to transmit solar radiation unless refinished every few years. If coated with an ultraviolet-resistant resin the fiberglass should last longer but cost more.

Aesthetically the main disadvantage of fiberglass is that you cannot see through it, but it does cast a pleasant, even light. If you want privacy, or the view consists of someone else's garbage cans, then translucency may be an advantage.

PLASTIC FILMS

Plastic films are not appropriate for a permanent structure attached to a house. They have a short life and a messy appearance. Ultraviolet light reduces their ability to transmit light and causes them to become brittle and tear easily. They expand when hot, so they tend to look floppy in the daytime. The labor involved in replacing the film and the amount of non-renewable energy they use (plastics are nearly all derived from oil) make film an undesirable long-term option. They are best used, if at all, for an inner layer of double glazing. Glass and the thicker rigid or semirigid plastics filter out most of the ultraviolet light, so a layer of plastic film will last considerably longer inside. Plastic film is especially good at reducing heat loss from air leaks. It can be installed just for the three or four coldest months of the year.

4.4 ▲ The Solar Room system provides an air-inflated polyethylene greenhouse during winter that can be removed when not required during the summer.

If you want to enclose the sunspace in winter and have it open in summer, plastic film might be worth considering since less ultraviolet light filters through the atmosphere in winter. A commercially available plastic film sunspace, called a Solar Room (Figure 4.4), is designed with temporary use in mind. A Solar Room consists of two layers of polyethylene film inflated by a small fan. It can be taken down in 15 minutes and either left open as a skeletal structure or replaced with an awning and a screen to form an instant screened-in porch for summer.

Polyethylene is the cheapest and most commonly used plastic film. It has a life expectancy of only 6 months (up to one year in cloudy climates if installed at the beginning of winter, but as little as 3 months in bright sunny areas). Some polyethylene comes with ultraviolet inhibitors, which help it to last up to twice as long.

More expensive plastic films exist that improve on polyethylene in various ways. The fluorocarbons, like Teflon and Tedlar, are less sensitive to ultraviolet degradation and should last for several years. They transmit over 90 percent of the solar energy striking them and they also absorb some infrared radiation, keeping the sunspace a bit warmer at night. Tedlar is extremely strong and can be used as an external glazing. Teflon has a low reflectivity, so less solar radiation is lost by reflection. Acetate is particularly vulner-

able to tearing but has good infrared absorption, so it can be useful as the inside layer in double glazing. Vinyl is quite sensitive to ultraviolet rays, but is initially quite strong. It absorbs some infrared radiation, so it too is worth considering for an inner layer. Acrylics and polyesters are strong and not very vulnerable to ultraviolet degradation. They can be used as an external glazing. Several laminated films, like Flexigard and Esifilm, combine two or more films to get both strength and ultraviolet resistance.

INSULATION

The construction of the solid walls, roofs, and floor of the sunspace is as important as the choice of glazing material. Everything needs to be carefully detailed, insulated, and draft-sealed so that the rate of heat loss from the sunspace is kept to a minimum. Considerable advances have been made in high-insulation construction over the last few years and most architects and builders are now becoming conversant with them.

The main aim is to ensure continuous insulation between the studs. To increase the overall insulation, clad the exterior of the studs with an insulating sheathing board. More heat escapes through solid roof structures than through walls, so try to incorporate at least 6 inches of fiberglass between rafters.

Make sure a continuous, lapped and taped vapor barrier, usually polyethylene film, is fixed on the warm side of all insulation. Be especially careful of any areas at high level and of the undersides of rafters. Seal carefully around any places where you have to puncture the vapor barrier, for example for electrical conduit and boxes, and ensure that the wall-vapor barrier joins the one in the roof. Warm moist air from the building must not be allowed to penetrate into the insulation. If it does, condensation will occur and cause problems where, initially at least, you cannot see them. By the time trouble is visible, it may be necessary to replace rotten structural timbers as well as the interior cladding.

Aluminum glazing bars that are continuous from inside to outside are fortunately becoming a thing of the past. Contemporary designs usually incorporate a "thermal break" of plastic joining the inner and outer aluminum extrusions. This prevents the glazing bar, with its very high rate of conductivity, forming a cold surface on the inside of the building and causing condensation. The same principle, however, applies to the entire building. Areas of particularly high conductivity form cold bridges in an otherwise well-insulated structure, and thus increase not only the rate of heat loss but also the incidence of condensaton.

Flooring to increase thermal storage should be constructed of concrete, with a heat-absorbent surface, ideally ceramic or clay tiles. It should be insulated underneath and at the edges. This is usually done with layers of rigid foam insulation, such as Styrofoam, immediately above the damp-proof membrane.

REDUCING INFILTRATION

In a traditional greenhouse much of the heat is lost through convection and infiltration—warm air seeping through the structure to the outside and colder air finding its way inside. Convection and infiltration increase dramatically as the speed of the air moving over the glass increases, so a windbreak can substantially decrease the heat loss in windy areas.

With the advent of more sophisticated glazing systems and better construction techniques, it is possible to build a sunspace with a very low infiltration rate. The problems occur, as they always have, at the junctions between different materials, such as between sloped glazing and roof or wall, between a gable wall and the roof, or simply at the edges of opening vents. Timber is not the quality it used to be, and shrinkage and warping can cause cracks to develop long after the sunspace is finished. You should design for a certain amount of movement and use draftstripping (such as EDPM or Neoprene) that can accommodate movement, and mastics (such as silicone and polysulphide) which retain elasticity over a number of years. Remember that extra dollars spent on insulation and draftstripping are generally repaid before the dollars spent on more complicated solar collection systems. Get the basic construction right.

MOVABLE INSULATION

However much care you take insulating the opaque structural elements of the sunspace, you will undoubtedly be left

WINDBREAKS

Evergreen trees provide good windbreaks, absorbing much of the force of the wind in the tossing of their branches. A windbreak planted in the path of the prevailing wind will be effective up to a distance of ten times its height. A solid wall is less effective than trees or a lattice-work fence because it merely deflects the wind, causing turbulence on the far side often equal to the force of the wind itself. A ratio of 50 percent solid to 50 percent space is ideal.

with a large area of glazing that constitutes the greatest source of heat loss. You can of course cut this down by using multiple layers of glazing and by using low-emissivity coatings on the glass, but such measures also inevitably cut down the incoming solar radiation. One answer to this dilemma is to incorporate movable insulation.

Over the last decade huge investments of time and money have gone into the search for a product that, on paper at least, should produce big energy savings. But conclusions drawn from a monitoring program of the Department of Energy and the Solar Energy Research Institute over the last few years indicate that movable insulation, though it has the capacity to produce savings, simply was not being used efficiently and effectively.

It takes a devoted owner to put up and take down movable insulation at the right moment every day, and any delays quickly eat away at the day's energy gains. Automatic systems for putting insulation in place are available, controlled either by a time clock or a light sensor, but the system is often more expensive than adding an extra layer of glazing and is also subject to mechanical failure. Movable insulation, however, is likely to create the most comfortable conditions for nighttime use by people.

The types of movable insulation fall into three basic categories: shutters, blinds, and conventional curtains.

Insulating Shutters.
The simplest form of movable insulation is a sheet of foam fixed in place on the inside of the glass during the night and removed during the day. Extruded polystyrene foam (Styrofoam) or Isocyanurate foam tends to be the most suitable, since both combine strength and rigidity with high-insulation value. The foam sheet can be kept in place by magnetic clips (obtainable from Zomeworks, which developed the idea), or with pieces of Velcro, obtainable at most fabric stores and glued to the frame and to the shutter. Or you can simply push it into place if it fits tightly. A strip of flexible foam around the outside of the panel will make up for any irregularity with a push-fit system. The shutter should be attached to the glazing bars rather than to the glass in order to leave a gap of ½ to 1 inch between the glass and shutter. This dead air space, sealed all round, adds considerably to the insulation value of the shutter.

4.5 ▲ Custom-made insulating shutters for high-level glazing by Boston Shutter and Door, Keene, New Hampshire. The timber-faced louvers pivot shut at night.

The foam should be covered with shiny foil or light-colored reflective cloth or painted to prevent deterioration in the sun's ultraviolet rays, and to reflect incoming radiation and stop heat build-up in the space between the glass and the shutter. When internal shutters are not removed on a sunny day, temperatures can reach over 150°F., harming the foam and damaging the edge seal on double-glazed sealed units.

The difficulty with these shutters is storing and handling them. Large slabs of foam are fragile and awkward to move. The foam should be covered to protect the edges and a small tab left on the back to form a handle to help ease out a tight-fitting shutter without damage. Putting the shutters in place without damaging plants can be a challenge and, when not in use, the shutters take up a great deal of room. If at all possible, devise beforehand some simple system for opening, closing, and storing them.

At the other end of the scale from the do-it-yourself foam slab, there are a number of manufacturers who produce custom-made insulating shutters that fold to one side (fairly common in prestigious eighteenth-century houses), but these are more suited to windows than to the large expanses of glass in a sunspace. InsulShutter of Keene, New Hampshire, produces insulating louvers for high-level glazing (Figure 4.5) that could easily be adapted for sunspace use. A similar product is available from Zomeworks in New Mexico. Developed many years ago by Steve Baer, the "Skylid" louvered system for controlling solar gain through rooflights can be operated automatically to track the sun for either maximum or minimum solar gain.

Shutters on the outside of the sunspace are theoretically a great idea (Figure 4.6). They could be used for reflecting more light in and for summer shading as well as for providing excellent insulation. But the difficulties of making shutters strong enough to withstand all the extremes of weather, in particular the occasional hurricane or tornado, make them impractical in most situations. Even where they can be secured against damage, the buildup of snow or ice can easily impede their operation, leaving you without insulation—or without sunshine—at the most critical point in the year.

Insulating Blinds.
Because of the space insulating shutters take up, much work has been done recently to develop insulating roller blinds or curtains that are made out of thin material and require less storage space than rigid shutters. Any opaque material will effectively halve the amount of radiation getting through. Only very shiny heat-reflective material, such as aluminum foil, can cut radiant heat loss by more than half. So a thin shiny blind is more effective at blocking radiant heat loss than a thick black one. A thick blind will cut conductive heat loss better, but takes more room to store. Shades or curtains can also reduce heat loss by convection but to do so they must fit tightly against the glazing bars of the greenhouse to enclose a completely dead airspace between the curtain and glazing.

If humidity from plants is likely to be a problem, padded material should be avoided. Even with a vapor barrier the padding is bound to get damp and lose much of its effectiveness as an insulator. And it is likely to get moldy if rolled up before it dries. Heat-reflective materials are less affected by humidity. Paradoxically, the shiny side should face the glazing as the most important function of heat-reflective materials is not to emit radiation. Having the shiny side out also helps if the blind is to be used for summer shading: much of the incoming solar energy will be reflected back out again.

Various manufacturers produce insulating blinds that can be adapted to sunspace design. Appropriate Technology Corporation, one of the leading manufacturers, produces the Window Quilt blind with a wide range of internal finishes (Figure 4.7). The quilted material incorporates a very thin layer of aluminized polyester film. This blind can be integrated into curved eave sunspace designs such as those produced by Four Seasons Solar Corporation. In their System Four the sill contains a built-in spring roller, which in conjunction with a motorized roller mechanism at the ridge enables the entire length of roof and front wall glazing to be sealed automatically with a Window Quilt blind, providing almost three times as much insulation as double glazing alone.

Thermal Technology Corporation produces a flexible, honeycomb-like blind made of aluminized plastic film that compresses to ⅛ inch of storage space at the top of the window for every foot of open blind. It operates like a pleated shade and can be fixed between vertical or sloping glazing bars.

Many types of roller blind or pleated shade can be adapted to suit sloping-roof glazing. Consult your local manufacturer on blinds and awnings, and select a material that will not be affected by moisture if you intend to grow many plants. If you are looking for maximum thermal efficiency, go for a material that is tightly woven to prevent air migrating from the blind's warm side to its cool side, and preferably one that has a high-reflective, low-emissivity surface on the outside (Figure 4.8). A tracking system that provides an airtight seal around the edges will improve the blind's performance substantially.

Curtains and drapes. Ordinary drapes or curtains can be used as movable insulation for vertical glazing. They will be greatly improved by the addition of a heat-reflective layer such as aluminized cotton curtain-lining material, with the shiny side out. If humidity is not a problem, a layer of fluffy dacron or polyester backing will help. Again, every effort should be made to avoid air leaking around the edges, particularly at the bottom and sides.

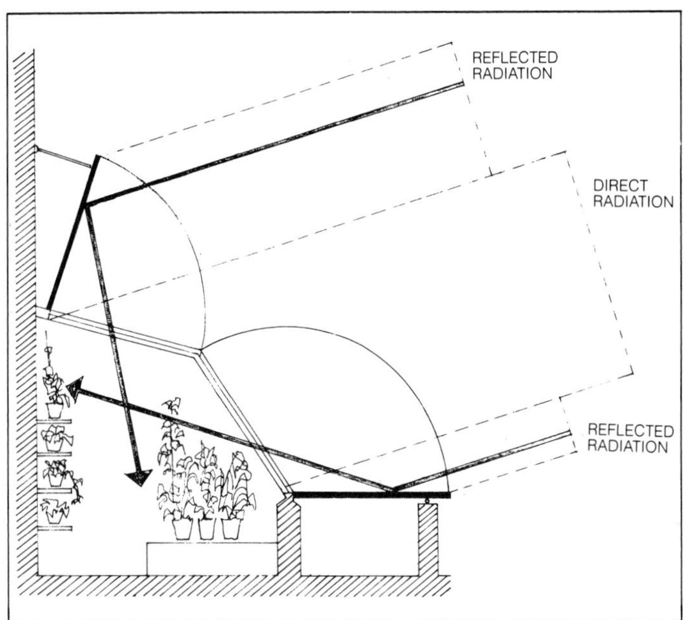

4.6 ▲ External insulating shutters with a bright white or mirrored surface could theoretically be used to increase winter solar radiation as well as to cut down heat loss.

Any movable insulation can also be used for shading in summer. This is especially useful for overhead glazing, which collects an enormous amount of heat from the overhead sun. Insulation left in place inside the glazing can cause drastic overheating there, so a gap should be left at top and bottom in summer and a heat reflective material should be used on the outside of the insulation to prevent heat buildup.

Shutters and blinds can reduce the heat loss from the sunspace tremendously. In most climates single glazing will collect almost as much heat as double glazing will if both have nighttime insulation because of the reduction in heat gain during the day with double glazing. In the Southwest it can actually provide more. But nighttime insulation is effective only if it is put in place and removed promptly. It all depends on the conscientiousness of the owner. People who are often away will find their movable insulation is not doing them much good.

4.7 ▲ Window Quilt insulating blinds by Appropriate Technology Corporation, shown partly rolled up.

4.8 ▲ Solar-reflective, low-emissivity blinds pulled half way down.

HEAT STORAGE

Any greenhouse quickly heats up when the sun shines on it and quickly cools down when the sun stops shining. It can easily rise to 110°F. on a sunny winter's day, and drop way below freezing the same night. If the glass area is small by comparison with the house, the house may be able to use all the daytime excess. But remember that the house is also being heated by its south-facing windows on a sunny day, and much of the extra heat may just have to be vented outside. By increasing the heat storage capacity of the sunspace, extra daytime heat can be saved for nighttime use and the efficiency of the system will be much increased.

HOW HEAT IS STORED

When any material heats up it is absorbing energy. As it cools down, it releases exactly the same amount of energy. Different materials require different amounts of energy to raise their temperatures the same number of degrees. The amount of heat needed to raise the temperature of a given material to a certain level is called its heat capacity. The more energy a material absorbs to bring about a given temperature rise, the more energy it will release when it cools down (Figure 4.9).

Dense materials tend to hold more heat than lighter weight materials. Concrete made with gravel aggregate, for example, will hold more heat than concrete made with lightweight aggregate such as vermiculite. Gypsum wallboard will hold more heat than wooden panelling. The other critical feature of heat storage materials is their rate of thermal conductivity; that is, the rate at which heat passes through them. When a material is heated its molecules heat up and gradually heat their neighbors by conduction. The higher the rate of conduction, the faster the heat will travel and thus the greater the quantity of material heated in a given time. Moreover, the surface of a material with high thermal conductivity will remain cooler, since the heat is being passed on to the rest of the material. Thus the surface will lose less heat by radiation as it is being heated up. Both these factors combine to allow a material with high thermal conductivity to absorb more heat than a material with low conductivity, assuming they both have the same heat capacity.When the sunspace cools down, a material with high thermal conductivity will lose its heat faster than a material with low conductivity. This can be an advantage or a disadvantage. Generally if there is enough of the material and there has been enough solar energy supplied in the day, it is an advantage, in that it passes stored heat back to the sunspace easily. But if there is not enough material or it it has been insufficiently charged with heat, it may give back all its stored heat in the early evening before the lowest nighttime temperatures.

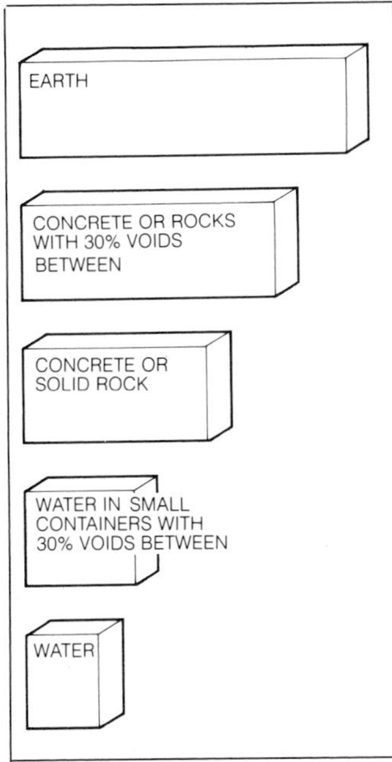

4.9 ▲ The relative heat capacity of common heat storage materials. The figure shows the volumes of different materials needed to achieve the same heat capacity.

Fluids, like air and water, have much greater thermal conductivity than most solids because convection currents form, mixing the heated molecules with the unheated ones, which greatly speeds up the rate of heat transfer. This not only makes much more of the fluid available to store the heat, it also reduces the surface temperatures so that less heat is lost by reradiation. Air has negligible heat capacity, that is, it can store very little heat. But water has both very high heat capacity and very high thermal conductivity, due to its convection currents.

The most effective way to charge any heat storage material with heat is to place it in direct sun. Materials not in direct sun will absorb some energy by convection and conduction from the heated air, but only at about one-quarter of the rate they would if in full sun. Heat storage materials not in direct sun need a very large surface through which to absorb the heat from warm air in the sunspace.

Dark surfaces absorb radiation better than light ones, and matt surfaces absorb better than shiny ones. So matt black is the best surface for heat storage materials. Dark red and dark blue absorb almost as well as black. They also reflect some of the red and blue parts of the spectrum, useful wavelengths for plant growth, so they are good compromises between using the energy for heat collection and for plant growth. Color is not so important in heat storage materials not exposed directly to the sun.

The more heat storage there is, the more even the temperature will remain. Heat storage materials both reduce high temperatures in the day and raise low temperatures at night. But you can reach a point when adding more water or masonry increases performance only slightly. Generally we recommend 3 gallons of water, or 3 square feet of exposed masonry, per square foot of south-facing glazing in sunspaces that will be used all winter long. In very cold and sunny climates more heat capacity should be incorporated. In mild climates, or when it does not matter if the sunspace drops below freezing on winter nights, half these quantities will be sufficient.

In very cloudy areas too much heat storage can actually cause problems. If it takes too long to reheat the storage material after a long cloudy spell the sunspace will remain too cold to use for a day or two even after the sun returns.

HEAT STORAGE MATERIALS

Masonry, such as stone, brick, concrete, adobe, and tile, and water are the two most common heat storage materials. Other heat storage materials are worth considering only where either the volume or weight of masonry or water would be too great.

Masonry.

The average brick or concrete block wall can store only half as much heat as the same volume of water. And it has a much lower thermal conductivity, so as much surface area as possible must be exposed to the sun. With most types of masonry even after ten hours of direct sun the heat will not spread more than 8 to 10 inches across the surface or penetrate more than 10 to 12 inches. So 12 inches is the maximum useful thickness, and generally 8 inches is adequate.

Because of its lower conductivity, the surface temperature of masonry is much higher than that of water when the sun shines on it. It radiates more heat back from the surface in the daytime; thus its effectiveness in preventing daytime overheating is reduced and some of the energy hitting it is wasted.

On the other hand, masonry is attractive, self-supporting, and will not rust or leak. Because of its strength it can act as a structural element in supporting a sunspace. Both the material and the greater building skills required to handle it well mean that it is more expensive than most water storage systems, though in many cases it is worth the extra cost. If you expect the sunspace to fall much below freezing on winter nights, then masonry is definitely preferable to water, which is apt to freeze.

If a masonry wall is to divide the sunspace from the house, it can be insulated on the house side so that it gives all its heat back to the sunspace. In this case the sunspace will be thermally isolated, that is, you can choose whether to open vents and share heat from one to the other. If the masonry wall is not insulated, the heat will slowly pass through it into the house automatically. Likewise the heat from the house will slowly pass back into the sunspace, if temperatures there are lower. The heat from this sort of direct transfer wall will be most useful at night when house temperatures are lower and there is no input of heat directly from the sunspace and house windows. It is important therefore to calculate the thickness of the wall to get the correct time lag, so most of the day's heat reaches the inner surface of the wall after dark. Eight hours is usually about right, so cold night temperatures in the sunspace do not begin to chill the house until the sun is up and warming the house next morning.

For an 8-hour time lag, the accepted rule of thumb is that a dense concrete blockwork wall should be about 12 inches thick. Adobe and brick have lower thermal conductivity, so adobe should be around 8 inches thick and brick walls about 10 inches. Dark bricks with added magnesium have better thermal conductivity than most, so up to 20 inches in thickness can be used and more heat can be stored.

4.10 ▲ Kalwall Sunlite fiberglass tubes designed to hold water for heat storage.

4.11 ◀ Translucent polyethylene containers by One Design Inc. built to contain water for increased thermal mass in a stud wall.

The storage capacity of masonry walls insulated on the house side is most effective close to the surface, so thickness can be reduced considerably. Normally, 5 inches of masonry in the floor is sufficient to store the amount of heat it is likely to receive. If you use brick paviers or quarry tiles, they should be dark-colored and bonded to the concrete screed for maximum conduction.

If you want a softer floor covering, try to steer clear of any kind of carpet. Vinyl or asbestos tiles, laid in a good bed of mastic to minimize trapped air underneath, are almost as good as masonry floor coverings, provided they are also dark in color.

Water.
In many ways water is an ideal heat storage material. It will store more heat per unit of volume than any other commonly available material. It maintains a relatively low surface temperature as it is being heated since the heat is transferred to the interior fairly quickly. It does not reradiate much heat to the space during the day. At night it maintains a relatively high surface temperature, giving off its heat more readily than masonry to keep the space at a higher temperature. Best of all, it is free, or at least very cheap.

The problems with water as a heat storge material all center around how to contain it. You can use either cheap recycled containers (which many people find quite ugly) or well-designed but expensive new containers. Remember that water-filled containers are quite heavy. Make sure the floor or structure you place them on is strong enough to take their weight without shifting. Place them exactly where you want them before filling.

Recycled containers.
Recycled containers may be

inexpensive, but they will not last forever. Eventually even the best recycled containers will begin to leak. This, combined with a rather uncouth appearance, makes them unsuitable for use in a sunspace intended primarily as an additional living area. A little extra water in a plant greenhouse is not a big problem, but it can ruin rugs, books, or even furniture. If economy is the overriding factor it may be necessary to use them in a living area, but take suitable precautions.

The most common recycled containers are 55-gallon steel drums, which cost about $10 each. Check local sources such as factories or garages for availability. Each drum holds a lot of water and hence a lot of heat. They are very strong and can be stacked on top of each other or used to support benches for plants or people (people will need a step up but will find the seat nice and warm after a day's sunshine). Steel drums tend to rust, so raise them a few inches off the floor to allow air to circulate. This will also increase the air currents, which help the drums give back their heat at night. Each drum should be carefully cleaned, checked for leaks, and painted a dark matt color. Oil or grease drums don't need cleaning because the residue will help to protect the steel from rusting. Eventually, despite your best efforts, steel drums will begin to leak. Fortunately they usually leak rather slowly, so you have time to find the culprit, siphon out its water, and replace it. Plastic-lined, or even all plastic, 55-gallon drums are sometimes available. Because these will not rust, they are considerably more desirable for water storage.

Small metal and plastic containers are available in many sizes. Glass should not be used because it is likely to burst if it freezes. The smallest containers are often free, but larger ones are generally more convenient and less likely to freeze. Square containers stack best and waste the least amount of space. The loose packing of containers offers more air circulation, which is helpful for heat transfer when the water is not exposed to direct sun. When stacked more than two or three high they will probably need some additional support, such as shelves. And for safety, the top layers should be tied back to the wall.

New containers.
Several large plastic containers have been designed specifically for heat storage. They tend to be expensive, but better looking—or at least less obtrusive—than recycled containers. They should not leak and they should last indefinitely.

The best known of these are Kalwall's Sunlite fiberglass tubes. They come in several sizes from 4 to 10 feet high. The biggest of them is 5 feet high and measures 5 feet across. It can be used for raising fish as well as for storing heat. Sunlite tubes are translucent. When used with plain water they transmit a soft, even light and can form a beautiful pale blue shimmering wall between the sunspace and the house. (Figure 4.10).

More expensive, but less space-consuming, are the flat 4-foot-square modules produced by One Design Incorporated. These are translucent polyethylene containers designed to be attached to alternate wall studs, fitting over the intervening studs. They are 7 inches deep and slightly ribbed like modern radiators (Figure 4.11). Fitted together they can form a wall of water between the house and sunspace or in front of a solid wall.

All opaque containers should be painted a dark matt color to help absorb radiation. Translucent or transparent containers should have some chlorine added to reduce the growth of algae. A dark dye added to the water will increase heat absorption considerably, but will of course transmit less light. Because they absorb heat throughout the water rather than just on the surface of the container, with the dye they will be slightly more efficient heat collectors than will opaque containers. As with paint, red and blue dyes will reflect some useful photosynthetic light back onto plants.

When filling any water containers leave a small gap at the top to allow for expansion. A little oil will form a thin layer over the surface of the water and reduce evaporation. Every few years they will need topping up to replace the water lost by evaporation. Metal containers also need a rust inhibitor (ask your local plumber where to buy this). If the sunspace is likely to freeze in the winter, either plan to drain the containers or add antifreeze to the water.

PROBLEMS WITH EXCESS HUMIDITY

Condensation occurs whenever warm moist air meets a cold surface. A little condensation on relatively dry, porous surfaces is acceptable, and in fact contributes to maintaining a good moisture balance in the house. Porous surfaces act as moisture storage, just as dense materials act as heat storage, modifying excessive swings of humidity. On impermeable surfaces like metal and glass, condensation will be much more evident. When outside temperatures are low, condensation may run down the glass and collect at the bottom. If the water does not usually dry during the day, then it is likely to cause problems with rotting, staining of soft furnishings, unsightly mold, and so on. Keeping interior surfaces warmer by better insulation, or adding additional layers of glazing will help reduce condensation. The alternative is to reduce the humidity in the air, either by severe pruning to reduce transpiration from the plants or by more ventilation to the outside.

An ordinary well-insulated house with double- or triple-glazed windows can withstand considerably higher amounts of humidity than a superinsulated house because of its higher air change rate. It also has fewer problems with humidity than a poorly insulated, single-glazed house because the interior surfaces remain warmer. In extremely cold weather condensation will occur even here, but water collecting on the bottom of windows can simply be mopped up on a temporary basis.

4.12 ▲ Openings through masonry walls to allow natural convection can be decorative.

Phase change materials. When a material changes from solid to liquid or liquid to gas, it is said to go through a phase change. Phase changes require a great deal of energy. It takes seventy times more heat to melt ice than to raise the temperature of either ice or water one degree. Changing phase from solid to liquid absorbs energy. Changing from liquid to solid releases energy. Special phase-change materials, mainly salt hydrates or paraffin wax, have been developed that change from solid to liquid at the temperatures usually found in sunspaces. When they reach the temperature at which they begin to melt, these materials absorb five to ten times as much heat as the equivalent amount of water before themselves heating up anymore. They release this extra heat as they cool down past their melting point and return to a solid form (usually as crystals). They are very effective at reducing overheating and can store a tremendous amount of heat in a relatively small volume. They also weigh much less than the equivalent amount of other heat storage materials.

Most commercially available phase-change materials melt at between 65° and 85°F., which is a good temperature range for human comfort, but wasteful if there is no need to heat the sunspace temperature at night. For plants the ideal phase-change material would start absorbing heat between 50° and 60°F. and would not release its heat until the temperature dropped below 50°. For maximum usefulness in winter, again a material with a relatively low melting point is best, so that it goes through its liquid/solid cycle even on cloudy days. Unfortunately, materials with lower melting points generally have slightly lower heat capacity; that is, they can actually store slightly less heat in a given volume. But extra volume may be worth the sacrifice, particularly in cloudy climates.

Phase-change materials are still relatively experimental, hence quite expensive and not totally reliable. Because they are passive heat-absorbing systems that depend on chemical changes, they should be utterly fail-safe. But in fact occasionally problems with supercooling and with salts forming insoluble precipitates have led to some or all of the material eventually failing to go through its liquid/solid cycle. New materials and new forms of packaging appear frequently. Find out what is available and what guarantees are offered before choosing.

Phase-change materials need a large surface area in relation to their volume in order to ensure that all the material changes its state. Generally no more than 1 inch of thickness is desirable, and performance falls off rapidly after 2 inches. These materials may be ideal in situations where it is impossible to incorporate heavyweight heat capacity materials. If there is already a stud wall beteen the house and the proposed sunspace, it can be adapted at relatively low cost to achieve a much higher heat capacity than masonry. Remember, however, that the rules of thermal storage still apply and try to insure that as much as possible of the storage material is in direct sunlight.

One of the most significant findings in the first generation of solar greenhouse design is that often there is not sufficient storage to prevent overheating even in winter. Another conclusion is that heat-storage rock beds, so popular ten years ago, have proved too expensive and too awkward—both to build and to get the heat into—to be practical. Vertical rock beds require very sturdy structures to contain them and take up useful internal space. Horizontal rock beds, generally beneath the floor, are difficult to get heat into and out of as needed. Both systems usually require large fans and complex and expensive ductwork and dampers to be successful.

"Keep it simple" is becoming a catch phrase in the passive solar industry. Just as active solar collection systems lost favor to passive systems, so active heat storage systems have lost popularity to simpler and cheaper passive methods. The commonest form of solar storage now is heavyweight masonry placed in direct sun, and, as a secondary measure, moving warm air from the sunspace into the house to heat up both the air and the thermal mass of the house itself. Air can be moved by natural convection but it may require fans, dampers, and thermostats to be efficient.

HEAT TRANSFER

In order to heat the house, it is usually most efficient to store heat in the thermal mass of the house itself rather than in the sunspace. The hot air from the sunspace can warm all the internal surfaces of the house, which will then release their heat exactly where it is needed as the house cools down. Moving warm air from the sunspace to the house also enables you to provide fresh air without heat loss. In many climates the additional humidity and higher level of oxygen produced by plants are beneficial as well.

Humid air has a higher heat capacity than dry air because the energy required to evaporate the water is still potentially present, ready to be released when the water vapor condenses onto a cold surface. This potential energy, called latent heat, makes moist air more effective for transferring heat from the sunspace to the house. But it also causes problems.

HEAT TRANSFER BY NATURAL CONVECTION

The simplest and most efficient way to use the heat collected in a sunspace is to let the hot air flow naturally into the house. Warm air rises and cool air falls, forming natural convection loops which gradually mix the heated air from the sunspace with the cooler air from the house (or the reverse at night, when the sunspace is cooler than the house). Three factors affect the speed with which the air flows by natural convection:

1) The temperature difference between the warmer and cooler air. The greater the difference, the faster the air flow.
2) The height of the loop. The further the hot air has to rise and the cool air has to fall, the faster the air flow.
3) The resistance to the air flow. The larger the opening, the less the resistance and hence the faster the air flow.

Because air has a low heat capacity, you need very large volumes of heated air to pass a significant amount of heat to the house. The air in the house will heat up fairly quickly by mixing with the heated air in the sunspace, but the structure of the house (which acts as heat storage, absorbing heat from the air in the day and giving it off at night) will heat up more slowly and will require much greater volumes of air.

When the sunspace is integrated into the house with no walls separating it, natural convection will automatically mix the sun-warmed air with the air from the rest of the house. Where there is an intervening wall, openings should be made, even if the wall is designed primarily for heat storage and the heat passes directly through (Figure 4.12). After a cloudy spell, the house wants the benefit of the returning sun quickly, and it will take the wall at least 6 to 8 hours to heat up again. Within half an hour of the sun coming out, the air in the sunspace could heat enough to make a valuable contribution to the house. Openings through the wall make the system more flexible, and the sun-heated air can be used directly, when necessary.

To reduce resistance to the air flow, openings to the house should be as large as possible. As a general rule of thumb, the total vent area should be at least 10 percent of the area of south-facing glazing, and 15 percent if the openings need to be screened against insects.

Ideally, about half the openings should be near the top of the sunspace and about half near the bottom. Frequently a door acts as one of the vents. A door will work as both a top and bottom vent, but not very efficiently due to turbulence in the middle section. So don't count the total door area in calculating the area of openings to the inside. Likewise if the top vents must be placed less than eight feet above the bottom vents, count them as somewhat smaller than their actual size because they won't be working as effectively. If the vertical distance between the vents can be significantly increased then the area of the openings can be decreased (e.g., if the vertical distance is 15 feet rather than 8 feet, only three-quarters as much vent area is needed). For the sake of good air circulation in the sunspace it is wise to have some vents at each end as well.

If all the vents in the common wall open into one large room, then the air flow pattern is likely to be fairly simple—hot air comes in through the top vent and cold air goes out through the bottom. But in more complicated arrangements, where more than one room is receiving hot air, the air flow patterns are likely to be rather complex, and the more convoluted the path the air must take, the larger the opening should be because of complications caused by turbulence and back drafts.

Natural convection has many advantages for moving heated air into the house. It is silent. The capital cost of making an opening in a wall is usually relatively low, and the openings often serve a dual purpose for access, visual connection, and so on. It is sun-powered, so the running costs are nil and it uses no fossil-fuel energy. It is self-regulating—as the sunspace gets hotter the air flow increases. It is unlikely to cause drafts since convection currents are relatively slow.

HEAT TRANSFER BY FANS

Where it is difficult to make sufficiently large openings in the wall between sunspace and house, a fan can increase enormously the volume of air moved. If most of the heat needs to be directed to one area, particularly if there is not a clear path for natural convection, a fan can help to push the air in the right direction. with the addition of a thermostat, the fan can form an automatic one-way heat transfer system, pushing heat into the house whenever the air in the sunspace rises above a certain temperature. With the addition of a second thermostat the fan becomes an automatic two-way heat transfer system, blowing hot air into the house when the sunspace is too warm and blowing warm air into the sunspace when it is

A 25¢ AUTOMATIC VENT OPENER

Windows, doors, and other large openings are usually opened and shut by hand, depending on whether heat is available to the house from the sunspace. You can render smaller openings automatic by hanging a sheet of very thin polyethylene film over the house side of the top vents and the sunspace side of the bottom vents. This backdrop damper works like a one-way valve. The plastic film over the top vent blows open when the hot air from the sunspace pushes against it and pushes shut when the sunspace cools and hot air from the house tries to flow into the sunspace. The bottom vent reverses the cycle, letting cold air from the house flow into the sunspace. A 1-1/2-inch mesh screen over the opening will prevent the film being sucked back through the opening without interfering much with the air flow. If you want heat to move from the house to the sunspace, you can tape the plastic film on the wall above or simply remove it until you want one-way heat flow again.

4.13 ▲ **These well-pruned grape vines will fill the overhang with leaves and shade the vertical glass in summer.**

too cold; e.g., for frost protection in winter. A reversible fan is not really necessary, since pulling cold air out of the sunspace will pull warm air in through the return air vents.

Integrating a fan into a home is more complicated than it first appears. The noise and the drafts they cause can be very irritating. Some people feel a fan is somehow a bit immoral in an otherwise passive house. Many people find they don't use them and even take them out after a few years, either because they seem ineffective or because the hum is so aggravating. A well-designed fan system should minimize these problems, but give careful consideration to choosing the right fan for the job.

The fan should be as large and as slow-running as possible. This will reduce problems with both noise and drafts. If the fan is used primarily to automate heat transfer while you are out and you can use some other method while you are at home, then the noise and drafts caused by high-speed fans won't be such a problem. If possible, choose a multispeed fan for flexibility.

Every fan needs a return air vent at least equal to the size of the fan. Without this, the chances are the fan will work less efficiently and will tend to draw in cold air from the outside rather than cool air from the house. The bigger the opening, the slower the speed of the air going through it and the less drafty it will feel nearby. The placing of the fan and the return air duct is not as critical as it is for natural circulation systems, but ideally they should be as far apart as possible, both horizontally and vertically, to maximize mixing of the air and to benefit from some natural convection. Placing the fan close to the ceiling will minimize the feeling of draftiness below, and the ceiling will then radiate the heat it picks up down to the rest of the room. All fans and return air vents should be fitted with backflap dampers or electronic shutters to seal the opening when not in use.

Various fans on the market are suitable for sunspace heat transfer. Ventaxia produces a range of models that can be controlled thermostatically or by adjusting the setting on a variable-speed switch. They have electronically operated draft-proof shutters that allow the fans to be fully reversible. Wesper fans, specifically manufactured for use in sunspaces, come with two differential thermostatic controls that allow you to regulate both airflow into the house during the day and into the sunspace for protecting plants at night. Wesper also produces a matching return air damper.

Fan thermostats are usually set to turn the fan on when

the air in the sunspace reaches 80°F. At 70°F. the air may be warmer than the air in the house, but it will feel cold because of the air movement. On the other hand, since air movement makes higher temperatures feel comfortable more heat can actually be stored in the house during the day with a fan. Air temperatures can get up to 85° or even 90°F. before people start opening windows to cool off. Thus the whole house gets several degrees warmer, which will help to keep it warm at night. The effectiveness of solar collection systems such as this can be increased dramatically if the house is unoccupied during the day and you can set the thermostats to push more heat into the house than would be acceptable if you were there.

Fans also reduce temperature stratification, circulating the warm air rapidly and thoroughly so all parts of the room are warmed nearly equally. The evenness of heat distribution also contributes to slightly greater heat storage, making better use of all available surfaces. Try to avoid taking the air to the far side of the house. Long tunnel-like ducts greatly increase air resistance, making the fan work harder and achieve less.

SUNSPACES FOR PRE-HEATING VENTILATION AIR

Finally, integrating a whole-house ventilation system with an attached sunspace should not be overlooked. Such systems use one fan to draw air out of moisture- and odor-producing rooms such as bathrooms and kitchen, and another fan to draw fresh air into living rooms and bedrooms. A heat exchanger transfers heat from the outgoing air to the incoming air. Whole-house ventilation systems are used on well-insulated airtight houses. They give an overall ventilation rate of about three-quarters of an air change per hour, but about 65 percent of the heat which would normally be lost at that ventilation rate is reclaimed. By drawing the fresh air from a sunspace rather than from outdoors, even more heat can be saved. Whole-house ventilation systems will undoubtedly become increasingly popular in cold climates, and we may well see them used in conjunction with sunspaces to produce well-ventilated and energy-efficient houses.

OVERHEATING CONTROL

Whether your sunspace is primarily for people, plants, or solar collection, you undoubtedly have to deal with the problem of overheating, not only in summer, but also in spring and fall—and maybe even in winter. If you have not lived with a greenhouse it is difficult to imagine the real power of glass as a solar heat trap. Plants of course suffer most, but people also wilt and need protection against overheating. The principles are the same whatever your priorities.

First, the best way to prevent overheating is to stop solar heat getting to the glass, by external shading. Second, if it gets through the glass, you can stop it getting to plants or surfaces in the sunspace by internal shades. And finally, you can ventilate away the excess heat.

EXTERNAL SHADING

External shading can be as simple as natural vegetation. Some deciduous trees will provide dense shade in summer and not cut out too much winter sun. But some deciduous trees have a density of branches and twigs that can cut out up to 50 percent of winter sun. Judicious planting of trees or shrubs to the east and west of the sunspace will cut out summer sun in early morning and late afternoon without affecting winter sun collection.

Some climbing plants, particularly annuals or herbaceous perennials, will provide good shade in summer and die back completely in the winter. Hops or morning glories will provide dense foliage by midsummer if you train them properly against the outside of the glazing. Deciduous vines like grapes will provide shade earlier in the year but cut out a percentage of winter sun with their bare branches (Figure 4.13).

External roller shades made of aluminum or cedarwood slats, which will cut out around 50 percent of the incoming radiation, are available for many makes of greenhouse, but they are expensive. They are by far the most effective form of shading because they can be adjusted day by day, hour by hour, to control the amount of heat and light coming in. Automatic controls are available but very expensive.

Non-adjustable external shading, applied in the spring and removed in the fall, can be very effective in reducing over-

4.14 ▲ Shading compound applied to the more horizontal surfaces of the glass reduces transmission of overhead solar radiation in summer. Some sections are not painted to allow more light in where lightloving crops like tomatoes and eggplants are growing.

heating but is likely to block out too much light on overcast days in summer. Plastic shade-cloth, if well anchored, can be used this way. But paint-on shading compounds are much cheaper and usually more effective, according to tests done by Gardening Which of England. One of the best, pbi Coolglass, blocks out 30 percent of the heat while letting in 70 percent of the light (Figure 4.14). That may sound only natural, but several others blocked out as little as 5 percent of the heat while letting in between 50 percent and 70 percent of the light. Varishade is more expensive but has the added benefit of becoming translucent when wet, so on rainy days almost all the available heat and light is allowed in. Paint-on shading resists the rain, so should last at least one season. In the autumn when

4.15 ▲ Push-fit shading screens can be fixed in the overhanging eaves to protect the sunspace from overhead summer sun.

light levels begin to drop, it can easily be rubbed off when dry, or washed off with soap and water.

With careful attention to design, you can incorporate overhangs to cut out high-altitude summer sun and admit lower-altitude winter sun (Figure 4.15) on vertical glazing. Morning and afternoon sun slants in beneath even the largest overhang, and sloped glazing sticks out too far for an overhang to be of much use, unless it can be extended as needed. Ideally what you want is a flexible overhang that can be extended weekly or monthly to cut out more and more sun as summer approaches, and can be gradually contracted with the onset of winter. An awning such as shops use to protect their sidewalk displays would be ideal for this purpose. As with movable insulation, the problem is—how reliable is the user going to be?

INTERNAL SHADING

The problem with internal shading is that the solar radiation is already inside the sunspace before it hits the shade itself. Some of it can be reflected back out again using a white or shiny blind, but the glazing will still act as a far-infrared heat trap and heat will build up between the inside face of the glazing and the blind. The effectiveness of the shading system will increase dramatically if this space can easily be vented to the outside either by roof ventilators or fans.

Big Fins, manufactured by Zomeworks, (Figure 4.16) are the one system that puts the waste heat collecting under the glass in summer to good use. They are a very simple form of solar collector used for preheating water for your domestic water heater. Because they are protected from the weather by the sunspace, they can be built more cheaply than ordinary solar collectors. Big Fins remove an enormous amount of heat from the sunspace by circulating water through large metal fins under the glass. They absorb the heat both from direct radiation and from the hot air. The 6-inch wide, flattened copper tubes produce dramatic stripes of sun and shade below. In summer this provides enough light for reasonable plant growth. Unfortunately, they cannot easily be removed in winter to allow in maximum sunshine. But because they are close to the overhead glass and the sun angle is low in winter, they shade mostly the back wall rather than the floor at that time of year. If the sunspace is allowed to go below freezing at night, they must be drained to avoid damage.

Blinds are often used for the benefit of both plants and people simply to reduce the intensity of light in the sunspace. A white venetian blind or a rigid paper material such as the Verasol shade will reduce the glare from the incoming sunlight. Fiberglass sunscreen material, available from greenhouse suppliers, has the same effect. Neither of these options will reduce the build-up of heat to any great extent.

The Pella/Rolscreen window system offers considerable flexibility of shading by incorporating a Slimshade venetian blind beteen two layers of glass (Figure 4.17). The inner layer of glass remains relatively cool when the venetian blind is closed, and the solar heat does not find its way into the sunspace. Another advantage is that being sealed in on both sides, the blind is less likely to collect dust. The blind can be adjusted to cut out from 20 to 100 percent of the incoming radiation. The flexibility of the Pella system is enhanced by the option of using three layers of glass with a gold-tone, low-E coated blind that can provide insulation as effective as a well-insulated wall when the blind is closed. The system can be adapted to skylights and French doors.

4.17 ▲ Integral venetian blinds (Slimshade) within the Pella/Rolscreen window system. Courtesy of Pella Windows and Doors.

4.16 ◀ Big Fin solar collectors make a striking effect.

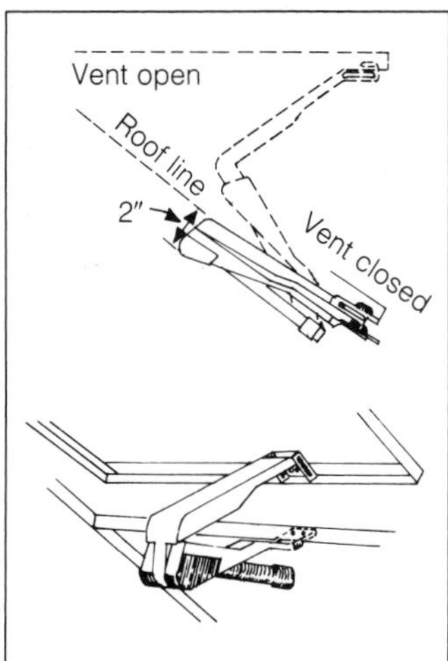

4.18 ▲ Heat-piston-operated greenhouse vent.

NATURAL VENTILATION

The last recourse in the battle against overheating is simply to remove the heated air in the sunspace. If the extra heat is not wanted in the house, the only recourse is to ventilate the sunspace to the outside. In summer this is standard procedure, but even in winter it may be necessary sometimes. Warm air should be exhausted at high level and replaced by cooler air at a lower level in order to get the maximum benefit from natural convection.

In custom-made sunspaces, great care must be taken with the detailing of any vents in a sloping section of roof or glazing. It is usually better to use a ready-made vent, such as those manufactured by Pella or Velux, in order to guarantee against penetration by driving rain. The Velux line includes a choice of two, three, or even four layers of glass, external awnings, and internal blinds, as well as a range of opening devices.

The position of any vents should be carefully considered to ensure that air movement is induced throughout the whole sunspace and that no hot spots occur where the air is stagnant. Vents placed at intervals along the bottom of the south-facing wall will greatly improve conditions for plants growing near the glass. Top vents should be staggered, not placed directly above bottom vents, so that cooler air circulates evenly throughout the space.

Vents can be equipped with automatic openers such as Heat-Piston motors (Figure 4.18). These consist of a small cylinder of wax which melts and expands when it warms up, forcing out a piston, which in turn raises the rooflight. When the air surrounding the wax cools, the wax solidifies and contracts, and the weight of the window, combined with an integral spring in the device itself, returns the rooflight to a closed position. The cylinder can be adjusted so the vent opens at any temperature beteen 68° and 90°F. Use these for overhead vents in sloped glazing, for vertical vents, or for louvers. The only limitation of automatic vent openers is the weight of the rooflight they will open, which in most cases is limited to standard, single-glazed greenhouse vents. Double glazing is usually too heavy. However, double-glazed Velux rooflights that are center pivoted can be adapted for use with Heat-Piston openers by removing the friction spring from the center pivoting mechanism and weighting the lower half of the window.

MECHANICAL VENTILATION

Mechanical ventilation is the last resort, though it does have the advantage of being easy to control. Exhaust fans such as Ventaxia units can be accommodated either in solid or glazed roofs or walls to provide high levels of ventilation. Their electronic shutters ensure that they are draftproof, and they can be controlled by a thermostatic switch. Standard greenhouse fans tend to be cheaper but also noisier and less draftproof when not in use. They are generally designed to be located at a high level in an end wall, working in conjunction with a low-level louvered ventilator in the opposite gable. The idea of using electricity to exhaust unwanted heat from a solar collection device is ironical to say the least, and with careful attention to heat storage, shading, and natural ventilation, switching on an exhaust fan should rarely be necessary.

REMOVABLE SUNSPACES

Finally, of course, the answer to summer overheating problems could be to take the sunspace down in the summer (see Kenin, page 132). Attached sunspaces made of plastic film need only operate during the heating season. Removing the sunspace for the summer will not only solve the overheating problem but also lengthen the life of the plastic.

Removable sunspaces do not necessarily have to be made of plastic film. We accept the idea of putting on and taking off storm windows; why shouldn't we design our sunspaces with removable glazing? For a plant-house-cum-solar-collector, the concept works fine and there is something to be said for an annual ritual welcoming the change in seasons with a major modification to your house.

CONCLUSION

From the vast array of sunspaces available and the variety of designs built over the last decade we can recognize several distinct trends.

First, architects and owners have come to realize that they are dealing with a powerful heat collector. Overheating can present one of the greatest problems in a sunspace, and the provision of additional thermal mass to soak up the heat, combined with carefully considered means of shading and ventilation should be high priorities at the design stage if you want to avoid roasting.

Second, there is obviously an increasing demand for higher quality glazings. Double glazing with low-E coating is on the increase primarily because it provides a higher radiant temperature on the inner surface of the glass. This, more than movable insulation, is likely to be used as a means of cutting down heat loss in the future.

Finally, a sunspace is rarely if ever economically justifiable on energy savings alone, but if it provides useful living space for a good 50 percent of the year it can save both money and energy. You do have to be a sun-worshipper to want one. If you are interested simply in cutting your heating bill there are many more mundane and sensible ways of investing in conservation. ■

PART II

WHAT SUNSPACE OWNERS HAVE LEARNED

Sunspaces generate enthusiasm. Almost everyone we spoke to loved their sunspace and would definitely build another if they were building a new house. Two nationwide surveys of sunspace owners, the Department of Energy's Class C Evaluation Program and the New York State Energy Research and Development Authority's (NYSERDA) Greenhouse Owners Survey found the same thing. Over 90 percent of the owners questioned in each survey were pleased with their sunspaces. The cheapest ones, under $5,000, caused the most dissatisfaction. In fact the more the sunspace cost, the more satisfied with it people were likely to be. In this chapter we will look at the problems sunspace owners most often encountered and at some ways to avoid or ameliorate them.

The main problem the people we interviewed mentioned was insect infestations. Insects "bugged" three-quarters of them. No doubt our choice of sunspace owners included a preponderance of plant addicts, but even those who were not particularly interested in plants found they had more problems with insects than they had had previously. Most people had been swamped by bugs at one time or another, but found they could keep the situation under control by carefully checking new plants, throwing out any plants that became badly infested, and keeping a watchful eye on the rest, ready to pounce at the first sign of trouble. Some people no longer grow plants particularly susceptible to those insects plaguing their sunspace. Usually a kind of balance is struck, and the insect population can be kept within reasonable limits. One man actually managed to run an insect-free greenhouse for three years by growing almost all of his plants from seeds. Any plant he could not resist buying had to spend a month in quarantine, waiting for problems to show themselves, before he would allow it in.

Nationally, overheating is far and away the most frequently encountered problem with sunspaces. About half the people we interviewed for this book found their sunspace got much too hot from time to time. Overheating is obviously more frequent in summer when outside air temperatures are high, but it also occurs in winter when a large glass area can let a flood of solar energy deep into the house. It is easy enough to lower the temperature in winter by letting in a little cold outside air, but some form of shading is usually needed on sloped glazing in summer to reduce the amount of heat coming in. Oddly enough, sunspaces with all vertical glazing overheat as often as those with sloped glazing according to the NYSERDA survey. Presumably spring and fall are more of a problem for them than summer.

Although overheating is common, it is not seen as a very serious problem. Usually the sunspace can be closed off, so the house itself does not overheat. It may be too hot to be used as a living space at times, but for the people we talked to, overheating was more of a problem for their plants than for them. Several people were considering adding external shades to the sunspace in order to cool it and reduce the rather overpowering light experienced on sunny days.

Excessive glare was often mentioned as a problem. In summer the contrast between the shaded interior of the house and the fully lit front section of the sunspace was too stark. In winter the reflection of sun off snow was sometimes almost blinding. By using the shade of large plants or installing an awning or some sort of light-diffusing blind, most people managed to find a shady spot where it was comfortable to sit even at the brightest times. A dappled effect halfway between the full sun under the glass and the full shade under the solid roof usually feels most comfortable.

Only about half as many people found their sunspace got too cold as found it got too hot. Again it was usually more of a problem for plants than for people. People accepted as natural the fact that it was usually too cold to sit in their sunspace on overcast winter days, and waited for the wonderful, jewel-like days of winter sun. For much of the year the space was too cold to sit in after the sun went down without some extra heat. Most people simply did not use the space at night in winter, and added only enough heat, usually with a portable electric heater or door open to the house, to keep the plants above freezing.

Very few of the sunspaces we saw had movable insulation. Of the six families who did, one used it only seasonally to keep summer heat out, two had expensive automatic systems that worked well, one had an inexpensive automatic system which, though crude and noisy, was both easy and effective. Two others had sophisticated systems for operating by hand. Both these families were scrupulously careful about opening and closing the blinds on time and so got a lot of benefit from them, but complained of difficulties in actually operating them. Nationwide, 60 percent of the families surveyed for NYSERDA who had movable insulation found it inconvenient to use. After a year or so, people quite often stop using it, which makes other forms of insulation, like multiple glazings, more effective in practice if not in theory.

Adding heat storage materials should keep the sunspace warmer at night and cooler in the day, but we found many of the people we talked to had taken out their water barrels in order to have more useful space. Usually they were unable to discern any difference in temperature, and a few commented that the extra space was worth more than the extra kilowatt or two of electricity which might be needed to maintain the same temperature without the water barrels. Several people also had removed or were not using fans that seemed too noisy.

Although not as common, the problems that annoyed people the most all had to do with leaking and condensation. Half the sunspaces with sloped glazing had at least some trouble with leaking (none of the vertical glazing leaked). Only one kit-built sunspace leaked and that had been deliberately installed at the wrong angle. Two-thirds of the custom-built ones had leaked at some time, but about half had been cured, some with a mastic gun, some by taking all the glazing off and reinstalling it with a better system. Many of the leaks were minor, an occasional drip that could be caught in a flower pot, but some were devastating, up to a gallon a day. The worst leaks, naturally, were on the shallowest slopes.

Few of the people we spoke to found they had too much humidity in the house; in fact, many of them commented on the healthfulness of living in a more humid atmosphere. Mold on north walls and windows is sometimes a problem for people who grow lots of plants. It can usually be cured by reducing the leaks in the sunspace, pruning the plants, and improving the insulation on the walls of the house.

By far the most annoying problem related to humidity was condensation between the layers of double glazing. As with leaks, this occurred mainly on sloped glazing. This was particularly galling when a beautiful view was one of the reasons for having a great expanse of glass. Often only one or two panes in an identical row fog up. Sometimes the condensation clears for a while in warm dry weather, but even then the glass remains streaked and there is no way to clean it.

Condensation between the layers of glazing was the main cause for complaint against manufacturers and in one case resulted in a prolonged lawsuit. Several installers of double glazing have gone out of business as a result of problems with sloped double glazing they installed. Manufacturers and installers are now generally very reluctant to guarantee any double glazing installed at an angle.

Cleaning the great expanses of glass in a sunspace is a major headache. A third of the people we interviewed said they found it difficult or impossible to get it all clean, and this is confirmed by the findings of the Class C report. Some people never washed the glass at all, some scrubbed the inside only. Several people built special supports to make acess to the highest panes of glass easier. Generally overhead glazing, which is both harder to reach and less noticeable, was washed less often. Long-handled hoses with a brush attachment make the job easier, but it is invariably messy and time-consuming.

The time needed to look after a sunspace full of plants is both a joy and a curse. People with lots of plants always mentioned how much pleasure they got from the time spent looking after them and also how endless the task was. An associated problem, often mentioned in mock horror, is the tendency of plants in sunspaces to keep growing until they take up all the available room. Some plants simply get too tall and must be either chopped down, given away, or thrown out. Others grow sideways, elbowing everything else out of the way. Some leap from pot to pot, colonizing all available space with either seeds or runners.

Oversized plants may be too much of a good thing, but for plant lovers, a sunspace often turns out to be too little of a good thing. A third of the people we spoke to definitely wanted a bigger sunspace. And only one person entertained even the possibility that it might have been a good idea to have made it smaller, and he had one of the biggest sunspaces we saw.

When we asked people to choose the single primary benefit of having a sunspace, they found the choice extremely difficult. Particularly the larger sunspaces are very much multi-functional. But when forced to choose, more people chose growing plants over any other single use. No doubt this reflects on our choice of people to interview, but it also confirms that the process as well as the end result of growing plants is a delight. As one man said, "A greenhouse is a very cheap form of therapy. What other therapist could you go to every day for five years for a total cost of $6,000 with free vegetables thrown in?" The NYSERDA survey confirms that nationwide most people find food and flower production the most useful aspect of their sunspaces.

Only two or three of the people we interviewed were not interested in plants at all. But in Davis, California, we saw many empty sunspaces used only for drying clothes or storing bicycles. With a nine-month growing season outdoors and very little frost even in winter, these homeowners obviously have less need for a protected plant environment. Moreover, most of them had traditional all-glass kit greenhouses that could not be kept below 100°F. for 5 months a year in that climate. The Davis, California, sunspaces were all built as solar collectors, to provide the extra heat needed during the coldest winter days. They were too hot and too bright for use by either people or plants most of the time. We saw a few empty sunspaces elsewhere, built by people who had received large tax allowances for them on the understanding that they would be used only for heat collection. These stand empty temporarily, in fear of the taxman.

Almost as many people as chose growing plants saw free heat for the house as the primary benefit of having a sunspace. Many people mentioned the pleasant quality of the heat. The air has not been dried out and depleted of oxygen by a fire. The radiant heat from thermal storage materials often feels more comfortable than circulating forced hot air. The money saved by supplying their own energy needs was the critical factor for some. But the fact that they are not depleting the world's nonrenewable resources is just as important to others. More often than not a woodstove was the only other heat in such homes.

Having a sunspace often improves the quality of light in your house. It makes the house feel bigger, airier, and more connected with the outdoors. The increased humidity and decorative value of a plant-filled sunspace also contributes to a pleasanter atmosphere in the adjacent rooms. Improving the feel of the rest of the house, though not considered a primary benefit, was actually cited more often than either plant growing or heat collection as one of the things people liked best about their sunspaces. Very often it came as a surprise, an unexpected bonus, once the sunspace was built.

No matter what the main purpose of the sunspace is, there is almost always an additional benefit to the rest of the house unless the sunspace is tucked away in an inaccessible corner. Therefore, it is worth locating the sunspace where it will have maximum impact on the other living areas, even if that involves sacrificing some sunshine. In living with a sunspace, people find aesthetic advantages more important than they expected beforehand. It is hard to put a price on the pattern of light and shadow that will greet you every morning, but in the long run it may be more valuable than a few gallons of oil or a few pounds of tomatoes. Both the light it casts into the house and the pleasure derived from looking into a sunny green space are important.

For many people the connection with nature is one of the main benefits of a sunspace. The sight of green living plants, the feel of the earth, the smell of growing things, provides a breath of life on a bleak winter's day. Sitting in warm sunshine when there is snow on the ground outside gives a unique psychological boost. Experiencing the wildest weather while well-protected indoors can be exhilarating. And just having so much glazing gives you a free, unrestricted view—mountains in the distance, deer grazing on the lawn, stars at night—nature feels very close.

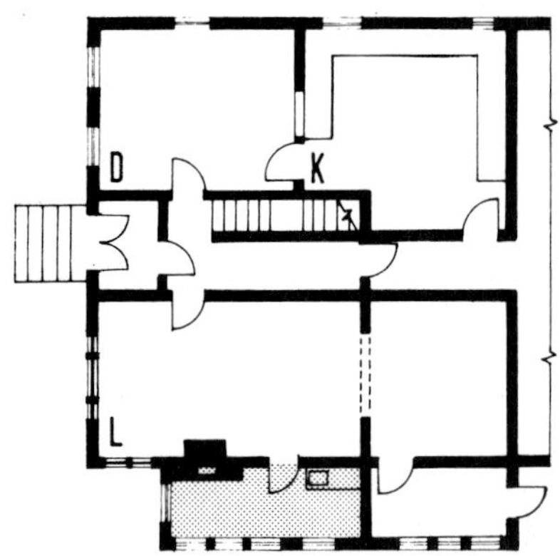

MRS. WILLIAM LANGER

CAMBRIDGE,
MASSACHUSETTS

Mrs. Langer's plant room is designed mainly for the delectation of the passersby. Separated by a yew hedge and a small strip of grass from the street, it glows like a jewel in the snow as the winter sun lights it from the side. When Derry was at college nearby, she used to make a special detour to bicycle by it on her way home. In her nineties now, Mrs. Langer has been tending her plant room for forty years. In the summer, when other people's gardens provide the color, her plant room is bare (she has to hire a moving van to take the largest plants with her to her summer house), but come October it begins to fill up again. From Christmas to Easter it is a blaze of color.

Date finished: 1870s

Floor area: 16 feet x 5 feet

Type of glazing: single glass, double hung, sash windows

Vertical glazed area:
south—63 square feet
west—18 square feet

Sloped glazed area: none

Orientation: SSE

Degree days: 6,300

Temperature in sunspace	**Day**	**Night**
summer average	(not in use)	
winter average	65°F.	40°F.
high	80°F.	50°F.
low	40°F.	35°F.

Special features:
Original glassed-in porch on old house

Glass shelves for display line all windows

Solid wall with single-glazed door between house and sunspace

It was rather amusing; I got started because somebody gave me a cyclamen which I put out in the hall and it started to die. I threw it out and a maid rescued it. She took it out into this porch room which we really had no use for. Two weeks later she said "Mrs. Langer, have you looked at the cyclamen?" I looked at it, and thought, "Well, our problem's solved, we will put flowers in here. We've got a flower that actually loves being here, and one that most people find very difficult to grow."

We started out with cyclamen. Then bit by bit we put in more and more shelves and tried different plants, some that didn't work at all, like African violets and impatiens, which need to be warmer than this

room was kept. It grew from very small beginnings to what you see now with all the camellias and the orange trees among the bigger plants and then the cyclamen and the kalanchoes and the Rieger begonias. I am very grateful for the dwarf cyclamen, which last. I get them in early December and they go right through to the middle of April at least. Not even ever fed, I just water them every day. People ask me "Isn't it a lot of work?" I say

"What do you mean by work?" because I think watering plants is a very pleasant occupation. You are surrounded by beauty.

It is particularly beautiful when it's snowing outside or when there is a lot of snow and the sun pouring in on these flowers. It's just lovely, the brilliance. The cyclamen seem luminescent. Oddly enough the cyclamen are never bothered by the sun there and they get a lot of it. I don't know whether it's because it's cooler at night than in the house or whether it's because there is more moisture. Many of the plants sit in water and that means the whole room is very humid.

I think what I love best is just the way it makes me feel in the morning when I come down and look at those plants. The sun comes in in the morning, pours in, and they just are so full of sunshine themselves, so bright. It's lovely. I can't imagine a house without a room like that.

▲ The Langer sunspace developed from an unused porch to an indoor garden over forty years of loving care.

ROBERT ORR AND MELANIE TAYLOR

NEW HAVEN, CONNECTICUT

Robert Orr and Melanie Taylor, architects and garden designers, bought a big Victorian house in New Haven and set about remaking it in their own image with allusions to the style and period of the original. One of the first things they did was to build a conservatory onto their bedroom. Originally designed as a stylish solar collector and an elegant additional room, it has gradually been taken over by plants so that now it is a steamy jungle resembling the creeper-bedecked swamps of Melanie's native Florida.

ROBERT: We thought of building it from the very beginning—an addition to a small room to make the smaller bigger and warmer. The big problem we were worried about was that it would be too hot in summer and too cold in winter, so we overdid it. We went to great lengths to have a wood frame (this was before they had the aluminum with a break in it so at that time aluminum was a real heat dispenser) and used Thermopane sliding glass-door units. And we also went to great lengths to make it have good ventilation for the summer. We put in ventilation panels and doors, windows in the top and all sorts of things

▲ **An extension of the bedroom, the sunspace brings beneficial humidity as well as the fragrance of growing things to the rest of the house.**

Date finished: 1979	**Orientation:** S
Designer: Robert Orr and Melanie Taylor	**Degree days:** 5,900
Builder: Robert Orr and Melanie Taylor	
Cost: $5,000	
Floor area: 10 feet x 8 feet	
Vertical glazed area: south—80 square feet; east—50 square feet; west—50 square feet	
Sloped glazed area: 96 square feet	
Type of glazing vertical double-glazed sealed patio door units sloped-double Plexiglas	

Temperature in sunspace	**Day**	**Night**
summer average	85°F.	65°F.
high	90°F.	
winter average	68°F.	50°F.
high	80°F.	
low	65°F.	50°F.

Special features:
Rock bed (no longer used)

Matchstick blinds (no longer used)

Classical detailing to complement house

Open to bedroom

Used for tropical plants

Fan for air circulation

because we were sure that it was going to be blistering in there in the summer. As a matter of fact we have a total of seven little venting hatches, but we never use more than one.

MELANIE: We don't need them, we use the window at the front on the south side and then the window up in the gable at the back and that convection is enough. We really don't need all these side flaps which look like secret doors.

ROBERT: We had one big problem with the construction. We put the greenhouse in the only place we could put it for code reasons. We never thought about the steep roof two stories above. We had just finished the foundations and put in all the ductwork that was going to go underneath the rocks when the first snowstorm came along and an avalanche occurred from the roof.

MELANIE: It really damaged the ducts, but fortunately the greenhouse with its glass roof hadn't been built yet so we were able to put the snow stays on the roof to take care of that.

ROBERT: On days when it gets particularly humid out there, perhaps I've just watered or it's a sunny day or something like that, we can blow humidity into the rest of the house.

MELANIE: And you can smell the water when it comes through the air. You know how it smells after rain, it smells a nice fresh smell.

ROBERT: We've woken up some mornings and there are actually clouds in our bedroom. We are waiting for it to start raining indoors.

MELANIE: Interestingly, we haven't had too many days when there has been condensation on the walls of the greenhouse. It is so well insulated there have not been many days when you cannot see out. Some greenhouses, you never see out of them. Usually in the early morning there is some condensation on the glass.

ROBERT: Where we do get lots of condensation is in all the closets, because the clothes sort of form a semi-insulation. The condensation comes between the clothes and the walls and all the clothes go moldy.

MELANIE: So what we have had to do is rip out the walls and insulate them very, very well to make the whole unit much more contained. But that moisture is great for sleeping in. We've had far fewer colds and winter diseases. The rest of the house doesn't get much more humid for some reason.

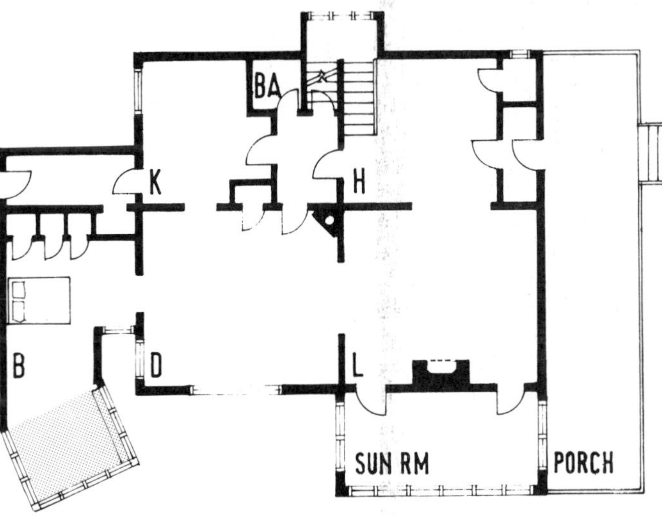

▲ The Orr/Taylor sunspace is a sophisticated and elegant addition to their Victorian New Haven home.

LISA AND PARRY JONES

EASTERN PENNSYLVANIA

When their children grew up and left home, Parry and Lisa Jones decided to move into their barn. They converted the stables below into a tiny apartment—just a kitchen/living room and a bedroom—heated by a greenhouse extension of almost the same size. The greenhouse is their main eating and sitting area in the daytime. Upstairs they have an enormous three-story-high room (the old hay barn) which is used only in warm weather or for special events in winter. Off this "Great Hall" they each have a compact, heated study to work in and there are spare bedrooms for the numerous visiting children and grandchildren. Many features of the original eighteenth-century barn have been left intact. The Great Hall in particular retains its spacious geometric character.

PARRY: The interesting thing is that a barn turns out to be quite suitable for solar heating, partly because you have such huge spaces you can turn into glass, and partly because you have such thick stone walls for thermal mass. It is very appealing because of the space differentials. We live here in a very cosy, ground-floor apartment. If the rest of the house blew away we could live here forever. But we also have access to that Great Hall upstairs (we call it "The Great Hall of the People" because we are a little Chinese-oriented) that we don't bother to heat all winter except if we are having a party.

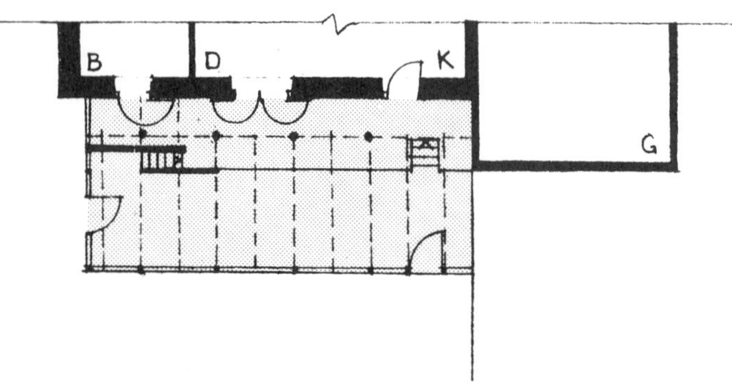

LISA: The amount of growing of things that we have done has varied a lot. There were years when we had trays of vegetables and things there and we were pottering around with them quite a lot. Radishes, of course are a sure cure. We have had lots of good lettuce. We had snow peas growing on this railing last year, that was fun. I have a little orange tree that at one time had so many oranges that I made nine jars of marmalade from one crop of oranges. They are little, but excellent oranges for marmalade because they are bitter but not full of seeds.

Herbs do well too, and next year I really want to do more with herbs. When you are using a greenhouse for solar purposes, there is a much bigger swing in temperature than is really good for most plants. That's one reason why growing vegetables is a bit chancy. On the very coldest nights of the year it can get down dangerously close to freezing and we sometimes run a little electric heater in here to make sure it doesn't freeze.

PARRY: From the beginning we intended to have a thermal curtain in winter and a shade curtain in summer. The winter curtain is about five or six times as heavy as the summer one. The winter curtain covers the vertical windows as well. The summer one just covers the sloping glazing. We change the timer so that in the summer the curtain is closed during the day and back at night. And in the wintertime it works in reverse.

Upstairs we have insulating shades that come down on all the windows. They work on a timer, too, with sixteen little motors. They are made of Mylar and they are very nice because they are semi-translucent. At night when it is dark inside you can see the stars through the shades.

The architects insisted we should have a wooden-frame, custom-built greenhouse. But it has never been waterproof. I think we should have gotten a standard metal-frame model.

LISA: Some of the acrylic panels leak. We had them replaced once and already there are new cracks. And it leaks around the vent, partly due to the insufficient angle of the roof. So it hasn't been entirely trouble-free, but it hasn't been unsatisfactory either.

We eat here, we sit and read there and I fiddle around with the plants. It takes me an hour just to water all the plants, then I might spend an extra hour or two pruning, repotting, whatever. I water with a hose

with a spray attachment so I can mist them at the same time. And at this time of year [March] when it is sunny we have to water almost every day, whereas in the fall and in the wintertime you don't have to water anywhere near as often. I usually keep the gravel in the trays under the plants wet as a way of humidifying the house. By the time I have watered and sprayed all the plants, there is quite a lot of humidity.

I think the light and the warmth are what we enjoy most from inside the house as well as in the greenhouse. The fact that you have this light and warm and green and bright space to look out at completely changes the quality of life inside this whole series of rooms.

▲ **The thermal curtain is bunched up at one end of the greenhouse during the day. A metal flap has been added along the ridge to reduce drafts.**

▶ **The Jones's converted barn provides excellent opportunities for solar heating.**

Date finished: 1979

Designer: Harrison Fraker, Jr.

Builder: Lucian Peebles

Floor area: 40 feet x 16 feet

Vertical glazed area:
south—300 square feet
east—45 square feet
west—65 square feet

Sloped glazed area:
487 square feet

Angle: 25°

Type of glazing:
roof—Cyro twinwall acrylic
walls—double glass

Orientation:
SSE

Degree days:
5,000

Temperature in sunspace	**Day**	**Night**
summer average	80°F.	
high	97°F.*	
winter average	63°F.	
high	85°F.	
low	50°F.	32°F.**

* (same as outside)
** (with heat)

Special features:
Retrofit on 200-year-old barn

Motorized thermal screen for all glazing and shade screen for sloping glazing

Push-in styrofoam shutters for east and west glazing

16 55-gallon water barrels

Floor steps down 3½ feet to form two levels: upper for sitting, lower for plants

Motorized vents to Great Hall above and to exterior

Date finished: 1980

Designer: Stephen Sparn

Builder: Stephen Sparn

Cost: $6,500

Floor area: 8 feet 6 inches x 14 feet

Vertical glazed area:
south—168 square feet
east—30 square feet
west—10 square feet

Sloped glazed area: 12 square feet

Angle: 45°

Type of glazing: double glass

Orientation: S

Degree days: 7,000

Temperature in sunspace	Day	Night
summer average	80°F.	65°F.
high	85°F.	
winter average	75°F.	50°F.
high	95°F.	
low	55°F.	35°F.

Special features:
- Retrofit on 80-year-old bungalow
- Victorian detailing to match house
- Recycled doors and windows
- Protruding glazed bay window
- Overhang and deciduous vines for summer shading
- Blinds on east windows no longer used
- Vents into master bathroom
- Fan to circulate heat

▶ **A new sunburst window set in used bricks. Baby's tears spread over the flagstones below.**

STEPHEN SPARN

BOULDER, COLORADO

Stephen Sparn was an architect with a problem. He had a nice little Victorian house on a tree-lined street. How could he extend it so it looked both contemporary and Victorian, felt both stylish and old-fashioned, and also collected some solar energy for heating his house? His solution is enchanting, proof that the narrower the constraints, the higher the leap of imagination called for. From the front it is still a conventional house much like any other on the street, but from the back it is a multicolored Victorian pastiche jewel. Using the right scale and many accurate details, he imparts a very modern sense of gaiety and fun to an otherwise ordinary house.

This whole neighborhood is very Victorian, and I wanted to make it more Victorian than it was before. I took some Victorian elements—the steep-pitched roofs, the brackets under the gable—and contemporized them a little bit. We did the initial greenhouse on the back four years ago. Two years ago we added a whole second story which comprised a master bedroom and greenhouse/bathroom that ties into the lower greenhouse.

It's a very small, concise greenhouse. At the peak, there are two windows into the house, so heat naturally flows up into the master bathroom. Up there a little fan on an air-conditioning thermostat turns on when it gets to a certain temperature and blows hot air into the back of the house, and the air just kind of migrates

◀ The Sparn two-story sunspace features Victorian detailing to achieve an addition well integrated into the existing house.

back in here. It's a very simple convective cycle. The purpose of the fan is not to cool the greenhouse but to circulate the warm air through the house. If you take the amount of energy gained through the glass and distribute it equally throughout the whole house it will bring it all up a few degrees, not enough to make it very warm, but some. It also humidifies and purifies the air for the house. The dry stale air goes in there and gets warmed, and humidity and oxygen are added to it. So when we come home our whole house tends to smell like a greenhouse. If we have a good sunny day I hose the greenhouse and then the whole house will be very steamy.

The design considerations override the energy considerations a little bit. It was very important to me that it be framed out of solid timbers as it is, with windows inset and filled with insulation. One of my hobbies has been salvaging old doors and windows from different buildings that get torn down. The whole greenhouse was designed around these two old windows. The sunburst window is new. The brick mass came from salvaged bricks, but the flagstones were new. They are laid on 6 inches of sand and 18 inches of gravel, so we can hose it down and it just soaks away.

The greenhouse is beginning to show its age. When we hose it down, the wood suffers. None of the wood inside is really sealed and I should have sealed it. The wood shrinks a bit, and then you get some cracks and air infiltration.

We had some interesting plants out there. One of our favorites we cut back severely last year. It was a huge New Guinea gold mine which had mealy bugs, but it really bloomed pretty in the spring. Spider plants just take over, and lots of succulents. I bought a clump of baby's tears four years ago and took a little soil and planted it by the step. It has spread over the floor and up the walls. Our dog comes in and eats it occasionally and trims it down.

On the other side of the deck I grow grapes, so it is nearly transparent in the winter and in summertime it completely fills out with leaves. It creates a kind of a leafy canopy all around the edges, gives a nice privacy and a bit of shade to the greenhouse.

Probably the worst time of the year for overheating is the fall when the earth mass and the outer air temperatures are equally warm and the sun angle is starting to drop. We have a little bamboo screen that I can cover the bay window with. The greenhouse doesn't have any movable insulation so it goes through a pretty radical temperature swing. We leave the door open just a crack on winter nights, so it gets cold in there.

If I did it again I think I would make it bigger. Maybe one of the reasons we don't use it more is because it's not an ideal size to put a table or chairs in. When there are two feet of snow outside and we want to go into a warm sunny spot, we do go out there. But the primary use is improving the environment in our whole house by circulating warm, purified, oxygenated air.

▼ Stephen Sparn enjoys collecting and using architectural features from other old buildings, such as the double window under the gable and this single-glazed door.

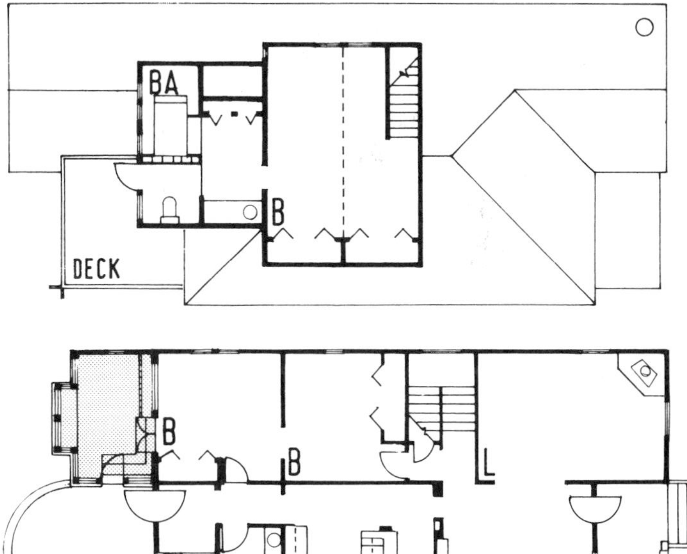

▼ **The Balcomb's central sunspace forms a kind of winter garden in the midst of their Santa Fe home.**

SARA BALCOMB

SANTA FE, NEW MEXICO

Doug and Sara Balcomb are two of the great pioneers of solar energy. He is a solar energy expert with the Los Alamos National Laboratories. Their house just outside of Santa Fe, New Mexico, was one of the first to be completely heated by the sun. It must be one of the most visited private houses in the country, with people coming from all over the world to see for themselves how well it works. They welcome all these visitors graciously as part of their never-ending efforts to popularize passive solar design.

The house is basically L-shaped, enclosing a triangular winter garden complete with trees and trickling fountains. Even in midwinter everything seems to grow and bloom in profusion. The brilliant New Mexico sun more than makes up for the bitterly cold temperatures outside.

The sunspace was one of the things that attracted us to the house. One of our visitors put it into words for me by saying: "Oh my, it's a hacienda." This feeling of the Mediterranean patio or the Spanish central courtyard, the fountain playing, flowers and green things all winter long, being able to have all that here in a very cold climate (there are over 200 days a year of freeze here), is what we wanted.

It took me a long time to find out what would and wouldn't grow in there. I have never been able to grow any member of the squash family, for example cucumbers, or any kind of legume, or any peas. That's because it's too warm, I guess. I have to grow only the heat-tolerant lettuces, although interestingly enough broccoli, which is a cold crop, does very well. Spinach does fairly well; beets are fantastic; chard grows well; the tomatoes are just fabulous. I have not had particularly good luck with root things, except the beets; carrots take too long to be worthwhile. Most herbs do very well in there. I've got everything but basil, and that I cannot grow. Marjoram, thyme, rosemary, chives, all those things do very nicely. Parsley and oregano will practically take over. I tried growing melons on the balcony which is the warmest place and I just didn't have any luck.

It's very strange. Things don't bloom when you think

▶ **Sara Balcomb chooses plants that flourish in climates like that of her sunspace—warm and dry.**

they're going to. I've just learned how to say "Okay guys, I'll try and deal with the water and the fertilizer and the insecticide and you do your thing!" I have roses in pots, and starting in early summer I prune them way down, put them all outside. Usually by August they are in bloom, and then comes the first frost. I cut them way down again, bring them inside, and by Christmas they are in bloom. I cut them down again about the first of the year, and by the spring they are in bloom again. So I get three blooms from my roses in any one year; it isn't really supposed to work that way but it does. I am learning to let the plants do what they want to do and me be the assistant.

What I did finally was to look around the world to find places that have a climate like my greenhouse. Basically my greenhouse has the same climate as San Diego—warm and dry. So poinsettias and bougainvilleas and roses and hibiscus, which all do well in San Diego, do well here. Now I'd like to get some plants from Western Australia which has the same sort of climate. They have crazy plants.

I don't like to spray with insecticides. I will use systemic insecticides in the soil if it's a particularly valuable plant, for example, hibiscus, but they smell bad. The main thing to do if you get a really bad insect problem is take it out and burn it. I hate to do that, and with the roses and the hibiscus and the things that I have not only a lot of money but a lot of time invested in, I just can't. So then I really need to get in there and work.

This time of year, March and April, is the worst time in the greenhouses. I've always got lots of bugs, particularly mealybug. Anybody that doesn't believe in the forces of evil and the powers of darkness has never dealt with mealybugs—terrible things. Somebody must have given me an infested plant. I had none for three years and then all of a sudden whammo. They are hard to get rid of. Alcohol works reasonably well. One thing that helps if you don't have too bad an infestation—and helps against the spidermites too—is spray-on leaf polish that the florists use.

We do have to refinish the floor every year or two, and also the wood. It's pretty intense heat and light in there,

Date finished: 1976

Designer: Susan Nichols and William Lumpkins

Builder: Communico

Cost: $8,000

Floor area: 350 square feet

Vertical glazed area: south—136 square feet

Sloped glazed area: 273 square feet

Angle: 53°

Type of glazing: double-glass, Sure-Seal

Orientation: S

Degree days: 6,500-7,000

Temperature in sunspace	Day	Night
summer average	80°F.	65°F.
high	90°F.*	
winter average	68°F.	
high	80°F.	
low	62°F.	55°F.**

* (94°F. highest ever recorded)
** (47°F. lowest ever recorded)

Special features:
Rock bed, fan assisted

Solid adobe walls with glazed doors between house and sunspace

Ground beds above floor level

Two-story space

Main entrance to house

and we need to oil the wood. The flagstone turns white if it gets a fair amount of water and sun, and then it doesn't absorb as much heat as it should. We paint it with a concrete sealer, to get it back to natural. For the first few weeks it makes it look shiny, then it gets to a matt finish and looks like stone again.

There was also a little bit of problem initially with leakage in the slanted overhead glass. More skylights leak than don't, and any overhead glass is liable to have leaks. Now they have used a new system for the mullions, SureSeal, and that seems to have stopped the leaks. The leaks would have mattered if that was a living room, but in a greenhouse, who cares? Most of the drips ended in a pot anyway.

We don't have any condensation on the north windows or walls, because we don't allow it. First of all our house is extremely well insulated, so the walls aren't terribly cold. On the couple of occasions we found heavy condensation beginning to form on the north windows, we did a lot of heavy-duty pruning in the greenhouse until it stopped. If there are too many leaves, we will get too much condensation. The roots of the first ficus we had escaped the pot and grew down into the ground. We were having to prune that tree three or four times a year to keep it from pushing up the roof. We finally had to cut it down, which broke my heart. But basically it was that tree which was causing the problem. You can't believe how fast a ficus will grow when it finds the world.

I guess the thing I like the very, very best is the winter garden feeling, that the house is focused on the greenhouse. Every room in the house opens onto it except the baths. I like winter, but I don't like the drab dreariness of it and this lets you avoid that. I like the smell and I like the sound and I like the feel, but best of all I like the idea that it lets me have my cake and eat it, too—summer and winter.

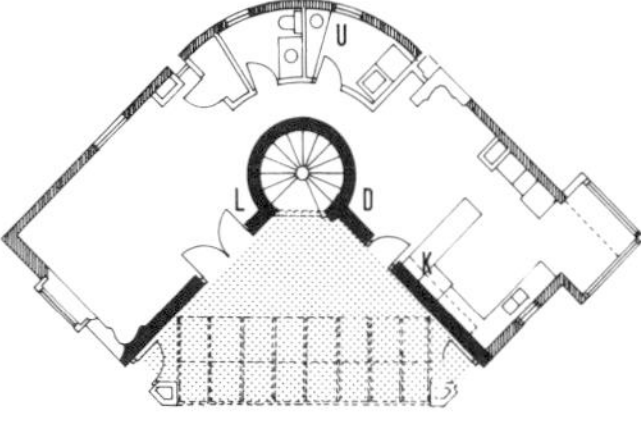

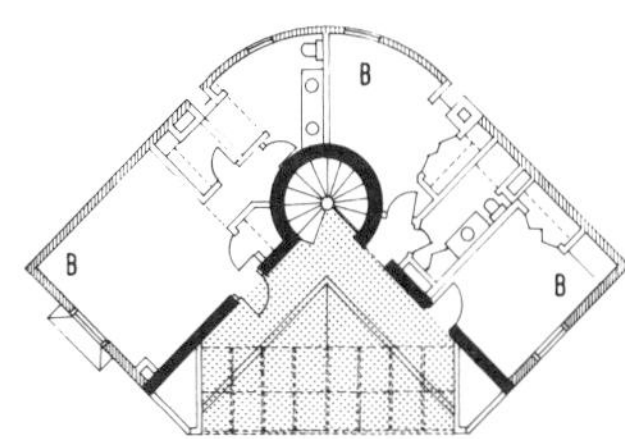

▶ **The pool cover (here shown rolled up) keeps the heat and humidity in when the pool is not in use.**

Date finished: 1980

Designer: Arvid Osterberg

Builder: Arvid Osterberg

Cost: $35,000

Floor area: 44 feet x 15 feet

Vertical glazed area:
south—244 square feet
east—15 square feet
west—15 square feet

Sloped glazed area:
144 square feet

Angle: 32°

Type of glazing:
roof—double glass, sealed units
walls—triple glass, sealed units

Orientation: S

Degree days: 6,800

Temperature in sunspace	Day	Night
summer average	70°F.	
high	98°F.*	
winter average	65°F.	
high	75°F.	
low	60°F.	58°F.**

* (105°F. outside)
** (-30°F. outisde, no auxiliary heat)

Special features:
36-foot swimming pool for heat storage and exercise

Shaded by deciduous trees

Open to house

Retrofit on 124-year-old farmhouse

▲ **The Osterbergs built a solar addition along the entire length of the south side of this old Iowa farmhouse.**

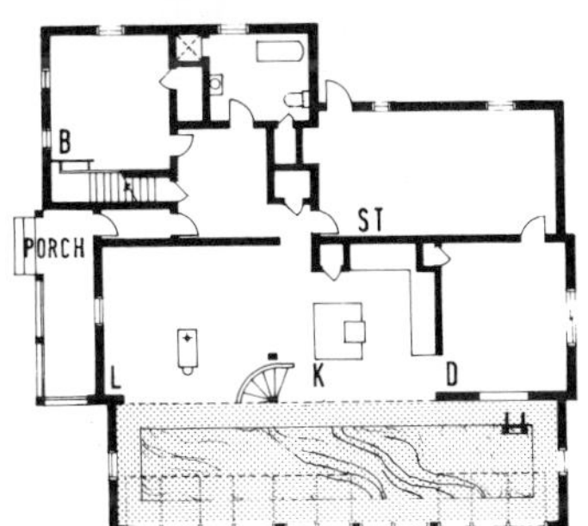

THE OSTERBERGS

IOWA

Arvid Osterberg is a professor of architecture. Against everyone's advice he and his wife Gayle bought a rundown old farmhouse. Even more outrageously, they wanted to convert it into a passive solar house using a swimming pool to store the sun's heat. After much travail, they have succeeded. Although the pool is in the main living area of the house, no problems of excessive humidity have arisen, no children or pets have drowned, and swimming is still a favorite pastime.

ARVID: When we were first married, I woke up in the middle of the night with a very vivid dream—an image of a house with a pool in it. I never got the notion out of my head.

GAYLE: We tried to be as self-sufficient as possible, to reduce reliance on burning fossil fuels. We did lots of gardening, recycling, and all this sort of thing. It kind of fits our philosophy.

ARVID: We have gotten a lot of publicity from this house. It is very gratifying to know that you are helping to promote the whole cause of solar design. I don't see any reason to build a new house now and not make it solar, or at least energy efficient with some passive features.

We had always wanted to build a new house with solar features, but couldn't afford it. Then we found this old farmhouse with a 44-foot long southern exposure. It was very rundown and everyone said it was beyond repair. But we got more and more excited by it. We wanted to build a solar addition with a swimming pool to absorb the sun's energy and act as a heat sink, but the whole south side was in particularly bad condition and had to be shored up first.

It was a nightmare. No professional contractors would take the risk, so with the help of a couple of students we dug out underneath the old house, jacking up the rotting floor joists and pouring new footings bit by bit. Then the entire south wall of the house had to be removed—a very delicate operation with such an old and shaky structure. Finally the new, mostly glass, addition containing the swimming pool was built on.

We had moved into the relatively sound north wing of the house before we started work. So we were there every day with the builders, and in fact found we modified the internal design to suit ourselves as it was being built. We probably lost money trying to save so many of the original bits of the house and using other recycled materials. It would have been cheaper to buy new doors and windows and so on, but they add to the character of the house.

The pool serves as dual purpose in the summer. Because we have no air conditioning in the house, we use the pool to cool ourselves off. When we get those extremely hot days in the summer, high humidity and unbearable heat, around 100°F, our house ventilates extremely well so you get nice breezes, and we take frequent dips in the pool. The pool doesn't reduce the air temperature much because we keep the windows open. But it seems to increase breezes.

GAYLE: I also think that a large body of water at 70° has a cooling effect.

ARVID: And the shading of course, with those south trees. South trees are a mixed blessing. We have tall deciduous trees that provide us good shading in the summer and filtered light which is marvelous. But they also block out some desirable sunlight in the winter. I estimate we are losing maybe 10 percent of desirable sun gain in winter. I think, overall, it is worth keeping these mature trees. We didn't want full shading because we wanted light to heat up that pool. So it is a matter of striking a good balance with what's the proper amount.

We had trouble with the double-glazed units when it got very, very hot. The glazing material would soften up and it would slide just slightly, maybe an inch, enough to create a gap at the top. So I put up steel brackets all along at the bottom. When I did this, there were no standard details, so I had to create my own flashing detail at the bottom of the line. It hasn't leaked since.

I don't think I would use quarry tile around the pool again. It looks nice, but it is difficult to lay and it is very porous.

GAYLE: It is hard to keep clean.

ARVID: I think I would search for another material, maybe exposed aggregate or brick. Everyone warned us that we'd have too much humidity with an indoor pool. First of all I knew I was going to have to have a cover and that I would have to control the amount of time that cover was on the pool. In fact the extra humidity in the wintertime is a benefit—less static electricity, more comfortable, plants thrive on it.

We reckon we have cut our heating bill in half with the solar addition, but our property taxes have tripled, so all the energy savings we have got are more than lost back in taxes.

▶ **The Spicer greenhouse wraps around the southeast corner of their Vermont farmhouse.**

Date finished: September 1981

Designer: Jeremy Coleman

Builder: Jeremy Coleman

Cost: $10,000

Floor area: 35 feet x 10 feet

Vertical glazed area: southeast—22½ square feet, southwest—30 square feet

Angle: 65°

Type of glazing: triple glass, sealed units

Orientation: SE and SW

Degree days: 8,000

Temperature in sunspace	Day	Night
summer average	80°F.	
high	100°F.	
winter average	65°F.	
high	75°F.	
low	55°F.	40°F.*

* (heater usually maintains 55°F. minimum)

Special features:

11 Kalwall water storage tubes

Five 55-gallon water drums

Retrofit to old farmhouse

Wraps around corner of house

Deciduous trees shade in summer

Intended to keep two sections at different temperatures, but found they were much the same

One-foot deep benches raised off ground

One, partly-glazed door in solid wall between sunspace and house

MARGARET AND JOHN SPICER

WILLIAMSVILLE, VERMONT

The Spicers bought an old Vermont farmhouse to retire to. Margaret, known as Targ, wanted to start a little herb business, so they built a greenhouse with two small wings enclosing the south corner of their house. The herb business fizzled, but Targ's passion for growing grew almost as fast as the plants themselves.

TARG: I saw an article in a magazine telling about a retired couple who moved up to Vermont, and she started her garden and planted herbs, which she then sold. I thought I could do the same thing, so we built our greenhouse and started the herb garden, but I found that it required fields of herbs in order to carry on a business, so I decided just to enjoy the herb garden and the greenhouse myself.

I've got two fans, one more powerful fan that pulls the air from one side, around the corner, and out the other side. It takes all the hot air off the top of it. And then there is a little fan into the house which is reversible. I have the little fan going all the time, all the year round. The greenhouse changed the temperature of the next room by about 10°F. The greenhouse is marvelous insulation. It still is cold around your feet, but the rest of the room is markedly different.

JOHN: The greenhouse really helps in heating the house.

TARG: I have just one heater, which is on only in the off-peak hours, except in really below-zero weather. The water tubes keep the temperature relatively stable, like the ocean. They never feel hot; they always feel the same temperature. We dyed the water in half the tubes blue, and in the others green, because blue and green happen to be my favorite colors.

The minute it gets hot, out come the aphids and all those people. The parsley gets the aphids started in the greenhouse every year. The more I thought about it, the more I thought, "I don't want to get these ghastly chemicals in the house." So I just use organic insecticide soap. But we do have the mask if we want to spray anything really bad.

We got a load of soil from the bottom of a pond, the sorriest stuff, big lumps. We had to put it all through screens. We mixed it with peatmoss and perlite and vermiculite and manure. I've fed it this year with manure and I have put some seaweed in it and some compost.

I wanted beds to grow things in, not just shelves. I didn't want it like a commercial greenhouse with just rows of pots on shelves. I wanted it to be more natural. I had big ideas about having the whole garden in here all winter. As it turns out it is not warm enough for most vegetables, but I enjoy having it. Using the raised beds, you can grow huge things if you plant them in the soil. If you don't want to, you just put pots on top of the soil.

So I can use it both ways.

I don't water every day. Once you water, it's usually good for two or three days. It takes me probably fifteen or twenty minutes to do it all thoroughly. This frame for seed trays is my own invention. You put them in there to soak, then pull the plug to drain it.

I brought this humidifier in from the living room. Everybody seemed to benefit from it right off. It put the humidity up from 30 percent to 50-60 percent in one day, so I figured it was a good idea. But I still try to mist it every day, even in the winter if the sun's out. And I hose down the floor in summer. Not in the winter because the pipes go outside, and they would freeze solid—and that would be it till spring.

I've tried growing vegetables over the winter, but it's a cold greenhouse so not too many like to grow there. Swiss chard does. Herbs do. But tomatoes, lettuce, all just sit there about 4 or 5 inches high and wait for hot weather, then they'll come on. It isn't really worth it, so I just have flowers and various ornamental plants.

One thing I have learned is not to plant all my seeds in early March. If I do then everybody gets so tall, it's like a race, and they aren't so healthy.

I like just being able to come out here and putter. I play with plants and experiment with them just to see what I can do. Sometimes I don't follow the books at all, but it works. I seem to be able to amuse myself for hours here.

JOHN: Targ lives out here. What we intend to do some day when we are old and doddering is to cut down the wall which we built between the guest room and the greenhouse, cut that down and make the whole thing into our bedroom.

▲ Targ Spicer enjoys the versatility of raised beds.

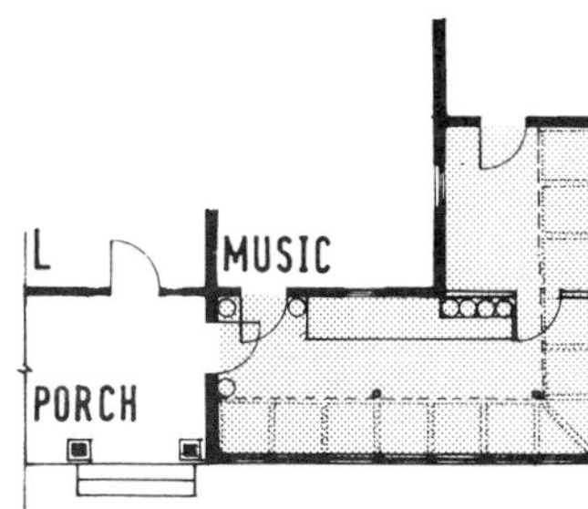

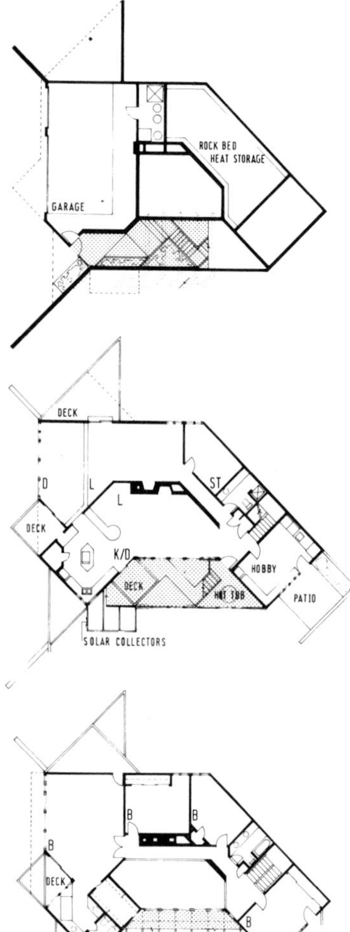

THE KEILS

LITTLETON, COLORADO

Art Keil is a plumbing contractor. He had been installing solar collection systems and was impressed with them. He and his wife Carol decided to build a solar-heated house. With the help of an architect they came up with a very dramatic modern house wrapped around a sunspace. In the foothills of the Rockies, near Denver, Colorado, it has lovely views of different mountains slightly obscured by condensation in the double glazing. The house is built on a hill with the main entrance at basement level. You enter through the sunspace, emerging up into the light from below ground. Greenery drips over every wall. The warm, moist smell of the tropics greets you.

CAROL: The thing that we were really looking at was a way to heat the house; we wanted passive solar and active solar. I had always wanted a place where I could paint and have my plants and have good lighting. The greenhouse makes the rest of the house feel alive. I just love plants; and out there they do so well, they just thrive.

ART: But you can't have anything too close to the glass, it just seems to burn.

CAROL: The ones downstairs in the entry are plants that like shade. They don't have to be watered so often. I would like to get some more cactus, I think the cactus like it up near the glass, they seem to do well.

Vegetables haven't done well at all. I tried tomatoes indoors in the top bed and they got real spindly and tall. They'd set their blossom, and then the blossoms would dry out and fall off. And pretty soon they went crazy with whitefly.

At first it was pretty sparse out there, and it didn't seem like anything would ever grow. And it was always so hot. Now that it's so green, they seem to do better when there are more of them. There is more humidity, especially with the swamp cooler now. It stays on whenever the temperature is over 80°, and that's quite a bit. Maybe the hot tub helps a little too, I don't know. Nights when we use the hot tub, you get all that steam. You don't have to worry about people looking in because the windows almost always fog up when we use it.

We have trouble with the slanting windows. They get moisture in between the glass. We were told by the architect, after he came out and inspected it, that they were installed wrong.

In such long lengths of glass you get a lot of expansion and contraction. When it cools off, you can hear it popping. Every time it does that, I know the glass is pushing against the caulking or pulling away from it. Eventually it's going to crack a bit.

ART: The sun is stronger than I thought it would be, and I think it is a little stronger than the architect thought it would be. Coming in through the glass, it really heats up out there. If you leave the doors open and the window shade up, then it gets real warm inside too. There is an air chase which takes the hot air off of the top of the greenhouse. A fan pulls the hot air through that chase and clean over to the outside wall and down into a rock storage bed underneath the study. It heats up those rocks and then there is a tube that goes under this floor and back out into the greenhouses. The study stays reasonably warm just from that.

CAROL: In the winter when it gets to a certain temperature in the morning, usually about 8:30, the thermal curtain will go up automatically. Then at night, depending on when the greenhouse cools off, it will shut. On the summer setting it comes down when it gets too hot out there. Then we close the doors to the greenhouse, turn the fans on and open the doors to the north, and the house cools off nicely. In the summer the plants do fine, even with the curtain shut because we leave the vents open all the time.

ART: I would like to have mechanically opened windows and vents, because the way it is now we have a hard time controlling the temperature out there. On days when the temperature only reaches 30° or 40° outside, it will get up to 100° in there easily.

CAROL: I think shades would help to keep the sun tempered so it would not get so hot out there. We thought about putting in shades when we built it, but they seemed ridiculously expensive. After living with it two years and putting up with that heat, maybe it would be worth it.

◀ **The Keil sunspace is the focal point of this contemporary home, the jutting profile of which echoes its Rocky Mountain background.**

Date finished: February 1983

Designer: Art Wise

Builder: McLawry Construction

Cost: $33,000

Floor area:
40 feet x 10 feet
(with corners chopped off)

Vertical glazed area:
south—36 square feet

Sloped glazed area:
295 square feet

Angle: 45°

Type of glazing: double glass

Orientation: S

Degree days: 6,300

Temperature in sunspace	Day	Night
summer average	100°F.	
high	110°F.	70°F.
winter average	80°F.	
high	100°F.	
low	55°F.	55°F.*

* (with heat)

Special features:
Hot tub

Main entrance to house (from basement level)

Rock storage bed with fan and ducts

Automatic thermal curtains on solid glazed wall between house and sunspace

Swamp cooler for humidity and cooling whenever temperature is over 80°F.

Two-and-a-half stories

▲ **The hot tub is a delight to see and to use, but it also adds beneficial humidity for people and plants.**

◀ **Plants thrive and bring life to the whole house.**

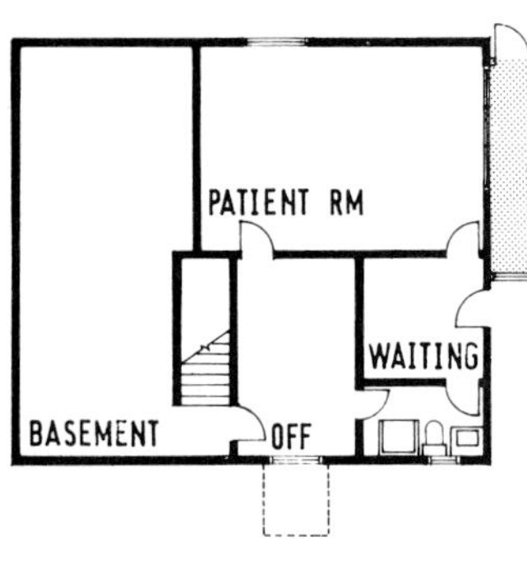

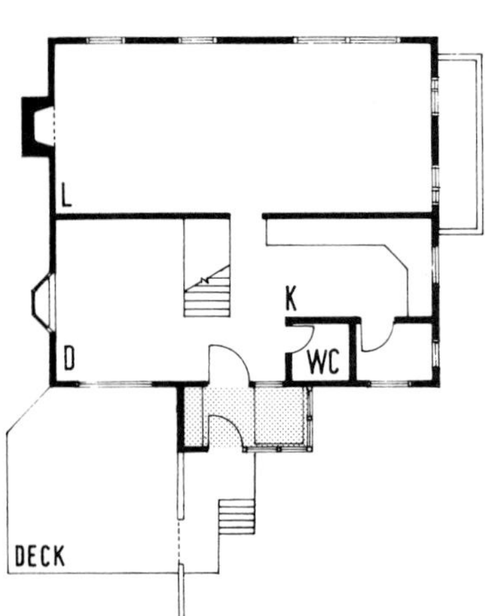

Date finished: 1983

Designer: Kent Bloomer

Builder: Irving Abel

Cost: $11,390

Floor area:
[1] 15 feet x 3 feet 8 inches
[2] 12 feet 3 inches x 5 feet 4 inches

Vertical glazed area:
[1] southeast—144 square feet
southwest—33 square feet;

[2] southeast—52 square feet
southwest—54 square feet

Sloped glazed area: none

Type of glazing:
double glass—Thermopane

Orientation: [1] SE [2] SW

Degree days: 5,800

Special features:
Shaded by deciduous trees in summer

Family entry includes lightwell for lighting back of basement office

Glazed wall between house and sunspaces

[1] *Main entrance to office*
[2] *Main entrance to house*

T. WAYNE AND JOAN DOWNEY

GUILFORD, CONNECTICUT

In the early fifties, Wayne and Joan Downey designed themselves a comfortable house. The interior of the house suited them perfectly and they did not pay much attention to the boxlike exterior. Then in 1980 Wayne Downey, a child psychiatrist, decided to move his office into his home. So with the help of a sculptor/designer friend they converted their basement garage into an office, and made two new entryways and a deck. The additions are elegant. Each entryway is an elaborate glass box designed to be a solar collector, to focus attention on the entrances, and to anchor the house visually to the ground. Together with the latticework shielding the deck from view, they break up a very plain facade and create a pattern of light and shadow that relates to the pattern of trees and branches surrounding the house.

WAYNE: Our prime motivation originally was to build something which would clearly differentiate the family's entrance from the public entrance where the patients enter the consulting room. But also from the beginning, we were very interested in passive solar heat collection, and in embellishing a house that was a plain, undecorated box from the outside.

We considered both active and passive solar collectors, and visited several demonstra-

tion "solar homes." It turned out two thin sunspaces were no more expensive than one prefab greenhouse addition would have been.

JOAN: We made the back door into the family's front door and emphasized and embelllished it with trelliswork and an "Alice in Wonderland" arch, as well as adding the sunspace on outside. The arch gives privacy to the family backyard and makes an exciting opening. The sunspaces also serve to ground the house, making the boxlike house look more attached to the ground, more embedded in its surroundings.

Inside the house we had already decided to convert a one-time garage area and basement playroom into a consulting room and office space

◀ **Elegant entryways, the Downey sunspaces add variety and interest as well as an opportunity for solar collection to their 1950s house.**

for Wayne. Because we did not want it to look like a cave, we added windows to the northeast wall and used the family entryway to create a light-well down into the back room of the office, which lets some light through into the consulting room. It was important to us to have light from different angles, not just from the glass wall where the garage doors had been.

Most days in the fall, winter, and spring, we open the doors into the house by 10 o'clock because it is warmer in the sunspace than in the house by then. In the summer we leave the top vents open or else the sunspaces get too hot for comfort. Because of the leaves on the trees and the vertical glazing, not as much sun gets into the sunspaces in summer.

In mid-winter and early spring, light from the sunspaces penetrates deep into the house, casting interesting shadows which change hour by hour. We do not spend time inside the sunspaces, we just pass through. But having them there makes the whole house seem larger and airier. It's a better house to entertain in than it was, it feels more welcoming.

WAYNE: What I like best about it is the aesthetic pleasure it gives me—the light and shadow, the sense of warmth, of the house opening out into the woods. The wooden glazing bars form a graduated geometric pattern repeated throughout the sunspaces and the trellis. This design picks up the window shapes in the house and the shape of the house itself. From inside, the glazing bars cut the view up into separate pictures. And each picture changes constantly. The angle of the light, the weather, the seasons, all affect the series of pictures. I have found myself taking pictures down from the office walls instead of putting them up. There are enough beautiful pictures through the glass.

When we designed this house we built it around a central fireplace, both literally and aesthetically a warm center for the house. If I were designing a house now, I would build it around the sunspace which would serve the same function—giving heat, light, and something endlessly fascinating to look at.

▶ **The finch's arched cage stands at the end of the room.**

BOB ENGEL

MARLBORO, VERMONT

The long cold winters of Vermont dismayed Bob Engel. He came from Southern California where things grow all year round. He and Lesley Reece, who came from Florida and so had an even greater adjustment to make, decided to create a tropical island amid the snow and ice. Their greenhouse occupies almost half the living area of their house. And all sorts of creatures live in it—insects and turtles and finches and people as well as an astonishing range of tropical and semitropical plants. A crocodile would not seem out of place peering out through the dense foliage at any moment.

I like tropical environments and I also like living in Vermont, so the appropriate blend was to make a tropical environment inside and live in a temperate environment outside. There is nothing better than skiing or being out in the woods in the snow and coming in here afterwards. The birds like it a lot; and we have turtles in here. I never once started out with the idea that I would be growing lettuce and radishes in a greenhouse and it would be part of my survival. I wanted to fool myself into thinking I was in Trinidad. I am surrounded by living things and that's my whole life, period. One wakes up, even in the dead of winter, to the sound of birds and recently to the smell of citrus blossom. Not only does it present a different visual phenomenon but other senses are informed that there is a living world out there.

The boards in the middle supporting plants cover a five-foot-deep hole underneath which, one day when I finally finish it, will be a pool with water hyacinths and maybe a snapping turtle, or carp, or I don't know what—something that is not too picky and doesn't need a lot of filtration and so on.

Insects remain the most difficult problem. If I can avoid poisons I do. However, I occasionally do use Malathion or something which has been demonstrated not to have any acute effects on warm-blooded things, but there are also cold-blooded animals here which are pretty susceptible, like the turtles. I generally try and find some tolerably warm day and take a plant outside and absolutely hose it down with a lot of spray velocity. All the bugs get whisked off and left outside. I used to be rather nonchalant

▲ **This large sunspace offers a tropical environment in the midst of the Vermont woods.**

▼ Under these boards is a five-foot-deep hole that will someday perhaps provide a home for water hyacinths and turtles.

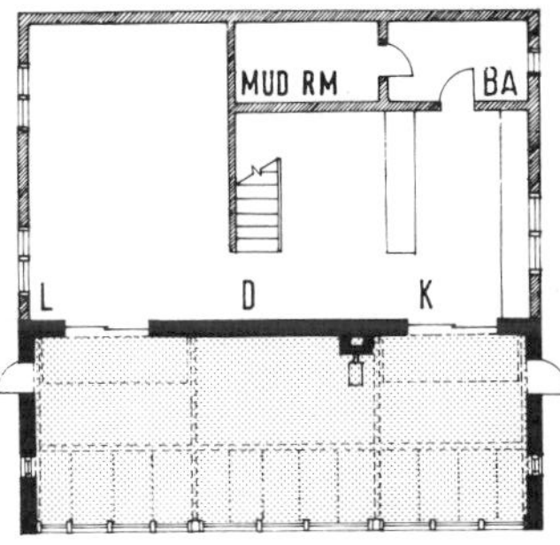

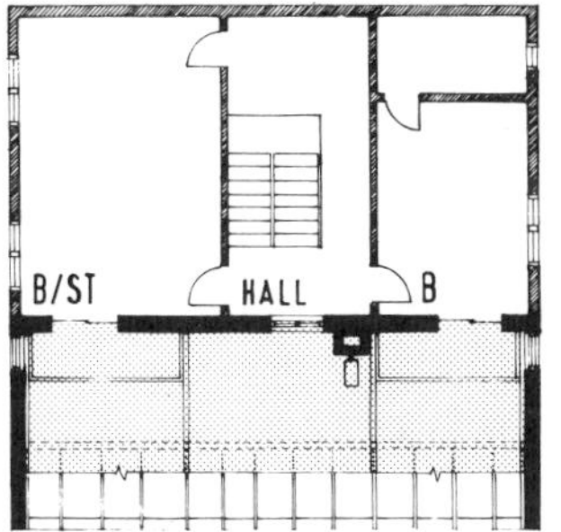

about pesticides. Now I use soapy water, and I buy some predators. But in general I can just brush them away with a water stream. I have not had any really ferocious outbreaks this winter. Winter is our difficult time. I see lots of ichneumon wasps and stuff in the greenhouse in the summer, but in the winter there aren't many predators. The relative humidity is a bit lower. Some of the insect pests—and I am thinking primarily of mealybug and spider mites—prefer those conditions or at least they are able to tolerate those conditions where some of the predators can't.

I have a couple of insectivorous plants that play hell with whitefly. They are close enough to the color that the adults are attracted to (a pale yellow green), so adult whitefly fly to them and stick on beautifully. I saw the finches on a citrus the other day pecking the bark, and when I went back I noticed that the scale mold which had developed was absolutely gone and they were working on the aphids on the hibiscus. That's why I don't want to apply pesticides. I don't want to start some sort of pesticide through a food chain in a greenhouse, because I'll never be able to eradicate the insects. I don't make any bones about it. It is simply not going to be possible. All I'm going to do is keep them from making loud noises.

We rely on this greenhouse to heat the house and dry the clothes. It is a passive house and it runs on a big convection cycle, so it would be very difficult to generate microclimates in here. Certainly some places get more light than other places, but the humidity is pretty even. All I do is water the plants and transpiration is enough to humidify the air. It almost feels like a summer day in here. I have never had the relative humidity drop below 60 percent. The construction of this house is post and beam. We used green timber, and if one doesn't have a moist house, there is a fair amount of cracking and twisting of these beams as they dry out. With our house we didn't have that problem at all because we were always running this sun-driven plant factory out here so we had a lot of moisture in the air. We do suffer, by the way, a great deal of condensation because of it, on cold winter days both in the house and in the greenhouse.

I like the fact that because of this greenhouse I use no fuel oil, no electricity, no gas, no nothing to heat this house except the wood that I collect off of my wood lot. And the fact that I use no fossil fuels, that is a very nice feeling for somebody who is worried about the way of the world. That's probably secondary to the feeling of growth going on, in a part of the world which is otherwise dormant for six months of the year. But the fact that I am doing something to reduce the consumption of fossil fuels is a close second. If I'm not careful it generates a sense of smugness; I want to avoid that, but it's a good feeling.

Date finished: December 1981

Designer:
Bob Engel, John Hayes, and MacArthur

Builder:
Bob Engel, John Hayes, and MacArthur

Cost: $4,000

Floor area: 40 feet x 15 feet

Vertical glazed area:
south—320 square feet
east—3 square feet
west—12 square feet

Sloped glazed area:
320 square feet

Angle:
60°

Type of glazing:
double glass, sealed units

Orientation: S

Degree days: 8,000

Temperature in sunspace	**Day**	**Night**
summer average	85°F.	
high	92°F.	
winter average	70°F.	
high	84°F.	
low	60°F.	60°F.*

* (with heat)

Special features:
Window quilts on sloped glazing

Woodstove in greenhouse (lit if below 15°F. outdoors)

Two balconies

Shaded by deciduous trees in summer

Sliding glass doors in solid wall between house and sunspace open all winter long

Two-story space

Date finished: April 1979

Designer: Massdesign

Builder:
Architectural Designers and Builders

Floor area: 13 feet x 10½ feet

Vertical glazed area:
south—84 square feet
east—6 square feet
west—6 square feet

Sloped glazed area:
104 square feet

Angle: 45°

Type of glazing:
double glass, sealed units

Orientation: SSW

Degree days: 6,500

Temperature in sunspace	Day	Night
summer average high	85°F.	60°F.
winter average		
high	75°F.	60°F.
low	58°F.	50°F.

Special features:
Rock storage bed

Shade curtain suspended under sloped glazing in summer

Sunspace open to all main living areas

Two-story space

▲ High openings into the next room allow hot air to circulate into the rest of the house from the Thompson sunspace.

▼ **The kitchen connects visually with the sunspace.**

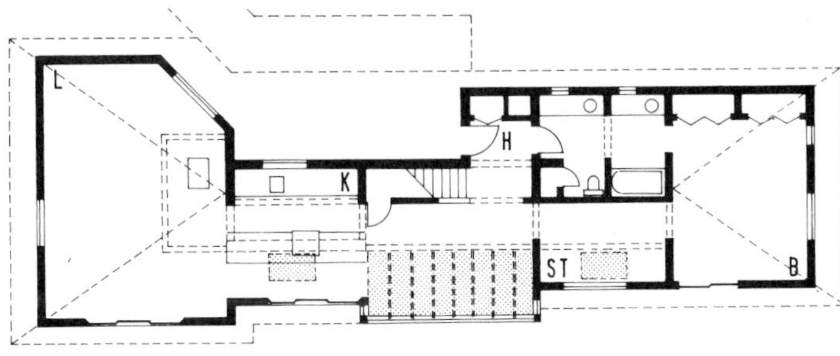

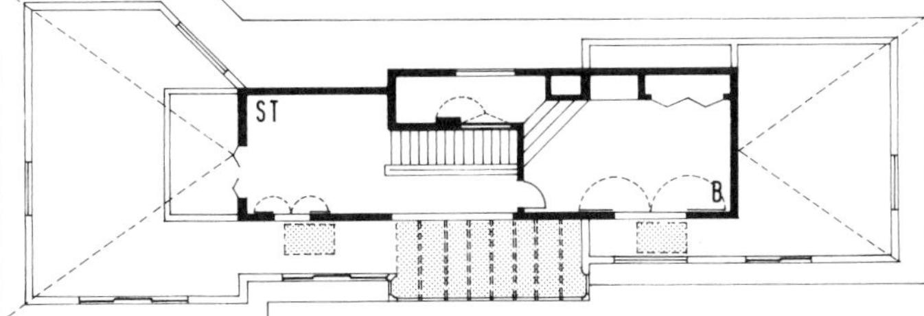

CLAIRE THOMPSON
WESTFORD, MASSACHUSETTS

William and Claire Thompson live half an hour outside Boston in a house they had built for themselves when they retired eight years ago. They wanted a house heated mainly by the sun and chose an architect with considerable experience in solar design. Together they decided to build the greenhouse into the house; there are no walls dividing it off, no doors that can be closed. It is part of the main living space including kitchen, dining, and living areas. The house looks across a marshy area to row upon row of young apple trees marching up the hill—the nursery for the neighboring orchard.

First of all we wanted heat, of course, and we wanted a place for plants. The fringe benefits are that we have an unobstructed view of moon and stars and that we feel much more involved with what's going on out there. It's just wonderful on a January morning with snow all over the place to sit there in the sun with flowers around.

There was a structural problem. We had some trouble with the glass popping and we had to have that replaced after it was finished. And there was steaming and condensation between the glass. Every time it rains I'm amazed that it doesn't leak. You sit there and watch the rain come down right on your head almost, and when the wind drives out of the southwest you really expect to be getting wet.

It is ventilated so that in summer we can open up both ends of the area and we have windows up over it on the north side of the house so that it is very pleasant. I do hang thin curtains underneath the glass and leave them there all summer.

It gets cold at night. We don't have any way of shutting it off from the rest of the house. It's a kind of a trade-off that we made for having it right there so that you can be involved. We don't use that area in the evening in winter. We come in here by the stove. But that's kind of nice, too, to have a retreat, to have a different place for different activities. I would say there are only ten or fifteen days a year when it gets so cold that I can't use it. We never run a stove during the day except when it's stormy or really bad.

The plants have done very well in that environment, even plants which aren't supposed to. I start all the vegetables there and have the flowers and of course I overwinter some herbs: rosemary, thyme, some chives and things like that, that I keep for cooking. There is nothing very thrilling that I grow, just ordinary stuff.

The best thing about it for me is the relationship with the outdoors. That is more of a bonus than we had thought it was going to be. The heat, of course, is lovely. We don't have a furnace. All we use for back-up heating is a cord and a half of wood in the wood-burning stove, which is adequate to heat the whole house. So it works much better than you would think, than we would have thought. Actually everyone was a little skeptical. The architects pictured us flapping around in sleeping bags here in the winter, in spite of the fact they talked us into it.

▼ The Champion sunspace seems to reach out to embrace sunlight and mountain views.

Date finished: March 1981

Designer: Dennis Holloway, architect

Builder: Erdkamp Construction

Floor area:
328 square feet
(or 20 feet x 16 feet with two corners cut off)

Vertical glazed area:
south—160 square feet

Sloped glazed area:
200 square feet

Angle: 45°

Type of glazing: double glass

Orientation: S

Degree days: 8,900

Temperature in sunspace	Day	Night
summer average	85°F.	60°F.
high	95°F.	
winter average	80°F.	
high	95°F.	
low	60°F.	47°F.*

* (42°F. lowest ever recorded)

Special features:
Three-story ventilation tower to help with cooling

Sidewalls of sunspace 8 inches concrete, act as Trombe walls

Sliding glass doors and windows that can be opened between house and sunspace

Bridge across sunspace upstairs

Earth floor

Two-and-a-half-story space

ELLEN CHAMPION

COLORADO

Perched on a rocky outcrop, Matt and Ellen Champion's house opens wide to greet the sun and the views of Colorado mountains. To the north, the house is buried snugly in the steeply sloping ground. Enclosed between the outstretched arms of the house is the large two-story greenhouse—Ellen's garden.

When they retired they designed this house, with the help of an architect, so that it exactly suited their needs. Upstairs is a kitchen/dining/living room and a large master bedroom, downstairs his office and her weaving studio. Only four lived-in rooms, but every room counts and every room opens into the greenhouse, which gives a sense of space and light. It is the largest room and is very much the heart of the house.

When we designed the house, we wanted a combination of heat-gathering space and a greenhouse for plants, just what it's turned out to be. With the mountain setting you can't do much with outside gardening, so that is my garden. I think most plants have done much better than I anticipated. Geraniums bloom constantly. The only time they are not in flower is when those stems get 7 feet long and I have to hack them back because they are just too bulky. And then it only takes a few weeks before they start putting out flower heads.

Compact plants don't stay compact in the greenhouse. Most of the pot plants I have can take quite a lot of sun and heat: orchid cactus, regular cactus, Thanksgiving cactus, things like that.

The running water down there comes from a rainwater cistern. I have a drip going. The faucet doesn't like to turn all the way off, so I have just taken advantage of it. I leave the end of the hose under the lime or under the hoya plant or under the bougainvillea for a week at a time. About once a month, or maybe two months in the wintertime, I water the whole thing with the sprinkler. But these plants, except for the lime tree—which produces real limes—are not things that really require very much moisture. Everything that is in pots I water once a week. For the whole house it takes about an hour and a half once a week.

Having most of the plants in the ground is less work because they don't have to be watered quite so carefully. The plants have a lot more vigor, they don't dry out as easily, and there is less chance of them freezing because that ground is not going to freeze.

Two things happen in a greenhouse, the insects love it and so do the plants—they just overcrowd. Whiteflies are the only big problem we have had. The main thing that's different from growing plants in the house is the abundance of insects.

We don't feel any need to add humidity. The plants that are out there have to be tolerant of very hot days and very cool nights. Of course we vent it in summer. Natural convection takes care of it. We leave these top windows open all summer long and we open and close the bottom ones as we need them. There's a lot of heat sink down there between the rock on the ground and the ground itself and the Trombe walls [glazed masonry walls which act as solar collectors].

People ask us whenever they see the house, or whenever we talk about living in a solar house, "Does it get too hot in the summer?" But it doesn't. A particular space can overheat. If this is all closed up then it gets hot, but we just open the windows and let it out. It doesn't really overheat as long as the windows are open, even when the sun is shining directly in in the summer.

It almost never freezes, but most of the plants go through a slower period in January/February when we have less light. In January we have hardly any tomatoes. You can grow them year round but they don't get quite enough light. The tomatoes were wonderful at first. It was just marvelous

▲ The two-story sunspace allows access to the pleasures of light and greenery from all parts of the house.

having all the tomatoes we could possibly eat. But once the whitefly got a stronghold we haven't been able to duplicate that. Most of the other vegetables we had were not very successful. Of course, in midsummer some things don't like that much heat. We tried to grow lettuce, radishes, carrots, spinach, and they can't tolerate summer heat at all. You have to work a lot more with vegetables than you do with perennials.

The sunspace is in visual use from everywhere. Every room in the house opens onto it. I like the smells. Right now the smell of geraniums has floated up here. The lime blooms almost all the time, and it has a nice fragrance. It's ideal for what it is, a garden space and a heat space, a solar space rather than a living space.

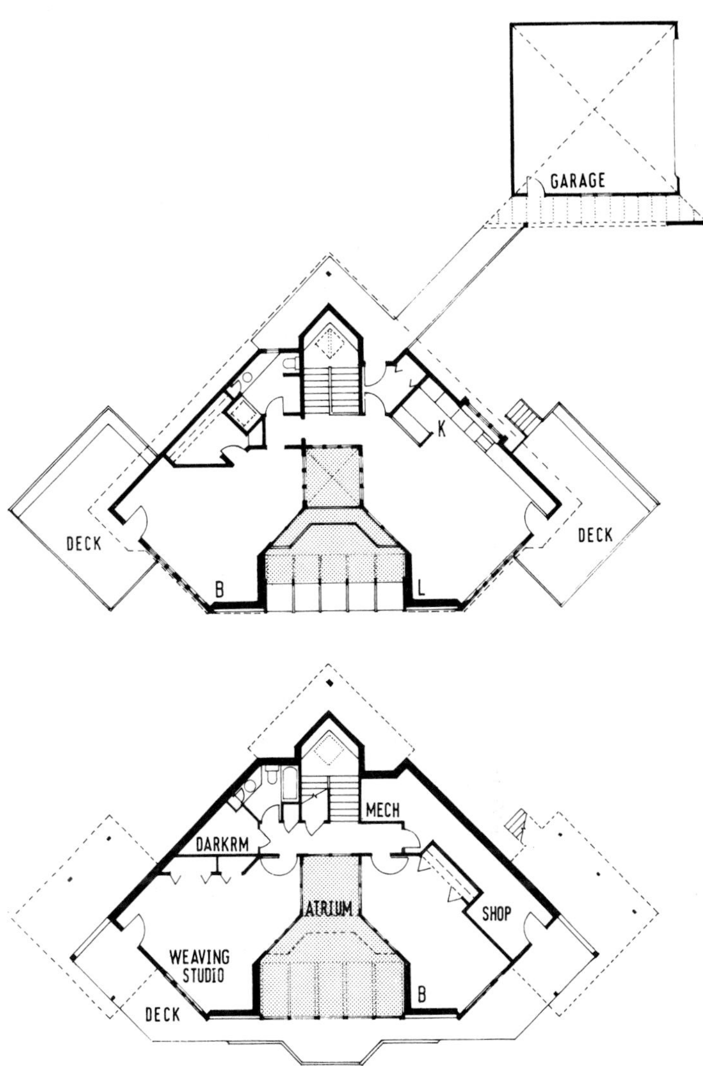

SUSAN YANDA

SANTA FE, NEW MEXICO

Bill and Susan Yanda are founding members of the solar greenhouse movement. Teachers by training, generous by nature, they devoted years of their lives to traveling around the country running workshops and training people in do-it-yourself design and construction of solar greenhouses. Their book, The Food and Heat Producing Solar Greenhouse, *resulted from several years of experience heating their own house and producing all their own vegetables from their greenhouse. When they finally came back to Santa Fe, they bought an old adobe house and immediately built a big attached greenhouse onto it. Together they now run Brother Sun, a company specializing in supplying equipment and materials for passive solar building. Vegetables now take a backseat to business, but their new greenhouse supplies virtually all the heat for their house.*

In the winter of '72 Bill and I built a growhole, just cutting a wedge out of a south-facing hill and glazing it, and we planted it. The only problem was that every insect in New Mexico decided to winter there, but what it produced was very, very good. That winter broke all records and got down to forty-five degrees below zero at night and only up to twenty degrees below zero in the day. But we were venting excess heat out of the growhole.

Bill had the idea of building growholes onto homes so instead of venting the excess heat out of doors, it could be vented into the house. Very few New Mexico homes are built on foundations so you cannot go digging deep holes right beside them, but by using very massive walls, usually adobe, we did an adaptation of a growhole above the ground. Eight of them are still being used as food-producing units. They were prototypes for what became known as a "Yanda greenhouse": built of pine and Lascolite (twin-wall fiberglass

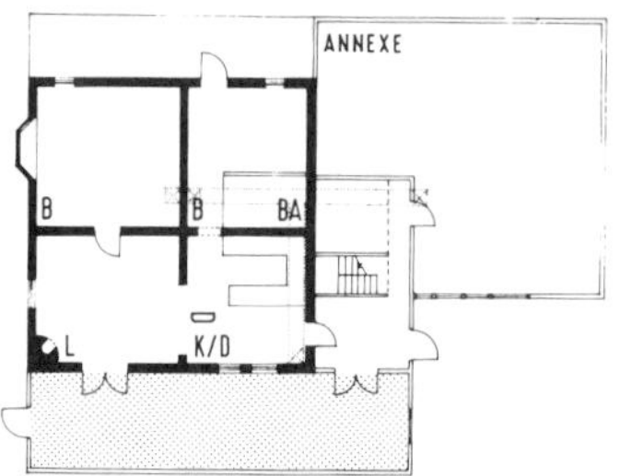

▲ The Yanda's sunspace provides 100 percent of their heat, as well as pleasant additional living space.

sheet), 55-gallon drums for thermal mass, always attached to a house, longer than they were wide, between a quarter and a half of the roof glazed with the rest insulated and the front face tilted.

Our own greenhouse was an add-on to a very big house. I found if I spent about ten hours a week in there I could get plenty of fresh things to eat. I found out things like, if you truly cut back the foliage of tomato plants they do much better. I was able to raise everything including an ear of corn in the greenhouse, but you soon find out things like it's not worth taking up that much space for an ear of corn.

I had to do some true learning with insects. We had aphids and whitefly and slugs and thrips and scale and those little rolypolies, those little armored tanks that roll up—pill bugs—and spider mites. The whitefly were the worst—that's when I started experimenting with encarsia formosa and ladybugs. The encarsia worked beautifully. The vacuum cleaner worked pretty well on whitefly, too. There is no way I can see to run an insect-free greenhouse, but we live in harmony now. I'm always on top of them and trying to work on them.

This greenhouse is working very differently from the last one we had. It was more added living space and heat producing that we were interested in this time. It's giving us 100 percent of our heat because we don't have anything else.

We have such heavy clay that it's going to take me a couple of years to build up that soil. I use bonemeal and bat guano from the Carlsbad Caverns. Bales of peat moss just get absorbed. I think it's critical to start with soil that is not too heavy because growing all the time you never give the soil a respite, and it packs down much more than it does out of doors. I dig fresh material in whenever I take something out. I've got drip irrigation underground in there which makes it more complicated, because I am forever slicing the hose in half when I forget it and dig in.

Through the wintertime probably once a month I spend a day really cleaning, moving any pots to get the insects that have nestled underneath. I prune back the tomatoes pretty drastically, try to turn over the soil to lighten it up and basically just give it a good clean. In the spring I spend a couple of days planting seeds that will go outside. In the fall again I will spend quite a bit of time starting seedlings to plant in the greenhouse, the cold weather crops. I plant everything except my leafy greens in the ground. I get the greens started in little six packs but I plant lettuce very intensively in a circle of nothing but lettuce. I thin it as we eat it instead of having each little lettuce plant develop.

I wish I could find more easy ways to hang things up. I can hang from the beams, but I don't have any way to use the back wall which is wasted space, although very important for the heating of the house because that adobe wall is basically the solar mass, it radiates a lot of heat into the house. I also wish I had knocked down the kitchen wall and made the kitchen more a part of the dining room and the greenhouse.

▲ An adaptation of the Yanda's earlier growholes, this sunspace addition to a large adobe house proved to have the potential to provide most of the food for a family. The photovoltaic cells in the middle of the roof power a fan to vent the space.

Date finished: 1983

Designer: Bill and Susan Yanda

Builder: Paul Williams and many others

Cost: $4,000

Floor area: 39 feet x 10 feet

Vertical glazed area:
south—246 square feet
east—6 square feet
west—9 square feet
(glazed door)

Sloped glazed area:
246 square feet

Type of glazing:
double glass with Sure-Seal

Orientation: S

Degree days:
6,500

Temperature in sunspace	Day	Night
summer average	80°F.	
high	85°F.*	
winter average	65°F.	
high	78°F.	
low	40°F.	29°F.

* (with shade cloth)

Special features:
Photovoltaic fan to take heat to north side of house

70% shade cloth inside sloped glass in summer

Half of roof solid

Ground beds

Solid adobe wall with glazed doors and opening windows between house and sunspace

Main entrance to house

▲ In the Nakosteen sunspace, heat storage tubes produce shimmering patterns of light.

FRANCES NAKOSTEEN
BOULDER, COLORADO

Frances Nakosteen added a curved sunspace, narrow in the middle and wide at each end, to the back of her house in Boulder. The curve encloses spaces on two levels joined by a narrow stairway in the middle. On the lower level is Frances's music room where friends come for musical evenings. The upper level has become the main sitting area for the house. A shimmering pale-blue wall of water tubes lines the center of the curve, reducing glare and storing heat to keep the space reasonably warm at night. Delicate patterns of light shift across the carpet behind the tubes. Seen from behind, the south side of her house has been transformed from a conventional suburban backyard to a rather extraordinary Japanese sweep of wood and glass.

For years I have been very interested in energy conservation; I guess since the oil embargo. So I desperately wanted to insulate the house, and bring in sun heat—and it is magnificent. It takes only the littlest bit of sun to make it comfortable in here in the daytime. If there is no sun, and it is very cold, that little wood stove makes it totally comfortable in about twenty to thirty minutes. Even when there is no extra heat out there, it is about 25° to 30°F. warmer after the coldest nights than it is outdoors.

My friend and I live in here. The rest of the house is just a superfluous back-up. We never sit anywhere else, unless it is in the living room in the mornings before it has heated up out here. In the middle of winter, of course, that isn't until 9:30. But by March it is pleasant by 8 a.m. We moved in and we haven't moved out, except to sleep and cook.

There used to be a porch all along here with vines growing up, so there wasn't much sun coming in from the south, in fact very little. The whole house is much brighter now. I don't grow many plants, but I am sure you could, it is just that I'm lazy.

I researched the curtains or thermal shades because I wanted to be able to sit out here in a storm and still see the storm, but be comfortable from it. These solar curtains darken the room a little bit, but still you

can see out. The tracking is a disaster but the curtains themselves are wonderful. At night, when it is bitter cold outdoors, it won't be comfortable with just the solar curtains shut, but that stove will make it toasty out here, so you can sit and watch the stars—it is wonderful. We have thick curtains as well for when we don't want to see out. And we put thin venetian blinds on these two windows, so we could control the sun streaming in where we wanted to sit, without closing out the heat coming in. When the sun is very hot in the middle of the winter, then we can put the heat downstairs with a fan and a duct.

I just adore it. It is perfect for two of us, though I think a big family would be a bit crowded. I wouldn't have a house without solar heating.

▲ **The rear of the Nakosteen house has been transformed by its sunspace addition.**

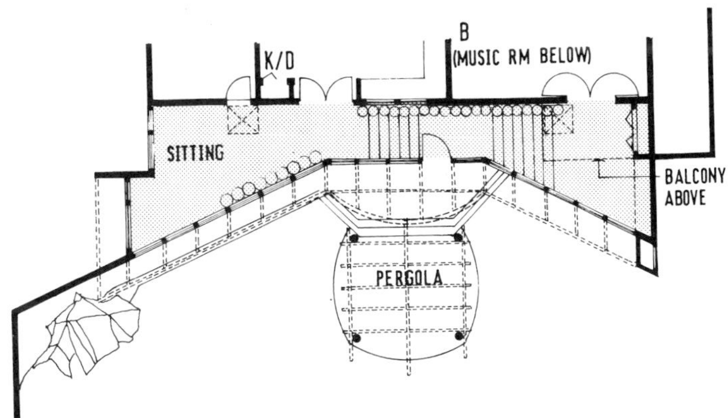

Date finished: 1983

Designer: Sunflower Design

Builder: Piccadilly Construction

Cost: $35,000

Sloped glazed area: none

Orientation: SSW

Degree days: 7,000

Temperature in sunspace	**Day**	**Night**
summer average	70°F.	
high	80°F.	
winter average	70°F.	
high	80°F.	
low	45°F.	35°F.*

* (when house unoccupied)

Special features:

Solid walls with glazed doors and windows between house and sunspace

12 Kalwall water tubes

Fan and duct to transfer heat downstairs

Semi-transparent heat-reflective blinds and lined curtains

Half of space is two-story with stairs to upper level

Date finished: 1975

Designer:
Doug Kelbaugh and Lord and Burnham

Builder:
Nathan Bard, Norm Servis, and Doug Kelbaugh

Cost: $5,000

Floor area: 20 feet x 10 feet

Vertical glazed area:
south—90 square feet
east—50 square feet
west—50 square feet

Sloped glazed area:
130 square feet

Angle: 26°

Type of glazing: double glass

Orientation: S

Degree days: 5,200

Temperature in sunspace	Day	Night
summer average	85°F.	
high	110°F.	
winter average	65°F.	40°F.
high	90°F.	
low	55°F.	30°F.

Special features:
Large opening to house, closed by thermal curtain at night

Big Fins for shading, cooling, and domestic water heating

Main entrance to house

▲ Meg Kelbaugh's mobile work station holds compost, sand, and peat below. A counter folds out for potting on and the top serves as a planter.

▼ **Looking down the stairs through the arch into the Kelbaugh sunspace.**

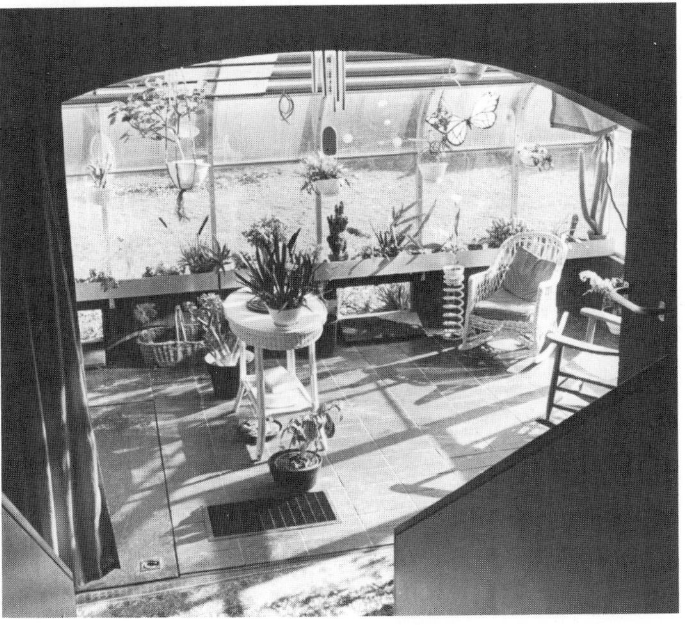

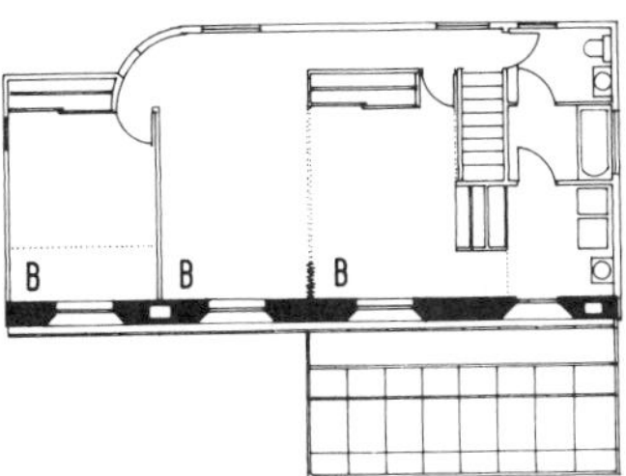

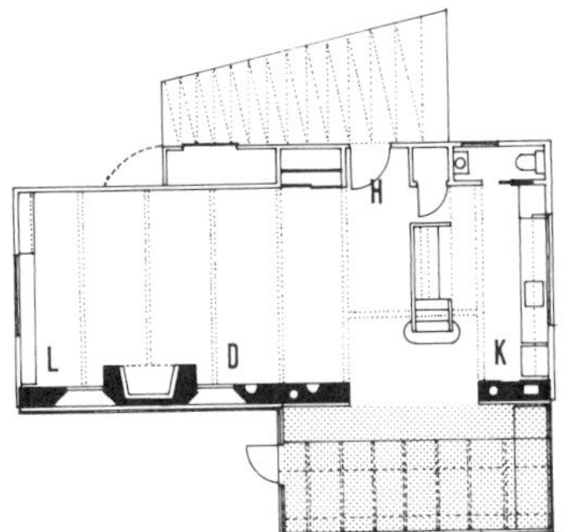

THE KELBAUGHS

PRINCETON, NEW JERSEY

Doug and Meg Kelbaugh's house has become famous as one of the pioneers of passive solar design. On a pleasant back street in Princeton, New Jersey, coming on the Kelbaugh's house can be quite startling. It makes no concessions to its neighbors' pitched roofs, white clapboard, and black shutters. The absolutely plain glass facade of the Trombe wall which covers the south side of the house is broken only by a Lord and Burnham greenhouse jutting out on one side. The greenhouse was the perfect solution to the problem of combining her interest in plants with his interest in solar energy.

MEG: At first it was very raw, unfinished. It took a while to get it looking green and growing. The initial idea was primarily a space for plants, a production area and work area. But the conditions are not really conducive to good growing. It has always been sort of awkward.

It used to have six or eight big black water barrels in it for mass. Because of that there was very little space for my plants, although they did grow up on top of the barrels. We took the barrels out when they started rusting and began to leak. I have transformed it into a place where I put things that I like, a collection of odd materials. I added chairs and stuff, so it is more sitting room, sunroom, than it used to be. It used to be just barrels and plants, functional, crowded, and very green. To me now it is open, airy, colorful, spacious.

It gets pretty chilly in the wintertime but that hasn't seemed to be too detrimental. Cacti and succulents do very well. It is hot and dry in the summertime. Just about anything will do well given proper care. I have lost a few plants to bugs, none to neglect. In the summertime they go out, it is pretty much empty in the summertime, except for the cactus.

DOUG: I liked the drums, though they weren't standard 55-gallon drums, they were corrugated drums, gloss black. They had a lot of presence. But in fact it works all right without them. We have a curtain we close every night, but it is not airtight. That is essential so that the greenhouse can rob back a little heat at night that it gave the main house in the day.

I think the Big Fins are one of the few breakthroughs in solar technology in the last five or six years. This is not the first installation, but I think it is the first on the east coast. They cost about a third to a half what regular solar collectors cost and they don't require a pump. It is all thermo-siphoned, no thermostat. They are smart, they know exactly when to start, how fast to go and when to stop. The extra heat, the heat that doesn't get into those black pipes and into the water, is lost into the space. A solar collector on the roof loses heat to the outside.

What they are, in fact, is a shading device that is water-cooled. The shade is welcome in the summer. It is not always welcome in the winter, but in this case it is welcome in the winter as well because Meg's plants don't want much sun. So it shades, it heats water at the same time, and it puts to use an otherwise horrible slope of glass which every greenhouse has. Big Fins don't solve the overheating problem—I mean, this is overheating right now and it's only March—but they certainly help. They take away a lot of heat, and they are cheap and should last a long time. The space can't go below freezing level for long or they will freeze up. But if you have a greenhouse, it is almost stupid not to do this, in my opinion. Most greenhouse slopes are about six in twelve which is not bad for domestic hot-water heating, though it is a lousy slope for space heating. It sees and transmits much more energy in the summer than in the winter, which is just the opposite to what you want for passive solar space heating.

MEG: On a sunny day in the wintertime, this is the nicest place to be, sitting out here. It is cozy, and it is nice to have the sun bathing the back and warming the spirit. Even on rainy days I like it. When the rain is pelting down outside and the wind is blowing, I come out here and I just feel very protected, I feel like a ship at sea but invulnerable to the elements. I don't think anyone else in the family except maybe our daughter Tess shares that feeling, but that makes it even more sacrosanct.

CANDIDA LYCETT-GREEN

WILTSHIRE, ENGLAND

Candida Lycett-Green and her husband bought a small eighteenth-century country manor twelve years ago. Set in its own rolling grounds with a river flowing through, it is a grand country house on a small scale. Attached to one side was a large Victorian conservatory with an alarming list. After winching it up until it approached vertical once more, she put plants in it and decorated it and left it to its own devices, returning only to water from time to time. The conservatory serves primarily to embellish the brilliant red drawing room/study to which it is attached. Full of seashells and mirrors, statues and chandeliers, jasmine and geraniums (and even a few plastic flowers) it achieves an effect of relaxed gaiety.

When we first saw the house, the conservatory was obviously an added attraction, but I didn't know anything about gardening so it didn't immediately conjure up images of rare banana trees and things growing in there. And twelve years later, I still have not got round to it.

When the children water it's quite frightening—even the chandeliers get watered. In the summer it's watered a terrific lot so the floor is always wet and the chair legs just disintegrate. I had a lunch party in there once, and somebody's chair just crumpled up underneath him and he sent the whole lunch flying. Now I've got the tin chairs I think we might be a bit safer.

I think the vents still work, but I don't use them, I just open the doors. I know you are meant to vent things; I am a terribly bad indoor gardener. I only choose tough candidates who survive all my neglect. It would be mean on delicate people to undergo my hard hands, my neglect.

For example I'd like to murder that jasmine, it just takes over. I have to cut it back drastically every year. It always has a lot of dead in it which is impossible to get out, it takes hours to pull the bits out from between the panes. But when the jasmine is in bloom, then the whole house smells. It's extraordinary; it completely permeates the house.

When I'm feeling generous I buy soil for the pots, otherwise I just use the earth I find in mole hills outside.

The conservatory gets terrible diseases and things. I'm sure everything is covered in little black spots, sort of soot; but I don't think it's worth worrying about really. I've given up spraying; now I think the best thing is just to feed them a lot with seaweed. If they are going to die of something, they will die, otherwise they will be able to combat the disease. That's my theory outside, so I use it inside, too.

I really only use the conservatory as an extension to the sitting room, so to me what matters is how it looks from there. I'm not a plant person, I'm after the effect of things together rather than individual plants. I do quite a lot of moving about of things as a Victorian conservatory owner is meant to do. You move things that look good into the front position, and then when they fade, you move them to the back. It's a bit like arranging furniture in a room.

I don't particularly crave exotic plants. I'm more interested in a plant's architecture than in its flowers. Orange and lemon trees I would like, but I could always tie false ones onto a bay tree, which would please me just as much. All I've got in winter basically is the variegated geraniums which I just let get bigger. Then I jolly it up; I buy a lot of stuff and tell people that I've grown it. If I'm passing a garden center I might buy some primulas, or I buy things for the house and then they go out there and just take their chance. I did grow lots of paperwhites this year for the first time.

There are all sorts of little treasures—statues, flowered pottery, elaborate boxes—in here, partly because I haven't got enough plants, just to add interest. Even in the garden I don't go for complete classical beauty. I like jokes and things that make people laugh.

▼ **The conservatory brings light and charm to the sitting room.**

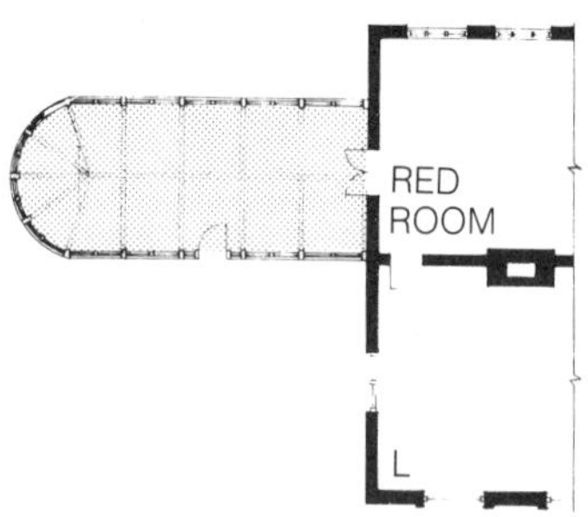

▲ **The Lycett-Green house boasts a Victorian conservatory.**

▲ **Candida Lycett-Green's use of chandeliers, statues, and other objets d'art gives her Victorian conservatory a whimsical ambiance.**

Date finished: 1890s

Floor area: 25 feet x 12½ feet

Type of glazing:
single, lapped glass

Vertical glazing area:
south—84 square feet
west—24 square feet
north—84 square feet

Sloped glazed area:
414 square feet

Orientation: N, S, W

Degree days: 3,300

Temperature in sunspace	Day	Night
summer average	75°F.	55°F.
high	90°F.	
winter average	55°F.	40°F.
high	70°F.	
low	40°F.*	

* (32 with heat; 20 without heat)

Special features:

Victorian conservatory with curved cast-iron roof structure

Added onto an eighteenth-century house, little altered

Groundbeds around perimeter, covered with benches, used only for jasmine

Solid stone wall with double-glazed doors, surrounded by mirrors between house and sunspace

Solid kneewall

Top vents with crank and side vents not used

Date finished: 1980

Designer: Tanya Olsen-Berger

Builder: Sweetwater Construction

Floor area: 25 feet x 10 feet

Vertical glazed area:
south—180 square feet

Sloped glazed area:
120 square feet (in four skylights)

Angle: 35°

Type of glazing: single glass

Orientation: S

Degree days: 3,000

Temperature in sunspace	**Day**	**Night**
summer average	80°F.	60°F.
high	90°F.	
winter average	55°F.	
high	100°F.	
low	48°F.	48°F.

Special features:
Double-glazed doors and windows between house and sunspace

Three 500-gallon water tanks form part of wall between sunspace and house

Fans for heat circulation not used anymore

Fans for heat removal in summer

Rolling shutters for skylights, used May–October

Awning to shade vertical glass, used May–October

Two-story space

▲ The height and brightness of the sunspace first attracted the Horners to this spec house in Davis, California.

THE HORNERS

DAVIS, CALIFORNIA

Gerald and Patricia Horner were looking for ways to make their traditional ranch house more energy efficient when they came across Village Homes in Davis, California. Village Homes is a development of assorted houses whose unifying theme is their dedication to energy conservation and use of the sun as the primary heat source. The Horners fell in love with and bought a new house there that had won a Housing and Urban Design Award for its energy-conscious design. Many of the houses in Village Homes have sunspaces used for heating, but very few manage to grow any plants in the intense sun. Those not empty mostly house old bicycles or lines of drying laundry. The Horner's two-story sunspace, however, succeeds in providing both a good growing environment and most of the heat for their house.

GERALD: This was a spec house and we just happened upon it one day with a real estate agent. I guess what we liked about it were essentially the solar features.

PATRICIA: I think the exciting design of the house made us feel we would like to live in it. I think that solarium, the height of it, and all the glass, was what made it so exciting.

GERALD: This is an entirely passive house and it performs as well as, if not better than, the active houses. That's the nice part of it, you just leave it alone, just close and open the drapes and vents when you should and that's about all you have to do.

PATRICIA: The whole functioning of the house depends on the solarium. It is the solar heart of the house. We use it as a garden area and an eating place and a sitting area, I would say, second to its function as a solar heat collector.

GERALD: Because it's so foggy here, we don't use the solarium very much in the wintertime. It's dead space most of the winter, but it's necessary to how the house works. It acts as a buffer even when the sun isn't out. When the sun does shine in the wintertime it's glorious.

We used to shut the insulating shutters on the skylights in the sunspace every night in winter. But we didn't really notice any difference, when we stopped. Now we just put the insulating shutters on the skylights down once a year in the spring and take them up in the fall.

The skylight shutters are plywood panels about 2-1/2 inches thick with a wheel in each corner. There is a channel iron track directly above the window so the weight of the shutter just slides it down onto the top of the glass. There is a crank to open them, that's no problem. They always go up. It's coming down that's the problem, because it catches. When I replace them I think I will use a much lighter substance, and I would attach some better wheels, maybe roller skate wheels.

In the summertime they stay down and we put the awning up so no sun gets in. It's much darker when they are down. But in the summertime it's very hot here; you want it cool and dark. At night you get a very cool breeze here and so you open up the house and it cools everything down.

PATRICIA: It's surprising, but that room is not really suited to a lot of plants and only certain types like it. So as plants go, they have to be very hardy.

GERALD: I think things would do a lot better if we had a humidifier. The air circulates through the house, so it's not like a greenhouse. There's a tremendous drying effect.

▲ Rolling white shutters can be seen above the skylights. Shading screens fit into the wooden structure in front of the house to keep the sun off the vertical glass in summer.

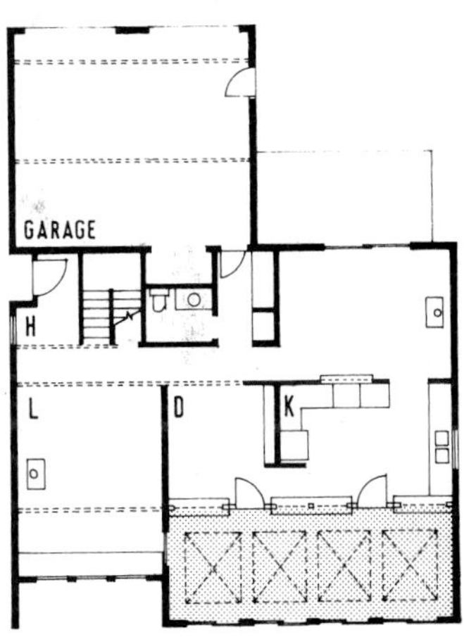

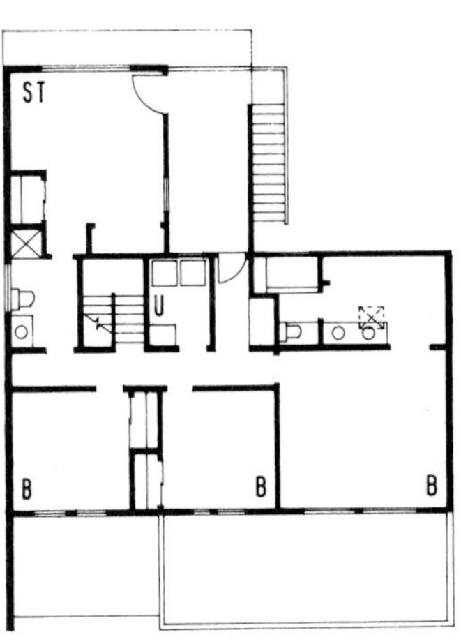

PATRICIA: It can't operate as a greenhouse can, because you have to open it up and you can't build up the humidity. Even if we filled it with plants, the air would still be dry. That's why we can use it also as a living area. I don't think you can eat in a greenhouse.

GERALD: We sit out there in the late afternoon, and we have a glass of wine out there most evenings before dinner in the summer. It's also a nice workspace. You put everything together and just leave it there; it doesn't get trampled on and it's not in anybody's way. And it's usually warm.

PATRICIA: I also love the effect it has on the rooms upstairs. I like the way the moon shines right into our bedroom. You can look out and see the stars and everything out our bedroom window through the glass panes in the roof.

GERALD: I wouldn't want to ever build a house without a greenhouse. What I like best by far are the winter days that have sunshine. It's incredible the lift that you get. It's just like going to Mexico.

▼ **Karen and Tom Huenink's sunspace is recycled from an old Lord and Burnham greenhouse from another site.**

KAREN HUENINK
MARLBORO, VERMONT

As a young couple, Karen and Tom Huenink, with the help of friends, built their own house in southern Vermont. They were keen gardeners and within a year had added a greenhouse for year-round vegetable growing. Like much of the house, the greenhouse was recycled from an earlier incarnation. Since then they have added two children, but the greenhouse still provides enough vegetables for them all and heat for the house as well.

We built our house with the idea that we would put a solar greenhouse on the front, and we did that the next year. We started off with a floor bed that went the entire length of the greenhouse, which is 10 feet by 16 feet, but two years ago we raised the bed, and divided it in two, making one side a bit higher by adding more earth. We built a big raised planter on the other side, right up off the ground; that is our warmer bed and we use it all the year round. The other peters out from about November. The raised bed is noticeably warmer and it is easier to handle—everything is more visible. I usually put the really deep-rooted plants in the ground bed.

We were mainly looking for a year-round vegetable garden. We designed it with growing in mind. And therefore we have much, much more glass than most solar greenhouses, so-called. We have a 45° and 50° angle on the glass to allow us to use the space for summer growing, and we put east and west glazing, too, for the same reason. I was concerned about drainage in the floor, but I need not have been—we have got plenty. We have a stone floor because I wanted to be sure that I could be good and messy and not have to worry about it.

In the summertime we open that vent, and half the side wall just pops out. We have no top vents, but the breeze in the summer comes right up the field and in the bottom vent, which is a big opening.

The whole frame of the thing including the vents and all those ribs, are from an old Lord and Burnham greenhouse that was taken down somewhere else. We bought the parts and put them up, which is very satisfactory except for one thing, it is not double glazed. We have tried twice to double glaze it, first with really thick, quarter-inch, rigid acrylic, which leaked, then with thin plastic film. We don't have so much problem with air leakage; this is much warmer, but we have bugs.

I thought I would be able to grow things in the back of the greenhouse, seedlings and stuff, because I thought it would be warmer sitting on top of the barrels, but it is too dark to grow anything but houseplants there. I wish now that we had less solid roof, more glazing overhead.

Lettuce does well in the fall and in the spring, but not in the winter. You can grow such a variety of Chinese and Italian greens, you don't really need lettuce. Orientals do wonderfully well. And last year a friend of mine went to Italy and brought back a whole bunch of salad greens from there—leekia, endive, Catalonia chicory, arugula, and I've got a bunch more. All greens in the greenhouse are milder than they are outside. Radishes can get to be the size of a baseball and still be edible.

Adding the greenhouse made this whole side of the house seem much bigger. Partly because it is sloping down, it really feels like you're almost outside, and that's what we wanted it to feel like: to feel we have a garden we can go to in the wintertime.

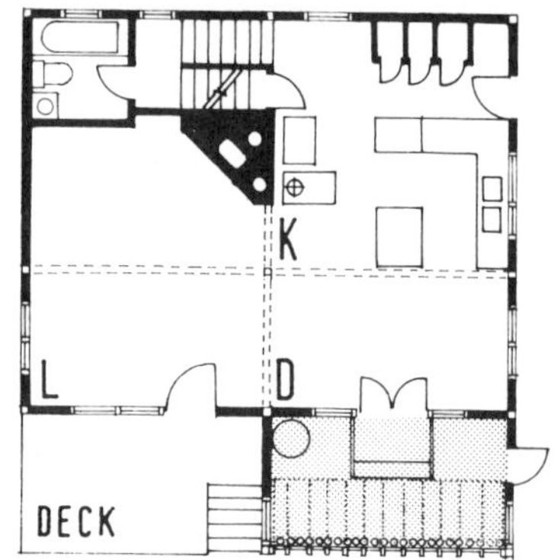

▲ **The Huenink sunspace provides a feeling of spaciousness and a garden-like atmosphere even in winter.**

◀ **Sweet peas and vegetables grow in this raised bed.**

Date finished: 1979

Designer:
Hueninks and Jeremy Coleman/
Lord and Burnham

Builder:
Hueninks and Jeremy Coleman/
Lord and Burnham

Cost: $1,500

Floor area: 16 feet x 10 feet

Vertical glazed area:
south—25 square feet
east—25 square feet
west—25 square feet

Sloped glazed area:
160 square feet

Angle: 50°

Type of glazing:
lapped single glass with inner layer of polyethylene film

Orientation: SSW

Degree days: 8,000

Temperature in sunspace	**Day**	**Night**
summer average	75°F.	65°F.
high	85°F.	
winter average	60°F.	50°F.
high	70°F.	
low	40°F.	28°F.

Special features:

Seven 30-gallon water drums

Many 1-gallon plastic water containers

glazed double doors in solid wall between sunspace and house

All vertical glazing on south side opens

One ground bed and one raised planter

Recycled Lord and Burnham greenhouse

▶ **Looking out through the Deye greenhouse.**

JERRY DEYE

PHILADELPHIA, PENNSYLVANIA

Jerry Deye is a born gardener who lives in the top half of a very old house in downtown Philadelphia. What does a high-rise gardener do without a garden? He grows on the roof. At first his roof bloomed only in summer, but since he built a greenhouse onto the attic room overlooking the flat roof, flowers have been blooming all year long up there. The attic itself has turned into an extension of the greenhouse. With fluorescent tubes striping the mirrored walls, ferns and palms and hanging baskets give the impression of an interior decorator's dream, but really the attic's visual excitement is secondary to its function as a place to winter-over foliage plants. Hiding behind the sofa, dormant fuschias and lantanas huddle like wallflowers. Every inch is in use.

Although I love this house and I love this area, it was very disappointing to me to have no garden. I always wanted an outdoor space, so in 1970 I constructed a large deck on the roof of the third floor. After I had the deck I realized that I needed some space to bring in for the winter all the things that I was growing on the deck in the summer. The room off of the deck was a large attic room and it was a little dark—it only had two dormer windows in it—and the greenhouse idea just seemed to fit in beautifully to tie that room and the deck together.

The greenhouse is set into the roof like a dormer, and while the roof was cut away to install it, Philadelphia had one

▲ **Jerry Deye's rooftop greenhouse provides growing space for an avid city gardener.**

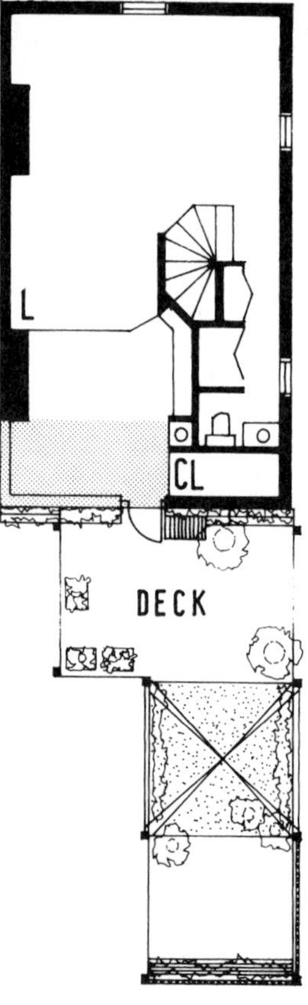

of its heaviest rainfalls ever—5 inches in less than seven hours. I received a phone call at work saying, "I think you'd better come home. See if you can find some plastic on the way." I had these dire premonitions that in no way matched the reality. The reality was horrendous.

Playing sorcerer's apprentice, I still was unable to prevent the water from totally wiping out the ceilings in two rooms, and all the woodwork in my bathroom, dining room, and bedroom. Ceiling moldings, doorframes all warped and twisted—it was unbelievable.

The greenhouse is basically oriented towards serving the deck. For example, I grow a lot of lantana trees, gerberas, hibiscus, gardenias, holding them from one year to the next in order to decorate the deck in the summer. They are brilliant sun plants that are trying to eke by in this dark winter. I grow a lot of things under lights in the rest of the room and I can do a reasonable job of tiding things over. I also winter over some of the shrimp plants and candelabra plants from the deck. I have ferns and green things up there, too, that I use as filler, some staghorn ferns, sea grape, false aralia, Ardisia crenata. It's full of scale right now, but it is a beautiful plant, wonderful at Christmas time, and it has always got some stage of red berries on it, as well as white flowers and pretty leaves.

Greenhouses up in the air turn out to be entirely different from greenhouses on the ground. On a good July day, four stories up, with 98°F. air rising up from below and all these brick buildings around, it is like a greenhouse sitting on an oven. It is very difficult to keep that greenhouse cool and moist shaded. The air up there is so hot and dry that things are just cremated. And by the same token you don't have any protection in the wintertime either.

Another trouble with a greenhouse in the city is that you have got a lot of pollution. It is difficult to grow plants in this environment; things that are sensitive get it really bad. Camellias and gardenias, hibiscus, seem to be affected by it.

The logistics of carrying everything up four stories are incredible. And you have to carry everything back down that you carried up, at some point or another. Dirt doesn't last forever. While you can keep adding to it, it just doesn't do the same as replacing it. I bought a ton of topsoil and had it dumped in the basement, and over the last ten years, in addition to what I brought up in the container of any plant I bought, I have totally used up that ton of top soil, plus innumerable bags of peat moss and some perlite.

You are also very limited on space. Most greenhouses on the ground you can grab everything and take it outside for a while. You can't do that in this one, you have got to deal with it more or less right there. I have always got more in this greenhouse than it could possibly hold, so that just keeping it clean is a real tough job. I have a tile floor with a drain and I can literally hose down the entire interior of the greenhouse. It's more difficult watering in the summertime because of the deck. I have to water the deck twice a day, once in the morning, once at night, and I should water it at noon if I could be here.

It's a place where you can go and sit and read or talk or listen to music. Day or night it's just wonderful. I particularly like it when it's snowing, or after it's snowed when it's sunny. You can sit there among all the flowers and just look out at the snow-covered rooftops. It's a place where people kind of relax, as a garden is in the summer. Plants are like fires, you can keep looking at them.

▼ Standard fuchsias and lantanas winter over behind the sofa.

Designer: Jerry Deye/prefab kit

Builder: Earl Springer

Cost: $6,000 plus water damage

Floor area: 8 feet x 10 feet

Vertical glazed area:
south—24 square feet
east—8 square feet
west—8 square feet

Sloped glazed area:
16 square feet plus
16 square feet curved

Angle: curved

Type of glazing: single glass

Orientation: S

Degree days: 5,100

Temperature in sunspace	Day	Night
summer average	85°F.	
high	110°F.	
winter average	65°F.	
high	80°F.	
low	50°F.	45°F.*

* (with heat)

Special features:
Retrofit on fourth-floor attic room overlooking flat roof garden

1000 cfm extract fan

Small fan for air circulation runs all the time

Sheer curtains under sloped glazing for summer shading

Open to room lined with mirrors and fluorescent tubes for additional growing space

▼ **Sunspaces provide settings for kids and turtles as well as adults and plants.**

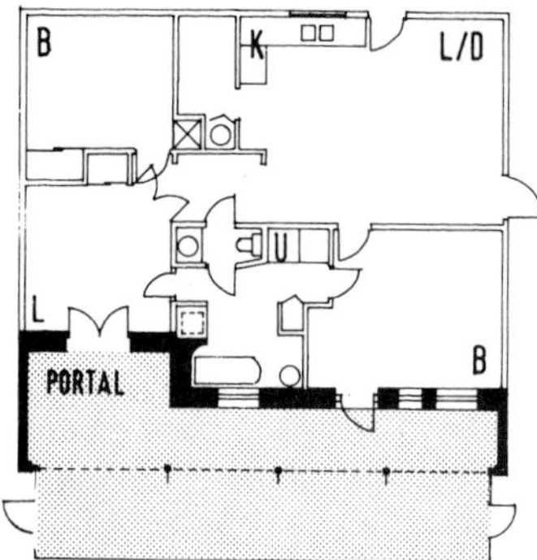

STEVE KENIN

TAOS, NEW MEXICO

Steve Kenin had a great idea: why not a zip-on, zip-off greenhouse? Put it up in summer, take it down in winter. He designed a simple, remarkably cheap, inflatable system which he has been marketing for several years. The whole south wall of his house is enclosed in a plastic bubble in winter. Every spring he takes it down and puts up an awning with screens to make it a screened-in porch for the summer. His enthusiasm for the heat produced, the extra living space, and the possibility of indoor gardening knows no bounds.

I tried to build a low-cost house, economically sound. I built the south wall out of adobe for heat storage, with a portal (which is a New Mexico porch), and attached to the porch is a greenhouse. The greenhouse is removable so it is year-round space, and it gets a workout. We use it for gardening, for chopping wood, and for storing firewood. It's an arboretum. It's a wonderful anteroom/mud room/boot room for the rest of the house. Obviously it supplies a lot of heat, and it's a play room for the turtles and my kids. It's an everything room.

But the main thing is, it's a heater for this house. It supplies about three-quarters of our heating requirements, probably more. We burn somewhat less than a cord of wood each winter. This is a pretty severe climate; we get some minus 20°F. of weather. We also get a lot of sun. We are facing somewhat east of south, so by 8 o'clock it's really very comfortable in there. And by 8:30 it's putting heat into the house.

In the summer we take the plastic off and put the green awning up. We can screen it if we want to. I think one of the key factors that differentiates it from other greenhouses is that you can remove the glazing in fifteen minutes. The fact that you can remove the glazing does away with overheating problems in summer.

It doesn't leak because it's one big piece of plastic which is folded over to make a double layer. Around here we have to replace the plastic about every four years. One man in New England had one for six years. I don't know many that have lasted less than three years.

It's translucent; the only time it looks quite transparent is at midday when the sun is shining right through it. At certain times of the evening as the temperature outside is dropping you get a layer of condensation inside the outer glazing and if we have just watered the greenhouse and it's real cold outside you might get condensation on the inside of the inner glazing, but then as things warm up it disappears completely.

The air for the blower comes from the inside, but it is only static pressure; that means it's like a balloon when it's blown up. It's not a continuous flow. With the blower it will withstand quite a few small leaks, about the equivalent of a 12-inch diameter circle in little holes.

I think it's important to have a substantial fan on a thermostatic control so that you can really move the heat around. Natural convection works in some cases when there are enough openings to let it work, but I have experienced so many houses that are cold with hot greenhouses. Having a thermostat on a fan is easy, and as long as it's a big enough fan, very effective. The house would have to be much bigger if we didn't have the greenhouse. We use it all the time. The kids use it after school as a playroom. Bernice [his wife] is a painter and she paints in there. I have a hammock in there I lie in. I could spend half the weekend out there helping the kids on various projects on the workbench or taking bicycles apart.

Our views are all to the north. If we had a superinsulated house, we couldn't afford to see those big mountains. But having a big collector on the south wall and having all our heat storage in it, we have the best of both worlds. We have enough heat in that massive adobe wall to support this loss through a north-facing picture window.

▲ **Steve Kenin's greenhouse zips off in fifteen minutes, yet it provides at least three-quarters of the heat for his New Mexico home.**

Date finished: 1978

Designer: Stephen Kenin

Builder: Stephen Kenin

Cost: $1,800 (plus two days labor)

Floor area: 39 feet x 12 feet

Vertical glazed area:
east—14 square feet
west—14 square feet

Sloped glazed area:
261 square feet and 156 square feet

Angle: 70° / 30°

Type of glazing:
two layers of ultraviolet resistant polyethylene, inflated with small fan

Orientation: SSE

Degree days: 7,500-8,000

Temperature in sunspace	Day	Night
summer average high	(cover removed)	
winter average	80°F.	
high	90°F.	
low	60°F.	40°F.

Special features:

2,000 cfm fan to transfer heat to house

Awning with screens in summer replaces polyethylene

Solid adobe walls with glazed doors and opening windows between house and sunspace

Main entrance to house

MARK CHALOM

SANTA FE, NEW MEXICO

Mark Chalom is an architect. Together with his wife, Betty Tsosie, he designed and built an adobe house for himself just outside of Santa Fe. A greenhouse is the hub of the house and the main passageway between living, working, and sleeping areas. It is an exciting space, full of life, both literally—with hundreds of plants growing in it, and architecturally—with its five doorways at different levels, a balcony, a spiral staircase, and assorted windows. There is also almost continuous music from built-in loudspeakers. With solid walls of adobe and a flagstone floor, it feels carved out of the earth, a light and airy cave.

We were looking for an architectural transition to separate the three main parts of the house, our upstairs bedroom (our sanctuary), my office space, and the family space—the living, kitchen, and dining rooms. This is a glorified hallway, an interior courtyard, to separate those main functions as well as a solar heater, as well as a garden room, which is something we had seen in books and never had before. We weren't necessarily green-thumb people in the beginning, but we brought in some plants, our friends gave us some plants, and it has "jungle-ized" since then. We have exterior stucco on the walls, and the floor is flagstone on sand, which has a fair amount of drainage, so we can hose the place down.

We have got ventilation (more than necessary) de-

▲ Speakers high on the adobe walls provide especially good listening in this sunspace.

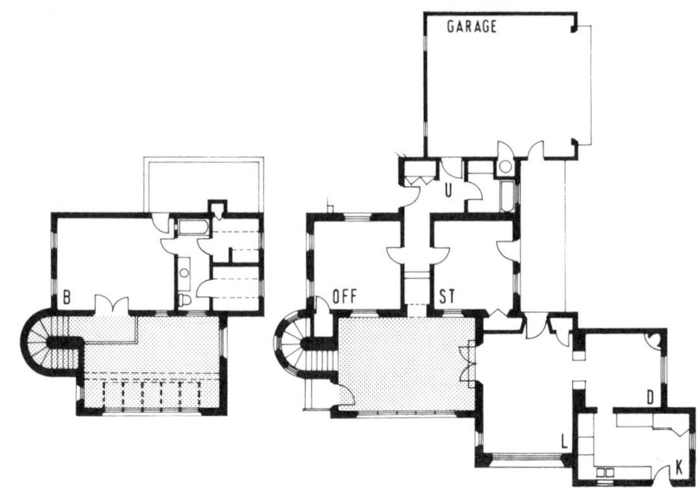

▲ **Courtyard, solar heater, and garden room, this sunspace forms an architectural transition to other living areas of the house.**

Date finished: 1982

Designer: Mark Chalom

Builder: Mark Chalom

Floor area: 21 feet x 14 feet 6 inches

Vertical glazed area: south—132 square feet

Sloped glazed area: 90 square feet

Angle: 45°

Type of glazing: double glass

Orientation: S

Degree days: 6,500-7,000

Temperature in sunspace	Day	Night
summer average	70°F.	
high	75°F.	
winter average	70°F.	
high	80°F.	
low	60°F.	50°F

Special features:
Solid adobe walls with glazed doors and windows between house and sunspace

Main passageway between all other rooms

Two-story space

Balcony

▼ **The Chalom sunspace is an integral part of their adobe home in Santa Fe.**

signed in, so we have no overheating problems with our sloped glazing. We minimized east and west glazing so we concentrate on the winter's southern sun. In fact plants grow better here in the winter and March/April/May than they do in the middle of summer because they get more sun. We decided to go with transparent glazing as opposed to translucent glazing because of the view; that was definitely important to us. To handle the phototropism (the plants growing towards the sunlight), we plant in pots and just turn the pots.

This greenhouse has not dropped below 51°F., so it's working quite well. As long as the sun is out or half out during the winter it's a comfortable space. We have no nighttime insulation. Come January it's a little too cool to sit in here so we just close it up and retreat, as opposed to trying to heat the whole thing. If we find that a plant can't take the temperature that the greenhouse provides, we get rid of the plant.

One nice thing about minimal east/west glazing is that there is always a shady spot. The texture of the wall and the floor absorbs and diffuses the light so we don't have a lot of glare.

We wash all the glass once a year. I put a piece of angle iron on the outside bolts and that gives me a three-inch level which I can climb off the ladder onto and caulk or wash or whatever. It's scary as hell but it works.

Gardening in the wintertime seems a luxury. On average we spend two hours a week doing maintenance—watering, picking off dead leaves, looking for insects, and just walking around. In the wintertime we water every eight or nine days. It takes up fifteen minutes at the most. We have a hose with a valve on a handle and a bubbler around the end so we don't wash the soil out, but we get a good volume of water. We go around not being that careful about water spilling over onto the floor or tables. In the summertime I would say every other day, or every third day, we put the bubbler on full blast and just wash the whole place down. It's beautiful, evaporative cooling as well. It adds some humidity, which is pleasant most of the year. In the very cold of the winter when we water we get a fair amount of condensation on the windows and I notice it on my drafting paper, which tends to wrinkle up a little bit right after we water, but it doesn't seem to be a problem. I haven't noticed any mold.

I don't know that we have had any major problems except for the insects. That's the one thing that kind of discourages us, some of the bugs. Scale is hard to get rid of. We give a plant as much maintenance as we can, and if it just gets worse we get rid of the plant. That is what is nice about planting in pots, you can take the whole mess out and get rid of it. We have a new child now so we are real nervous about using any kind of insecticide. I think if we go away for a weekend, then I will spray those spider mites as we walk out the door.

I like to listen to music in here. It has a real bassy, vibrant sound. When we have parties this is an extension of the living room; people are in here dancing. It's really fun and it works.

I think an interesting part of living is being in a space that is alive and growing. Every time a plant goes through one of its changes, starts putting out a flower or starts sprouting, you get all excited. This cactus did nothing for years then all of a sudden it's doing something. I threw in a lot of barbed wire plant seeds, and they are all coming up. I'm excited by that.

▼ **Peter Reason added space to his Georgian rowhouse by building on a second-floor bathroom and a third-floor greenhouse over the front portico.**

Date finished: March 1982

Designer: Feilden Clegg Design

Builder: Wraxall Builders Ltd.

Cost: $3,500

Floor area: 7 feet x 4 feet 6 inches

Vertical glazed area:
south—22 square feet
east—22 square feet
west—22 square feet

Sloped glazed area:
35 square feet

Angle: 30°

Type of glazing:
double glass, laminated in roof

Orientation: SW

Degree days: 4,000

Temperature in sunspace	Day	Night
summer average	85°F.	70°F.
high	100°F.	75°F.
winter average	70°F.	65°F.
high	85°F.	70°F.
low	60°F.	50°F.

Special features:
Built-on third floor above entrance and bathroom extension

Open to hall and stairway

PETER REASON

BATH, ENGLAND

Peter Reason and Elizabeth Adeline have a classic Georgian row house that they love, but with two teenage boys it was not big enough. The impressive front of the house faces out over a garden with views of the city of Bath below. It could not be altered without destroying the aesthetics of the whole row. The entrance to the house is from behind, with the doorway opening directly onto the sidewalk and protected by a stone portico. Unable to build on at ground level, they decided to expand upward, by building a bathroom over the portico and a greenhouse on top of that.

I think honestly the real reason we built a conservatory up in the air is because the idea was such an exciting one. I had always wanted a conservatory as a place for my plants. The house never seemed to be quite right for houseplants. I wanted something that had proper light for growing plants, and I wanted to be more ambitious about the sort of plants I could grow. I suppose I was interested in flowers as well as green plants, so I wanted more light for that. I also had problems of where to put my geraniums in the winter so I thought I could have a greenhouse or conservatory for that. I had thought of putting a greenhouse in the garden, but it is too far away and it would not have been heated.

I didn't imagine it would be as swish as it is. All this double glazing and the elegance of it and the amount of light it has are much nicer than I ever thought it would be. It's just wonderful how it has opened up the whole top area of the house and made it light. The neighbors were really worried about what it would look like, "not in keeping." I was worried about the glass getting broken, a slate falling off the roof, but that has not happened. It was quite a major operation to the house, taking that wall out—it's a two-hundred-year-old wall. I was quite worried about what the house thought about it.

The conservatory was part of a whole extension including a new bathroom on the floor below. The whole structure was much more expensive than we thought it would be. But when it was finally ready it felt wonderful, absolutely wonderful. I started putting plants in before the builders had left. The house was always stuffed with plants and I never had enough space to put them, never. I thought the conservatory would solve that problem, but it only made them grow

◀ Though small, the space is brimful of plants.

▼ The Reason greenhouse, approached from below.

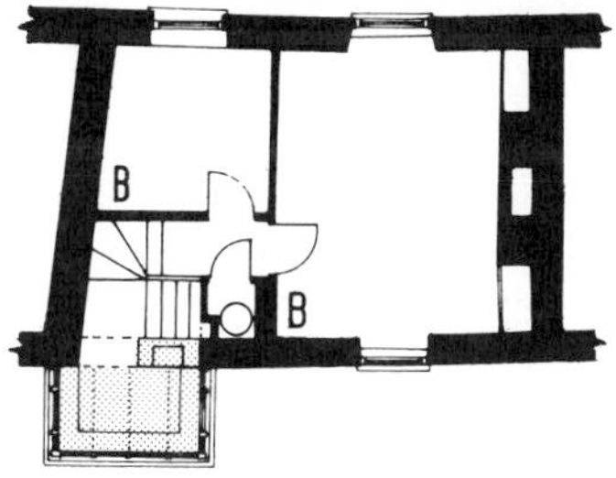

bigger still, until they were too big for that space as well.

My ideal now is to have a calendar and to be growing something particular for each time of the year. Like at the moment to have freesias and cyclamen in February is just so glorious. In the summer I am not so worried about it. I just keep it shaded and as cool as can be because of all the plants outside. The conservatory is most important in the winter, and maybe early spring and late autumn when I haven't got the outdoor pots or the garden.

I didn't know enough; I hadn't thought enough beforehand. I thought it should be really warm, but I didn't realize how much it needed shading in the summer. It's a terribly hot place; there is no shade at all. It doesn't have any blinds, outside or in. It doesn't have any automatic cooling, which probably would be a great help. I think it is underventilated if anything, but if I had had opening windows in the glass I would have had problems with it being weatherproof. It's got the fan for external ventilation and I don't use it very much because it's not automatic. I don't like fans anyway. They are noisy and they are not natural.

I wouldn't have these plastic-coated cork tiles again. They get wet so often, I think the water gets in the cracks (they are not sealed between the joints) and they are beginning to bubble. I think it needs quarry tiles. Or just sheet vinyl would be better.

I believe that plants recycle toxic wastes as well as human psychic waste. Perhaps that's why we have them, apart from the fact that they are beautiful—they are important. They are a kind of opposite, and so my experience in the conservatory at its best is like a lot of relaxation or the parasympathetic healing stage when blood flows to the extremities rather than to the organs. Things drop off me.

Date finished: October 1981		
Designer: Peter Clegg/English Aluminum Greenhouses		
Builder: Wraxall Builders		
Cost: $8,000		
Floor area: 7 feet x 44 feet		
Vertical glazed area: east—56 square feet		
Sloped glazed area: 198 square feet plus 264 square feet		
Angle: 75° / 15°		
Type of glazing: single glass		
Orientation: S		
Degree days: 3,200		

Temperature in sunspace	**Day**	**Night**
summer average	75°F.	58°F.
high	90°F.	
winter average	55°F.	40°F.
high	70°F.	
low	40°F.	28°F.

Special features:
Internal glass wall and door to divide into two temperature zones/two uses (entryway and greenhouse)

Solid stone wall with several glazed doors and opening windows between house and sunspace

Designed to be one-third living space but taken over by plants

Front wall buried in sloping ground

Roof whitewashed in summer

Main entrance to house

DERRY WATKINS

CHIPPENHAM, ENGLAND

We have a house like a train, and a greenhouse to match. Forty feet long, it covers almost the whole south side of our long, thin house. It is very much a working greenhouse, with pots and boxes and dirt everywhere. Filled to bursting with plants, there is rarely room enough to squeeze in a chair despite Peter's best efforts. Propagating is Derry's passion, she grows innumerable plants, both tender and hardy, from seed and cuttings. What started as a way of getting rid of involuntary excess production has grown into a small business selling unusual plants.

I had always wanted to have a greenhouse, desperately. And I had written a book about greenhouses in order to learn everything I possibly could before I actually got round to building this one. We built it very long so that there would be enough room for me and my plants and enough room to sit in and eat in. Well, it turns out we vastly underestimated my appetite for plants. I could use twice as much space for a working greenhouse for plants, easily. Every now and then I get shoved back into my allocated greenhouse space. But most of the time plants take over the whole length of it.

And I love it—I love the blooming things, I love the way it looks. But what I really love best about it are the tiny things coming on, all my babies. Now, they're not very beautiful, and I try to keep them primarily down at the other end. But just at the moment, for example, the only bench in the greenhouse, the only thing you can sit on, happens to be full of geranium cuttings. I am not very good about keeping my separation.

▼ **Stretching the length of her Cotswold house, author Derry Watkins's 40-foot greenhouse beckons through a door or window from almost every room in the house.**

We finished the greenhouse in September. It was glary and hot and bright and empty and uncomfortable—a big, flat, barren space—and I didn't like it. I felt daunted by it; I would put a plant out there and it would just look miserable, uncomfortable and lonely. It wasn't really until the next spring when I started my seeds in there that I began to feel a little more comfortable with it. I put a few things in; I had one or two treasures I had been saving for when the greenhouse was ready—I had bought the white plumbago and the winter-flowering jasmine a year before. They looked just ridiculous in there for the longest time, but along about May or June the following year they started to take off; they just grew their hearts out. And it started to fill up with the seedlings and cuttings. From then on I have absolutely adored it. It took on a completely different character once it got full of plants. And the more it got full of plants, the more I loved it.

I do most of my potting and my work in the greenhouse at the sink which is directly in front of a big window into the house. The children will often be working or playing or drawing at the table on the other side of the window, and I will be on my side of the window potting my plants. It is very, very nice, because we are each doing our own thing and we are not interfering with each other, yet it is very companionable.

It is my place of meditation, my quiet place, my peaceful place. I come out here frazzled and tense and anxious and full of a million things I have to do, and I gradually slow down and start breathing a bit more deeply and stop running. I start wandering, just going from plant to plant, investigating each one carefully. You can't deal with plants in an anxious way; it just doesn't work. The greenhouse slows me down in a way that I really like; I feel more centered here than anywhere else.

The only thing I don't like is cleaning it. Scrubbing the glass is the most enormous job. Once a year the cleaning lady and I try to wash the whole thing down with bleach. It is a vast job, and I never feel I have done it thoroughly enough. I have permanent plants in here that I can't remove. There is no way I can scrub behind the jasmine. We do what we can. I think it helps, but I wish that was easier.

We have just tiled the floor, which makes the greenhouse look completely different; it's like a room now. Until then we had a rough concrete floor which always looked a mess and was always dirty, but I didn't mind because it was a working greenhouse. I like the new floor, but I am aware that in a way what I have done is added to my burden of housework—now it irritates me when it is dirty whereas before it didn't bother me at all.

I was very worried about whether to have absorbent tiles or glazed tiles. Glazed tiles are much easier to clean, but the absorbent tiles obviously will hold quite a lot of moisture that helps keep the humidity up in the summer. These are unglazed and they have an informal, grubby look even when they are clean, which I like. You can hose these down, but they water mark. The floor is so dirty you probably can't tell, but where it has dripped from the condensation we are getting a mark on the tiles right down the greenhouse. And we have very hard water, so that will leave calcium deposits all over, which will be very hard to get off. They are gradually going to turn white on these nice rosy tiles.

The greenhouse insulates the whole south wall of the house from cold weather, like an enormous bit of double glazing. But what's much more noticeable is that as soon as the sun comes out, even in the middle of winter, within minutes you can feel it warming the house. This morning, for example, it was below freezing outside, there was frost on the ground, and beautiful thick frost patterns inside the greenhouse, but by ten o'clock it was absolutely delightful in here without any other source of heat. And there is still frost on the ground outside.

One thing about having the greenhouse attached to the house is you become so conscious of the sun. As soon as the sun comes out, wherever I am in the house, I am aware of it. And almost immediately I rush down and start opening doors and windows and vents. I become very responsive to the weather. Is the sun out? Is it windy? Is it cold? In swing seasons, the early spring and late fall, I can rush round opening and shutting all the windows and doors three, four, five times a day, as the sun dashes in and out and the temperature rises and plummets. And it is not just for the greenhouse or for the heat for the house. There is something so merry and gay about it when the sun comes out, you want to be part of it, you want to open the house to it. And then as soon as the sun goes in, within seconds it is cold inside and you start dashing round shutting the windows for self-preservation.

Having the top vents automated made a huge difference. I didn't feel like I had to be so desperate from the plants' point of view. The top vents will take care of most of the overheating except in the middle of summer. But in order to get heat to the inside I have still got to run round opening and shutting things. If I'm not here, then the heat can go outside, I don't care.

We were surprised at how much heat we got out of it on sunny days, but even more surprised at how few sunny days there are in winter. We often go for two weeks without a single bit of sun. You don't want to go out there, and you certainly don't want to open the doors to the house, unless the sun is out. It is very unappealing on gray winter days. It doesn't get much above 50°, 55°F. It is sort of damp and chilly. I have no trouble not watering it and not fussing with it on those days.

It frequently gets down to freezing in there on winter nights, and it occasionally gets down a bit below freezing. (I think 27°F. is the coldest it has ever been in there.) I would have expected that to kill a lot of plants. The greenhouse is full of geraniums and fuchsias and other theoretically tender plants, but they live in there so they are used to it getting pretty cold. I guess they just get very hardy because I have never lost any of them to frost—even last winter when we had the worst-ever cold snap of two weeks when it never got above freezing in the daytime. Then I put a heater in at night for about seven or eight nights, the only time I have put extra heating in it.

I had thought that we would leave the door from the house open a crack, and the windows open a bit, to let a little heat go out at night. But in fact I find I can't bear to do that because it makes the house so cold when you come down in the mornings. We have no central heating, just two woodburning stoves which are usually lit only in the evenings. If it is cold enough outside for the greenhouse to need heat, it is cold enough for the house to need it. And I just can't stand coming down to a house that is 50°. I would rather put an electric heater out there.

It is too hot in the summer. I grow hops up the front for summer shade, and I paint the top section of glass with Coolglass, to shade the bit that faced the sky. You don't notice it too much because all that is above your head. The glass you actually look through I leave clear. The shading helps some, but it still gets too hot. I would love to have proper big bamboo blinds on the outside to cool it. And to be able to adjust it so if there is a three-week cloudy period in the middle of summer you don't have to live without any light in there. But they are very, very expensive, too much for us.

I think we didn't actually design in enough vents; we didn't take into account the fact that because we raised the base onto a knee wall, there isn't enough vertical separation between the high vents and the low vents. In any case, it turns out that the high vents can't open all the way because they bump into the wall behind them when they get about half-way open. I thought because there were doors at each end and so many openings into the house, there would be enough through ventilation. The house never gets too hot, but the greenhouse can get much too hot.

We were a little worried about the glass breaking, or the children running along the path and falling into it. It is all single-glazed with very thin horticultural glass. But nobody has ever broken a pane by falling into it. Several panes have cracked, just from temperature stress, without any impact. Then those panes leak a bit, but it doesn't seem to be much of a problem.

It makes horrendous noises sometimes. Especially the first year, when the sun would come out after a gray period it cracked and banged like shotguns going off as the glass expanded. It doesn't seem to do that quite so badly now. It creaks, but it doesn't bang anymore. I hated that.

I think I had assumed it was going to be blissful, everything was going to work wonderfully. I don't think it dawned on me that there would be any problems with it. But there are. To begin with, it leaks like a sieve. It pours in around every vent if it rains hard. We took an ordinary lean-to greenhouse and attached the top of it about where you would normally, but we set the bottom up on a knee wall about hip high. As a result the slope of the glass is very much less steep than it should be, so the water doesn't run off fast enough. It sort of collects and finds its way in; it seeps in around every joint. Peter tried to stop the leaks and failed. I had premonitions of disaster, all the plants were going to rot, etc. In fact not only does it leak, but condensation adds a pint or two of water on cold days. It hasn't rained in the last few days, but, because it has been frosty, when I come out in the morning there has been a puddle the entire length of the greenhouse under the middle glazing bar from condensation which has dripped off. So I assumed it would be much too humid in there in the wintertime and that would encourage fungal diseases and so forth. Well. I don't know how it happens, but I have hardly ever had any fungal diseases in there.

The leaking is annoying, but since it isn't in fact a live-in greenhouse, it is not nearly as bad as it might be. In some ways I have had it all my own way because you can't leave good furniture out there to be leaked on continually. So there was never any very serious attempt at furnishing a living area. The leaks can cause some problems if you get a plant directly underneath one of the worst drips, but I have never had a plant die or look really damaged because of it.

The other major problem is the insects. I try to be organic and not use any wicked sprays, and I just assumed that, as in the garden, I would not have any serious problem with insects. But the insects love it. In the winter it is all right; winter is almost the best time in my greenhouse because it is too cold for the insects. But come April they just take off, there is such a population explosion it isn't true. Now this year, for the first time since I have had the greenhouse, I had very little problem with insects; we had a cold, damp, foggy summer exactly like the winter, and I suppose they didn't like that. Also, I got the whitefly predator early this year. I had bought encarsia before and it hadn't worked when the whitefly had too much of a hold before I got the predator. But this summer I actually thought that the whitefly had died out and disappeared; there just weren't any in the greenhouse all summer long. I thought, "What a waste of ten pounds just to buy the predator." But when the sun came out in September, blimey, if the whitefly didn't come out. And within two weeks there were the encarsia formosa as well, to my amazement. The only problem was, I knew perfectly well that the encarsia would die in a month because it would get too cold for them, and the whitefly wouldn't die, they would winter over. So I knew I had got whiteflies for life. And I will have to buy predators every spring.

I think it was the cool, damp weather kept the red spider mite down. In some ways red spider mite is a more bitter problem for me than whitefly. It is the red spider mite that kills things. Whitefly are just annoying, they drive me crazy, they look revolting, and they leave this black mold behind. But red spider mite actually decimate some things—cucumbers and melons I have given up growing. I find that really sad. And morning glories, I love morning glories, and they only grow inside here. Occasionally we have had years when they have done really well and we have had 150 blossoms one morning, but usually by the time they are 6 or 8 feet tall, they are beginning to get the red spider mite, and by the time they really get into blooming they are dead, so I don't grow those anymore. I am thinking hard about giving up tomatoes and fuchsias, they always have whitefly, but I can't grow outdoor tomatoes, and I don't know if I can live without homegrown tomatoes. The peppers and eggplants get red spider mite as well, so I probably ought to give up growing them.

Summer before last was the first time in my life I have ever given in on the subject of organic growing. Everything seemed to be dying and I actually bought some nasty insecticides to use in here. I can't face the thought of using a systemic insecticide. The idea of putting poison in soil and the poison going up through the plant gives me the complete heebie-jeebies. But there are various contact insecticides that are supposed to be inactivated on contact, and I thought I would try although it scares the living daylights out of me. Even that didn't seem to work though, and in the end I got a smoke bomb. That helped, but it didn't work altogether. I think the encarsia are just as good, if not better, at keeping the whitefly down than all those horrible chemicals. I am so glad not to be using them any more.

I ought to get myself a proper sprayer, but because I think of myself as somebody organic who doesn't do spraying, I only have a little tiny hand-pump sprayer. And I can tell you by the time I have finished spraying this greenhouse and trying to get underneath ever leaf in it, my hand aches and there is soap dripping down my elbow and I am really fed up with it.

The greenhouse isn't built directly on the ground, it is on a concrete base. Because it was dug out of a hillside, and we are way down into the subsoil here, there didn't seem any point in leaving a connection to the ground. We built in one big bed against the back wall, about 14 feet long, 2 feet across, and 15 inches deep, and that makes an enormous difference. Tomatoes grow in there at twice the rate and produce twice the crop of tomatoes that they do in any pot, even one 2 feet across and 2-1/2 feet deep. And the plants stay healthy for much longer. They seem to be more resistant to insects, and they withstand the frost better. The ones in pots all packed it in by Thanksgiving; they all turned yellow and have been thrown out. The ones in the bed are still green and producing tomatoes. I don't really know whether it is that the roots stay warmer, or they have more moisture, or what. I think maybe they just like a big root run. Moreover, the bed doesn't take nearly so much care; it has to be watered only once or twice a week as opposed to every single day for even the big pots in a hot summer.

Theoretically watering is a big problem. It can take me up to an hour and a half to water all the plants in the house and the greenhouse. Now that sounds like a big problem, and it is a big problem to anyone who has to do it for me. But it is not a big problem to me; I love it. It is just part of my day. I go around and I look at, and feel, and think about, each and every plant in this whole place, and there must be hundreds of them altogether. I look for insects and I pick off dead leaves. I am not a very efficient waterer—I idle about, I have a good time out there with them. If I am in a hurry I can do it probably in half an hour, forty minutes if I have to do the house as well. In a pinch I can do the greenhouse in fifteen

▲ An in-ground bed, 14 feet long and 2 feet wide provides excellent space for tomato plants.

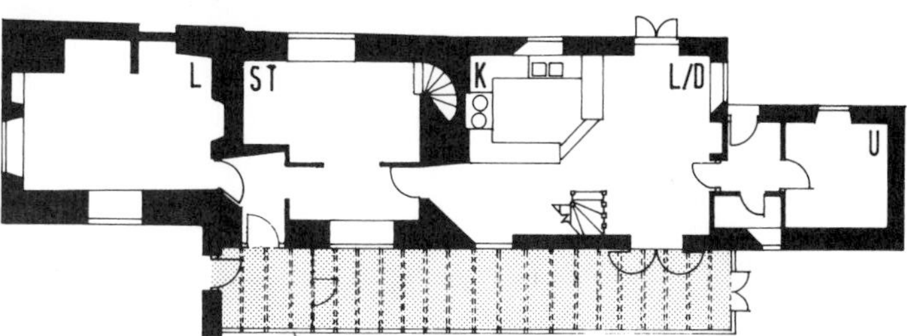

minutes with a hose. But I don't like doing that, and I don't feel the plants thrive on that. It compacts the soil too much. At least twice a week you have to have a really good look at everything, I reckon. And I get pleasure from doing it, so it is not a problem. Plants bloom better and look better if the old flowers are removed quickly, and I think there is less disease.

I keep a big galvanized bathtub under one of the benches, for soaking pots and boxes. Most days in summer, there's something in it. If I'm potting on, I can fill it four or five times a day, settling the plants into their new pots. I couldn't manage with just the sink. The bathtub doesn't have a drain so it is always full of dirty water which I hope is adding to the humidity and fear is passing diseases from pot to pot. I clean it out two or three times in the summer and empty it in October.

I buy soil for this greenhouse. The compost I make seems precious to me out in the garden, and I am really worried about bringing in insects and diseases. Also, because I sell plants, a huge amount of soil passes through every year. So I buy sterilized, loam-based compost (1,400 pounds of it last year). I add peat and bonemeal to it. For fast-growing, well-established, easy-to-grow plants like geraniums I will often mix the fresh soil half and half with soil I used for something else the year before. The old tomato bed is my big soil extender until I plant new tomatoes in May.

Originally I thought that the greenhouse would be full of large and beautiful plants. It does have a big jasmine and a passionflower and various other things, but I thought that it would mostly be things like that. In fact, plants that look beautiful are very much secondary to plants that either I find particularly interesting, or my babies. I allow the jasmine an enormous amount of space because I love it, and I think it looks beautiful all the year round. It doesn't get any pests or diseases. And I have my beloved little rhodochiton which looks enchanting and crazy, quite obscene. Hardly anyone has ever seen one before, so I couldn't possibly live without that. I bring in things, if a geranium or a big petunia plant is flowering particularly well outside in the summer, I bring it in to make the greenhouse look better. It isn't so full in the summer, so there is more room for things like that. Alyssum and lobelia self-sow all over the greenhouse, so that cheers it

▲ Early spring—seeds sprouting below, bulbs blooming above. The clogs stay in the greenhouse to avoid tracking dirt into the house.

up. Alyssum manages to grow and bloom profusely in cracks in the concrete floor. In the autumn, when I bring in mother plants of all my stock, geraniums and so forth, they decorate it for a while. They do much better than they ever did outside in the summer.

We definitely don't get the living space from it we originally wanted. Peter complains bitterly. From time to time I push the plants back, but basically we don't live in there. I put a chair in sometimes but the glass leaks so much that the chair tends to rot. We sit here at the dining table with the French doors open and the sun pouring in, and it feels like we are in the greenhouse, but not quite. I do all my paperwork here, and of course we eat here. It is not a good place to read (even at the dining table, but particularly not in the greenhouse). It is too bright if the sun is out, and if the sun is not out it is too cold.

We use it very differently at different times of year. In the summer it is mainly growing vegetables, tomatoes, eggplants, peppers, and big, permanent, ornamental things. Actually I think we probably sit in it more in the summer, not in the middle of the day of course—evenings and mornings. We often have breakfast out there in the summertime. There is more room in the summer to sit in it for one thing; it is not so full of plants. Almost everything does better outdoors actually, apart from the really tropical things like the tomatoes. It doesn't need much work apart from watering. I try to hose it all down two or three times a day in hot weather.

In the autumn it is bursting with geraniums and fuchsias, petunias, felicias, etc., that I've brought in, and it looks really nice. I always take masses of cuttings, so sporadically I have to spend half a day potting them, but the greenhouse doesn't seem too demanding in autumn. When it gets too cold to sit outside, I usually bring a couple of deckchairs in, so it's the most comfortable time of year for sitting there. It's the time I'm most likely to just sit quietly and enjoy being there, enjoy the fruits of my labors.

In winter I often don't go out for a week or more if the sun doesn't shine. When the sun does shine in winter that can be the best time of all in the greenhouse. It's usually too cold to just sit still and relax, but it's very comfortable to work in. A lot of the most fragrant things bloom in winter. The whole house will be suffused with the smell of jasmine if any window is open into the greenhouse. It is lovely in winter and it is no trouble. I probably don't water it even once a week, unless we have several sunny days in a row, which is rare.

The spring, of course, is the time I am totally devoted to it, when tending it requires all my waking moments. And I think it is almost too much even for me in spring, almost too many plants and too much to do. No room to breathe. Cuttings and seeds don't take any room at all when you are trying to get them to root. You can put them under the bench and out of the way. They are no problem, and so I always take too many. I love doing it, and I love watching them root, and I love fiddling around with them. But come time to pot them on, they can take so much room, they can just take the entire greenhouse. About November I have to start finding tables and benches and shelves and anything I can lay my hands on to put them on.

Things such as geraniums and fuchsias don't mind it being really quite cold, but they like a lot of sun, otherwise they get scraggy. And the competition for sun becomes so fierce by about April, it is driving everybody insane. I need two greenhouses this size in April. And I have to put a desperate amount of effort into rushing them all off to market to sell them, in order to get rid of them to make some more space.

I would never, ever, again live in a house without a sunspace. If I could, I would have it twice as big, and hope there would be enough room to get a little living space in it. When I say twice as big I mean twice as long, because it is the effective growing area I am really interested in. On the other hand, I would really like to have one that was taller, so that it vented better and so that I could grow a few trees in it. I would love to grow a lemon tree. So I would like one twice as long, twice as tall, and a little bit wider, so you could fit in chairs and a table more comfortably.

In some ways building this greenhouse has changed my life. I knew I wanted the greenhouse very much. I was a very keen gardener, and I have practically abandoned my outdoor gardening in favor of the greenhouse. That is not quite true, but my heart is mainly in my greenhouse now and not in the outdoor garden. It has given a whole new sort of emphasis and organization to my life. It never dawned on me that I would be spending three or four hours a day out there whenever the sun was out.

I grow these plants because I love them. I can't help myself. Once I really like something I have to get a little and see if I can't grow it and propagate it and make more of it and give it away.

In the beginning I was didactic about, "I don't like this" and "I don't like that." "I don't like big gaudy, vulgar flowers —amaryllis and chrysanthemums and fuchsias and gladioli—they are too bold." I have gradually come to realize that there are at least one or two beautiful varieties of almost everything. I can't be nearly so sweeping anymore about all the things I don't like. There are plenty of individual things I don't like. But there is probably a beautiful representative of every family lurking somewhere in the shadows.

I almost need to make this into a plant nursery in order to support the enormous number of plants I want to grow. I am bursting out of a 40-foot long greenhouse. And there is no way I can justify that as just pleasure. I feel foolish devoting this huge amount of time to my idle pleasure, to things I happen to like. And running a little nursery makes it all make sense. The only trouble is I have to convince everybody else that these plants they have never heard of are beautiful and worth buying. I could make a fortune just selling geraniums and lobelia and alyssum, bedding plants for the spring. There is an endless demand for them. But what I really love are my rare things, my little alpines, and my tender perennials, special things that I think are really beautiful, that I want other people to grow, that I want to spread around. In some way I think I feel proud of them. The greenhouse and the plants in it are like my children in some funny way. And they are very responsive, unlike real children! You do something nice for them and they are grateful! ■

▶ **Top. Jeremy and Caroline Walsh's sunspace near Bristol, England, extends on a 45-degree angle from the house, to bring sun and garden views to the kitchen and living room.**

▼ **Bottom. A cornice line of stained-glass panels diffuses its colors into all corners of the interior.**

Photographer, Simon Doling; Architect, Feilden Clegg Design (Katy Duke and Richard Feilden)

Photographer, Simon Doling; Architect, Feilden Clegg Design (Katy Duke and Richard Feilden)

Orr and Taylor

▲ **Above. Candida Lycett-Green restored the old conservatory on her eighteenth-century country manor house in Wiltshire, England, in order to enjoy it as an extension of the sitting room.**

▲ **Top and right. Architectural detailing relates Robert Orr and Melanie Taylor's conservatory addition to their Victorian home in New Haven, Connecticut. The jungle-like plantings moisturize and refresh the air of the entire house.** ▶

Orr and Taylor

Barbara Norfleet

◀ **Top, left and below.** As winter sun streams through Mrs. William Langer's plant room windows in Cambridge, Massachusetts, plants glow like jewels, providing delight for both passers-by and those within. ▼

Suzanne Dworsky

◀ **Bottom, left and right.** Peter Reason and Elizabeth Adelaide extended the stone portico of their classic Georgian row house in Bath, England, upward to add a bathroom below and a greenhouse above. The greenhouse is already overflowing with plants. ▶

▼ **Top, left and right. Art and Carol Keil's dramatic contemporary house is set in the foothills of the Rockies, near Denver, Colorado. Entering the upper sunspace from the main entrance a floor below, one encounters a world of sunlight and greenery and the warm, moist smells of the tropics.** ▶

Krebs Uptown Photography

Krebs Uptown Photography

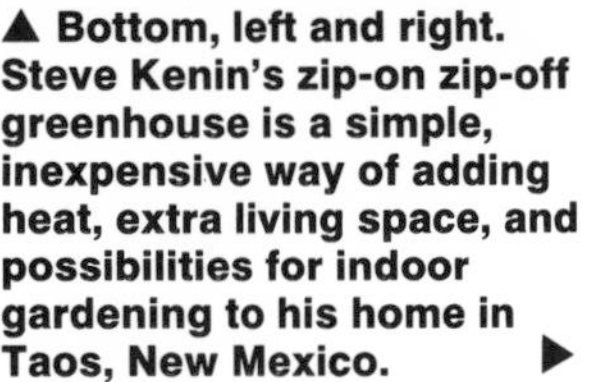

▲ **Bottom, left and right. Steve Kenin's zip-on zip-off greenhouse is a simple, inexpensive way of adding heat, extra living space, and possibilities for indoor gardening to his home in Taos, New Mexico.** ▶

Sara Balcomb

Sara Balcomb

Douglas Kelbaugh

▲ Above. Doug and Meg Kelbaugh's greenhouse combines growing space for plants with more than adequate heat collection for their Princeton, New Jersey house.

▲ Top and left. In spite of over two hundred days per year of below freezing temperatures, Doug and Sara Balcomb's Santa Fe, New Mexico, home is always filled with light and a profusion of bloom. The triangular winter garden, with trees and trickling fountains, reminds visitors of a Spanish central courtyard. ◀

▼ **Top, left.** Plants overflow into potential living space in authors Derry Watkins and Peter Clegg's greenhouse.

▼ **Bottom, left.** Derry enjoys the connections from all parts of the house to the greenhouse and the sunshine outside.

▲ **Above.** Geraniums, fuschias, petunias, and felicias fill this quiet corner where Derry can enjoy the fruits of her labor.

▲ **Derry and Peter's trainlike greenhouse extends forty feet along the south side of their old stone house in the Cotswolds.** ◀

Arvid E. Osterberg

▲ Above. Karen and Tom Huenink's recycled greenhouse provides extra space and a winter garden for the house they built themselves in southern Vermont.

▲ Top and right. Arvid and Gayle Osterberg's solar addition forms the entire south side of their Iowa farmhouse. The full-length swimming pool acts as a heat collector in winter and a cooling device in summer, as well as a means of exercise year-round. ▶

Arvid E. Osterberg

PART III
CARING FOR SUNSPACE PLANTS

CHAPTER 5

GROWING CONDITIONS

Most plants are eager to grow and will survive all but the most adverse conditions. But to produce beautiful, healthy plants, each species dictates certain general conditions. Some of course are more flexible than others. Some are willing to tolerate poor conditions and resume growing with renewed vigor when things improve, while some will be permanently damaged or even killed by prolonged adversity. In particular, many vegetables that survive a drought or a long, dark cold spell will become tough or bitter. Ideally, everything should grow as quickly and strongly as possible for best flavor and for most handsome appearance. Herbs are an exception—slow, stunted growth concentrates their flavor.

Healthy plants in a greenhouse can provide beauty and pleasure indoors and out. Plants in bloom can be brought into the house to be admired; a few weeks of dim light and dry air in the dining room won't hurt them. Hundreds of annuals can easily be started in the greenhouse to bloom outdoors from June to frost. And remember that healthy vegetables in the greenhouse can be as beautiful as any foliage plant.

Growing your own vegetables is a considerable contribution to saving fossil fuel energy. Fresh vegetables bought in a store are fairly sound ecologically, but any processed vegetables are among the most energy-intensive food we eat. Growing your own flowers and vegetables can also make a big saving in cash. An inexpensive packet of seed can produce as many lettuces as a family of four could eat in a year. And a packet of celery seed could produce enough celery for a village. A pot of bulbs about to flower costs more than several dozen bulbs ordered in advance. And one bouquet would pay for all the flower seed you could use.

Unless you are lucky, you will have to reach some sort of compromise between the requirements of different plants you want to grow and the conditions you can afford to maintain in the greenhouse. It is sensible to grow only those things that you are fond of, that are compatible with each other, and that do not make inordinate demands on your money or time. Local conditions—cloudy days, subzero winter weather, scorching summers—will have a strong influence on your choice of plants. But remember that different areas of the greenhouse can provide fairly different microclimates. Grow the heat-lovers at the apex, the light-lovers that can withstand cold nights at the front, the cold-sensitive light-lovers in the middle or against the back wall, and the shade-lovers down below.

Experiment with different types of plants and different regimes. You may find certain plants do better with less water or extra light or a greater drop in night temperature. Beg cuttings and young plants from your friends and see what grows well for you. You will almost certainly be able to pay them back in kind.

The tables of growing conditions that follow are only a general guide; modify them as you go along. Every greenhouse has its own peculiarities of orientation, shading, ventilation, and/or soil composition. Only you can know what will grow well where and under what conditions in your greenhouse.

TENDER PERENNIALS

Tender perennials include most common houseplants, but also many flowering plants that could not stand the dry heat of an ordinary house. They are grown for the beauty of either their flowers or their foliage. Those that are usually grown from bulbs or as annuals are included in separate sections. Almost any attractive, hardy garden plants can also be brought indoors to bloom a few weeks early. You will appreciate them more indoors, and the blooms will be protected from the ravages of the weather.

Most ornamental plants will grow well in a mixture of two parts loam to one part peat to one part sharp sand. Variations from this are noted under individual entries. Seeds can be started in the same mix with some extra peat and sand. Cuttings do best in half peat and half sharp sand or in pure vermiculite.

▶

The temperatures given are what the plants would prefer. They will accept the minimum temperature, but will often stop blooming or look unhappy if kept at that for long. If tender plants get frozen, spraying them with cold water before the sun hits them will sometimes save them.

"Good indirect light" ideally means a northern exposure with plenty of sky light and no direct sun, but partial shade cast by other plants or a place at the back of a greenhouse with a solid roof will do almost as well.

"Partial sun" ideally means shade for a few hours at midday and direct sun the rest of the time, but good indirect light all day will often do instead. Generally, foliage plants prefer, or at least accept, indirect light. Most flowering plants need lots of sunshine. (African violets, begonias and impatiens are the major exceptions to this rule.) They will continue to grow with less light but will get long and spindly, and will soon stop flowering.

Keeping leaves clean will increase photosynthesis as well as make the plants more attractive. Wipe the leaves with a damp cloth whenever they begin to look dusty. Avoid hard water, which will leave lime spots. Half water and half skimmed milk gives the leaves a good shine. Large plants can be put outside in a gentle rain or even given a shower to clean them off.

The pot sizes given are those normally used for mature plants. Extra large specimens will of course need bigger pots. But don't put small plants into large pots. Wait till the roots have used up the available soil, then pot into the next size pot. If that is not convenient, just shake as much soil as possible off the root ball, cut 1/4–1/3 the roots off with a sharp knife, and repot it with fresh soil in a clean pot of the same size. Prune the top back by about one quarter at the same time. Most plants need to be repotted or to have at least the top few inches of soil replaced annually in the early spring.

TENDER PERENNIALS

Name	Propagation by Seed	Vegetative Propagation	Growing Conditions	Comments
Abutilon *(flowering maple)* *Malvaceae hybridum* *A. megapotamicum (trailing)*	Seedlings will not be identical to parents. Sow in February (60-70°F.) for autumn flower. In July for spring flowers.	* Take 3-4" tip cuttings (60-65°F.) Pot into 3" pots when rooted.	55-75°F. (min 50°F.). Full sun. Water moderately, keep nearly dry in winter. Don't overfertilize.	Can grow to 5 feet. Prune by 1/3 in March. Discard after 2-3 years. Look out for scale and whitefly.
Achimenes, *see* **Gloxinia** *under* **Bulbs and Corms**				
African violets, *see* **Gesneriads.**				
Aralia, *see* **Fatsia**				
Asparagus Fern *Liliaceae* *Asparagus plumosus* *A. sprengeri*	Sow seed in April or May (60-70°F.). Soaking for 48 hours helps germination, which may take up to 2 months.	* Divide plants in spring.	55-70°F. (min 50°F.). Good indirect light. Keep moist except in winter.	Attractive, feathery foliage. New stems often bare at first.
Azalea *Ericaceae* *Rhododendron indicum,* syn *R. simsii and others*	Sow seed in early spring on moist peat, sprinkling sand over top (55-60°F.). Keep shaded and moist.	* Take 2-3" cuttings in spring or summer, inserting in 1 peat/2 sand (60°F.). Takes 2-3 months to root. Layer by making small slit in young stem and burying 2" deep. Sever after 2 years.	45-55°F. (min 35°F., max 70° F.). Partial sun. Does well in all-peat mixture. Keep thoroughly moist; avoid hard water.	Likes acid soil, moisture, semi-shade and cool conditions. Prefers to be somewhat potbound. Spray daily when buds form, and keep atmosphere humid. Put outdoors in shade and keep moist in summer.
Begonia (fibrous-rooted) *Begoniaceae* *Begonia semperflorens ("wax-leaved")* *and others*	Sow seed in early spring (60-70°F.) on surface of soil in good light. Sprouts in 2-3 weeks. Blooms in 4-6 months. Or sow in August for winter.	* Take 3-4" cuttings any time. Root in peat-sand or water (60-70°F.). Flowers in 2 months.	60-70°F. (min 50°F.). Good indirect light. Add extra peat or leaf mold. Do not firm the soil.	Very easy to grow. Prefers warmth, and indirect light, but very tolerant. Water well. Pinch back for bushy plants. Some tall species have dramatic stems and foliage. Look out for powdery mildew.

** Preferred method of propagation*

▶

Name	Propagation by Seed	Vegetative Propagation	Growing Conditions	Comments
Begonia (rhizomatous) *Begoniaceae* *Begonia rex, and others.*	Sow seed in early spring on surface of soil. (65-70°F.).	Divide plants in April. * Take leaf cuttings with 1″ of stalk in spring (65-70° F.). For *B. rex*, nick underside of main veins and place flat on peat-sand mix; will root from each wound. When 2 or 3 leaves each, separate seedlings and pot. Take 2-3″ stem cuttings of rhizomes.	60-70°F. (min 50°F.). Good indirect light.	Easy to grow. Culture as for fibrous-rooted begonias.
Begonia (tuberous) *Begoniaceae* *Begonia cheimantha (Lorraine)* *B. heimalis* *B. tuberhybrida, and others*	Sow seed on surface of soil in February (65-70°F.). Blooms in 4-5 months.	Divide tubers in March, one shoot per section. Take stem cuttings in early summer in peat-sand mix (65°F.). Pinch back and remove buds until November, then treat as ordinary tubers.	60-65°F. (45°F. in winter). 50-60° F. for Lorraine and *B. heimalis* varieties when flowering. Good indirect light. Add extra peat or leaf mold or use all-peat mix. Use high potash feed. Plant tubers concave side up, half their depth in soil.	When leaves die back naturally, overwinter tubers at 45°F. giving little water. Can store tubers in damp peat over winter. In March increase heat to 60°F. and increase watering to start growth. Keep atmosphere moist and avoid drafts. Stake large flowers. Some varieties become only semi-dormant and retain leaves. *B. heimalis* and Lorraine are winter-blooming.
Beloperone (shrimp plant) *Acanthaceae* *Beloperone guttata*		* 2-3″ tip cuttings in spring (65°F.). Pot 3-4 cuttings together when rooted.	60-70°F. (min 50°F.). Partial sun. Water moderately. Add extra peat. 6″ pot.	Flowers over long period. Pinch regularly. Prune by 1/3 in March and pot.
Bougainvillea (paper flower) *Nyctaginaceae* *Bougainvillea x buttiana hybrids* *B. glabra* *Other varieties take several years to flower.*		* 3-6″ cuttings in spring or summer, with bottom heat (70-75°F.). Or 6″ cuttings of dormant shoots in January (55°F.).	60-70°F. (50°F. in winter). Full sun. Water moderately; keep nearly dry in winter. 6-8″ pot or deep bed.	Colorful bracts around insignificant flowers. Usually loses leaves in winter. Can get very large; prune by 1/3 in early spring.
Bromeliads *Bromeliaceae ananas (pineapple)* *Billbergia and others*	Sow fresh seed on surface in 2 peat/1 sand (80°F.). Germinates quickly, but takes many years to reach flowering size.	* Offsets produced after flowering; should be potted when leaves are 3-4″ and have formed a rosette. Cut close to parent. Best done in early spring.	60-75°F. for most. High humidity; mist in warm weather. Full sun in winter, partial shade in summer. Thin-leaved varieties need less sun. Use half loam and half coarse leaf mold for soil mix. Avoid lime. Use rainwater if possible.	Most have watertight reservoir at base of leaves from which they absorb food, therefore need relatively small pots. Ethylene gas from ripe apples or banana skins will induce flowering. Most plants die after flowering.

* *Preferred method of propagation*

▶

Name	Propagation by Seed	Vegetative Propagation	Growing Conditions	Comments
Brunfelsia (yesterday, today, and tomorrow) *Solanaceae* *Brunfelsia paucifolra calycina*	Sow in summer.	* Take 3-5″ tip cuttings in spring or summer (70°F.). When rooted, fertilize weakly, but do not pot for 3 months.	60-80°F. If you want the plant to rest, then keep nearly dry at 50-55°F. (min 40°F.) in winter. Partial shade in summer; full sun in winter. Maintain high humidity. 5-6″ pot.	Flowers change color with age from purple to lavender to white; sometimes fragrant. Flowers better when root-bound. Replace soil in early spring without increasing pot size. Prune by 1/3 to 1/2 in early spring and pinch growing tips during summer.
Cactus (except epiphytes) *Cactaceae*	Sow fresh seed on surface of soil (70-80°F.). Sprouts in about 1 month. Transplant when 1/2″ (may take a year). Some bloom in 3 years, some take much longer.	Divide varieties which produce offshoots in spring. Take cuttings in late spring or early summer. Cut at joint or 4″ from tip. Dry for 24 hours then pot in sand or peat-sand mix.	55-70°F. (45°F. in winter) (min 35°F.). Full sun. Water moderately in summer; keep nearly dry in winter. Add extra grit for drainage. Feed only when in bud and flower; use high potash feed.	Likes well-drained soil and lots of light. Do not overpot. Make a paper collar to hold spiney plants with when repotting. Do not firm the compost, just tap the pot to settle it into place. Avoid repotting in winter. Needs very little plant food. Best outdoors in summer. Look out for soft rotting spots which must be cut away completely.
Cactus, epiphytic *Cactaceae* *Schlumbergera* *(Christmas cactus)* *Epiphyllum* *(Orchid cactus)* *and others*		Take cuttings at joints in spring or summer. Dry for 24 hours, then pot in ordinary cactus mix.	60-70°F., night 55°F. (min 50°F.). Partial sun in summer, full sun in winter. Add extra grit. Keep moist and maintain humid atmosphere when in bud and flower. Decrease water after flowering, but do not allow to dry out completely. Avoid hard water and excess nitrogen. 4-5″ pot.	Tropical jungle plants with spectacular flowers. Good in hanging baskets when large. Can place outdoors in semishade in summer. Christmas cactus need long nights to set buds; beware of electric lights. A cold period at the end of summer will encourage bud formation of all epiphytic cacti. Do not turn plants in bud, as buds may drop off in effort to turn towards light.
Camellia *Theaceae* *Camellia japonica* *C. reticulata* *C. williamsii,* *and many hybrids*		* Leafbud cuttings or 3-4″ cuttings of side shoots in summer (55-60°F.).	40-60°F. (min 25°F.; max 65°F.) Partial sun. Maintain humidity. Water well, but keep nearly dry for 6 weeks after flowering. Use lime-free soil, and add extra peat or leaf mold. 8-12″ pots or deep bed.	Shiny, evergreen leaves with showy flowers. Early varieties will flower in winter. Will survive freezing, but buds may be damaged. Can grow to 12 feet. Trim if necessary in April. Look out for scale insects.
Capsicum, *see* **Solanum**				

** Preferred method of propagation*

▶

Name	Propagation by Seed	Vegetative Propagation	Growing Conditions	Comments
Carnations & Pinks *Caryophyllaceae* *Dianthus* *See also* **Pinks,** *under* **Annuals**	Sow carnation seed in late winter (65°F. until it sprouts, then 50°F.). Sow pinks seed in spring or in August for winter flowers (65-70°F.). Blooms in 4 months.	* Take 3″ cuttings of perpetual carnations in winter (though will root anytime). Insert in sand (65°F. reducing to 50°F. when begin to grow). Take 3-4″ cuttings of pinks in summer. Pot in 1 peat/1 loam/1 sand mix. Keep in partial shade. Cuttings bloom in 4-8 months. Layer side shoots of pinks, border, and annual carnations in midsummer. Sever after 6 weeks, transplant 1 month later.	60°F., night 50°F. summer 5°F. higher (min 45°F. for perpetual carnations, others are frosthardy). Full sun.	Pinch young plants at least once (except for border and annual carnations) to ensure many flowers and bushy plants. Remove all but one bud on each stem if you want large flowers. Support stems with canes or string. Ventilate freely.
Chrysanthemum *Compositae* *Chrysanthemum frutescens* *C. morifolium*	Sow seed shallowly (55-60°F.). Sprouts in about 2 weeks.	Divide perennial species in early spring. * Take 2-4″ cuttings and pot shallowly in sand or peat-sand mix (55-60°F.). Roots in 1-3 weeks. Blooms in 6 months.	50-65°F. (min 45°F.). Partial to full sun. Buds form only if continuous darkness for 10 hours daily. Maintain humidity. Give good ventilation. Water thoroughly, but allow to dry out between waterings.	Plant shallowly and support large plants with canes. Pinch out the growing tip for more flowers and bushier plant. Or, on standard mums, remove all but one main bud to produce a single enormous flower. Do not grow too close together or few flowers will appear. Time of flowering (2 months from beginning of 10-hour nights) can be accurately controlled by lengthening dark period in summer or giving extra light in fall. Outdoor plants are often lifted in fall to bloom indoors after frost.
Cineraria *Compositae* *Senicio cruentus hybrids*	* Sow April to July (55°F.) for flowers January to May. Prick out and grow outdoors over summer, avoiding hot sun.		45-50°F. until buds form, then 50-60°F. (65°F. max). Water well, but don't let them get waterlogged. 6-7″ pots.	Usually bought in winter and discared after flowering. Keep cool and humid. Look out for aphids and whitefly.
Cissus and Rhoicissus *(kangeroo vine, grape ivy, etc.)* *Vitaceae* *Cissus antartica* *C. rhombifolia* *Rhoicissus kapensus*		* 3-6″ tip cuttings or layered stems.	60-70°F. (55°F. in winter). Indirect light. Water moderately; keep barely moist in winter. 8-10″ pots.	Easy foliage plants, will climb or trail. Can grow to 10 feet. Pinch often. Can prune hard in spring. Look out for spider mites.
Clivia *Amaryllidaceae* *Clivia miniata*		* Remove 8-10″ tall offsets after plant flowers. Insert in 4″ pot of peat-sand (60-65°F.). Water sparingly. Flowers in 1-2 years. Old plants can be divided with a knife. Try to avoid damaging roots.	60-70°F. (45-50°F. in winter). Partial shade. Water and feed well in summer. Keep nearly dry in winter till buds appear. 8-10″ pot.	Spectacular flowers in early spring. Prefers being pot bound. Replace top few inches of soil annually in late winter. Repot after flowering every 2-3 years. Remove fruits as flowers fade. For maximum effect do not remove offsets.

** Preferred method of propagation*

▶

Name	Propagation by Seed	Vegetative Propagation	Growing Conditions	Comments
Coleus (flamenettle) *Labiatae* *Coleus blumei*	Sow seeds in late winter on surface of soil in good light (70-75°F.). Sprouts in 2-3 weeks.	* Take 2-3″ cuttings in late summer or early spring (60-65°F.).	55-70°F. (not over 60°F. in winter). Good indirect light. Keep moist in summer, fairly dry in winter.	Brilliantly colored, fast-growing foliage plants. Pinch back for bushiness and remove any flowers which form. Best to start new plants from cuttings or seed each year.
Crassula *Crassulaceae* *Crassula argentea (jade tree)* *C. falcata* *(propeller plant)* *C. rupestris* *(rosary vine) and others.*		* 2-3″ stem cuttings or single leaf cuttings in spring (70°F.).	55-75°F. (45-55°F. in winter). Partial sun. Water moderately; keep nearly dry in winter. Add sharp sand to potting mix. 6-10″ pots.	Succulents with unusual leaf forms. Need rest period in winter.
Crown of Thorns *Euphorbiaceae* *Euphorbia milii*, syn. *E. splendens*		* 3-4″ tip cuttings. Dip in powdered charcoal and allow to dry for a day. Insert in barely moist peat-sand. Do not overwater.	65-80°F. (min 55°F.). Full sun. Water moderately; less if below 60°F. Add extra sand to soil mix and pack in firmly.	Very spiny plant with red or yellow bracts over a long period. Lower leaves eventually fall, leaving bare spiny stem.
Cyclamen, *see under* **bulbs**				
Episcia, *see* **Gesneriads**				
Euphorbia, *see* **Crown of Thorns** *and* **Poinsettia.**				
Fatshedera and Fatsia *Araliaceae* *Fatshedera lizei* *Fatsia japonica*	Sow fresh fatsia seed 1″ deep in April (55-60°F.).	* 3-4″ tip or lower stem cuttings (60-70°F.).	Fatshedera 55-75°F. Fatasia 45-65°F. Both 40-50°F. in winter (min 35°F. except variegated—60°F.). Water moderately, less in winter if cold. Extra peat. 8-10″ pots.	Easy, nearly hardy, foliage plants. Fatshederas climb or trail. Fatsias make rounded bushes. Can prune hard in spring and will sprout from below. Will survive some freezing, but may be damaged.
Felicia compositae *Felicia amelloides* *F. pappei*		* 2-3″ cuttings. June for winter bloom; August for spring and summer.	45-65°F. (min 35°F.). 5″ pots.	Sky-blue daisies all winter. Pinch twice before set buds. Remove flowers as they fade.
Ferns *many genera and species*	Reproduce by spores that produce prothalli that in turn produce little ferns.	* Some species can be divided. Best done in early spring. Take 2″ tip cutting of above-ground rhizomes.	Tropical species, 65-70°F. Temperate species, 55-65°F. Medium indirect light. Maintain humid atmosphere. Spray with fine mist in hot weather. Keep soil moist, except in cold weather. Avoid cold or hard water. Use humusy soil (add extra peat or leaf mold) and do not overpot. Apply weak liquid feed. Wide pots better than deep ones.	Avoid direct sunlight. Many ferns are sensitive to pollution in either air or water and to chemical insecticides. Most become dormant below 50°F.

** Preferred method of propagation*

▶

NAME	PROPAGATION BY SEED	VEGETATIVE PROPAGATION	GROWING CONDITIONS	COMMENTS
Ficus (fig) *Moraceae* *Ficus Benjamina* *F. elastica (rubber plant)* *F. pumila (creeping fig)* *F. sagittata and others*		* *F. pumila* and *F. sagittata* 4-6″ cuttings in spring (60-65°F.). Larger ficuses are better air layered (see page 000).	60-70°F. (min 50°F. for *F. Benjamina* and *F. sagittata* min 35°F. for *F. pumila).* Indirect light. Water moderately (except *F. pumila,* keep moist).	An enormous range of foliage plants from trees to creepers. Shiny-leaved ficuses must be kept clean. To encourage branching of rubber plants, cut off tips and sprinkle with powdered charcoal to stop flow of latex sap. Variegated ficuses need more light.
Fuchsia *Onagraceae* *Fuchsia*	Sow seeds in spring (60°F.).	Take 3-4″ cuttings. Pinch at 3″	50-65°F. (40-50°F. in winter) (min 35°F., max 70°F.). Partial sun. Feed well. 5″ pots.	Pot lightly. Keep moist, but water less in winter. Too much heat will cause buds to drop, so give partial shade in hot weather. Cut back in fall or late winter. Keep cold and dry over winter. Will lose leaves. Standards need a little more heat to be sure the head is not damaged. Look out for whitefly.
Geranium *Geraniaceae* *Pelargonium domesticum (regal pelargonium or Martha Washington geranium)* *P. hortorum (zonal or ordinary geranium)* *P. peltatum (ivyleaf geranium) and many scented-leaf geraniums*	Sow seeds in early spring (60-65°F.). Flowers in 5-9 months.	* Take 3-4″ cuttings in late summer or early spring, in sand or peat-sand mix (60-65°F.). Flowers in 6-8 months (3-4 months if taken in spring). Summer cuttings bloom all winter if not too cold.	60-70°F. (winter 45-50°F.) (min 35°F.). Full sun. Water thoroughly but allow to dry out between waterings. Keep almost dry in winter. Use high potash feed.	Shade only if necessary to prevent overheating in summer. Will stop flowering if too hot. Does well out of doors in summer. Cut back in fall before taking in. Pinch tips of young plants, except regals. Regals give best show of bloom but have briefer season and should be kept fairly dry for 2 months after flowering.
Gesneriads *Gesneriacea* *Episcia (flameviolet)* *Saintpaulia (African violet)* *Streptocarpus* *(Cape primrose)* See also Gloxinia and Achimenes under Bulbs and Corms	Sow seed on surface of peat-sand mix (70°F.) in good light. Sprouts in about 3 weeks. Blooms in 6-10 months.	Take African violet leaf cuttings (70°F.). Blooms in about 1 year. Cut *Streptocarpus* leaves in 3″ sections; insert top end up. Blooms in 6-9 months. Pot rooted *Episcia* plantlets at end of stolons. Divide mature plants in early spring.	60-75°F. (min 55°F.). Good indirect light. Maintain humidity. Water from below to prevent splash marks on leaves and possible rotting. Keep moist but not sodden, and use tepid water. A light, free-draining, humusy soil is essential. Does well in all-peat mixture. Give very weak feed at every watering. 5-6″ pots.	Does well under fluorescents. Likes warm nights. Pull off any damaged leaves; do not cut. Look out for aphids and mealybugs.
Gloxinia, *see under* **Bulbs**				
Hibiscus *Malvaceae* *Hibiscus rosa-sinenis*		* 3-4″ cuttings, with heel if possible, in spring or summer. (65°F.). Give weak feed for a month or two after rooting before transplanting.	60-70°F. (45-55°F. in winter). Partial sun. Water moderately when in growth; keep nearly dry in winter. 8-12″ pots.	Big flowers on big plants. Pinch young plants. Can grow to 6 feet plus. Prune hard in early spring.
Hoya *see* **Wax Plant**				

* *Preferred method of propagation*

▶

NAME	PROPAGATION BY SEED	VEGETATIVE PROPAGATION	GROWING CONDITIONS	COMMENTS
Impatiens *(Busy Lizzie)* *Balsaminaceae* *Impatiens sultanii*, syn *I. wallerana*	Sow seed in spring or summer on surface of soil in good light (65-75°F.). Sprouts in 2-3 weeks. Blooms in 3-4 months.	* Take 3″ cuttings any time. Root in water or peat-sand mix (60°F.). Flowers in 1-2 months. 3 cuttings in a pot quickly makes a bushy plant.	60-75°F. (min 50°F., 55°F. to flower). Good indirect light. Keep moist, but water less if below 55°F. 5″ pots.	Can bloom all year. Pinch back young plants. Prune old plants hard in early spring. Look out for spider mites and aphids.
Ivy *Araliaceae* *Hedera, Helix, and others*		Take 3-4″ cuttings in summer. Root in water or peat-sand mix.	45-65°F. (50°F. in the winter) (min 30°F.). Keep only just moist in winter.	Will climb or trail. Wide variety of leaf shape and variegation. Look out for spider mites.
Jasmine *Oleaceae* *Jasminum officinale* *J. polyanthum*	Sow seeds in fall.	3-5″ tip cuttings or heel cuttings after flowering (40-50°F.). Pinch 10″. Will flower the following winter. Layer shoots in early fall; sever a year later.	5-6″ post. 40-60°F. (min 30°F.; *J. officinale* min 20°F.). Full sun. Keep moist, especially in summer. Ventilate well. 8-10″ pots, or better in deep bed.	Fragant climber. *J. polyanthum* winter blooming. Train up wires or canes. Can be set outdoors in summer. Very vigorous. Can grow to 15 feet. Prune after flowering. For small plants, replace every 3 years.
Kalanchoe *Crassulaceae* *Kalanchoe blossfeldiana*	Sow on surface in light (70°F.). Sow February for winter bloom. May for early spring. Difficult.	3″ tip cuttings in May.	55-70°F. (min 50°F.). Full sun in winter. Water moderately, less after flowering. 5″ pots.	Bright red, orange, or yellow winter flowers with shiny succulent leaves. Usually bought in bud and discarded. Need long nights then short nights to flower. Look out for mealybugs and spider mites.
Lantana *Verbaenaceae* *Lantana camara*	Sow February (60°F.) for summer.	3″ stem cutting in August (60-65°F.).	60-70°F. (winter 50°F.) (min 45°F.). Partial to full sun. Maintain humidity. Keep moist in summer, nearly dry in winter. 6-8″ pot (up to 12″ for standards).	Bright colored, fragrant summer flowers. Can grow as annuals. Pinch overwintered cuttings in late winter. Prune old plants hard in February. Look out for whitefly.
Monstera (Swiss cheese plant) *Araceae* *Monstera deliciosa*		Tip cutting in April or May (75-80°F.) or air layers, see page 000.	65-70°F. (min 45°F.). Good indirect light. Water sparingly and maintain humidity. Add leaf mold to soil. 10-12″ pots.	Large, shiny leaves that develop holes with age. Can grow to 15 feet, but needs staking. Train aerial roots around damp moss-covered pole if possible. If not, let them root in pot.

** Preferred method of propagation*

▶

Name	Propagation by Seed	Vegetative Propagation	Growing Conditions	Comments
Orchid *Orchidaceae*	Propagation by seed is a difficult, highly specialized business.	Mature plants can be divided. Each piece of rhizome should have at least 1, preferably 2 or 3, pseudobulbs attached.	Temperature depends on species. Full sun in winter. Partial shade or good indirect light in summer. Terrestrial orchids—1 coarse peat/1 loam/1 sand/1 sphagnum moss. Epiphytic orchids—2 osmunda fiber or shredded bark/1 sphagnum moss, or 1 coarse peat/1 perlite/1 sphagnum moss. Allow soil nearly to dry between watering, then soak well. Needs little plant food. A foliar feed once a month should be enough.	Avoid stagnant air. Most species like a lot of heat if there is sufficient humidity (from 70% up to 100% for tropical species). Remove damaged roots and pack soil in firmly when repotting. Do not water newly planted orchids; mist daily for 3-4 weeks. Many orchids have a dormant period in fall or winter when they require very little water. Epiphytic orchids grow naturally on trees and suffer greatly if their roots are kept wet. Grow them on a piece of bark, a wooden basket, or special perforated pot for sufficient aeration.
Orchid Cactus, *See* **Cactus, epiphytic**				
Palm *Palmae* *Howea*, syn *Kentia* *Washingtonia and others*	Sow seed in February (80°F.). May take months to sprout.		55-70°F. Partial shade in summer, partial sun in winter.	Water well in summer, keep fairly dry in winter. Keep atmosphere moist in spring and summer. Dislikes drafts. Difficult to propagate, easiest to buy small plants. Look out for scale insects.
Passiflora (Passion flower) *Passifloraceae* *Passiflora caerulea* *P. edulis*	* Sow in spring (65-70°F.).	* 3-4″ stem cuttings in summer (60-65°F.). When rooted give weak feed till winter, then keep fairly dry. Pot in early spring.	60-70°F. (winter 50°F.) (min 40°F.). Partial sun. Keep moist in summer, nearly dry in winter. Maintain humidity. 8″ pot.	Extraordinary flowers, thought to represent the Passion of Christ. *P. edulis* has more attractive leaves and delicious fruits like pale green eggs. Fast-growing climbers. Prune hard in early spring, cut side shoots to 2-3″. If frosted, plant will often send up new shoots from base. Look out for spider mites.
Pelargonium, *see* **Geranium**				
Philodendron *Araceae* *Philodendron*	Nonclimbing varieties can be propagated by seed. Sown in April (75°F.).	3-6″ cuttings in June or October (70°F.). Some species can be divided.	55-65°F. (min 50°F.). Good indirect light. Add extra peat to soil. 10-12″ pot.	Keep soil and atmosphere moist, especially in summer. Most need staking; damp moss on stake will encourage aerial roots.
Pinks, *See* **Carnations** *and under* **Annuals.**				
Plumbago *Plumbaginaceae* *Plumbago capensis*, syn *P. auriculata*		* 3-4″ heel cuttings in June (60-65°F.). When rooted, feed weakly till 12″ high then pinch and pot.	55-75°F. (winter 45-50°F.) (min 35°F.). Partial sun. Water well in summer; keep nearly dry in winter. 8-10″ pot (better in ground bed).	Pale blue or white flowering climber. Must be tied to support. Will survive, but loses leaves at 30°F. Can grow to 15ft. Prune new growth by 2/3 February.

** Preferred method of propagation*

▶

Name	Propagation by Seed	Vegetative Propagation	Growing Conditions	Comments
Poinsettia *Euphorbia Pulcherrima*		Take 3-6″ cuttings in spring; dip in powdered charcoal (60-65°F.). Keep fairly dry until well-rooted, then water young plants freely.	Winter 55-50°F., rest of year 60-75°F. Full sun in winter, partial sun in summer. Allow soil to dry between waterings, then water well.	Not really worth keeping for a second year, but if you want to try, keep just moist in winter; gradually dry off after flowering. Cut back to 2″ from base. Start watering again in April. Keep humid atmosphere when growing. Can be put out of doors in summer. Needs long nights to flower. Provide 2 hours extra darkness from October on to produce flowers by Christmas. Commercial growers use dwarfing hormones to keep plants short.
Primulas, *see under* **Annuals**				
Salvias *Labitae* *Salvia argentea* *S. fulgens* *S. patens* *S. rutilans*	Sow seeds in March (65°F.).	3″ cuttings April or September (55-60°F.).	50-60°F. (min 35°F.). Water well in summer; keep nearly dry in winter. 6-8″ pots.	Brilliantly colored red or blue flowers. Can be made to bloom indoors in winter, or grown for summer garden. Pinch. Prune to 4-6″ in February. Look out for spider mites.
Schefflera *Araliaceae* *Schefflera actinophylla,* syn *Brassaia actinophylla*	Sow fresh seed with bottom heat (70-75°F.).	Air layer.	60-70°F. (min 55°F.). Good indirect light. Water moderately; keep nearly dry in winter. Maintain humidity. 8-10″ pots.	Shiny leaves and attractive structure. Keep leaves clean. Can grow to 6 feet. Difficult to propagate, easiest to buy small plants.
Snapdragon, *see under* **Bedding Plants**				
Solanums and Capsicums *Solanceae* *S. capsicastrum (winter cherry)* *S. pseudocapsicum (Jerusalem cherry)* *C. frutescens (ornamental pepper)*	Sow shallowly in March (60-65°F.). Pinch.		70-80°F. (55-60°F. in winter) (min 50°F.). Full sun. Water well. Maintain humidity. 4-6″ pots.	Ornamental fruits in winter. Will fruit again if pruned hard, potted, and put outside for the summer. Keep fairly dry to rest in spring. Mist plants while flowering to encourage fruit set. Look out for spider mites and whitefly.
Sparmannia *(room lime or zimmer linden)* *Tiliaceae* *Sparmannia africana*		3-6″ cuttings in April (60-65°F.). Pinch.	55-65°F. (45°F. in winter). Good indirect light or partial sun. Keep humid if over 60°F. Water well in summer; keep barely dry in winter. 6″ pot (10″ for 6 foot plant).	Fast growing, bushy plants with large leaves and white flowers. Can grow to 10 feet. Prune hard in March. Replace overgrown plants with cutting.
Spider Plant *Liliaceae* *Chlorophytum* *Elatum variegatum*		Set small plants on surface of soil in separate pots. Sever when well rooted. Divide large plants in spring.	50-60°F. (min. 45°F.). Partial shade. Good in hanging baskets.	Easy trailer. Keep moist in spring and summer, somewhat drier in fall and winter. Avoid drafts. Invasive, will root in other plants' pots.
Streptocarpus *see* **Gesneriads**				

▶

Name	Propagation by Seed	Vegetative Propagation	Growing Conditions	Comments
Wandering Jew *Commelinaceae* *Callisia* *Setcreasea* *Tradescantia* *Zebrina Purpusii*		Take 3" cuttings in summer. Root in peat-sand mix or just water (60-65°F.). Three in a pot will quickly produce a bushy plant.	60-75°F. (min 50°F.). 4-6" pots.	Hard to keep for more than a few years, but easy to propagate. Pinch young plants to promote bushiness. Remove any nonvariegated shoots. Water freely in summer, less in winter.
Wax Plant *Asclepiadaceae* *Hoya carnosa* *H. bella (miniature)*		Take 3-4" cuttings of mature stems in summer. Root in peat-sand mix (60-65°F.). Layer shoots in spring.	60-70°F. (winter 55-65°F.) (min 45°F.). Full sun in winter, partial shade in summer. Maintain humidity 6-10" pots.	Fragrant flowers drip sweet nectar. Pinch back young plants, but do not prune older ones. Keep moist in summer, cooler and drier in fall and winter. Dislikes root disturbance. ■

BEDDING PLANTS, OR ANNUALS

In general, these plants are started in flats in the greenhouse to be planted out of doors in summer, but most of them can also be sown in late summer or fall to bloom indoors in winter or spring if sufficient light and heat can be given. If winter-flowering or indoor varieties are available, use them for forcing indoors in winter.

Sow the seed of annuals thinly and shallowly. Use ordinary potting mix with a bit of extra peat and sharp sand. If the seed needs light for germination, just press it gently into the surface of the soil. Otherwise cover it with a thin layer of fine peat or soil.

Cover the seed box with plastic or glass to retain humidity until the seeds have sprouted, then remove the cover and allow air to circulate. Most annuals germinate in about two weeks; bottom heat will speed them up by a few days. Transplant or thin them as soon as the leaves touch. Pinch out the growing tip to encourage branching. Gradually harden off those that are to be planted outside. Annuals are usually planted out two or three weeks after the last possible date of frost in your area.

Name	Growing Temp.	Sowing Conditions	Date to Sow for Blooming Season
Ageratum *Compositae*	45-60°F.	65-75°F. in light	August for spring February-March for summer
Alyssum *Cruciferae*	45-60°F. TPS	65-75°F. in light	August for winter March for summer
Aster *Compositae*	60-70°F.	65-75°F.	August for winter December for spring February for summer
Baby's breath *Caryophyllaceae* *Gypsophila elegans*	60-70°F.	70-75°F.	September for November
Begonia, *see under* **Tender Perennials**			
Black-eyed Susan *Acanthaceae* *Thunbergia alata*	65-70°F.	70-75°F.	March for summer
Browallia *Solanaceae*	55-70°F.	70°F. in light	February for summer July for winter
Calendula *Compositae*	40-55°F.	65-75°F. in dark	January for spring March for summer August for winter
Candytuft *Cruciferae* *Iberis*	45-60°F.	60-65°F.	December-February for summer Fall for spring

▶

Name	Growing Temp.	Sowing Conditions	Date to Sow for Blooming Season
Carnation **Chrysanthemum** **Cineraria** **Coleus** *See Under* **Tender Perennials**			
Cosmos *Compositae*	55-65°F.	60-70°F. (max 70°F.).	March for summer October for spring
Dusty Miller *Compositae* *Artemisia* *Stelleriana*	50-70°F.	60-70°F. in dark	February-March for May-June
Forget-me-not *Boraginaceae* *Myosotis*	40-60°F. TPS	70-75°F.	Use early flowering variety Takes 4 months to bloom August for winter
Geranium, *see under* **Tender Perennials**			
Heliotrope *Boraginaceae*	45-65°F.	60-65°F.	February for summer July for winter Cuttings bloom in 4-6 months
Impatiens **Kalanchoe** **Lantana** *see under* **Tender Perennials**			
Lobelia *Campanulaceae*	50-60°F. TPS	60-75°F.	February for summer September for winter December for spring
Marigold *Compositae* *Tagetes*	50-65°F. (min 45°F.).	65-70°F.	February for spring April for summer August-September for winter
Nasturtium *Tropaeolaceae*	45-60°F.	55-65°F. Hard to transplant, use peat pots.	August-September for winter February for summer
Nemesia *Scrophulariaceae*	50-65°F.	60-65°F. in dark	July for winter March for summer January for spring
Pansy *Violaceae*	45-60°F.	60-70°F. in dark	December for spring March for summer July for winter
Petunia *Solanaceae*	45-60°F. TPS	60-70°F. on surface	November for spring March for summer
Phlox *Polemoniaceae*	50-60°F.	55-65°F. in dark	March for summer September for spring
Pinks & Sweet William *Caryophyllaceae* *Dianthus*	50-60°F.	65-75°F.	March for summer
Portulaca (moss rose) *Portulaceae*	50-70°F.	65-70°F. in dark	March for summer
Primula *Primulaceae* *P. kewensis* *P. malacoides* *P. obconica* *P. vulgaris*	45-60°F. TPS Add extra peat *P. vulgaris* will stand frost.	60-70°F. in light	March for winter

▶

Name	Growing Temp.	Sowing Conditions	Date to Sow for Blooming Season
Salpiglossis *Solanaceae*	55-65°F. (min 50°F.) TPS	65-70°F. in dark, on surface	February for summer September for winter December for May
Salvia *Labiatae*	55-60°F.	70-80°F.	March for summer
Scabious *Dipsacaceae*	50-60°F.	65-75°F.	March for summer
Schizanthus *Scrophulariaceae*	45-60°F.	in dark	August for spring June for winter; pinch often
Snapdragon *Scrophulariaceae* *Antirrhinum* *Majus*	45-65°F. TPS	70-75°F. in light	Sow anytime for flowers in 3-4 months (up to 6 months in winter)
Stock *Cruciferae* *Matthiola*	50-55°F. (min 45°F.) (max 65°F.)	70-75°F.	January for summer August for winter
Sweet Pea *Leguminosae* *Lathyrus* *Odoratus*	45-55°F.	55-60°F. in dark	January for spring June for fall August for winter
Sweet William, *see* **Pinks**			
Tobacco Plant *Solanaceae* *Nicotiana*	45-60°F. TPS	65-70°F. in light	March for summer August for spring
Zinnia *Compositae*	60-75°F.	65-75°F.	April for summer August for winter

TPS - tolerates partial shade

■

BULBS

Bulbs, corms and tubers are all included here. In general, plants grown from bulbs will not come true from seeds. It is fun to experiment, but you are unlikely to improve on the parent variety.

Hardy bulbs (like crocus, hyacinth, narcissus, tulip) need a cold, dark rooting period. They can be forced to flower at any time of the year if the cold period can be given. Some people put pots of bulbs in the refrigerator in August or September to be sure of flowers by Christmas. For later blooming bulbs are better left outside under a pile of leaves or straw once the weather turns chilly. You can buy specially preconditioned bulbs that need less time in the dark, so they will bloom earlier.

When the bulbs are well-rooted and leaves 1-1½″ tall, the base of the leaves should be fat with the emerging bud. At this point they are ready to come into the light, but some can be left for several weeks longer to give a succession of blooms. Give some shade for the first week indoors as the white leaves green up, then full sun at 45-50°F. After a few more weeks you can increase the temperature to 60°F. to speed them up, but never let them get really warm until the buds have opened. Even then, cold will prolong the life of the flowers.

Any good, free-draining greenhouse soil is suitable for growing hardy bulbs. Equal parts of peat, sand, and loam (or compost) is a good mixture. Many bulbs can be grown successfully in bulb fiber, peat moss with some charcoal, or even plain gravel, but they will use up all of their stored energy and are unlikely to survive to bloom another year out of doors. They are also more difficult to stake in these materials. When flowers fade, cut off only the flower head, leaving the green stalk to help feed the bulb for next year.

Name	Planting Time	Planting Depth	Growing Conditions	Propagation	Comments
Achimenes, *see* **Gloxinia**					

▶

Name	Planting Time	Planting Depth	Growing Conditions	Propagation	Comments
Amaryllis *Amaryllidaceae* *Hippeastrum*	September-October for February-March (treated bulbs for January)	Half bulb depth	60-70°F. (min 55°F.) Full sun. Feed after flowering.	Detach 1½″ offsets as growth begins. Grow on, will flower when 3-3½″. Sow seed in March (60-65°F.), takes 2-8 years to bloom.	Keep fairly dry after leaves yellow, very dry if below 55°F. Water sparingly when new growth appears, usually early winter. Water more after bud appears.
Anemone *Ranunculaceae* *Anemone*	September-October for January-March	2″	50°F. (60°F. when in flower) Full sun.	Sow seed in late summer; takes several years to bloom.	Needs good drainage. Water sparingly until growing well. Reduce water in winter.
Begonia, tuberous, *see under* **Houseplants**					
Crocus *Iridaceae* *Crocus*	September-October for December-February (8-10 weeks in dark plus 2-4 in light).	Just cover corm	35-45°F. in darkness until well rooted. Then 50°F. in full sun.	Offsets will bloom the following year. Sow seed in summer, takes 2-4 years to bloom.	Winter-flowering varieties will be ready first. Species crocus have smaller but more plentiful flowers than hybrids. Do not try to mix colors as they are likely to bloom at different times. Chionodoxa, snowdrops, and scillas can be grown like crocuses.
Cyclamen *Primulaceae* *Cyclamen*	August for winter	Leave half of corm showing	Day, 55-65°F. Night, 50-55°F. Good, indirect light or partial sun. Use ordinary potting mix. Maintain humidity, especially if over 65°F.	Sow seed in August or September (60°F.). Takes up to 2 months to sprout, 15-18 months to bloom Can take leaf cuttings with a bit of corm attached.	Keep moist but provide good drainage and avoid wetting corm. Keep fairly dry and allow to rest after blooming. In August, as new leaves appear, repot if necessary and begin watering to restart growth. Do not feed if repotted. Twist off faded leaves and flowers to remove all of stalk.
Daffodil, *see* **Narcissus**					
Freesia *Iridaceae* *Freesia*	August-November for December-April	1″	Day 65°F., night 50°F. (min 45°F.). Full sun.	Sow seed in spring (60°F.). Do not transplant. Takes 9-12 months to bloom.	Water sparingly until buds appear. Best discarded after blooming. Support leaves and flowers with canes or grow in hanging baskets.
Gloxinia and Achimenes *Gesneriaceae* *Sinningia speciosa* *Achimenes*	January-April for summer	Gloxinia crown level with surface. Achimenes 3-4 rhizomes per 4″ pot. Lay horizontally ½″ below surface.	Day 65-75°F., night 65°F. (min 60°F., max 70°F.) Partial shade or good indirect light. Water well. Maintain humidity. Give high potash feed after flowering. Use ½ peat, ½ vermiculite mix with extra lime. 5″ pot.	Divide tubers or rhizomes in March. Root 2-4″ stem cuttings in June with sliver of tuber attached. Or take leaf cuttings of gloxinias nicking the main veins and laying flat on peat-sand mix. Sow gloxinia seed in fall or winter (70°F.) in light. Takes 6-9 months.	Needs humid warm atmosphere, but avoid wetting leaves. Gradually dry off when leaves yellow, then store at 50-60°F. in darkness. Repot and begin watering sparingly in early spring.

▶

Name	Planting Time	Planting Depth	Growing Conditions	Propagation	Comments
Hyacinth *Liliaceae* *Hyacinthus*	Prepared bulbs: September-November for December-February. Unprepared bulbs: October for March-April (both bloom 3-5 weeks after being brought into light).	Leave tip of bulb showing.	35-45°F. in darkness until well rooted and buds showing, usually 10-14 weeks. Then 50°F. for 10 days in semishade. Then 55-60°F. in full sun till blooms; then 60°F.		Specially prepared bulbs should be used for very early flowers. Can be grown in sand, sand and peat, bulb fiber, pebbles, or just water. Large flowers will need staking. Bulbs grown in soil can be planted outdoors (6″ deep) after flowering. Grape hyacinths are more difficult to grow.
Iris *Iridaceae* *Iris reticulata and others*	November-January for February-April	Leave tip of bulb showing.	40-50°F. until buds color, then 60-65°F.	Divide tubers after leaves die back. Offsets will bloom in 1-3 years.	Buy specially treated bulbs for forcing. Not so easy to grow as hyacinths and narcissi.
Lily of the Valley *Liliaceae* *Convallaria majalis*	October-November for February-March	Leave tip of bulb showing.	40-50°F. until January then 60-70°F. Partial shade.		Buy specially prepared pips for forcing. Keep moist.
Narcissus *Amaryllidaceae* *Narcissus*	September-November for December-March. (Tazettas 5-8 weeks after planting; others 8-10 weeks in dark, plus 3-4 weeks in light).	Leave tip of bulb showing.	35-45°F. in darkness (except for Tazettas, which can be placed immediately) until well rooted, then 50-55°F. in full sun till bloom, then 60°F.	Offsets will bloom in 1-2 years. Sow seed in summer when ripe; takes 3-7 years to bloom; usually poor quality.	Buy specially prepared bulbs for very early flowers. Tazetta narcissi (with several flowers on one stalk, e.g., Paper white or Soleil d'Or) will bloom sooner than others. Plant in sand, gravel, bulb fiber, or soil. Keep some in dark longer for succession of blooms. Flowers may need staking if too hot, last longer if cool. After blooming, hardy varieties potted in soil can be grown on, gradually drying off as leaves yellow, then planted outside (6″ deep).
Orchid, *see under* **Houseplants**					
Tuberose *Agavaceae* *Polianthes tuberosa*	Plant late autumn or winter. Keep frost free. Tubers will wait till 60-65°F. to sprout.	1″ deep 3 in a 7″ pot	65-80°F. after leaves appear. Full sun.	Offsets, but unlikely to bloom.	3′ tall, extremely fragrant and beautiful flowers. Buy tubers and discard after flowering. Plant in moist soil, but don't water unless bone dry until leaves appear.
Tulip *Liliaceae* *Tulipa*	September-October for January-February (8-12 weeks in dark, plus 3-5 weeks in light).	Leave tip of bulb showing. Put flat side of bulb toward outside of pot.	35-45°F. in darkness until well rooted, usually 8-10 weeks; then 50-60°F. in full sun.	Some produce offsets that will bloom in 2-3 years. Sow seed in summer to bloom in 5-7 years; usually poor quality.	Single and double earlies will bloom soonest and are easiest to force.

VEGETABLES

Virtually all vegetables require full sun for optimum growth. But those that are grown for their leaves or roots rather than for their fruit will usually grow moderately well, though more slowly, when partially in the shade. Winter vegetables should be well advanced by midautumn. They will stay in good condition but won't make much more growth in the depths of winter.

Most vegetables are grown in the standard soil mix of two parts loam to one part peat and one part sand. The depth of soil needed depends on the final size of the plant and whether most of its growth takes place above ground or below ground (carrots will obviously need deeper soil than lettuce, even though they take up less room above ground). Generally, 10-16 inches is sufficient, with a 2-4 inch layer of gravel or other free-draining material below.

Most vegetable seed will germinate at 50-60°F., though it will sprout sooner with more heat. A few plants absolutely require more heat to germinate and this is noted in the individual entry.

Name	Planting Seeds	Growing Conditions	Time from Seed to Harvest (in ideal conditions)	Comments
Artichoke,[a] globe *Compositae* *Cynara scolymus*	½″ deep 1″ apart 60-70°F.	35-75°F. 30″x30″ TPS in summer	6 months	Perennial related to thistles. Cut buds before they open. Likes rich deep soil. Can grow from basal suckers cut off in November or March. Takes a lot of room but handsome plant.
Beans[b] *Leguminosae*	2″ deep 5″ apart 60-70°F. Inoculate seed with nitrogen-fixing bacteria	50-70°F. 10″ apart. Full sun.	bush 2-3 months pole 3-4 months soya 4-5 months broad 2-4 months	Bush beans take less space and crop sooner, but produce less and have less flavor. Broad beans can be grown as winter crop.
Beets[a] *Chenopodiaceae* *Beta vulgaris*	½″ deep 1″ apart	40-70°F. 2″ then 4″ TPS	2 months (greens in 1-1½ months)	Quite hardy. Greens are good to eat. Efficient user of space if every other plant is pulled for greens when 4-5″ high. Likes lime. Roots won't swell in late autumn or winter.
Cabbage family[c] (broccoli Brussels sprouts cabbage cauliflower collards[a] kale kohlrabi, etc.) *Cruciferae* *Brassica* *see also* **Chinese Cabbage, Chinese Greens, & Turnips**	½″ deep ½″ apart 60-70°F.	40-65°F. 18″x18″ Brussels & cauliflowers 24″x24″ TPS	broccoli 2-3 months Brussels 6-7 months cauliflower 2-4 months cabbage 3-5 months kale 5 months	Quite hardy, but worth starting plants indoors February or March. If hardened off, can plant outdoors quite early, before last frost. Probably not worth growing inside because they take a lot of space for a long time. If you have enough room, they are reliable producers, but need deep soil and should be fed well with manure or fish emulsion. Overwintered plants likely to go to seed in spring.
Carrots[a] *Umbelliferae* *Daucus carota*	¼″ deep, thinly. Slow to germinate. Don't transplant.	45-65°F. 1½″ (3″ for large carrots) TPS	2-4 months	Quite hardy. Keep cool and moist. Likes deep sandy soil. Use stumprooted varieties.
Celery & Celeriac[c] *Umbelliferae* *Apium graveolens*	½″ deep, thinly. 60°F. Slow to germinate.	35-60°F. 12″x12″ TPS	celery 5-6 months celeriac 4-5 months	Needs rich, moist soil and cool conditions. Not easy or quick to grow.
Chard[a] (swiss chard or seakale beet) *Chenopodiaceae* *Beta vulgaris*	1″ deep thinly	8″x8″ TPS	2 months	Easy to grow. One of the best winter crops. Pick outside leaves continuously. Rhubarb chard is a beautiful deep red, slightly smaller and sweeter. Break leaves off at base; do not cut.

TPS—tolerates partial shade (almost all vegetables prefer full sun, especially in winter, but these will grow in some shade).

[a] Good winter crop in a cool greenhouse (min 35°F., average 40-45°F.).

[b] Difficult to transplant, but often worth starting indoors to extend the growing season. Use peat pots (2 seeds per pot, removing the weaker seedling) to reduce transplanting shock.

[c] Commonly started indoors in flats in early spring to be planted out in the garden after the last frost.

▶

Name	Planting Seeds	Growing Conditions	Time from Seed to Harvest (in ideal conditions)	Comments
Chicory, *see* **Endive** *or* **Escarole**				
Chinese Cabbage[a] *Cruciferae* *Brassica cernua*	½″ deep 1″ apart 60°F. Don't transplant.	50-65°F., 40-50°F. at night. 18″x18″ TPS	2-3 months	Difficult, but worthwhile. Needs rich, moist soil and coolness. Sow in early fall for early winter crop.
Chinese Greens[a] *Cruciferae* *Brassica* *Pac Choi* *(syn Bok Choy)* *Osaka and many others*	½″ deep ½″ apart 60°F.	35-60°F. 2″x2″ then 8″x8″ TPS	2-4 months	One of best cool greenhouse crops. September sowings can be harvested all winter. Use thinnings, then pick outside leaves.
Cress[a] *Cruciferae* *Lepidium* *Sativum*	¼″ deep thinly (in dark)	50-60°F. Likes shade.	10 days-3 weeks	Very easy and quick to grow. Does not need much sun but likes rich, very moist soil.
Cucumbers[b] *Cucurbitaceae* *Cucumis* *Sativus*	½″ deep in 4″ pot. 70-85°F.	65-85°F. (min 50°F.) 36″x36″ Full sun	2 months (sow 5 weeks before planting date).	Needs deep, rich soil, warmth, humidity, and some shade in the height of summer if grown insde. Pick frequently. Use European, seedless, all-female varieties for best yield and flavor. Other varieties need to be hand-pollinated, but can stand slightly lower temperatures and are better for pickling. Remove old leaves and fruitlets near base. Also remove any male flowers that appear on all-female varieties. Pinch shoots at second leaf. Allow only one, or on mature plants two, fruits to develop at each joint. Best grown up trellis or wires to take less room. Look out for spider mites and whitefly.
Eggplant[b] *Solanaceae* *Melongena* *Ovigerum*	¼″ deep 2″ apart 75-80°F.	65-75°F. 24″x24″ Full sun	3-4 months (sow 8 weeks before planting date)	Needs lots of warmth, light, and rich soil. May have to be potted before being planted outside. Needs hand pollinating indoors.
Endive[a] **(chicons, Belgian or French endive)** *Compositae* *Cichorium intybus*	½″ deep thinly outside in June	45-60°F. (60°F. max) In dark when forcing.	7 months (3-5 weeks of forcing)	Grow outdoors. In fall cut off leaves to about 2″, dig up and store in damp, dark cold place. To force, plant roots vertically, close together, in damp sand or soil. Cover with 6″ of dry sand or just invert a box over the top. Keep in dark until ready, when leaves 5-6″ long. If broken rather than cut, more will grow. Start a new crop of roots every few weeks.
Escarole[a] *(chicory or curly endive)* *Compositae* *Cichorium endivia*	¼″ deep thinly in light	40-65°F. 9″x9″ TPS	3 months	Quite hardy, a good winter crop. Bitter, but the heart can be blanched for 2-3 weeks when plant is almost full grown to reduce bitterness. Just tie the outside leaves together or cover with a box. Many Italian salad vegetables are closely related and can be grown in the same way.
Lettuce[a,c] *Compositae* *Lactuca sativa*	¼″ deep thinly in light	55-70°F., night 45-55°F. (max 70°F.) 4″x4″ then 8″x8″ TPS	2 months (up to 4 months in midwinter)	In winter use varieties bred for low light, low temperature. Looseleaf usually better. Needs moisture, light soil, and good ventilation. Foliar feed. Harvest every other plant when leaves touch, or pick outside leaves continuously. Look out for aphids and fungus diseases.

▶

Name	Planting Seeds	Growing Conditions	Time from Seed to Harvest (in ideal conditions)	Comments
Melons, *see under* **Fruit**				
Mushrooms[a] *Agricaceae* *Psalliota campestris*	Sow fine spawn thinly & shallowly. Or plant 1″ lumps 1½-2″ deep, 10″ apart.	50-60°F. In dark	2-3 months	Keep moist and dark. Grow in composted manure (horse manure is best). Should be able to harvest for several months.
New Zealand spinach *Chenopodiaceae* *Tetragonia expansa*	¼″ deep thinly 55-60°F.	45-80°F. 18″x18″ TPS in summer	1-1½ months	Perennial and productive almost all year. Tolerant of wide range of conditions. Can be trained up a trellis or allowed to trail.
Okra[b] *Malvaceae* *Hibiscus esculentus*	1″ deep 2″ apart 65-75°F. Soak seeds.	60-80°F. 18″ apart Full sun.	3½ - 4½ months	Very tall, heat-loving plant with pretty flowers. Pick pods when 2″ long. Uses a lot of space for a small return.
Onion family (leek, onion, scallion, shallot, etc.) *Alliaceae* *Allium*	½″ deep thinly	40-70°F. 2-5″ apart (scallions & leeks TPS)	From seed—4 months From cloves, sets or plants—3 months Leeks—5 months	Quite hardy, but not usually worth growing indoors because they store well. Bulbs grow slowly in winter, so scallions, leeks, and chives will do better than onions or garlic.
Chives & Garlic, *see under* **Herbs**				
Peas[a] *Leguminosae* *Pisum sativum*	2″ deep 1″ apart Inoculate seeds with nitrogen-fixing bacteria.	40-60°F. 2″ apart TPS	2 months	Quite hardy, needs cool, damp conditions. Give even dwarf varieties some support. Not much yield for space taken, but delicious. Snap peas produce a larger crop. Look out for powdery mildew.
Peppers[c] *Solanceae* *Capsicum annuum*	¼″ deep 1″ apart 70-80°F.	70-85°F., night 55-65°F. 12″-18″ apart Full sun.	3½ - 4 months Sow 8-10 weeks before planting date.	Needs a long season and quite a lot of warmth and sun, but not difficult to grow. Needs hand pollination indoors. Can overwinter at 50°F.
Radishes[a] *Cruciferae* *Raphanus sativus*	½″ deep thinly	55-65°F. 1″ apart TPS	3-5 weeks	Easiest and quickest of all crops to grow. Will grow in shade of other crops. Good between rows of larger, slower plants. Dislikes heat.
Spinach[a] *Chenopodiaceae* *Spinacia oleracea*	½″ deep ½″ apart 40-60°F. Sow early fall and early spring. Don't transplant.	40-50°F. 3″ then 6″ TPS	2 months	Quite hardy; will withstand moderate freezing. Dislikes heat. Good winter crop. Can harvest whole or pick outside leaves continously.
Squash[b] *Cucurbitaceae*	½″ deep 3″ apart	60-75°F. (min 55°F.) 36-48″ Full sun.	Summer squash—2 months; winter squash—3-5 months	Needs rich soil, lots of water, sun, and heat. Takes a lot of space, but bears prolifically. Use bush varieties. Pick summer squash when young for more and better yield. Needs hand pollination indoors. Gold Rush is a good variety with easy-to-see, bright yellow fruits.

TPS—tolerates partial shade (almost all vegetables prefer full sun, especially in winter, but these will grow in some shade).

[a] Good winter crop in a cool greenhouse (min 35°F., average 40-45°F.).

[b] Difficult to transplant, but often worth starting indoors to extend the growing season. Use peat pots (2 seeds per pot, removing the weaker seedling) to reduce transplanting shock.

[c] Commonly started indoors in flats in early spring to be planted out in the garden after the last frost.

▶

Name	Planting Seeds	Growing Conditions	Time from Seed to Harvest (in ideal conditions)	Comments
Tomatoes[b,c] *Solanaceae Lycopersicon esculentum*	¼″ deep 1″ apart 75-80°F. Plant in final position just before first flowers open. Choose plants with sturdy stems. Needs 12″ pot or, better, deep bed.	60-80°F. (max 90°F., min 55°F.) 24″ apart Full sun.	2-4 months.	Needs rich soil, lots of water, sun, and a fair amount of heat. Hand pollinate indoors. Use high potash feed. Look out for magnesium deficiency. Stake or wind around strings tied to roof. Avoid bush varieties. Remove suckers. Does well all fall if transplanted indoors from the garden. Summer-sown tomatoes should produce in the fall and again in the spring. Cherry tomatoes produce over a longer period and are likely to be healthier. Sweet 100s, Sugar Lump, and Gardener's Delight are particularly good ones. Most areas in U.S. have insufficient light in winter to set fruit.
Turnips[a] *Cruciferae Brassica Rapa*	¼″ deep ½″ apart	55-70°F., night 45-55°F. 2″ then 4″ TPS	2 months (greens in 1 month)	Needs cool conditions. Pull every other one for greens when the leaves touch. ■

HERBS

All herbs, except possibly mint, prefer as much sun as they can get. They have more flavor if given a lot of sunlight and a relatively slow rate of growth. Be careful not to plant in too rich a soil or to overfertilize. Many herbs will make large, handsome shrubs lasting several years, if given greenhouse protection in winter.

Generally, herb seed is slow to germinate, and often the plants do not make enough growth for a significant harvest until the second year. It is interesting how many apparently unrelated herbs are in the genus *Labiatae,* the mint family.

Name	Propagation	Growing On	Comments
Basil *Labiatae Ocimum Basilicum*	Sow seed thinly ¼″ deep, 55-60°F.	8″ apart min 45°F. Full sun.	Very vulnerable to cold. Look out for whitefly.
Bay Leaves *Lauraceae Laurus Nobilis*	Can take cuttings, but usually bought as a small tree.	Min 45°F. Full sun.	Can be put outdoors in summer, brought in for winter.
Chives[a] *Alliaceae Allium Schoenoprasum*	Sow seed thinly ¼″ deep. Divide mature clumps.	8″ apart Min 35°F. TPS	Two years from seed. Keep cut back and remove all flowers.
Comfrey[a] *Boraginaceae Symphytum*	Plant roots 6″ deep.	36″ apart TPS	Large vigorous plant, keep cutting.
Dill *Umbelliferae Peucedanum Graveolens*	Sow seed thinly ¼″ deep, every few weeks.	8″ apart Full sun.	Do not transplant. Both leaves & seeds good. Takes 2 months.
Garlic *Alliaceae Allium Sativum*	Plant cloves 1-2″ deep.	6″ apart Full sun.	Pull and dry when leaves die. Takes 5 months.

[a] *Fairly hardy perennials, often grown outdoors, will overwinter quite far north if given some protection. But also often brought inside or grown inside to insure active growth and harvesting in winter.*

▶

Name	Propagation	Growing On	Comments
Marjoram *Labiatae* *Origanum* *Majorana*	Sow seed thinly ¼″ deep. Take cuttings or divide.	6″ apart Full sun.	Grows slowly, milder than oregano. Likes lime.
Mint[a] *Labiatae* *Mentha*	Plant section of root 1-2″ deep.	8″ apart Likes shade.	Keep moist. Grows rampantly.
Oregano[a] *Labiatae* *Origanum* *Vulgare*	Sow seed thinly ¼″ deep. Divide or take cuttings.	6″ apart Full sun.	Grows slowly, is perennial. Likes lime.
Parsley *Umbelliferae* *Carum* *Petroselinum*	Sow seed thinly ½″ deep (60°F.). Soaking speeds germination.	4″ apart TPS	Very nutritious. Flat leaf or Italian better flavored. Young plants can be wintered over, but will bolt in spring.
Rosemary[a] *Labiatae* *Rosmarinus*	Sow seed thinly ¼″ deep. Take cuttings in late spring.	8″ apart (36″ when full grown) Full sun.	Slow growing, but if frostfree will grow up to 4′ in several years.
Sage[a] *Labiatae* *Salvia* *Officinalis*	Sow seed thinly ¼″ deep. Take cuttings in spring.	6-12″ apart Full sun.	Will last 2 or 3 years, then should be replaced.
Savory (winter)[a] *Labiatae* *Satureja* *Montana*	Sow seed thinly on surface in August (in light). Take cuttings in spring.	12″ apart Full sun.	Perennial, stronger flavor than summer.
Savory (summer)[a] *Labiatae* *Satureja* *Hortensis*	Sow seed thinly ¼″ deep.	6″ apart Full sun 45-50°F.	A more subtle-flavored annual.
Sorrel[a] *Polygonaceae* *Rumex*	Sow seed thinly ¼″ deep. Divide mature plants.	9″ apart TPS	Two years from seed. A hardy perennial with lemony leaves.
Tarragon[a] *Compositae* *Artemisia* *Dracunculus*	Transplant runners in early spring. Take cuttings in fall. Sow seeds of Russian tarragon.	12″ apart Full sun.	Best to start new plants every few years. Russian is bigger and hardier, but has less flavor. French is better.
Thyme[a] *Labiatae* *Thymus* *Vulgaris*	Sow seed thinly ¼″ deep. Divide or take cuttings.	6″ apart Full sun.	Likes lime. Lemon thyme very fragrant.

[a] *Fairly hardy perennials, often grown outdoors, will overwinter quite far north if given some protection. But also often brought inside or grown inside to insure active growth and harvesting in winter.*

FRUIT

Use dwarf varieties indoors. It is generally better to buy fruit trees as young trees rather than starting them from seed (do not use seed you have saved because it is unlikely to produce edible fruits). All fruits need a lot of sunlight to ripen properly.

NAME	PROPAGATION	GROWING ON	COMMENTS
Citrus fruits (grapefruit, lemon, orange, tangerine) *Rutaceae citrus*	Sow seeds in March (60°F., ½-¼ deep). Take 3-6″ cuttings in summer (60-70°F.).	Days 60°F. (65-70°F. for fruit). Nights 45°F. (min 40°F.) Full sun. Maintain humidity. Give high-potash feed.	Often bears fruit and fragrant flowers at some time. Likes acid soil. Water sparingly in winter and repot if necessary. Needs only frost protection, not much heat unless you want fruit in winter. May be pruned in early spring. Pinch for bushiness. Move outdoors in partial shade for summer. Needs hand pollinating indoors. Tangerines are the hardiest, lemons the most likely to ripen fruit. Look out for spider mites and scale insects.
Figs *Moraceae* *Ficus* *Carica*	Layer (sever in 12 months). Take 4-6″ cuttings (may take months to root).	50-65°F. (min 40°F.). Full sun.	Takes a lot of space. Move outdoors in summer. Keep frost free in fall and winter (will often lose leaves). Can be given longer season by moving into warmth in late winter to restart growth early. Keep fairly potbound. Likes humidity when hot. Will often produce two crops a year.
Grapes *Vitaceae* *Vitis* *Vinifera*	Take 2″ cuttings in February, bury except for eye (55-60°F.). Or take 12″ cuttings in fall.	50-65°F. (min. 40°F., max 80°F.). Full sun.	Prune hard in autumn and train up a trellis. Allow each plant to produce only after 2 years and then only a few bunches until well established. Ventilate well. Look out for powdery mildew.
Melons *Cucurbitaceae* *Cucumis* *Melo*	Sow seed on side ¼″ deep, 2″ apart, or 2 per pot thinning to 1 (75°F.).	60-80°F., (min. 60°F. except cantaloupes 55°F. (min 35°F., max 80°F.) Full sun. Keep humid atmosphere 36″x36″	Takes a lot of space. Ogen and Minnesota Midget are good varieties. Can be trained up trellis if fruits are supported (can then be 24″ apart instead of 36″). Hard to transplant. Needs hand pollinating indoors. Limit to 6 fruits per plant. Ripe when fragrant or comes away from stem easily. Look out for powdery mildew.
Peaches & Nectarines *Rosaceae* *Prunus* *Persica*	Sow stones 1″ deep in fall (45-50°F.).	45-55°F. until fruit sets, then 55-70°F. (min 35°F., max 80°F.) Full sun.	Comments as for figs (except do not keep potbound).
Strawberries *Rosaceae* *Fragaria*	Plant rooted runners. Sow seed for alpine varieties.	50-70°F. Full sun. 9-12″ apart.	Likes rich, well-drained soil, plenty of water. Pick off all blossoms the first year. Next year allow one runner to develop from each plant to make replacement. Needs hand pollinating indoors. Pot garden plants in August. Bring indoors after frost. Keep cold and sunny. Will fruit 1-2 months early. Look out for aphids.

■

COMPANION PLANTING GUIDE

It has been known for centuries that some plants grow better when certain other plants are growing nearby. Science has gradually unearthed reasons why some combinations of plants are successful, but many other combinations that can be observed to be beneficial have as yet received no explanation.

In general, herbs and other aromatic plants like tomatoes, marigolds, and onions are helpful in warding off insects. Usually, the more powerful the smell of the plant, the more effect it has. Certain colors, like the orange of nasturtium and marigold flowers, are thought to repel some harmful flying insects.

Sometimes, one plant's physical structure benefits that of another. Melons or cucumbers will provide dense shade for the roots of corn, while the corn provides a windbreak and some shade for the vines below. Many plants produce root exudates that discourage burrowing insects, or that cause chemical changes in the soil that benefit other plants. On the other hand, some plants produce root exudates that are hostile to other plants. Sunflowers, for example, tend to inhibit the growth of nearby plants. And some plants seem to lower the resistance to disease of others grown nearby. Potatoes—which you are unlikely to grow in a greenhouse in any case—are vulnerable in this respect because their resistance is lowered by many other plants.

Some plants are used as "trap" crops so that when grown near more valuable plants, they will attract harmful insects away. But as a general rule, plants that attract the same harmful insects should not be grown close together or they will invite a proliferation of the pest.

Even fairly large animals can be discouraged by companion planting. Rabbits dislike onions, so garlic and chives are usually grown with the leafy greens rabbits like so well. Rue, a hardy blue-green herb, is said to repel cats, and pot marigolds keep dogs away.

Some of the plants that are commonly believed to benefit each other are in the accompanying chart. Those that do well when grown together are shown by a +. Those that should *not* be grown near each other are marked by an 0.

	Basil	Beans, bush	Beans, pole	Beets	Cabbage family	Carrots	Celery	Corn	Cucumbers	Eggplant	Lettuce	Marigolds	Melons	Nasturtiums	Onions	Parsley	Peas	Peppers	Pigweed	Radishes	Sage	Spinach	Squash	Strawberries	Tomatoes
Beans, bush				0	0	0	0	0	0	0	0	0			+		0			0				0	
Beans, pole						0		0	0	0	0	0			+		0			0					
Beets		0			0										0						0				
Cabbage family		0		0			0					0		0	0						0			+	
Carrots		0	0								0				0		0			0	0				0
Celery		0			0										0							0			0
Corn		0	0						0				0				0		0				0		+
Cucumbers		0	0					0			0	0		0	0		0			0	+				
Eggplant		0	0																0			0			
Lettuce		0	0			0			0						0					0				0	
Melons								0						0						0					
Onions		+	+	0	0	0	0		0		0						+	0	0				0	0	0
Peas		0	0			0		0	0						+					0					
Peppers	0														0				0						
Radishes		0	0			0			0		0		0	0			0		0				0		
Spinach							0			0														0	
Squash								0						0	0					0					
Strawberries		0			+						0	0			0							0			
Tomatoes	0					0	0	+				0		0	0	0			0						

+ *Good Companions*

0 *Bad Companions*

CHAPTER 6

PLANT PROPAGATION

For Derry, one of the major joys of having a greenhouse is plant propagation. Watching the leaves of seedlings unfold day by day, feeling the resistance of the well-rooted cutting as you try to ease it out of its compost, even the lumpy swellings of callous at the base of an unrooted cutting where the roots will soon break forth, touch her in the same way as the faces of our sleeping children. But unlike children, young plants are appreciative. They respond quickly to your care and don't whine or argue. Infant plants want to grow; all you have to do is supply the bare necessities of life—moisture, air, warmth, and, once growth has begun, food and light—then step back and bask in their grateful response.

SEEDS

There are basically two ways in which new plants are created: sexually, by seeds, and asexually, by the rooting of pieces of the original plant. Making seeds is the primary way plants reproduce themselves. Because seeds are the result of a sexual union between the pollen and the ovary of (usually) different plants, the genes of the parent plants are combined in the offspring. The enormous number of possible combinations of genes produces a wide range of offspring, all slightly different, some of which may be better suited to the prevailing conditions. This possibility of genetic variation is one reason why seeds are the primary form of reproduction for most plants. Other reasons are the very large number of seeds one plant can produce, the ease with which they can be dispersed (spread over the widest area to maximize their chances of success), and the fact that pests and diseases are not passed to the offspring.

For thousands of years people have saved the seeds produced naturally by plants useful to them. By saving seeds from the best plants each year, any accidental genetic improvements were fostered. Strains of plants that grow better in a particular area were developed locally by continual selection of the strongest plants.

SAVING YOUR OWN SEEDS

Seed saving from open-pollinated varieties of plants is well worthwhile. Almost all old-fashioned varieties are open-pollinated and a good seed catalog will state which of their new varieties are hybrid. Gather the seeds when fully ripe, usually when the husk has dried. Remove any husks,

F-1 SEEDS

F-1 seed has been very carefully pollinated from specially bred plants and should be almost completely uniform (the range of genes has been much reduced by inbreeding) and very vigorous. It is very expensive compared to open-pollinated seed (which is produced in abundance in nature without human assistance) but it is often worth using in a greenhouse where space is limited and you want every plant to be as nearly perfect as possible. If you can get three crops of hybrid lettuce from the same ground in the same time it takes to grow two crops of open-pollinated lettuce, then it is definitely worthwhile.

Some of the advantages bred into F-1 seeds are very valuable. Improved color or shape in flowers, improved flavor in vegetables, earlier cropping, or improved disease resistance, may be well worth paying extra for. But some characteristics bred into F-1 hybrids are only of value to commercial growers. Uniformity of size and cropping dates, ease of machine harvesting and long shelf life after harvest are not important factors for most home gardeners. So choose your variety with care. One drawback to F-1 hybrids is that you cannot save seeds from your own plants for use next year as they do not breed true.

SILICA GEL

Silica gel is a dessicant, that is, it absorbs moisture from other things, drying them out. It usually comes with blue indicator paper that turns pink when the silica has absorbed all the water it can. If this happens, a warm place (on a radiator, or in an oven set at 200°F.) to dry out. It is an inert material and can be used over and over again indefinitely. It is very good for drying flowers as well as seeds.

leaves, or bits of extraneous matter by rubbing the seeds between your hands to break up any large pieces, then blowing the debris away. Most seeds are relatively heavy so this crude winnowing works just as it does for grain in traditional peasant cultures. Tomatoes and other watery fruits, however, are gathered dead ripe, allowed to stand until they ferment a bit, mashed and washed through a sieve. When the seeds are clean, dry them in a thin layer of newspaper.

STORING SEEDS

Traditionally the seed is then put in paper bags, labeled and hung up in a cool, dry, dark place until needed. Cool, dry, dark places with room for festoons of paper bags are not much in evidence in our house, so Derry uses a more modern and spacesaving technique. Put each kind of seed into a small envelope, seal it and write the name of the seed, the date harvested, and the date to be sown on the front (this last saves looking it up in the mad March rush). Have ready a plastic container with about half a cup of silica gel in a fabric bag at the bottom. Derry buys the gel in a two-pound bag and makes smaller bags for it out of old sheets.

Put the seeds in one box with the silica. After a few days, assuming the indicator paper is still blue, you can be sure the seeds are perfectly dry. They can now be stored in any cool place; in fact, the colder the better. An outdoor shed, an unheated bedroom, the refrigerator are all fine. Derry keeps hers in the deep freeze where they should last for at least a hundred years. They can be removed from the freezer, used, resealed, dried out again, and replaced in the freezer over and over again without appreciably diminishing their lives. The only proviso is that they must be perfectly dry when frozen or else the moisture may burst the cell walls, killing the seed. Derry keeps one box of silica in the freezer and one next to the freezer for seeds in transition. There are very few seeds that do not like being dry frozen. Magnolias and nuts won't stand for it, and lettuce is not perfectly happy about it, but almost all other seeds survive beautifully. The seeds for worldwide gene banks are stored in this way, using liquid nitrogen to reduce the temperature even further.

GERMINATION

For storage, seeds need to be cold and dry and ideally short of oxygen. To germinate they need the opposite conditions—warm, moist, and plenty of oxygen. When a seed begins to grow it is working very hard. It burns the carbohydrates stored inside it to get the energy for growth. Respiration uses oxygen and gives off carbon dioxide. So a germinating seed needs to have free access to air, which will supply oxygen and allow the carbon dioxide to diffuse.

SEED COMPOST

The ideal compost for starting seeds is always described as "well-drained and moisture-retentive," which sounds like a contradiction in terms. This really means compost that will hold both air and water. A well-drained compost has many fairly large holes in it, holes too big to hold water by capillarity. Water will drain out of these holes due to the force of gravity, and air will then fill them. Water is held in the smaller holes by capillary action. The ideal compost then is made up of moisture-retentive material which does not pack together tightly, but leaves plenty of large pore spaces between the particles.

Any moisture-retentive material—such as peat, vermiculite, or compost—can be used. Usually the drainage needs to be improved by adding some sharp sand, coarse grit, or perlite. Seeds do not need nutrients to germinate but they do need nutrients soon after. A rich soil should not be used as the salts in the soil solution (the nutrients) will exert too much osmotic pressure and make it difficult for the seedling to take in the water it needs. Phosphorus is the first thing the growing roots need, so a sprinkling of superphosphate is usually added to seed compost.

Derry uses her ordinary potting compost with an equal amount of cutting compost left over from her last batch of cuttings (this is equivalent to a mixture of two parts potting compost: one part peat, one part sharp sand by volume). If using garden soil, then pasteurize it and use a mixture of one part soil, two parts peat, and one part sharp sand. Pure vermiculite is quite good for getting seeds to germinate, but they need to be fed a very dilute fertilizer or transplanted to something a bit more nutritious as soon as they germinate.

Young seedlings are very prone to damping-off disease, a group of fungi which cause the stem to rot at soil level and the seedling (or sometimes the whole tray of seedlings) to collapse suddenly, never to recover. Overcrowding and lack of air movement contribute to damping-off disease, but the basic fungal spores are much more likely to be present in unsterilized soil. Sphagnum peat inhibits damping-off fungi, so it should always be included in seed composts. Many people use finely milled peat to cover the seeds as an added precaution, but if it dries out it is a nuisance to rewet. Chamomile tea or a 10 percent solution of vinegar watered on seed flats also helps the battle against fungi.

Seedlings are more susceptible to almost all pests and diseases than are mature plants. Not much soil is needed to produce many small plants, so it is well worth sterlizing seed compost. Weeds have a way of germinating faster and thicker than prize seeds, and to the inexperienced eye they can be difficult to distinguish.

Some seeds have very specialized requirements for periods of hot or cold, wet or dry, light or dark, or even just the passage of time, before they will germinate, but the vast majority of seeds will burst into life very readily given a few weeks in that "well-drained, moisture-retentive" warm compost. Most germinate more readily at a temperature slightly higher than the temperature at which they like to grow.

SOWING SEEDS

Given fresh, or well-stored, viable seed and a sterile, well-drained, moisture-retentive compost, what next? Take a clean shallow container, about 2 inches deep, with plenty of holes in the bottom for the water to drain, and fill it to overflowing with compost. The container should not be too flexible or cracks will develop in the compost from being readjusted every time the container is moved. Sturdy seed trays designed for the purpose are wonderful, but the shallow wooden flats used for transporting peaches and tomatoes are fine. Sometimes a few extra bits of wood or newspaper are needed to block up any large holes in the bottom. If no shallow containers are available, build up the level with a sheet of styrofoam or a layer of perlite or whatever is handy. The top of the compost should not be more than 1/4 inch below the top of the container or air circulation will be impeded and fungal diseases will be encouraged. And there is no reason to waste the compost by making it too deep, since the seedlings should be transplanted to a richer soil before their roots get 3 inches long. Fastgrowing plants such as squash, and ones that do not like being transplanted, such as beans and corn, are best started in individual 3-inch pots.

Fill the container, tap it sharply to settle the compost, level it off, preferably by scraping off the excess with a straight board laid across the top of the container, then tamp the compost down. Derry usually just pats it with her hands, but the best thing is to make a tamping board just slightly smaller than the container and press that gently onto the compost. The idea is to get the compost level and evenly firmed without compacting it too much (Figure 6.1).

Next comes a very important step. Write your label with the name of the seed, date, and any comments, like "two-year-old seed" or "pinch at 2 inches" or "shade lightly." It is astonishing what you can forget in two months. You are almost sure to find something to confuse it with, if it isn't carefully labeled.

Then sow the seed thinly. It is an art to use few enough seedlings. They will be healthier and you will be happier if you have twelve rather than twelve hundred. Very fine seeds like impatiens and primrose are just sprinkled on the surface and pressed gently in. Most seeds are sprinkled on and about 1/4 inch of compost sieved or sprinkled over them. Larger seeds need a tiny trench raked for them so they will be covered to about twice their depth when the tray is filled. Tamp the surface down very gently, with the tamping board if you have one.

Water with a very fine hose or, better, set the container in a tub to soak until the surface glistens. Some people soak the compost before sowing the seeds, but Derry finds it much easier to work with soil which is just damp. Leave to drain thoroughly, then put in a warm place (60° to 80°F. depending on the seeds).

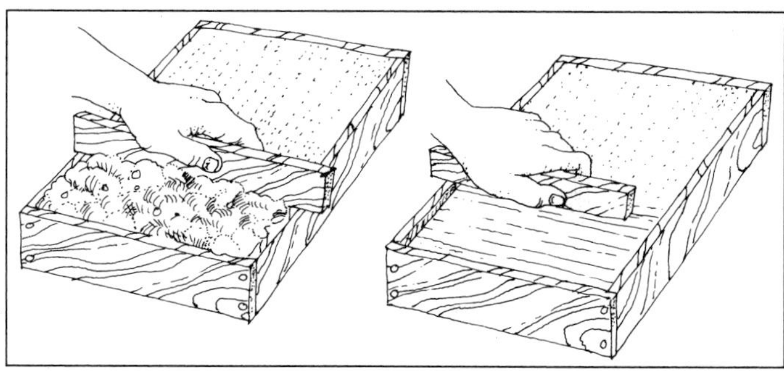

6.1 ▲ Fill the container with compost, tap it on a hard surface, level it off, and tamp down gently and evenly.

Most seeds don't mind if it's light or dark at this point, but some are fussy, so check the seed packet or a garden encyclopedia. Don't leave them in full sun as the surface of the compost will dry out too rapidly and strong sunlight may scorch emerging seedlings. Old books recommend covering with a layer of glass and turning the glass daily to keep the humidity high until they germinate. Derry just puts the container under a bench in the greenhouse with any other seed trays, with a sheet of plastic in front of the bench to make a damp, shady tent for them. In winter and early spring she puts a heating cable under the trays to keep the soil temperature up. Seeds that need a lot of heat (usually those from tropical climates), she brings into the warmest part of the house.

After five or six days the seeds should be checked daily and *as soon as* they begin to germinate they should be brought into an area of good indirect light where it is still fairly warm and moist. Within a week they should be given the best conditions you can find. Warmth and sunshine at this early stage will pay dividends later.

As soon as they are big enough to handle, usually when the first true leaves as opposed to seed leaves have developed, transplant them individually into potting compost. For most plants use a similar tray, perhaps 3 inches deep, and "prick out" the seedlings about 2 inches apart (Figure 6.2). Fast-growing plants such as tomatoes can be set in individual 3-inch pots at this point.

Hold the seedlings by a leaf—use a seed leaf if possible as these will never grow very big—to avoid damaging the stem. Any check to their growth now will have permanent effects. The aim is to create sturdy, bushy seedlings growing steadily, each one with plenty of air, light, and food. Given this they can astonish you with the speed at which they grow.

CUTTINGS

Nature does not use many cuttings. Occasionally a broken-off bit of branch will root, or a piece of root dug up by an animal will grow somewhere else. Some plants root where a stem touches the ground, some make runners and small plantlets and some send up suckers or underground stems to colonize new areas. But by and large most plants reproduce by seed in nature.

For the gardener a cutting has certain advantages. Because it is an asexual form of reproduction, the new plant has the same genes as its parents and is therefore identical. Usually a plant from a cutting will reach maturity sooner than a plant from seed. Many special, highly bred plants do not set seed, or the seed won't germinate or won't come true to type, so they can only be reproduced from cuttings. Other plants are reluctant to set seed in the particular climate you live in, or may not have ripe seed at the moment you have access to them in a friend's garden. (Derry hardly ever walks around a gardener's garden without wanting a little piece of this or that. A cutting is the ideal gift from one gardener to another—no trouble to the giver and highly desired by the receiver.) Ideally cuttings should be taken at the appropriate time of year for that plant, but it is always worth trying if you are offered a bit of something special.

The two major disadvantages of cuttings are the possibility of spreading disease by propagating from a diseased plant, and the reluctance of some plants to root. By taking care to use only healthy plant material and by avoiding fussy plants you should avoid most of the problems. Unfortunately most books are not very helpful about the ease with which cuttings root—but you can be sure common plants are easy to propagate either by seeds or cuttings, and with unusual plants, sad experience will gradually teach you.

HOW CUTTINGS ROOT

Both new roots and shoots are produced from meristem tissue, specialized areas where cells divide, producing new cells. Meristem tissue can develop into roots, shoots, or flowers depending on the needs of the plant. It is found mostly in leaf axils and at nodes on both roots and stems, as well as at the growing tips of roots and shoots. Special plant hormones are present near the meristem tissue to encourage faster cell division. For most plants, if the right kind of cutting is taken at the right time of year, sufficient hormones will be present for quick rooting. But as an insurance policy many people dip the cut end into a hormone rooting powder. Use the recommended strength for each plant, usually .3 to .8 percent, as too strong a concentration can dehydrate the base of the cutting. Tap the cutting after dipping it to knock off any excess powder. A good rooting powder will include a fungicide, which is at least as important as the hormone in increasing the cutting's chance of a success.

6.2 ▼ Make a hole in the compost. Holding the seedling by one leaf, lower it until it is at the same level it was before. Firm compost around the roots.

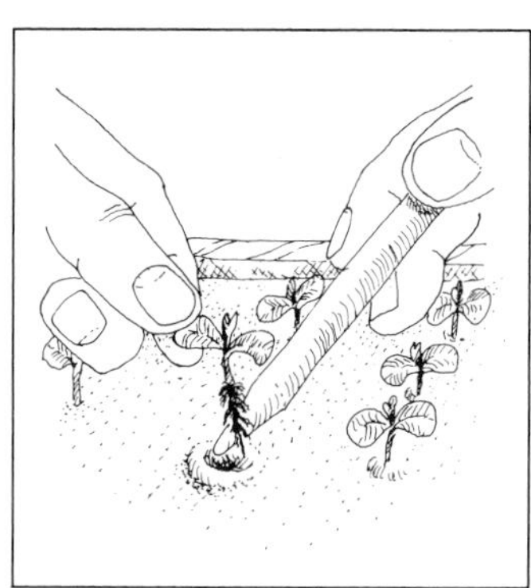

6.3 ▲ Take softwood cuttings just below the fourth or fifth node, and remove bottom leaves and stipules.

TYPES OF CUTTINGS

There are endless types of cuttings depending on the part of the plant—leaf, stem, branch, root—the time of year, the size and shape of the cutting, and so on. But all basically involve taking a small piece of the mother plant and keeping it warm with plenty of air and water while it produces roots and shoots, i.e., stems and leaves.

■ STEM CUTTINGS are the most common and there are three basic types:

Softwood cuttings.
Two to 5 inches taken from new soft growth in April or May. With easy-to-root plants like fuchsias, geraniums, and impatiens, they can be taken at any time the plant is in active growth. Usually best cut just below a node. Need considerable warmth (Figure 6.3).

Semihardwood cuttings.
Four to 6 inches, slightly older, firmer growth, taken in summer. Shoots are ready if they snap when bent. Basal cuttings (cut through the swelling at the base of the shoot, where it joins the stem), and heel cuttings (pulled off with a tiny bit of the stem wood attached to the base of the shoot—especially good for evergreen and hollow-stemmed plants) are usually taken from semihard wood. The soft tip of the cutting can be removed if de-

sired. Benefit from some warmth (Figure 6.4).

Hardwood cuttings.
Six to 10 inches of fully ripened mature wood of this year's growth taken after leaf fall and before growth resumes in the spring (generally November to February). The soft growth at the tip of the stem is often removed just above a node. Hormone rooting powder is not needed. Usually buried to half their length or more in a cold frame and left until the following autumn when they should be ready to transplant. Need to be kept cold initially to prevent leaf buds from developing before roots. Bougainvillea and many hardy shrubs and trees are propagated from these dormant shoots (Figure 6.5).

Eye cuttings
are a special form of stem cutting using just one or two nodes. A short section of thick, fairly mature stem is placed horizontally in the compost so just the "eye," the dormant bud on the stem, shows. A strip of bark is sometimes removed from the opposite side of the stem to facilitate rooting. Where propagating material is scarce, every node can be made to produce a plant with this method, but for most plants it is slower and less reliable than ordinary stem cuttings. Grapes, however, are often propagated from eye cuttings taken in early spring. Cordylines and dracaenas also respond well (Figure 6.6).

Layering
is another special form of stem cutting. The stem is induced to root while still attached to the parent plant—an uncut cutting, so to speak. Many stems will root wherever they happen to touch the ground, but more resistant plants can be induced to root by slitting the stem, dipping it in rooting powder and burying it in the compost. Bend up the tip to make it vertical. The slit should be on the outside of the curve so it tends to stay open. It often helps to pin

6.4 ▲ Heel cuttings are pulled off the parent plant. Trim off the ragged bits.

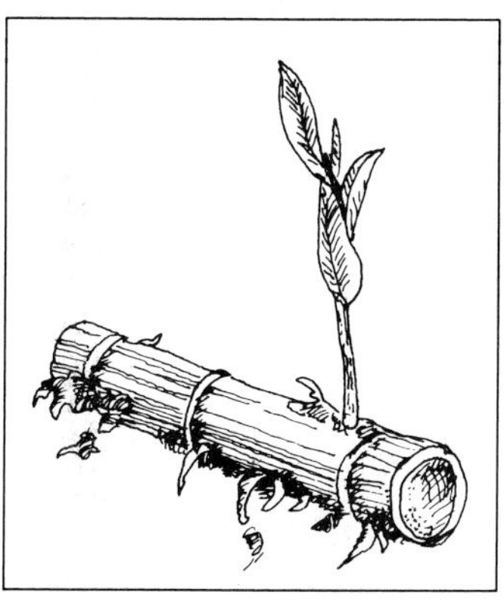

6.6 ▲ A thick section of mature stem is laid on one side to make an eye cutting. Roots emerge from the bottom and shoots from the top, often from the same node.

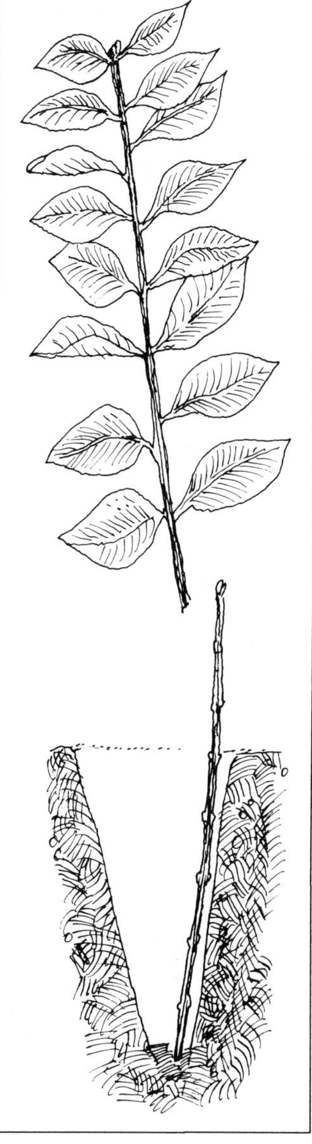

6.5 ◀ Hardwood cuttings are taken when the plant is dormant. Remove all leaves and bury most of stem.

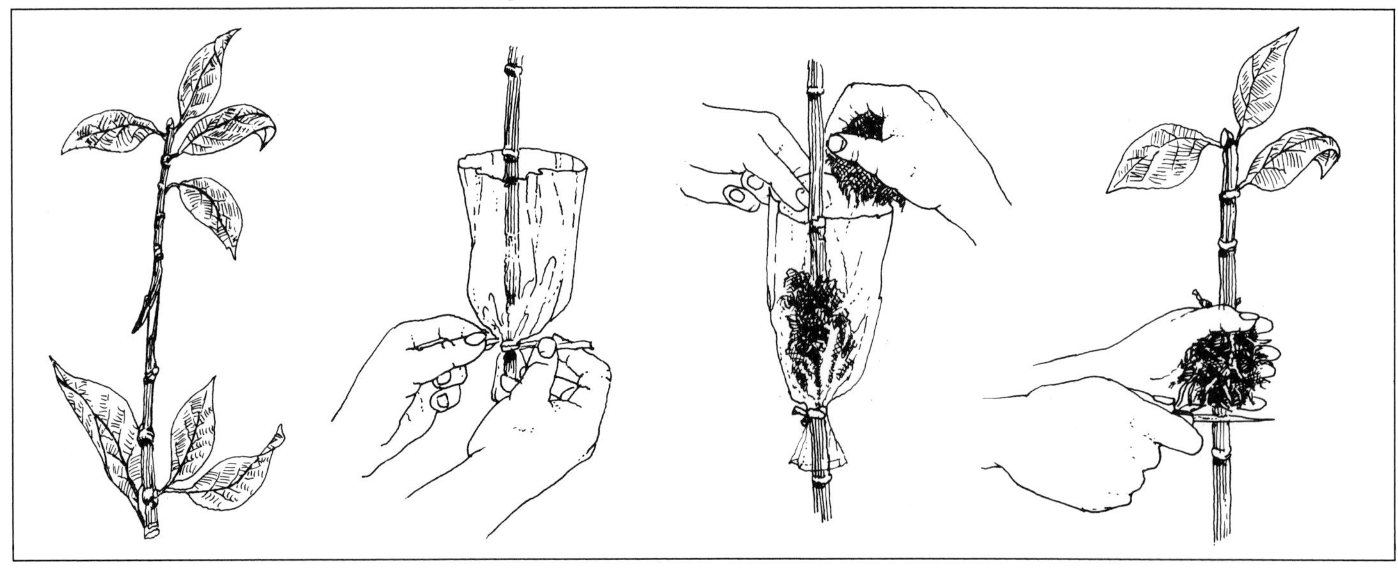

6.7 ▲ **Layering is an easy form of propagation. Tying the tips to little stakes helps to prevent the young roots being disturbed.**

the stem in place with a piece of wire or a stone (Figure 6.7).

If the stem cannot be attached to the earth, the earth can be brought up to it in an "air layer." Cut upward into the stem at an angle without severing it and stuff a matchstick or a bit of peat moss into the slit to hold it open. More drastic, but often more effective, is girdling the stem by removing a 3/4-inch strip of bark all the way around it. It seems as though this should kill it, but actually it builds up big food reserves above the wound by preventing carbohydrates formed in the leaves from being transported to other parts of the plant. A piece of plastic is then tied around the stem below the wound. It is stuffed full of cutting compost or peat moss and is tied again above the wound to make a neat package (Figure 6.8). Rooting may take over a year. When good roots have formed, the stem attaching the layer to the parent plant is severed; when that wound has healed, the layer is potted in seed compost.

6.8 ▲ Air layers are stems that are wounded, then encouraged to root while still on the plant.

■ LEAF CUTTINGS.

Many tropical and subtropical houseplants with fleshy leaves (begonias, streptocarpus, African violets, etc.) are best propagated by leaf cuttings. A single leaf is inserted in the compost, stalk downward. Large leaves may be cut into sections. By nicking the large rib veins on a rex begonia or cutting the whole leaf into small squares, many small plants can be produced from one leaf. Leaf cuttings, like the plants they come from, need considerable warmth (Figure 6.9).

Leaf bud cuttings
are rather like heel cuttings of a single leaf. They are often used for camellias. Cut off a mature leaf by slicing a sliver of wood from the stem. The dormant bud nestling at the base of the leaf stalk will form the new plant (Figure 6.10). A short section of stem with a leaf attached may be used instead if you don't mind cutting into the stem. This is called a "mallet cutting" and seems to help reduce the likelihood of rotting. Bury the bit of stem and leaf stalk in the compost so just the leaf shows.

■ ROOT CUTTINGS.
Many herbaceous perennials and especially shrubs are propagated by root cuttings, eliminating any pests or diseases that infect only the upper part of the plant. Use neither the smallest nor the largest roots; generally 1/4 to 1/2 inch thick is best. Cut straight off at the top and on a slant at the bottom, to be sure not to put them in upside down. They are inserted slanted end down in the compost and can be left in a cold frame until they are ready to transplant. Thin, fibrous roots, like phlox has, are cut in 2-inch sections and laid horizontally on the compost, then covered with 1/4 inch of sand. Root cuttings are usually best taken in winter when the plant is dormant. They need no extra heat (Figure 6.11).

■ DIVISION.
Division is really a crude form of cutting that takes advantage of the fact that as most herbaceous perennial plants grow they throw out new shoots from

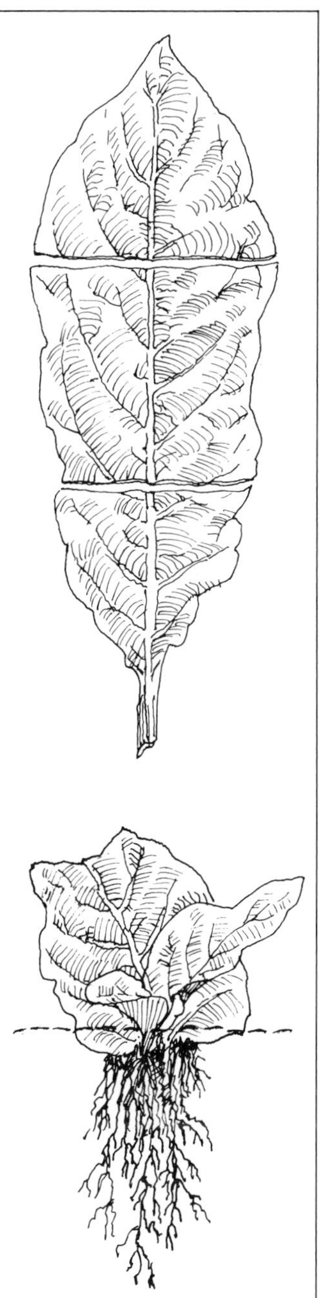

6.9 ▲ Leaf cuttings usually root easily; some, like African violets, will root in water. Large leaves can be cut into 2-inch sections, but be sure to insert them the right way up.

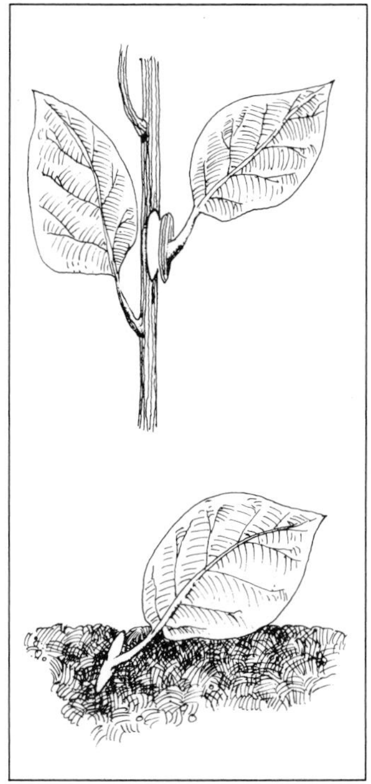

6.10 ▲ Leaf bud cuttings use a mature leaf attached to a sliver of the parent stem.

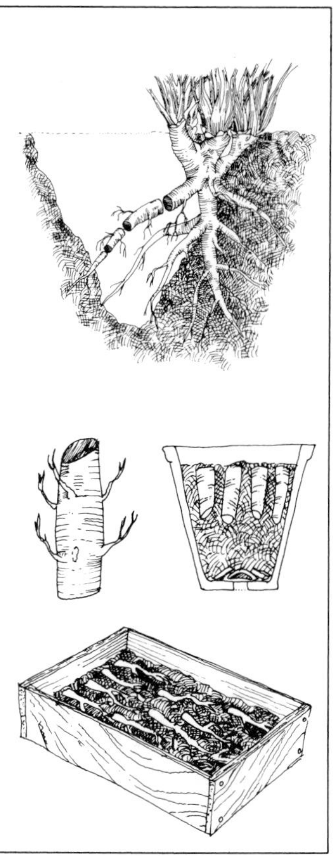

6.11 ▲ Root cuttings are always cut straight across the top and angled at the bottom so you know which way up to plant them. Bury them so just the top is exposed, then cover with 1/4 inch of sharp sand.

the base and spread sideways. These shoots form ready-rooted cuttings. Simply knock the plant out of its pot (or dig it up) and break it into several pieces, each with roots attached. A knife may be necessary to cut through the woody center section, which should be discarded. The young shoots round the outside will be more vigorous. Each shoot, or bunch of shoots, can then be potted. They will need protection from full sun for several days, but since they already have roots, they will not need to be cosseted nearly as carefully as ordinary cuttings. Not so many new plants can be made by dividing one plant as by taking cuttings from it, but they are easy and grow to flowering size very quickly (Figure 6.12).

TAKING CUTTINGS

Take cuttings only from healthy plants. Select sturdy shoots typical of the plant, unless you want to propagate an interesting variation. Usually juvenile shoots root better than mature ones. Commercial greenhouses keep "stock plants" specially for producing cuttings. They are pruned hard so they produce many young shoots. Once flowers have begun to form, root-inhibiting hormones begin to circulate in the plant, making propagation more difficult.

The larger the cutting the quicker it will grow into a mature plant, but above a certain size it will be more difficult to keep it alive while it is rooting. Too large a cutting will need more water than the naked stem can absorb. Too small a cutting will have insufficient food reserves to tide it over. For every plant there is an optimum size of cutting. Generally about six buds, or nodes, are needed—three above ground to make shoots and three below ground to make roots.

For all cuttings cleanliness is important to reduce the risk of disease. Spraying the plant with a fungicide before taking cuttings or immersing the cuttings in a fungicide solution is a useful precaution to reduce disease. A clean and very sharp knife is essential. Professionals dip their knives into a sterlizing solution between cuts to avoid passing disease from one plant to the next. The sharper the knife, the cleaner the cut and the smaller the area which must heal over before rooting can begin.

Cuttings are best taken in early morning the day after a plant has been well soaked so that the stems are fully turgid. Try to take cuttings with one quick, clean slice just below a node. Some people find it easier to make them slightly too long and then cut them to the right size later using a razor blade on a hard surface.

Cuttings of succulents are usually allowed to dry for a day or two in a shady place so the cut end can heal over. All other cuttings should be inserted in a rooting compost as soon as possible after they are taken. They do best in a very moisture-retentive, free-draining compost, pasteurized if possible to reduce the fungal infections which cause rotting. Cuttings need no nutrients until their roots have developed; in fact, any nutrient in the compost will impede their ability to take up the water they need. Half peat and half sharp (gritty, coarse) sand is the usual mixture for cuttings, but pure vermiculite or perlite does just as well. Some cuttings can be rooted in pure sand or even in pure water. They are not fussy as long as there is plenty of air and moisture and no competition from pests and diseases.

The compost should be leveled off within a quarter-inch of the top of the container. Pick up the container and knock it gently on a hard surface once or twice to settle the contents. Then make a hole with a dibber about the same length of the stem to be inserted. Any clean object about the diame-

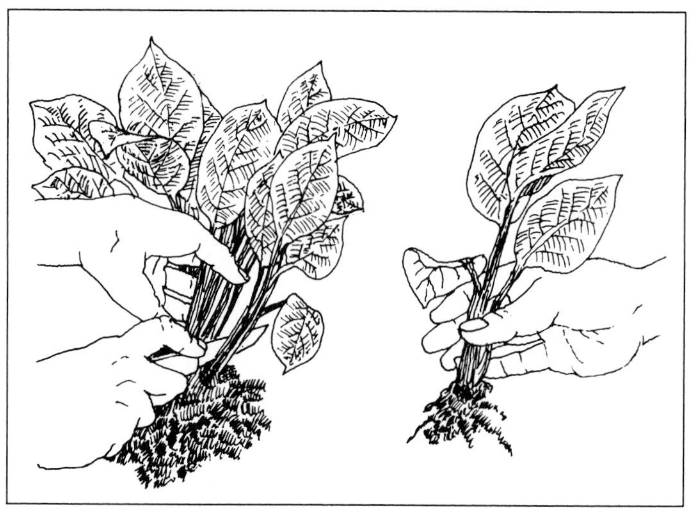

6.12 ▲ To divide a plant, dig it up and break it into several pieces each with some roots and leaves (or growing points, if the plant is dormant) attached.

6.13 ▲ To make a miniature propagating case, bend two wires into a U-shape and insert the ends in the container. Cover with a plastic bag, and tie it around the bottom to keep it airtight.

KEEPING CUTTINGS FRESH

If the cuttings cannot be dealt with immediately, put them in a plastic bag. Blow the bag up like a balloon and seal it. The humidity and carbon dioxide from your breath will help keep the cuttings in good condition for a few days, if kept cool. A refrigerator will help to keep them fresh longer. (Salad greens dipped in water and shaken off will keep much better if treated the same way, and limp greens will revive to some extent.

ter of the stem of the cutting will do, but a proper dibber for small cuttings is like a pencil with two ends, 1/8 inch in diameter at one end and 1/3 inch in diameter at the other.

Remove the bottom few leaves and stipules (the little leaflike growths at the base of the leaf stalk) from the cutting so that one-third its length is bare. If the remaining leaves are very large, one or two can be removed or reduced in size. Dip the bottom end in rooting powder, knock off any excess, and insert it in the hole. Firm the compost in around the cutting so that it makes good contact. Place cuttings close together but not touching. Label carefully, including date. Soak the container until the compost glistens, and drain well.

The cuttings should be kept in a moist, warm atmosphere, in good light but out of direct sun until the new roots are well developed. If only a few cuttings are being taken, a shallow plastic bulb pot can be used with four or five cuttings inserted around the edge. Put the whole thing in a plastic bag and blow the bag up like a balloon, sealing it when it is fully inflated. Alternatively two wires bent into a U-shape and inserted in the pot will ensure that the bag does not accidentally touch the leaves (Figure 6.13). For larger numbers of cuttings a propagator should be used. This can be as simple as a tomato box filled with compost and inserted in a large plastic bag. Two wire coat hangers bent to shape and inserted along either side will keep the plastic up off the cuttings. Commercially available propagators, consisting of a plastic seed tray and clear plastic domed top with adjustable vents, are very useful (Figure 6.14).

Cuttings root best with "warm feet and cool heads," so try to apply any heat from below. Pots or boxes or propagators can be placed on soil-heating cables, on a propagating mat, or on top of water storage barrels to provide a bit of bottom heat. For a slightly larger initial investment, you can buy a heated propagator with its own soil-warming cables on a thermostat.

Most cuttings of garden plants are taken in July, August, and September. For this busy period Derry rigs up a special propagating case by draping plastic sheets around a big folding table. Box after box of cuttings fit under there, and though it is quite dark they seem to root fast enough to survive on their summer food reserves. For use later in the year Derry puts a set of soil-heating cables under the boxes, but lack of light seems more critical then. A pair of fluorescent tubes under the table would perfect the set-up. A few plants, like geraniums, prefer a less humid atmosphere. Any warm corner out of direct sun will do for them.

The cuttings can safely be left unattended in a warm place away from direct sunlight for two to three weeks. After that time check weekly to be sure the compost has not dried out. It will dry very much faster if there is a source of bottom heat or if the cover is not airtight. The cuttings need water, but the soil can be allowed to get dry enough to feel barely moist when pressed. If it is too wet and soggy for long the stem won't get the air it needs and will quickly rot. Forming roots is hard work. It uses up the oxygen in the soil. This will be replenished from the oxygen given off by the slowly photosynthesizing leaves, but only if air can get in and out of the compost.

MIST UNITS

For more difficult cuttings, faster rooting, and closer to a 100 percent success rate with easy cuttings, you can set up a mist propagating unit. Fine misting creates a film of water on the leaves of the cuttings so water loss is reduced almost to zero. As a result the cuttings can be placed in full sunlight and will continue to photosynthesize. All the cutting's energy goes into rooting rather than just into staying alive. A few plants, particularly those with woolly leaves, don't like mist and will rot, but most thrive. Bottom heat and good drainage are essential. The misting can be controlled by a time clock, or more accurately with an "artificial leaf" that causes the mister to turn on whenever its surface dries out. Soft water is a must for success with a mister, as the fine nozzle is easily clogged. It should be checked regularly.

POTTING

When new growth begins to appear—two to three weeks for some softwood cuttings, a bit longer for most cuttings, but up to a year for some resistant shrubs—ease a cutting up from below, taking care not to damage any small roots (vermiculite is particularly good at releasing the new roots without damage). If any roots are visible the cutting can be potted, but it is best to wait till the roots are 1/2 to 1 inch long. If no roots are showing put the cutting back and wait a few weeks before checking its neighbors. If conditions are good, most cuttings of a particular plant should be ready to pot within a week or two of each other.

Carefully pot each cutting individually, disturbing the roots as little as possible. Half-fill the pot with a potting compost which is not too rich (Derry usually uses a mixture of one-third to one-half cutting compost mixed with ordinary potting compost). Insert the cutting, fill in around it with more compost, trying to keep the cutting centered and upright. Give the pot a sharp tap to settle the soil and lightly firm the compost with the tips of your fingers (Figure 6.15).

Soak the newly potted cuttings and allow to drain. Then put them back in a humid, warm atmosphere for a few days to recover from the shock. Gradually harden them off, moving them out into the open, but shade from direct sun for a few weeks until well-established.

Softwood cuttings usually root very quickly, often within a few weeks. The harder the wood of the cutting, the longer it takes to root but the less heat it needs. If semihard or hardwood cuttings root but fail to grow well when potted, next time try leaving them in the rooting compost for a growing season before potting. They will need to be fed regularly as there are no nutrients in the compost, but make sure the fertilizer is very dilute so that it does not burn the young roots.

With even a modicum of success you should soon have enough plants to supply yourself, your friends and neighbors, and most of the people you meet. ■

CHAPTER 7

PESTS AND DISEASES

From time to time every greenhouse gardener finds a plant overrun by insects or infected with some serious disease. Greenhouses provide good growing conditions for pests as well as for plants, but a well-run greenhouse is much less susceptible to calamity. Healthy, fast-growing plants are less attractive to insects and can resist many diseases.

Good ventilation and good sanitation are probably the two key factors in reducing the incidence of pests and diseases in the greenhouse. Fungus diseases especially, but also many pests, are encouraged by stagnant, moist air conditions. Open the vents for half an hour in the afternoon even on cold days to dry out the air before the night chill sets in. A slow circulating fan is helpful in winter to keep the air moving when the vents are closed.

A clean, tidy sunspace will house fewer problems than a messy one. Dead leaves, bits of litter, even old pots left lying about form breeding places for pests and harbor the spores that will reinfect even the most carefully pasteurized soil. Weeds allowed to grow under the benches can hide pests you have eliminated in the rest of the sunspace.

Once a year scrub the sunspace from top to bottom with a 10 percent bleach solution, making sure you clean all the glass and get into all the nooks and crannies. Empty the greenhouse first if possible; otherwise cover the plants with sheets of plastic to protect them from drips and splashes. Fumigate if you have had a bad infestation. Washing the glass periodically during the rest of the year will improve light transmission and decrease chances of condensation dripping on plants.

Use only clean pots for repotting. After scrubbing used pots, sterilize them by soaking in a solution of one part bleach to nine parts water. Old clay pots covered with a hard white encrustation, due to hard water or excess fertilizer salts, should be scraped clean if possible. Otherwise the crust will prevent air and water from passing through the clay, and roots are more likely to be torn when repotting.

Using pasteurized soil for seeds and cuttings will help eliminate almost all the diseases young plants are prone to. Once they are growing sturdily, potting in pasteurized soil is not necessary, but it is still a wise precaution, especially if you have had a serious disease in your greenhouse in the last year. Pasteurized soil also eliminates the problem of weeding for some time until new weed seeds gradually drift in. The same crop should never be grown for more than a year or two in the soil of the border unless you are able to pasteurize it in some way, because the pests and disease that attack that plant are bound to increase year by year.

Set newly potted plants in water halfway up the sides of the pot until the soil glistens with moisture. Leave clay pots in a few hours longer to be sure the pot itself is thoroughly wet and will not draw moisture from the soil. When bringing in plants that have spent the summer outdoors, soak them to the rim overnight to drown any insects in the soil.

Besides the damage they do in their own right, sucking insects such as aphids and whitefly frequently carry diseases from one plant to another, so controlling the insect population is another way of preventing the spread of disease. Because plant sap contains relatively few amino acids, most sap-sucking insects must drink a great deal of sap in order to get enough amino acids to manufacture proteins for growth. Plant sap is rich in simple sugars, so they get more sugar than they need and they excrete the excess, which drips onto lower leaves, forming "honeydew." The sugary honeydew dries on and clogs the pores in the leaf. It is also an ideal medium for the growth of unsightly black molds. These "sooty molds" will not harm the plant themselves, but they reduce the amount of light reaching the leaf and so the amount of photosynthesis. Sooty molds are a classic sign of insect trouble, so always investigate the cause.

Checking each plant individually and thoroughly at frequent intervals will almost always reveal any problem at a stage where it can easily be dealt with. Once an infestation is allowed to run rampant it is much more difficult to control, requiring strong chemicals or even the destruction of some of your favorite plants. If you can catch it when it is just beginning, most problems can be cured, and they can certainly be prevented from spreading to other plants. For this reason it is important to check any new plant carefully before allowing it into your greenhouse. It is a good idea to keep new plants separate for a week or two to be sure they do not develop any problems they might pass on to their neighbors.

An isolation ward is also a good idea for any of your plants that look unhealthy. By keeping them separate until you have identified and dealt with the cause of their distress, you are sure to keep the problem under control. Badly infected plants should be destroyed. Even if you can cure the problems they have, they are likely to be so weakened that they will be susceptible to other problems for some time.

After inspecting a sick plant, wash your hands and any tools you have used before touching other plants, to prevent the problem from spreading. Do not handle plants when they are wet because diseases are transferred more easily then. And don't smoke in or near a greenhouse. If you have handled tobacco, wash your hands in skimmed milk before touching any tomato, pepper, petunia, or other related plants to avoid spreading tobacco mosaic virus.

Sprays are generally better than dusts for getting rid of insects, because they can reach the underside of leaves where most pests hide.

The addition of a little soap will make most sprays adhere better and penetrate the thin skins of many insects better. It is best to spray in the late afternoon when the sun is off the plants and the greenhouse can remain shut till morning. Always shut any doors and windows into the house. Wear a respirator, not a dust mask, even for relatively safe "botanical pesticides." Even ordinary soap is not very good for your lungs, and in the enclosed environment of a sunspace quite a high concentration of spray builds up in the air. Wear goggles if spraying overhead.

Be sure to dilute any spray to the recommended strength. More is *not* necessarily better. It is best to spray a few leaves of any unusual plant first to see if it has an adverse reaction. Flowers are often marked by sprays, but are usually quickly replaced. Wash out the sprayer thoroughly afterwards and wash off any exposed areas of the skin.

IDENTIFYING THE PROBLEM

The following tables list the most common symptoms that trouble plants indoors and give some of the possible causes. Only those causes that affect many varieties of plants are included. Every plant has some diseases or pests that are specific to it but that are not likely to occur unless you grow masses of that one plant. Commercial growers who have whole greenhouses devoted to a single crop are subject to all sorts of problems that hardly ever arise in the mixed culture of a domestic sunspace. If you want to concentrate on just one crop, or are especially interested in the health and well-being of one particular kind of plant, then it is worth investing in a specialist guide to growing that plant.

Those symptoms common to almost all plants affected by a particular insect or disease are listed first. But the same insect or disease sometimes produces different symptoms in different varieties of plants, and some of these distinctive symptoms follow, divided into vegetables, flowers, and fruits.

Each possible cause of a symptom is followed by a (P) or a (D) to indicate whether that problem is described in the Pests section (P) or the Diseases section (D). Some symptoms are due neither to a pest or to a disease, but rather to the wrong growing conditions, such as too little sun, too much water, or some imbalance in the soil fertility.

In the Pests and Diseases sections that follow we describe each problem and suggest some simple natural remedies. Several natural insecticides are described in the Natural Insecticides section and beneficial insects that prey on greenhouse pests in the Beneficial Insects section. For severe outbreaks it may be necessary to use stronger methods, but only resort to the really powerful chemical poisons in desperation. They are dangerous to you as well as to the beneficial insects, fungi, and bacteria in the sunspace. Beware of using poisonous chemicals on a plant you intend to eat.

SYMPTOMS COMMON TO MANY PLANTS

■ *Seedlings collapse*
Damping-off disease (D)
Fungus gnat larvae (P)

■ *Seedlings cut off at base*
Leatherjackets (P)
Millipedes (P)
Slugs (P)
Wood lice (P)

■ *Rot at base of stem, plant wilts and dies*
Stem rot or root rot (D)

■ *Plant pale and spindly*
Not enough sun

■ *Stunted growth*
Root aphids (see Aphids) (P)
Eelworms (P)
Fungus gnat larvae (P)
Leatherjackets (P)
Mealybugs in roots (P)
Symphilids (P)
Vine weevils (P)
Wireworms (P)

Aspermey (D)
Mosaic viruses (D)

■ *Bluish leaves*
Symphilids (P)
Phosphorus deficiency
Excess potash
Too cold

■ *Yellowing leaves and/or wilting in strong sun (probably the most common symptoms of distress in a plant, generally associated with some damage to the root system)*
Aphids (P)
Eelworms (P)
Leafhoppers (P)
Leatherjackets (P)
Millipedes (P)
Scale insects (P)
Spider mites (P)
Thrips (P)
Vine weevils (P)
Whitefly (P)
Wireworms (P)
Gray mold (D)
Stem or root rot (D)
Viruses (D)
Wilt (D)
Soil too alkaline
Soil compacted
Soil too dry
Soil consistently too wet
Cold soil and warm air
Sudden, excessive drop in temperature
Nitrogen deficiency
Too little light

■ *Yellowing leaves, but veins remain green*
Excess alkalinity
Iron deficiency in young leaves
Magnesium deficiency in older leaves

■ *Unusual color in leaves*
Viruses (D)

■ *Mottled leaves (usually light and dark green)*
Mosaic viruses (D)
Manganese deficiency (often due to excess acidity)
Spider mites (P)
Thrips (P)

■ *Unusual streaks on leaves*
Thrips (P)
Viruses (D)

■ *Yellow patches on leaves*
Aphids (P)
Leafhoppers (P)
Scale insects (P)
Whitefly (P)
Downy mildew (D)
Mosaic virus (D)

■ *Brown patches on leaves*
Eelworms (P)
Fungi (D)
Powdery mildew (D)
Too much sun on wet leaves
Prolonged magnesium deficiency

■ *Small brown spots on leaves*
Capsid bugs (P)

■ *Black specks on leaves*
Thrips (P)

■ *Brown patches on stem*
Eelworms (stem) (P)
Gray mold (D)
Stem rot (D)

■ *Brown, orange, or purple patches between leaf veins*
Eelworms (P)
Magnesium deficiency

■ *Watery spots on leaves or buds*
Eelworms (P)

■ *Pale swellings under leaves or on stems*
Prolonged overwatering
Air too humid

■ *Corky patches beneath leaves or on stems*
Prolonged overwatering
Air too humid

■ *Yellow, orange, or brown spore masses on leaves*
Rust (D)

■ *Stippled leaves*
Leafhoppers (P)
Spider mites (P)
Thrips (P)
Whitefly (P)

■ *Silvery leaves*
Thrips (P)

■ *Edges of leaves scorched*
Potash deficiency

■ *Tips of leaves withered*
Air too hot
Air too dry
Physical damage from being brushed against

■ *Growing tips pale and spindly*
Aphids (P)
Cuckoo spit (P)
Spider mites (P)

■ *Pale wiggly lines in leaf*
Leaf miners (P)

■ *Distorted leaves and buds*
Capsid bugs (P)
Cyclamen mites (P)
Eelworms (P)
Spider mites (P)
Thrips (P)
Viruses (D)

■ *Leaves curl*
Aphids (P)
Leaftiers (P)
Thrips (P)
Viruses (D)
Temperature fluctuates too much

■ *Malformed flowers*
Aphids (P)
Capsid bugs (P)
Cuckoo spit (P)
Cyclamen mites (P)
Eelworms (P)
Midge larvae (P)
Thrips (P)

■ *Buds or flowers drop, or fail to set fruit*
Thrips (P)
Not enough sun
Temperature fluctuates too much
Air too dry
Soil too dry
Too many drafts
Excess nitrogen

■ *Brown spots or patches on flowers*
Aphids (P)
Cyclamen mites (P)
Thrips (P)
Gray mold (D)

■ *Unusual spots or streaks on flowers*
Viruses (D)

■ *White spots on flowers*
Cyclamen mites (P)
Thrips (P)

■ *Raggedly chewed leaves or flowers*
Caterpillars (P)
Cockroaches (P)
Earwigs (P)
Slugs or snails (P)

■ *Stem gnawed*
Caterpillars (P)
Earwigs (P)
Leatherjackets (P)
Millipedes (P)
Slugs or snails (P)
Springtails (P)
Symphilids (P)
Woodlice (P)

■ *Only lower leaves chewed*
Springtails (P)
Wood lice (P)

■ *Small holes in leaves*
Capsid bugs (P)
Earwigs (P)
Flea beetle (P)
Springtails (P)
Vine weevil adults (P)

■ *Galls on leaves, deformed buds and flowers*
Midge larvae (P)

■ *Galls on roots*
Eelworms (P)

■ *Corky patches on roots*
Symphilids (P)

■ *Sticky leaves (often covered with black mold)*
Aphids (P)
Scale insects (P)
Whitefly (P)

■ *Black mold on leaves*
Funguses (D)
Often result of insect infestation

■ *White powder on leaves*
Powdery mildew (D)

■ *Fruit and/or flowers rot, may show gray fuzz*
Gray mold (D)

■ *Thin white mold on soil*
Funguses (D)

■ *White wooly covering on roots*
Root aphids, see Aphids (P)
Root mealybugs, see Mealybugs (P)

■ *Sticky wooly white bumps*
Mealybugs (P)
Scale insects (P)

■ *Brown or whitish waxy bumps on stems or leaves*
Scale insects(P)

■ *White froth in leaf axils or on stems*
Cuckoo spit (P)

■ *Pale webbing in leaf axils or growing tips*
Spider mites (P)
Caterpillars, possibly (P)

■ *Leaves held together by fine webbing*
Leaftiers (P)

■ *Clouds of tiny white insects fly up when plant disturbed*
Whitefly (P)

■ *Roots or tubers eaten*
Leatherjackets (P)
Symphilids (P)
Vine weevils (P)
Wireworms (P)

SYMPTOMS IN VEGETABLE PLANTS

LETTUCE

■ *Edge of leaf scorched*
Too dry
Excess fertilizer

■ *Watery spots on leaf*
Gray mold (D)

PEAS

■ *Roots and then stem turn black*
Wilt (fusarium) (D)

SQUASH, MELONS, AND CUCUMBERS

■ *Pale spots on leaves turn brown, leaf edges watery*
Stem rot (D)

■ *Watery spots at leaf nodes*
Gray mold (D)

■ *Slimy, bad-smelling spots on fruit, split fruits*
Gummosis (D)

■ *End of fruit withered*
Irregular watering

■ *Fruits bitter*
Too much nitrogen
Irregular watering

TOMATOES

■ *Seedlings purplish*
Mosaic virus (D)

■ *Plants purplish, wilt easily, fibrous roots*
Potato cyst eelworms, (see Eelworms) (P)

■ *Pale lower leaves, wilt easily, fibrous roots*
Root knot eelworms, see Eelworms (P)

■ *Mottled leaves, bushy plants, small seedless fruits*
Aspermey (D)

■ *Shoestring leaves*
Mosaic virus (D)

■ *Leaves eaten except for veins*
Caterpillars (P)

■ *Pitted leaves*
Leaf miners (P)

■ *Brown patches on stem*
Excess manganese

■ *Flowers drop off*
Soil too dry

■ *Fruits do not develop*
Air too dry
Air too hot
Nights too cold

■ *Bronzing of fruit*
Boron deficiency
Too hot
Mosaic virus (D)

■ *Green shoulders on fruit*
Excess sunlight
Potash deficiency

■ *Green or yellow patches on fruit which remain hard*
Irregular feeding
Irregular watering
High temperatures
Too little nitrogen
Too much sun on fruit
Too little potash

■ *Pale round spots on fruit ("ghost spots")*
Botrytis (D)

■ *Round, dark, sunken spot at blossom end of fruit*
Soil too dry

■ *Fruits split*
Irregular watering
Temperature fluctuates too much

SYMPTOMS IN FLOWERING PLANTS

AFRICAN VIOLETS

■ *Yellow spots on leaves*
Too much sun
Water splashes

BEGONIAS

■ *Yellow patches with brown spots between veins of leaf*
Mosaic virus (D)

CACTUS

■ *Brown corky patches*
Too much light
Too little light
Too little humidity

CARNATIONS

■ *Small white spots on leaves*
Spider mites (P)

CHRYSANTHEMUMS

■ *Yellow/green spots above, brownish warts below*
Rust (D)

■ *Flowers small and distorted*
Aspermey (D)

■ *Flowers raggedly chewed*
Earwigs (P)

■ *Cone-shaped, 1/8-inch galls on leaves and stems*
Midge larvae (P)

■ *Yellowing of lower leaves, few flowers*
Overcrowded

CYCLAMEN

■ *Weak yellow plants*
Root rot, see Stem rot (D)

■ *Buds rot, outer leaves curl up*
Cyclamen mites (P)

GARDENIAS

■ *Yellow leaves*
Too cold

GERANIUMS

■ *Watery spots on leaves*
Stem rot (D)

■ *Rings of brown spore masses under leaves, yellow patches above*
Rust (D)

■ *Rough swellings under leaves (ivy leaf geraniums)*
Overwatering
Air too humid

■ *Purple spots on leaves*
Too cold

■ *Red leaves*
Too sudden an increase in sun

■ *Leaves curl*
Viruses (D)

ROSES

■ *Yellow or purple spots on leaves, gray fur below*
Downy mildew (D)

SYMPTOMS IN FRUIT TREES

■ *Red or yellow leaves, twig or leaf distortion*
Aphids (P)

■ *Yellow, spotted leaves turning brown*
Spider mites (P)

■ *Young shoots wilt and die, fruits rot*
Gray mold (D)

■ *White grubs in fruit*
Midge larvae (P)

SYMPTOMS IN STRAWBERRY PLANTS

■ *Red spots on distorted leaves*
Mosaic virus (D)

■ *Younger leaves stunted and wrinkled, older leaves silvery brown*
Cyclamen mites (P)

■ *Young leaves crinkled, midribs swollen below*
Stem eelworms, see Eelworms (P)

■ *Young leaves distorted with rough gray-brown spots*
Leaf and bud eelworms, see Eelworms (P)

PESTS

■ *Aphids (also called Blackfly, Greenfly, and Plant lice).* Very small, juicy-looking creatures. Usually pale green, but sometimes red, black, yellow, brown or gray. They are normally wingless and crawl slowly over the plant, but when overcrowded, later in the season, they can develop wings and fly to a new host. As they grow they shed their skins, which are sometimes mistaken for whiteflies but on closer inspection are clearly immobile white shreds. Aphids suck plant sap and can transmit virus diseases from one plant to another. Some species of aphids feed on the roots of the plant, producing a white, wooly fur on the roots. Another species, the wooly aphid, produces a white wooly fur on shoots and branches. Both can easily be mistaken for mealybugs, but a closer look will reveal the typical aphid shapes under the fur.

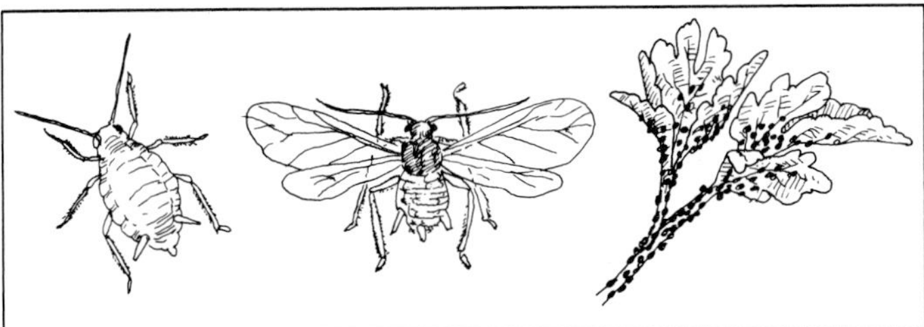

Almost all aphids are female and, as their eggs do not need to be fertilized in order to develop, they can reproduce at an astonishing rate. One aphid can easily become over two hundred thousand aphids in six weeks' time.

The first sign of an aphid attack may be the sticky honeydew that they excrete, or may be just the pale, sickly appearance of the leaves. Close inspection will usually reveal dozens of aphids on young shoots and the underside of leaves. Leaves often curl as a result of aphid damage and plants soon become stunted.

Aphids are easy to kill. Almost all botanical insecticides work, but one or two aphids usually escape to start the colony anew, so be persistent and spray at five-day intervals. Aphids are also common out of doors, so reinfection is fairly frequent.

Washing or spraying a plant with soft soap and water twice, about a week apart, will usually check an aphid invasion. Three times five days apart will be even more effective. Garlic and red pepper solution will make the plant unappetizing for new aphids (see Natural Insecticides). Either solution can be poured on the soil to control root aphids. Since aphids are often brought to a plant by ants, tansy, mint, and other ant-discouraging plants planted around the greenhouse should help to reduce the number of aphids coming in from outside. Ladybugs and their larvae (which look like tiny spotted crocodiles) are aphids' biggest predators and should be encouraged. Many other predators such as lacewing flies, hover flies, and praying mantises include aphids in their diet.

■ *Broad mites. See Cyclamen mites*

■ *Capsid bugs (including Tarnished plant bugs and Bishop bugs).*
Bugs which suck the sap from many kinds of plants, producing tiny brown spots. As the leaf grows, the spots develop into small ragged holes with brown edges. Both leaves and flowers are likely to become stunted and distorted. Fruits may develop pale corky patches and may crack open.

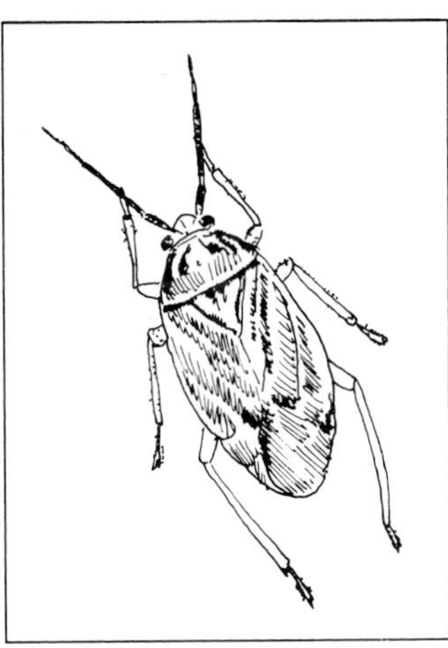

The young nymphs are green and wingless. The adults are greenish or brownish with two wings and are about 1/4 inch long. They are usually troublesome only in late summer, spending most of the year outdoors in weeds. Screening doors and windows to keep them out will prevent any problem. George and Katy Abraham's book *Organic Gardening Under Glass* suggests spraying with a red pepper solution should they get in.

■ *Caterpillars.*
The larvae of any moth or butterfly, often greatly attracted to the succulent plants growing in a greenhouse. They are usually voracious eaters, chewing great holes in the leaves. They sometimes pupate in the greenhouse, emerging to lay more eggs and produce more caterpillars. Cutworms are some of the most damaging, encircling the stems of young plants and gnawing through them at ground level.

Screening the doors and vents to prevent the first moth getting in and handpicking any caterpillars or egg clusters you find are the best methods of control. Most caterpillars are susceptible to a disease caused by the bacteria *Bacillus Thuringiensis,* (see Natural Insecticides section). *See also Leaf miners and Leaf tiers.*

■ *Click beetles. See Wireworms*

■ *Crane fly larvae. See Leatherjackets*

■ *Cockroaches.*
Not uncommon in heated greenhouses, they are rapacious feeders. One to 1 1/2 inches long, and dark brown, cockroaches can move startlingly fast when disturbed. They can be trapped by burying bottles level with the soil and putting a small amount of beer or any sweet syrup in each. Removing possible hiding places near the source of heat will hinder their breeding cycle.

■ *Cuckoo spit.*
What appears to be a gob of spittle is in fact the protective white foam covering the young of the froghopper. The adults are 1/4 inch long, yellow or brown, and able to jump long distances as their name implies. The young are yellowish green, but are usually hidden in a frothy mass of cuckoo spit. It is the young that do the most damage by sucking the plant sap, so find and squash the culprits in any patches of foam

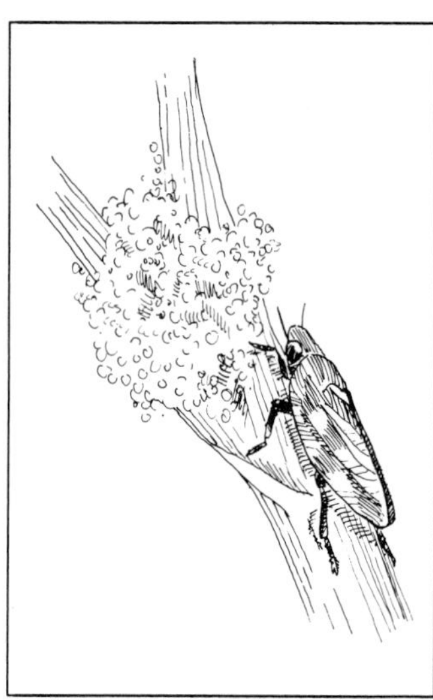

you see. But froghoppers are rarely a serious problem. A hard spray of water will get rid of those that are hard to reach.

■ *Cyclamen mites (also called Strawberry mites or Tarsonemid mites).*
Minute, colorless mites that feed on very young leaves. They live inside leaf and flower buds. Leaves and flowers become small, distorted, and spotted with brown. Leaves sometimes become distorted into long spoon shapes. The eggs and mites, like a fine white powder, can sometimes be seen among the tightly folded leaves and buds.

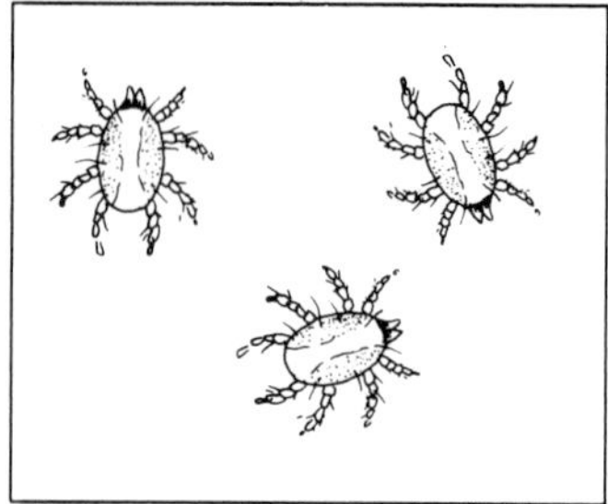

Cyclamen mites affect African violets, begonias, fuchsias, geraniums, impatiens, ivies, and strawberries, as well as cyclamen. Broad mites are very similar and affect an even broader range of plants. Both are difficult to control. Affected plants are best burned. If this is unacceptable, Abraham's *Organic Gardening Under Glass* suggests immersing the whole plant in 110°F. water for two minutes.

■ *Earwigs.*
Dark brown shiny insects about 3/4 inch long with a pair of curved pinchers for a tail. They chew ragged holes in leaves, flowers, and fruit during the night. In the daytime they hide in dark, dry places, usually under bits of rubbish. They can easily be caught in an earwig trap—a bit of dry moss or straw stuffed into a flowerpot or other container that is turned upside down and balanced on

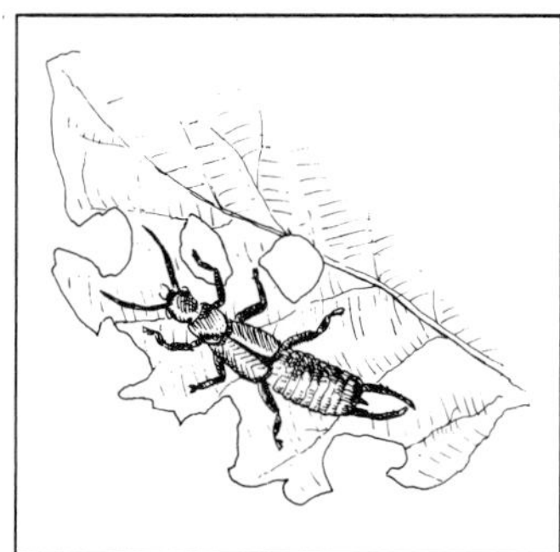

a stake. It will attract earwigs as a safe refuge after a night's feeding. They can then be knocked out of the pot during the day and killed. Large flowers such as dahlias provide a natural earwig refuge, and if shaken vigorously can be used as an earwig trap. Not usually a very serious problem, but they should be killed when found in order to prevent the population expanding.

■ *Eelworms (also called Nematodes).*
Many, many varieties of this microscopic worm exist. Some of them are a serious menace to growing plants both in the greenhouse and in the garden. Other nematodes are innocuous or even beneficial, feeding on harmful insects in the soil. A soil rich in humus will encourage the beneficial nematodes and discourage the harmful ones. Most of the nematodes that damage plants live in the soil and attack plant roots, causing them to form small cysts, which gives rise to their common name of root knot eelworms. One of the worst species is the potato-cyst eelworm, attacking the roots of all solanaceous plants (tomatoes, peppers, eggplants, potatoes, petunias, etc.). If your plants are weak and stunted, check the roots for any abnormal bumps that might be caused by eelworms. A few nematodes feed on leaves and buds causing them to distort or sometimes to show color streaking.

Eelworms are difficult to control. Soil must be pasteurized to 200°F. to be sure of eradicating them. Hot water treatment (115°. for five minutes) will kill leaf-feeding nematodes if the plant can stand it. Best tried during a dormant phase. Several fungi and some predatory nematodes attack root-feeding nematodes. Compost may contain these, but a more reliable source is the Necessary Trading Company. Marigolds are said to repel many nematodes, especially if grown as a crop and turned under in the fall. Many plants have varieties that are resistant to nematode attack.

■ *Flea beatles.*
Minute, shiny black or black and yellow insects that jump away when disturbed. They are not such a pest in the greenhouse as they are in the garden where they eat tiny round holes in the leaves of seedlings and young plants, especially brassicas. Seedlings look as though they have been peppered with buckshot. A fast-growing plant will not be seriously harmed by them since they will leave it alone when tissues begin to mature, but young or weak plants can be killed. Nettle tea (see Natural Insecticides) will drive them away when sprinkled on the plants. But this is necessary only if you have a real epidemic.

■ *Froghoppers. See Cuckoo spit*

■ *Fungus gnats (also called Sciarid flies).*
Tiny black gnats which lay their eggs in the soil. Sometimes you can see them running across the soil or flying slowly around a plant. The larvae (about 1/8 inch long, pale with black heads) burrow down and feed on root hairs and decomposing organic matter. Not often a very serious problem, but when there are many of them, the plant stops growing and may wilt and eventually die. They sometimes bother cuttings. The larvae can be drowned by immersing the pot in water to soil level for six hours. Adult gnats may be discouraged from laying their eggs by spraying the plant with pyrethrum or tobacco solution (see Natural Insecticides). Plants in peat-based composts are more susceptible.

■ *Gall midges. See Midge larvae*

■ *Leafhoppers.*
Yellow-green, fast-jumping insects 1/8 inch long that suck the sap from leaves, producing pale specks and weakening the plant. The pale specks may merge together to form irregular, colorless blotches in a bad attack. The damage is usually

more unsightly than serious, but they can spread virus diseases so should not be allowed to multiply. After molting the empty skin remains attached to the leaf, leading to the name "ghost fly." Leafhoppers are especially fond of chickweed, which should be removed from the vicinity of the greenhouse. Spray the underside of the leaves of infected plants with pyrethrum or tobacco solution every two weeks if they are a problem.

■ *Leaf miners.*
The larvae of any of several flies or moths that live inside the leaf itself. Their tunneling trails are visible from outside the leaf as light-colored wriggling lines or blotches. The older trails gradually turn brown. The little grub can often be seen through the semi-transparent skin of the leaf, nestling at the end of a trail. Different species attack different plants, tomatoes and chrysanthemums being the most common. Affected leaves should be picked and burned as they may contain eggs in addition to the visible larvae.

■ *Leaftiers (also called Leaf rollers).*
The caterpillars of various moths which twist a leaf about themselves for protection. The tortrix moth caterpillar is the most common leaftier. If the

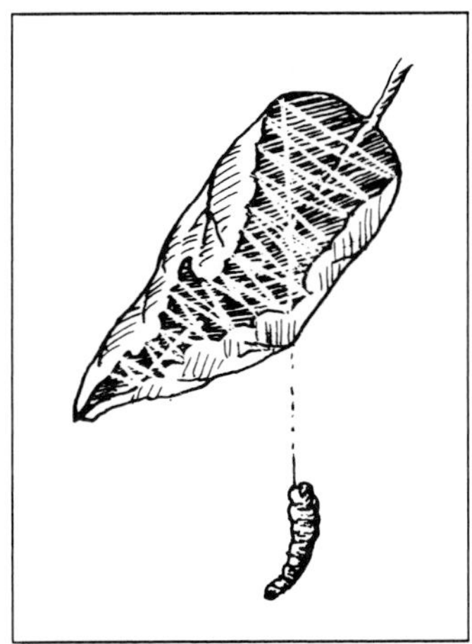

leaves are fairly stiff they may simply glue two leaves together with the fine white webbing they produce. Usually you will find a small caterpillar inside each twist or leaf sandwich. Even if they are empty, pick off any stuck together leaves and burn them because there may be eggs hiding there. Nearby leaves often show ragged holes where the caterpillar has fed.

■ *Leatherjackets (larvae of Crane flies).*
Thick, dark, greyish brown, worm-like creatures, 1/2 to 1 1/2 inches long with a tough skin. The adults are large delicate flies with gauzy wings and long dangling legs. In late summer they are common out of doors and may find their way inside. Catch any you see, because they will be looking for places

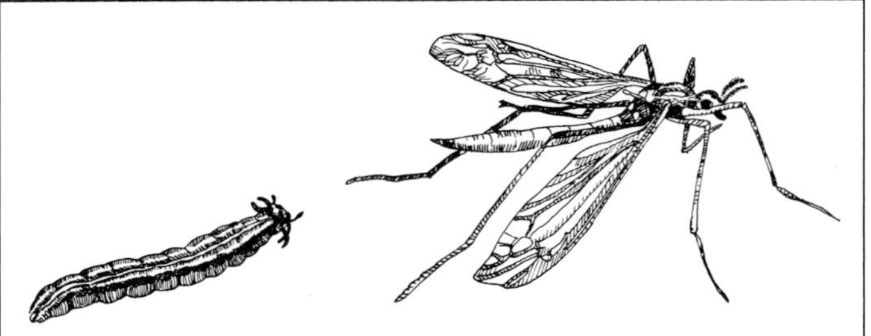

to lay their eggs. The larvae live just below the surface of the soil, feeding on roots and stems. They like damp soil and dense vegetation, so clearing out weeds, cultivating the soil surface and letting the soil dry out between watering should all help to discourage the adults from laying their eggs.

■ *Mealybugs. See Scale insects.*

■ *Midge larvae (the larvae of Gall midges).*
Little white maggots which develop into small flies. The

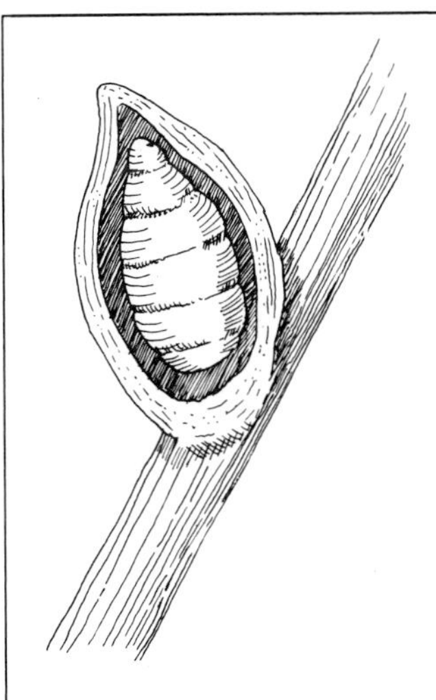

larvae feed inside leaves and flowers of chrysanthemums, causing them to distort. They pupate in warty growths called galls on leaves, and any such growths should be burned immediately. One kind of midge larvae, Aphidoletes, (see Beneficial Insects section) is very helpful to gardeners, but as these pupate in cocoons on the ground, they will not be harmed by destroying the galls formed by other midges.

■ *Millipedes.*
Many-legged insects with segmented bodies, 1/3 to 1 inch long. They may be cream, brown, or black. Distinguished from centipedes (which are usually beneficial) by having two pairs of legs on each body segment instead of one. Also millipedes are less active, often curling up rather than running away when disturbed. At night they feed on the roots and stems of seedlings and occasionally eat the seeds

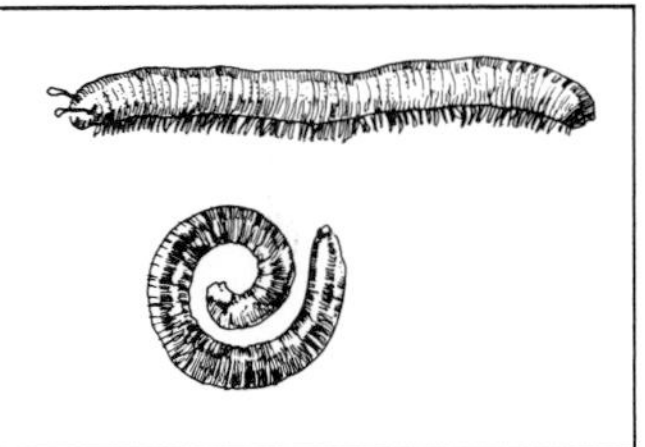

themselves. During the day they curl up in decaying humus or rich soil. Scratch around near affected plants and kill any millipedes you find. Using pasteurized soil for seed sowing usually eliminates the problem, since millipedes are only fond of very young plants or those previously damaged by some other pest. Drenching the soil with tobacco solution helps, especially if more tobacco solution is sprayed on those that come to the surface. Clearing up dead leaves and other organic rubbish will reduce their hiding places.

■ *Mites. See Cyclamen mites and Spider mites*

■ *Nematodes. See Eelworms*

■ *Pill bugs. See Woodlice*

■ *Plant bugs. See Capsid bugs*

■ *Red spider mites. See Spider mites*

■ *Scale insects (including Mealybugs).*
Small insects that move very slowly if at all. They look like reddish or yellowish brown

bumps on stems or leaves. If a bump rouses your suspicions try to scrape it off. It should squash fairly easily and no

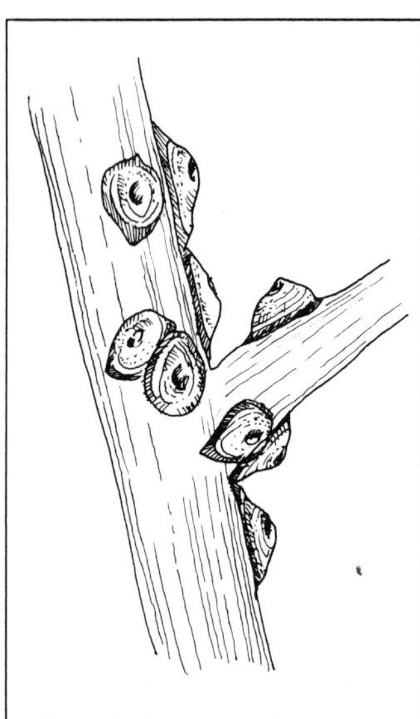

mark should be left on the plant if you are right. Mealybugs are closely related to scale insects, but can move slowly over the plant. They are white and furry or waxy-looking and are easy to scrape off or squash on the plant. Some mealybugs feed on roots, where their white wooly nests are visible only when the plant is repotted.

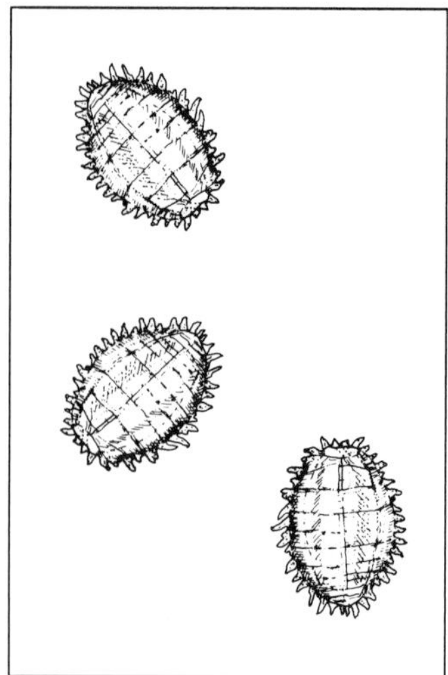

All scale insects excrete a sticky honeydew that encourages mold. They suck the sap of the host plant, causing the leaves to turn yellow and wilt. Washing the plant, and if possible scrubbing it, with Safer Soap (see Natural Insecticides section) twice two days apart and again a week later, or spraying with tobacco solution a few times at two week intervals will usually get rid of the pests. The problem with them is that their young are so well protected by the mother's body that it is almost impossible to kill them, so you have to wait until the next generation are big enough to attack and repeat your efforts. If there are only a few adults present, touching each with a dab of rubbing alcohol, turpentine, or kerosene will kill them. A relative of the ladybug (see *Cryptolaemus montrouzieri* (in Beneficial Insects) eats mealybugs and, to a lesser extent, scale insects. *Thrip stick* (see Thrips) painted on the stem will help to prevent the young scale insects from migrating to other plants. Drenching the soil with Safer Soap solution (see Natural Insecticides) will keep root mealybugs in check, though it won't usually eliminate them.

■ *Sciarid flies. See Fungus gnats*

■ *Slaters. See Woodlice*

■ *Slugs and snails.*
Closely related, slow-moving, slimy creatures, one with a shell and one without. They can quickly chew large ragged

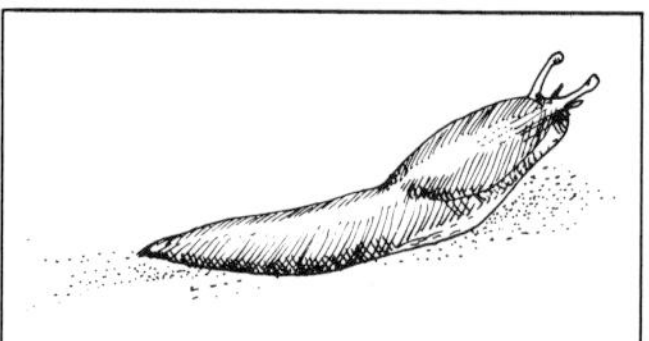

holes in leaves or fruit, or destroy a large number of seedlings overnight. They usually spend the day in dark, damp hiding places, coming out to feed at night. Their soft bodies leave behind a shiny trail of mucus as they move. Their eggs look like clusters of small, transparent balls, a pale version of caviar. These should be destroyed whenever found.

Any rough or dehydrating surface is irritating to their tender bodies, and they will try to avoid it. Cinders, lime, or ashes will discourage them and salt will kill them outright, dissolving them into slimy puddles. Diatomaceous earth scattered on plants makes them unappetizing to slugs or snails (see Natural Insecticides section). They can easily be trapped in saucersful of honey or beer, which stimulate them to a fatal overindulgence. Looking under empty flowerpots or seed flats will often disclose a few slugs which can be quickly dispatched with the shake of a salt cellar. A nighttime raid with a flashlight will yield the majority of any slugs living in your sunspace. Mulching gives them plenty of cool, damp places to hide so is better avoided if slugs are a problem. Fertosan, if you can find it, is supposed to be more effective than poisonous slug baits and is harmful only to mollusks (see Natural Insecticides).

■ *Sow bugs. See Woodlice*

■ *Spider mites (also called Red spider mites or Two-spotted mites).*
Tiny, almost invisible pests that turn red in autumn, but are usually yellow, green, or tan. They are so small their color is not usually visible without using a magnifying glass. Mites suck the plant's sap, causing a fine pale speckling on the leaves, which eventually become mottled yellow with a papery texture. When they begin to get overcrowded they start spinning their webs. Several individuals will hang at the end of a long strand of silk waiting to be carried to another plant by catching a ride on a passing animal or just by swinging in the wind. Often the first signs of trouble are the small pale cobwebs in leaf axils and on growing points, but by then many mites are already present. Careful examination will reveal the mites like a dusting of meal under young leaves. With a magnifying glass they are easy to identify.

Spider mites are one of the commonest problems in greenhouses and are hard to eliminate, though good management will keep them in check. They hibernate in cracks in the walls and floors, so a good scrub in late autumn will help to reduce the problem next year. A hard spray of water (especially on the underside of leaves) will dislodge many mites and should be re-

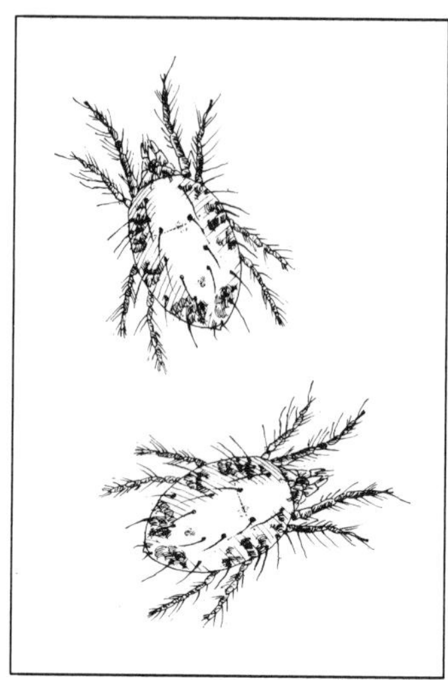

peated frequently. Dipping affected plants in buttermilk is supposed to drive away spider mites. Ced-O-Flora, rotenone, pyrethrum, and Safer Soap (see Natural Insecticides) are all moderately effective against mites, but treatment needs to be repeated four or five times at five day intervals. Maintaining a cool, humid atmosphere and misting the affected plants whenever possible will go a long way towards preventing a serious attack. Spider mites are resistant to chemical insecticides and in fact often benefit from them because their predators are killed off. For severe infestations a supply of predatory mites known as *Phytoseiulius persimilis* can be purchased (see Beneficial Insects).

■ *Springtails.*
Tiny white insects that jump violently when disturbed. They do not usually do much harm but occasionally they feed on root hairs or young seedlings. Tiny holes may appear on the surface of young leaves. When a pot plant is heavily watered,

springtails float to the surface of the soil where they can easily be seen. They thrive in damp soil on decaying plant matter, so keeping a tidy greenhouse and avoiding overwatering should prevent an

extensive number of them. If they are a problem, drench the soil with Safer Soap solution and be sure to pasteurize any garden soil you use as it commonly contains springtails.

■ *Strawberry mites. See Cyclamen mites*

■ *Symphilids.*
Soft, white, centipede-like creatures about 1/4 inch long, they live in the soil and feed on young roots, leaving corky patches behind. Occasionally they gnaw leaves that touch the soil. If the plant is weak, wilts easily, and has bluish leaves, take it out of its pot and look for symphilids in the soil. They quickly burrow back into the soil when exposed, so look carefully. Dunking the roots in a bucket of water should bring any symphilids to the surface. If you find them, kill them, cut off any damaged roots, and repot in pasteurized soil.

■ *Tarnished plant bugs. See Capsid bugs*

■ *Tarsonemid mites. See Cyclamen mites*

■ *Thrips.*
Very tiny, fast-moving winged insects, yellow, green, or dark brown. They have fringed wings, which look fuzzy, but they ordinarily jump rather than fly. They attack both leaves and flowers causing small pale scars that give an overall silvery look. They also leave behind a deposit of black specks. The most troublesome variety is the onion thrip, which sucks the sap of members of the onion family and for some reason also fancies carnations,

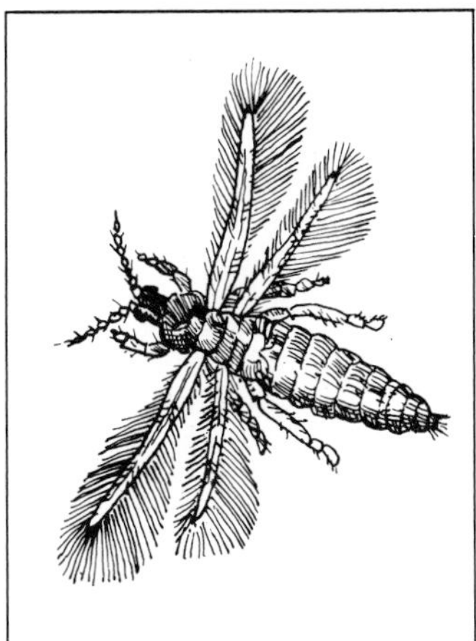

chrysanthemums, and several other flowers, as well as cabbage and spinach.

Spraying with soft soap, pyrethrum, derris, or garlic and red pepper (see Natural Insecticides) should help to control all thrips. Reducing the heat and increasing humidity will also help. A fungal parasite practically eliminates them if the floor is kept wet.

Lacewing larvae and two kinds of predatory mites (*Amblyseius californicus* and *A. mackensie*) eat thrips and can keep the population down to a reasonable level.

■ *Tortrix moths. See Leaftiers*

■ *Two-spotted mites. See Spider mites*

■ *Vine weevil grubs.*
Plump white grubs, 1 to 1 1/2 inches long, with brown heads. They live in the soil, eating bulbs, tubers, corms, and sometimes roots. If a plant wilts suddenly, suspect their presence. Shake the earth off its roots over a flat surface; the grubs should be visible amid the soil.

Adult vine weevils are 1/2 to 1 inch long, dull black beetles with rather long heads and thoraxes. They feed at night, chewing neat holes out of the edges of leaves, producing a characteristic notched edge. Both adults and grubs should be destroyed on sight. Adult vine weevils cannot fly so any sticky substance painted on stems will catch them as they climb upward to feed. During the day they hide near the base of the plant they are feeding on, so search around

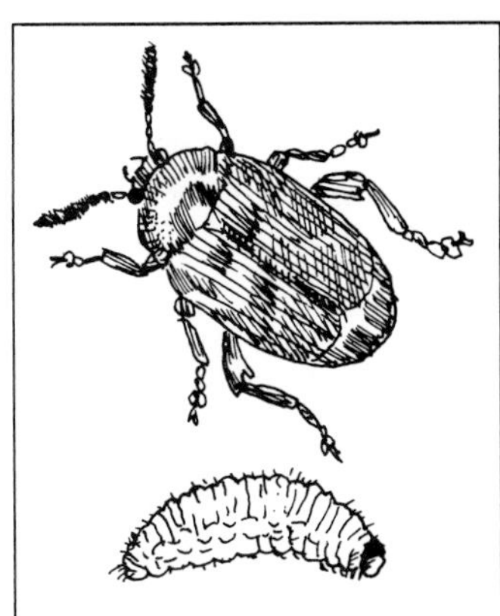

under any mulch or leave corrugated paper lying near damaged plants and shake that out during the day.

■ *Whitefly.*
A tiny, white, moth-like, sap-sucking insect usually found on the underside of leaves, which rises in clouds when disturbed. Infested plants are weakened, the leaves becoming mottled with yellow and often covered with a sticky honeydew. It is commonly found in greenhouses and is difficult to control.

Spraying with Soft Soap, tobacco solution, Ced-O-Flora,

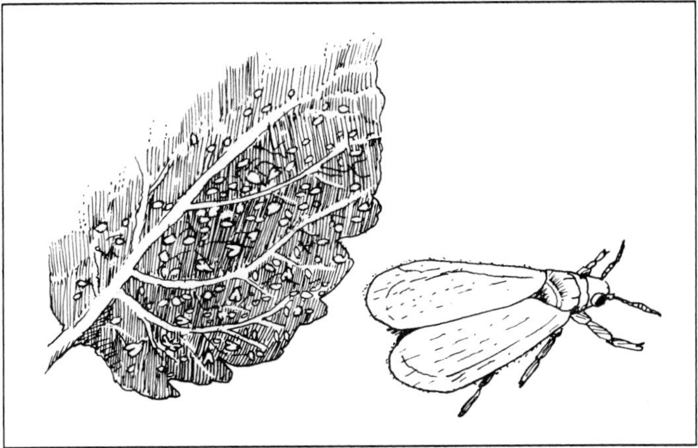

or pyrethrum (see Natural Insecticides) is effective if begun early enough, before many adults are present. Spray every four days, paying special attention to the underside of leaves, until no more whiteflies are visible, and even then keep a sharp eye out for reinfestation. Whiteflies are attracted to the color yellow, so coating yellow strips of paper or plastic with Ced-O-Flora or Tanglefoot or even thick engine oil will trap large numbers. Hang the strips nearby, and gently shake the affected plants. Wipe off and repeat until you are not catching many. A vacuum cleaner hose will suck up hundreds of whiteflies if held nearby when the plants are disturbed.

There is a special wasp called *Encarsia formosa* (see Beneficial Insects) which is parasitic on whitefly larvae (the tiny, round, nearly transparent scales on the back of leaves). Encarsia are very effective at getting rid of whiteflies, provided they are introduced early enough. Two types of fungus are also successful whitefly parasites, but these are not yet commercially available.

■ *Wireworms (the larvae of Click beetles).*
They look like hard, shiny, yellow-brown worms about an

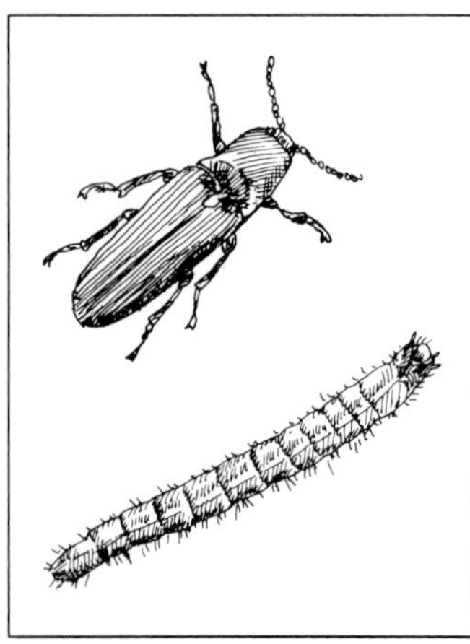

inch long, but have three small pairs of legs and powerful jaws. The adults are dark brown beetles, about 1/2 inch long. When they fall on their backs they can right themselves with a loud snap; hence the name. The larvae feed on roots and bulbs of many plants, tunneling through them rather than gnawing on the outside. They are very slow moving. They are most common in soil that has not previously been cultivated, so be sure to pasteurize any soil taken from pastureland or waste patches of ground.

■ *Woodlice (also called Sow bugs, Slaters or Pill bugs).*
Gray-brown creatures about 1/2 inch long that roll up in a

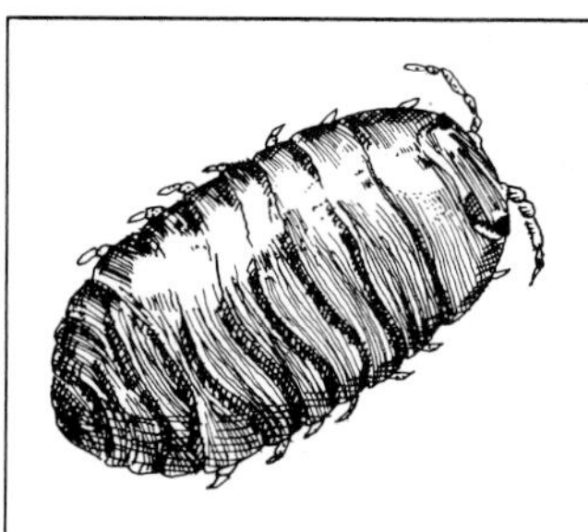

ball when disturbed. They are fond of damp, decaying matter and are usually found out of doors under rocks or old pieces of wood, emerging at night to feed. It is unnerving to discover them in the greenhouse under old pots or seed boxes, but they do not often do much harm, although they may attack seedlings. If you suffer from infestation of these queer creatures (with their hard, segmented shells and many legs, they are most closely related to lobsters!), clearing out their hiding places and getting rid of any you find will go a long way to reducing their numbers. If you want to get rid of more, try using an earwig trap with the addition of a piece of fruit as bait, or dust pyrethrum in dark corners where they might congregate. Dipel II, a bacterial disease of caterpillars available as spores, is said to affect wood lice as well (see Natural Insecticides).

DISEASES

■ *Aspermey.*
A virus disease of tomatoes which also affects chrysanthemums. The plant becomes bushy and somewhat stunted. The leaves become mottled and distorted. Tomato fruits are small, often seedless. Chrysanthemum flowers are small, distorted, and show color changes. Aphids are the commonest carrier of this virus, so be sure to deal with them. Destroy infected plants and take cuttings only from healthy stock.

■ *Bacterial diseases.*
Many kinds of bacteria attack plants, given the right conditions. Symptoms are similar to those caused by fungi (wilting, rotting spots, etc.). As bacterial infection is commonly followed by an invasion of fungi into the damaged area, the two are hard to disentangle. If the typical fuzzy or powdery fungal growths are not present, it is likely to be a bacterial problem.

Bacterial diseases are less omnipresent than fungal diseases so good sanitation, and getting rid of infected plants is more successful. They can be passed by insects and on seeds from infected plants. Like fungi they are most virulent in moist, warm conditions, but they are not so dependent on the right conditions, and will continue to grow, though more slowly, even in drier conditions. Keeping the humidity moderate (below 70 percent), not letting any water splash on plants, and ensuring good drainage and fertility are preventive measures. (See also *Wilt.*)

■ *Blight.*
Early and late blight are fungus diseases affecting mainly tomatoes and other related plants such as petunias. *Early blight* causes small brown spots on older leaves or stems. These spots gradually enlarge, creating a pattern of concentric rings. Affected leaves eventually die and fall off. Some tomato varieties are resistant.

Late blight (also called potato blight). Causes water-soaked spots on leaves surrounded by rings of white powder underneath the leaf in damp conditions. If the air is dry, brown patches on the edge of leaves dry up and shrivel. Sometimes black patches appear on the stem. Brown patches on green fruits spread until the fruit rots, often destroying an entire crop of tomatoes. The disease gradually spreads over the whole plant, usually killing it in the end.

As with most fungi, lowering the humidity is the main defense. Make sure plants are getting adequate trace elements.

■ *Botrytis. See Gray mold*

■ *Damping-off disease.* Any of a variety of fungus diseases that cause seedlings to collapse suddenly and completely, the stem and/or roots having rotted. Plants cannot be revived, but good ventilation and drier soil and air

conditions will prevent the fungus from spreading. If damping-off has been a problem, look out for seedlings with damaged stems when transplanting; they may survive but will never grow well (see also *Wire stem).*

Use pasteurized soil to prevent initial infection. Peat moss is said to inhibit damping-off disease, so add some to seed soil mixes. Avoid overcrowding and overwatering and remove any sickly seedlings quickly. Spraying with chamomile tea or a 10 percent vinegar solution may help. Maintain optimum growing conditions because fast-growing seedlings are much less liable to infection.

■ *Downy mildew.*
A white or gray fungus growing in fuzzy patches on the underside of leaves. The part of the leaf above the mildew is usually yellow but eventually turns brown and dies. Destroy infected leaves. Reduce

humidity and consider raising nighttime temperatures. Avoid splashing the leaves when watering and try adding some extra phosphorus to the soil mix. Chive or chamomile tea sprays may help. Avoid overcrowding. For similar symptoms on tomatoes or potatoes, see Blight, late.

■ *Funguses.*
There are hundreds of varieties of fungus diseases that attack plants causing molds, mildews, or rotting spots on leaves, flowers, fruits, roots, or soil. Fungus diseases are common in greenhouse plants. Their presence usually indicates overwatering or too high a level of humidity in the air. The plant will usually revive if the infected part is cut off and humidity is reduced. Fungus growths on the soil should be scraped off and watering reduced. A black mold on leaves is usually caused by a fungus that grows on the honeydew secreted by sapsucking insects; the treatment is simply to get rid of the insect and wash the sticky coating off the leaves.

Chamomile flowers, chives, equisetum (horsetail), nettles, and horseradish leaves are said to help prevent mildew. Pour a quart of boiling water on a handful of one of these and steep for fifteen minutes. When cool, strain and use as a spray.

Wilts and funguses which cause the plant to rot (see damping-off disease, gray mold, gummosis, stem rot and wilt) are a much more serious menace than the unsightly molds and mildews that frequently occur in winter greenhouses. Generally, using pasteurized soil, removing any dead or infected leaves, and maintaining good ventilation will greatly reduce the likelihood of fungus infections.

■ *Gray mold (also called Botrytis.* A fungus disease encouraged by high humidity, it usually appears in winter when light levels are low. Brown rotting spots covered with a gray fur develop on leaves, stems, fruit, and/or flowers. Gray mold can also cause "ghost spots" on tomatoes. Small watery rings appear on the skin of the fruit without affecting its quality.

Reduce humidity, increase ventilation, and remove infected parts of the plant. Make sure not to overwater the soil or spill water unnecessarily. Wash your hands after handling infected plants because it spreads easily. The spores enter most easily through damaged tissues, so avoid pruning in winter and remove fading flowers promptly.

■ *Gummosis.*
A fungus disease affecting cucumbers, melons, and squash. Gray or brown sunken spots develop on young fruits. The spots begin to ooze and eventually split open, exposing a green fungus inside. Destroy any infected fruits. Reduce humidity by increasing heat and ventilation. If gummosis is a persistent problem, you can grow resistant varieties.

■ *Mosaic viruses.*
There are several kinds of mosaic, some specific to certain plants, others more widespread. One of the commonest forms is tobacco mosaic virus, which is often spread by people who handle tobacco. Tomatoes, peppers, and other solanaceous plants are particularly susceptible to tobacco mosaic, but orchids, cacti, and other plants can get it also. Cucumber mosaic virus affects all members of the squash family and several flowering plants as well. It causes tomatoes to produce narrow string-like leaves, similar to hormone weedkiller damage. Most mosaic viruses cause yellow patches on leaves, giving a mottled appearance overall. They sometimes stunt and distort leaf growth as well.

Skimmed milk is quite good at inhibiting mosaic viruses. Washing your hands in skimmed milk after smoking will prevent the spread of tobacco mosaic virus, but smokers should not really work with tomatoes and peppers and eggplants. Some people won't let smokers in their greenhouse at all, for fear of tobacco mosaic. Spraying a plant with skimmed milk helps to protect it against all mosaic virus diseases. According to Miranda Smith's book *Greenhouse Gardening,* a week of temperatures over 95°F. will kill mosaic viruses, but the plants won't like it much either. Destroy any plants suspected of mosaic virus and don't try to compost them.

■ *Powdery mildew.*
A fungus that covers leaves and young shoots with a gray or white powder. Brown patches on leaves with gray powder underneath are another sign of powdery mildew. Very common in the garden late in summer. Grapes, chrysanthemums, begonias, and squashes are most susceptible. Don't let the soil get too dry as thirsty plants are more vulnerable. Avoid overcrowding. Prevention is the same as for Downy mildew. Shane Smith's book *The Bountiful Solar Greenhouse* suggests spraying with a mixture of one tablespoon baking soda to one quart of water.

■ *Root rot. See Stem rot*

■ *Rust.*
Any of several fungus diseases affecting many flowers and mint. Yellow, orange, or brown swellings form on the underside of leaves. These are the spore masses of the fungus. Mint leaves become severely distorted. Destroy any infected leaves or severely infected plants. Keep plants and atmosphere fairly dry, being careful not to splash the leaves or stems when watering. Make sure there is sufficient potassium available in the soil.

■ *Stem rot and Root rot, including Blackleg.*
One of several fungus diseases, including gray mold, which cause either the stem or the root (usually both) to rot. Dark brown or black patches can often be found at the base of the stem and part or all of the roots may turn black and die. The lower leaves turn yellow, and the whole plant wilts increasingly easily, until it finally collapses.

Blackleg is a disease mainly affecting geranium cuttings, but sometimes mature plants also. The base of the stem turns black and rots. Cuttings can safely be taken from the tops of mature plants with blackleg, but the plant itself cannot be saved.

Remove any infected plants immediately. Use pasteurized soil to prevent the initial infection. Be sure the soil is well drained and not too cold. Space plants well apart. Tomato plants can often be saved by removing lower leaves and mounding fresh, pasteurized soil around the stem for the plant to root into.

■ *Viruses.*
There are many kinds of virus diseases that affect different plants. Some of the most virulent are the mosaic viruses. Once a virus infects a plant the whole plant will be diseased and cannot usually be saved. Most viruses are first indicated by mottled or discolored leaves. Dispose of weak or stunted plants and those with distorted or mottled leaves. Insects, tools, or even your own hands can spread a virus disease, so wash your hands and tools after handling any plant you suspect and control insect populations. Aphids and other sucking insects are common carriers of viruses.

■ *Wilt.*
Irreversible wilting when the soil has not been too dry and there is no obvious damage to the roots is usually caused by a fungus, but occasionally by a

bacteria. Verticillium wilt and Fusarium wilt are the two most common fungus diseases causing wilting. Leaves gradu-

ally become yellow or grayish and wilt, usually old leaves first and gradually progressing up the plant. Growing points may wilt during the day. Eventually the whole plant wilts simultaneously. If you cut through a stem lengthwise you will find the characteristic brown streaks.

Pasteurizing the soil and keeping a clean greenhouse go a long way towards preventing these fungi. Resistant varieties of most plants can be obtained.

Bacterial wilt produces similar symptoms and also affects many plants. It too is spread through the soil, so be sure to use pasteurized soil for young plants. Cucumber beetles can infect young plants, so controlling them helps to control bacterial wilt.

■ *Wire stem.*
A fungus disease mainly affecting brassica seedlings. The base of the stem shrivels and

darkens. Most affected seedlings topple over and collapse as in damping-off, but some survive with shrunken, wiry stems. These should be discarded as they will remain stunted all their lives.

BENEFICIAL INSECTS

■ *Amblyseius californicus. See Phytoseiulius persimilis*

■ *Aphid Lions. See Lacewings*

■ *Aphidoletes aphidimyza.*
A tiny gall midge (2 millimeters long), sometimes known as an aphid midge, whose larvae are very effective aphid predators. The females lay their minute,

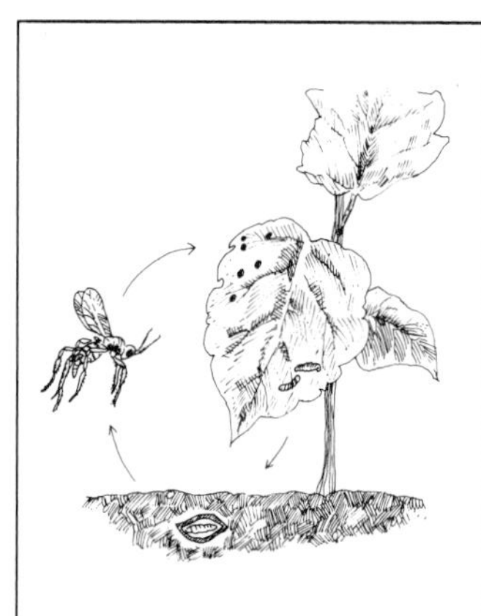

shiny orange eggs near colonies of aphids. Because they can fly, they will find any large populations of aphids. When the larvae hatch they feed on all the aphids they can find, searching them out very effectively and often killing more than they can eat if many aphids are present. The dead aphids turn black and often hang off the leaf as a telltale sign.

The larvae are pale orange to red and about the size of the aphids they feed on. When fully grown the larvae drop off the plant and pupate just under the surface of the soil. Their cocoons will survive the winter so it should be possible to establish a permanent population. They exist in the wild all over the United States and may enter your sunspace spontaneously. "A Guide to the Biological Control of Greenhouse Aphids" has a good description of how to collect them from the wild. Otherwise, the best method is to buy cocoons if possible, but they are only just beginning to become commercially available. A large number of cocoons is needed early in the season before the aphid population explosion begins. Given an early start the aphid midge can keep the aphids within acceptable limits.

■ *Braconid wasps.*
A very useful family of small wasps, about 2 millimeters long, almost all of which are parasites on less helpful creatures. The most common varieties of braconid wasps lay their eggs in caterpillars. The larvae make tiny white cocoons which stick out all over the caterpillar like fat spines. Up to 150 larvae may be attached to a single caterpillar, which is gradually eaten alive. The wasp larvae then hatch out and go on to lay their eggs in other caterpillars. They often occur naturally and may enter your greenhouse spontaneously.

Several other braconid wasps are parasites on aphids. The female lays her egg in an aphid, and as the larva develops, it eats the aphid from

within. The dead aphid becomes very round and turns a coppery or pearly color with a distinctive shiny luster, but is still recognizably aphid-shaped. When the larvae are ready to hatch out, they glue the mummified aphid to the leaf and emerge through a small round hole that is just visible. Some larvae overwinter inside mummified aphids. If you happen to notice any of the little coppery globes among the aphids in your garden, bring them in because new wasps will hatch out and go on to lay their eggs in other aphids.

A third sort of braconid wasp is parasitic on carrot fly.

■ *Cryptolaemus montrouzieri.*
A relative of the ladybug that specializes in eating mealybugs. When very hungry they will eat scale insects as well. The adult looks like a plain brown ladybug; the larvae resemble mealybugs themselves. All stages of this beetle

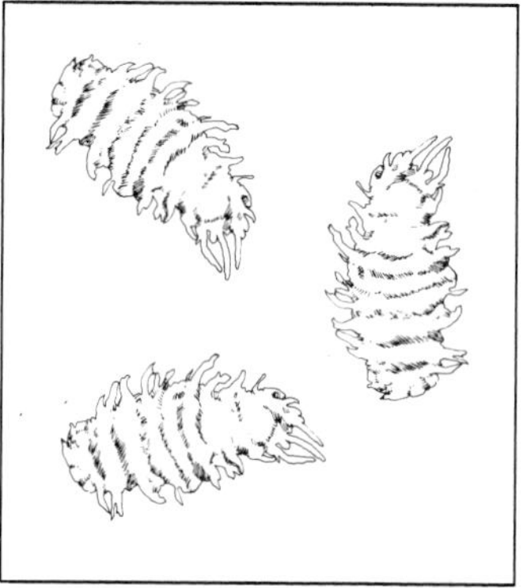

eat mealybugs and can keep large populations of mealybugs in check, but will rarely eliminate them altogether. They are most effective between 68 and 85°F.

Cryptolaemus montrouzieri are available commercially, but distribute them carefully when they arrive as they will eat each other as readily as mealybugs.

■ *Encarsia formosa.*
A tiny (almost invisible) parasitic wasp that can decimate the whitefly population in a few months. It lays its eggs in whitefly larvae, turning them black. Black specks on the back of whitefly-infested leaves are your guarantee that *Encarsia* is doing its job. The specks should appear two to three weeks after introducing the parasites. The wasp takes three to four weeks to develop inside the whitefly larvae, so any prunings with the telltale specks on should be left in the sunspace for a few weeks until all the *Encarsia wasps* hatch out. Once they have hatched, if you hold the leaf up to the light, you will see a tiny round hole in each of the blackened

scales where the adult wasp emerged.

Encarsia are attracted by whitefly honeydew and can search out every last one. But if the whitefly population becomes too dense the excess

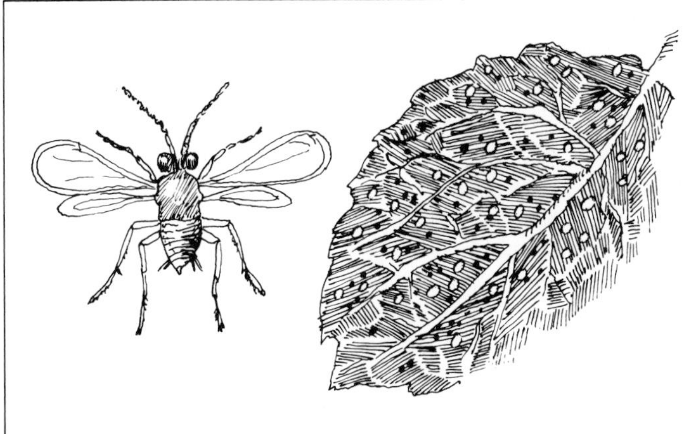

honeydew hampers them. (Certain plants with hairy leaves such as cucumbers and tobacco plants also make them less effective.) Once there is so much honeydew that sooty mold has begun to develop, *Encarsia* will have a hard time controlling the whitefly, and some other method should be used first.

As long as the whitefly population is not too high to begin with, *Encarsia* are so effective they can starve themselves by eradicating the whitefly altogether. It may be worth keeping one badly infested plant elsewhere to be sure the wasps will have enough whitefly to reproduce on. *Encarsia* don't like tobacco plants so one of those in the sunspace can act as a trap plant, breeding enough whitefly to ensure the *Encarsia* don't starve themselves out of existence.

It usually takes about two months for the wasps to completely control the whitefly, but if numbers are small to start with, they will stay fairly small during this period. Like whitefly itself, *Encarsia* does best in warm, humid conditions, 65 to 80°F. with at least 50 percent humidity. They normally die out during the winter and have to be reintroduced in the spring. But if the sunspace stays above freezing all winter it will be worth checking for black specks before ordering next year's batch of *Encarsia.*

Deciding when to introduce *Encarsia* is critical. If there are not enough whitefly scales or if temperatures or light levels are too low, they will die out. If too many whitefly, particularly too many adults, are already present, they will not be able to multiply fast enough to catch up. Usually the first whitefly you see after February should be the signal to order immediately. Ideally there should be no more than one or two whitefly per leaf distributed fairly evenly throughout the sunspace. Any badly infested plants should be thrown out or treated (see *Whitefly* in Pests section) to bring the numbers down to a reasonable level before introducing *Encarsia.* The best suppliers send two or three batches of *Encarsia* at two-week intervals in order to increase their chances of success.

It is vital to avoid using any permethrin-based insecticides with *Encarsia.* They are lethal to the little wasps for up to three months after spraying. Safer Soap, pyrethrum, rotenone, derris, and bioresmethrin can all be safely used up to a week before introducing *Encarsia.* If a whitefly population explosion occurs on a particular plant after the wasps have arrived, it may be worth spraying the worst-affected plants with one of these to reduce the population of adult whiteflies. If possible spray the plants outside the sunspace. A few predators will be killed but more whitefly, and this should help to bring the two back into balance so that the *Encarsia* have a fair chance. Pyretherum and derris are safe for the larval forms of *Encarsia* and will harm the adults only on the first day.

If aphids become a problem while *Encarsia* are present, try to remove the plant from the sunspace and spray it with one of the less harmful sprays. Pirimicarb is the only insecticide which is totally safe to use with *Encarsia* and with most other beneficial insects. Fortunately, it is an extremely effective aphid killer.

■ *Fireflies.*
Besides being the delight of summer evenings, fireflies eat slugs and snails for you, and their larvae eat cutworms. So if your children catch any of these dull, black, elongated beetles with their phosphorescent, green tail lights, ask them to release them in the greenhouse. They may not stay long, but they might eat a few pests on their way out.

■ *Hover flies (also called Syrphid flies).*
Adults look like small black- and yellow-striped wasps but are actually flies. They hover

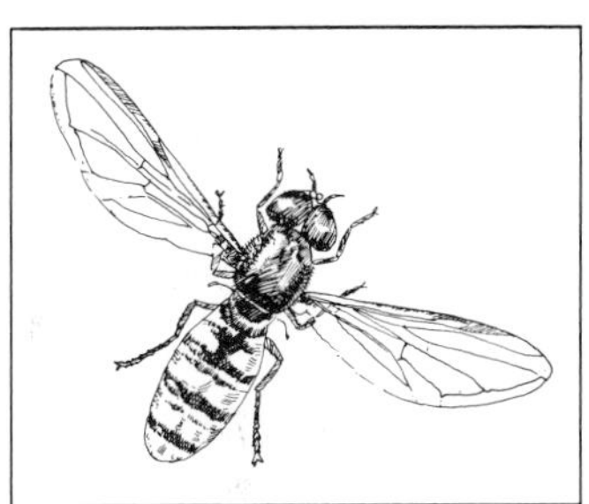

over flowers before darting in to feed on the nectar. Their larvae look like tiny semitransparent slugs and eat enormous quantities of aphids. They are more effective predators than ladybugs, eating up to nine hundred aphids before they mature. It might be worth planting their favorite food, Convolvulus tricolor, a small relative of the morning glory, in the greenhouse to attract adult hover flies. The females search out aphid colonies by smell and always lay their single, white, cylindrical eggs close by.

■ *Ichneumon flies.*
Really a long, slender, delicate wasp, up to 2 inches long. It looks like it might sting but it does not; it uses what appears to be its stinger to lay eggs in many kinds of caterpillars. The

larvae eat the caterpillar from within.

■ *Lacewing flies.*
The adults have large, gauzy green wings and golden eyes. They lay their eggs on thin,

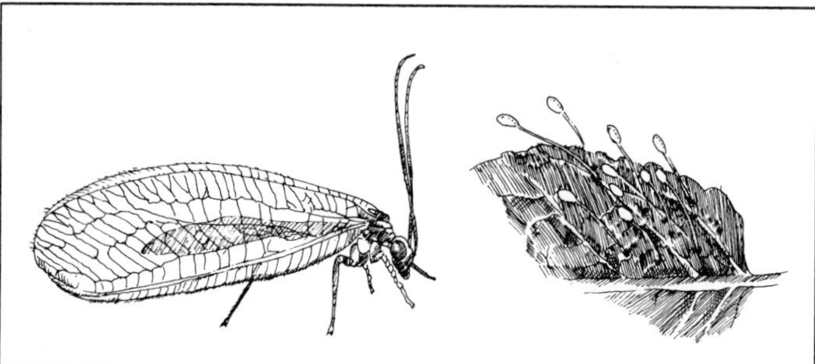

threadlike stalks attached to leaves. The larvae, nicknamed *Aphid lions*, are small ferocious-looking creatures that eat aphids and many other small insects with gusto. When mature, they pupate in round, white, silken cocoons. They are very cannibalistic, so space them as far apart as possible when releasing them.

■ *Ladybugs.*
A prime predator of small soft-bodied insects, epecially aphids. Their cheerful red shells with black spots are a common

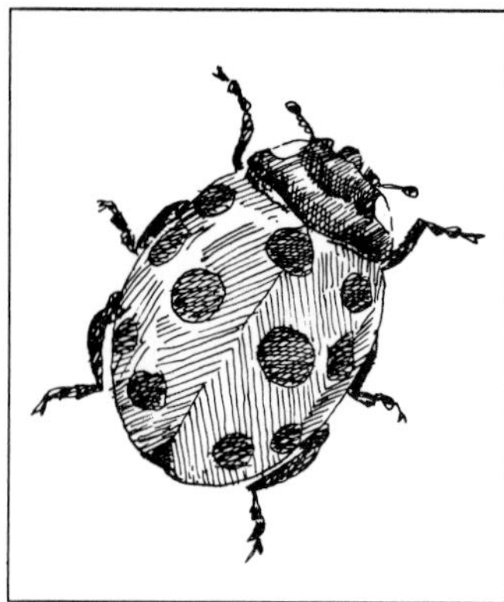

and welcome feature of most gardens and greenhouses. Less well known but almost equally voracious are their larvae—like small black crocodiles with yellow, red or orange spots down their backs. Ladybug eggs are bright yellow and come in clusters usually on the underside of leaves.

Ladybugs are not as effective indoors as many other predators, but they should be protected and encouraged. Bring in any you find outside. If you decide to buy ladybugs for a severe infestation of aphids, keep some in reserve in the refrigerator. They will live several weeks there. Release a few more from time to time as needed. It is best to release them in the evening. Screens will prevent them wandering off into the garden.

■ *Phytoseiulius persimilis and Amblyseius californicus.*
Two kinds of predatory mites, both so small as to be almost invisible. They are hard to distinguish from spider mites, but both nymphs and adults eat spider mite eggs. The predatory mites reproduce rapidly and keep the greenhouse spider mite population well under control. They cannot fly, only crawl from leaf to leaf, so they need to be carried to plants that develop spider mites later.

Under the right conditions *Phytoseiulus persimilis* will eliminate red spider mites within two months and starve itself out. They may need to be reintroduced later if reinfestation occurs. They are less effective if temperatures get too high or the air gets too dry. Above 85°F. the spider mites will breed faster than the *Phytoseiulus* mites.

Amblyseius californicus is useful at higher temperatures. It has the additional advantage of eating thrips as well. *Phytoseiulus* and *Amblyseius* can be used together, though they will prey on each other a bit. Both kinds of predatory mites can be bought from commercial sources.

■ *Praying mantises (also called Stick insects).*
Large, awkward-looking insects, surprisingly able to blend into their surroundings and look like twigs. Their narrow, stick-like bodies can be anywhere from 2 to 5 inches long, with long legs and big green eyes. They eat many varieties of insects. The egg cases can be bought in winter. They should be attached to the stem of a large plant or to an out-of-the-way part of the greenhouse and let alone. In

spring they will hatch out and begin foraging.

■ *Spiders.*
Very useful in catching endless small flying insects. Unless you can't bear the untidy look their webs should be left alone.

■ *Syrphid flies.* *See Hover flies*

■ *Tachinid flies.*
Look like large house flies but move more quickly. They lay

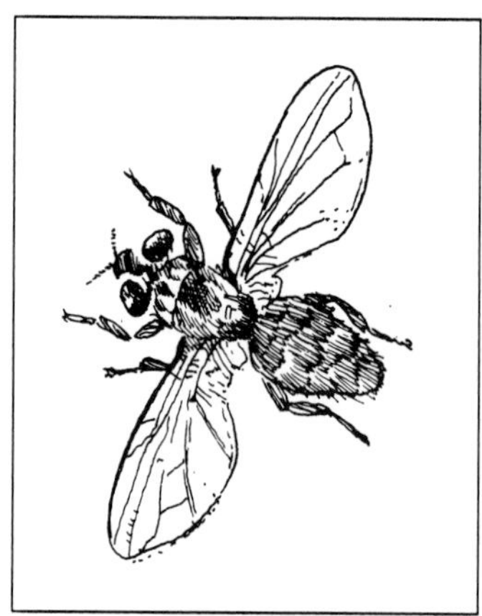

their eggs in many species of caterpillar, in Japanese beetles, earwigs and grasshoppers, so they are decidedly helpful.

■ *Trichogramma wasps.*
Minute wasps, 1/50 of an inch long, which are parasitic

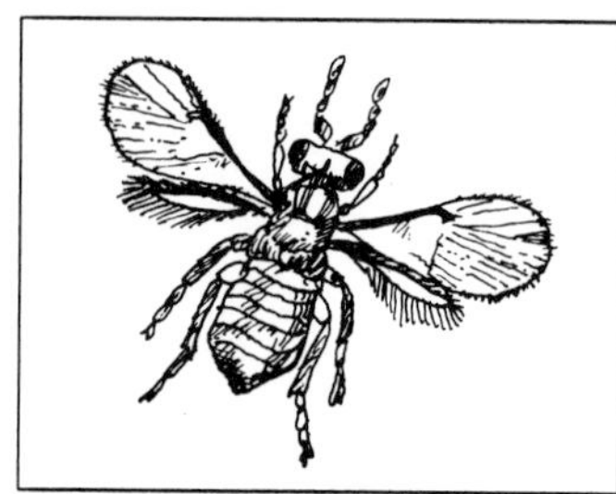

on the eggs of most varieties of caterpillars. The larvae of *Trichogramma* wasps can be bought, but they are more useful outdoors than in, unless you are subject to severe attacks of caterpillars. One pack contains up to four thousand wasp larvae, which should be able to control an area of seven acres. Ideally the wasps should be released at the time the moths are laying eggs.

FROGS, TOADS, AND OTHER SMALL CREATURES

Toads, frogs, newts, salamanders, chameleons, and snakes—if you can find them—will all do a magnificent job of eating a variety of insects in the greenhouse. It is a good idea to leave out saucers of water for them and perhaps provide extra food in winter when the insect populations are low.

NATURAL INSECTICIDES

■ *Ammonia.*
Household ammonia is a good fumigant to get rid of woodlice and earwigs in a greenhouse. Simply shut all the vents, sprinkle ammonia liberally over the floor and leave the greenhouse shut tight overnight.

■ *Bacillus thuringiensis (trade names: Thuricide, Dipel, or Biotrol).*
A bacterial disease which affects several varieties of caterpillars. It is long-lasting, effective, and harmful only to caterpillars, but is probably more useful in the garden than in the greenhouse. Unfortunately it is not very effective on cabbage moths, which usually cause the biggest headache for home gardeners. The spores of the disease are available from any of the major seed companies. Dipel II is said to be effective against woodlice, too.

■ *Ced-O-Flora.*
A natural insect repellent made of pine oils and other plant essences. Very effective against aphids and mealybugs and fairly effective on whiteflies and spider mites. Available from most garden shops.

■ *Derris.*
The roots of a South American plant, which is the main ingredient in rotenone. Good against chewing and sucking insects, especially aphids, but harmful to fish, nesting birds, and some beneficial insects including bees and ladybug larvae. Effective for about 48 hours. Available from garden stores.

■ *Diatomaceous earth (also called Tripoli).*
The fine silica remains of the skeletons of millions of prehistoric one-celled creatures. Kills on contact, probably by dehydration after the silicon pierces the insect's body. Very effective against caterpillars and thrips and harmless to other creatures including earthworms. Can be sprinkled on or diluted with water and sprayed on.

■ *Fertosan (aluminum sulphate).*
This powder has been found to be more effective than poisonous slug baits. It works on contact by damaging the slug's ability to form slime. It is harmful only to mollusks so all animals and beneficial insects are safe. It can be dusted over the soil or diluted with water and sprayed on, and is effective for several months. Avoid contact with plants if possible, especially seedlings, but safe to use on seed flats before sowing. Spraying walls and floors, especially near doors and vents where slugs might enter, should be very effective.

■ *Garlic and red pepper.*
The organic gardener's standby. Many combinations are possible but a typical recipe would be:

3 cloves of garlic or 1 Tbs. garlic powder

1 large onion

1 Tbs. ground cayenne, or 2 whole hot red peppers, or 1 Tbs. Tabasco sauce
½ oz. soft soap (which see) or 1 Tbs. liquid detergent
1 quart water

Blend, strain, and use immediately or store in a glass container in the refrigerator. Mint, horseradish leaves, or ground mustard are sometimes added. Sprayed on plants, it deters most insects, but will not eliminate them.

■ *Hot water.*
Potted plants can be dipped in hot water (140-150°F.) for five minutes to kill aphids, scale, and most other pests, but it may damage the plant as well. It is best to try this when the plant is relatively dormant. Experiment on a single leaf and then on smaller, less valuable specimens before immersing your most treasured plants.

■ *Kerosene. See Rubbing alcohol*

■ *Nettle tea.*
An old biodynamic recipe used both as a fertilizer and an insect repellent. Fill a bucket with stinging nettles and water (preferably rainwater), cover it and leave it in the sun to ferment. In about a week the nettles will have rotted to a slimy mass and the brew will smell terrible. Strain and dilute it with five parts of water to one part nettle concentrate. Use it to spray on plants or drench the soil around them. Excellent against aphids and flea beetles, and said to inhibit fungal diseases. Nettle tea is also a good stimulant for sickly plants.

■ *Nicotine. See Tobacco*

■ *Pirimicarb.*
Not a natural insecticide but the one aphid killer which is completely harmless to all predatory insects.

■ *Pyrethrum.*
The dry flowers of a plant closely related to chrysanthemums. Good against many insects including aphids, thrips, and whitefly, somewhat effective against spider mites, but harmful to fish, bees, and ladybugs. Kills adult *Encarsia* for a period of 24 hours. Harmless to warmblooded animals, but some people are allergic to it and develop a rash.

It is best to grind the flowers yourself as they are most effective when freshly ground. The dust can be sprinkled directly over the plants, or a spray can be made by steeping one teaspoon of ground flowers in one quart of hot water for three hours. Strain, add ½ ounce of soft soap, and spray. Loses its potency twelve hours after the flowers are ground. Pyrethrum plants may be grown outdoors near the greenhouse to discourage pests from coming in. You can collect and dry the flowers yourself. Commercial sprays often combine pyrethrum and rotenone.

■ *Quassia.*
The ground wood of a South American tree with an intensely bitter taste. Makes a good spray against aphids, thrips, slugs, and small caterpillars. None of them like the taste. Soak 2 ounces of quassia in 1 gallon of water for three days. Then simmer slowly for three hours. Strain and mix with 2 ounces of soft soap before spraying.

■ *Red pepper. See Garlic and red pepper*

■ *Rotenone.*
A combination of the roots of two South American plants, derris and lonchocarpus. Kills most pests, but harmful to fish, birds, and most beneficial insects.

■ *Rubbing alcohol, turpentine, or kerosene.*
Effective against mealybugs and almost all other insects. Individual pests can be dabbed with a Q-tip dipped in rubbing alcohol, turpentine, or kerosene, but be careful not to get any on the plant. In heavy infestations, the plant may be sprayed with the mixture of one tablespoon of rubbing alcohol and one pint of water. A teaspoon of camphor dissolved in the alcohol makes it even more effective. Check the effect of this spray on a single leaf before spraying the whole plant, as some plants are sensitive to it.

■ *Ryania.*
Made from the ground wood of a tropical shrub, it is effective at getting rid of aphids. Said to be less harmful than most things to beneficial insects, but no one seems to know for sure.

■ *Safer soap. See Softsoap*

■ *Salt.*
Effective dry, sprinkled on slugs, and it can also be used in a weak solution (1 teaspoon salt to 1 quart water) sprayed on brassicas against cabbage worms or on other plants to combat spider mites. Be careful not to get too much salt on the soil because it reduces fertility.

■ *Soft soap.*
Fels Naptha, ordinary hand soap (chopped up or leftover slivers), green soap, or Ivory Flakes, left in enough water to cover for a few days will form a jelly-like solution that can be added to other aromatic ingredients for a spray that adheres better and will penetrate the protective coating of many insects. If you are in a hurry you can boil the soap and it will liquefy faster. Liquid detergent can be used instead, though some people think it may be harmful to plants.

Diluted with water (2 tablespoons per gallon) soft soap can be used by itself as a spray. Small potted plants can be dipped in the suds: cover the soil and turn the pot upside down, swishing the plant through the suds; rinse well afterwards. Good against aphids and cabbage worms, moderately effective against scale and mealybugs.

Safer Insecticidal Soap, which comes in an easy-to-use liquid form, is a bit more expensive, but it has been specially formulated to be effective against a wide range of insects including aphids, spider mites, whitefly, mealybugs, and scale, and is probably worth the extra money. Although a build-up of soap spray should theoretically clog the pores in the leaves, organically run nurseries often spray weekly with Safer Soap as a preventive measure without having any noticeable effect on plant growth. Be sure not to use too concentrated a solution, though.

■ *Tobacco.*
Every form of tobacco is an effective insecticide. It is also highly toxic to most other creatures including humans, so use with care. Do not breathe it or get it on your skin or in your eyes, and be sure to wash your hands after using. Fortunately, its toxicity dissipates gradually and is pretty much gone in two or three days. It is especially useful against caterpillars and does no harm to ladybugs. Nicotine is the active ingredient in tobacco and can be bought in concentrated form.

You can extract the nicotine yourself by steeping tobacco dust, tobacco stems, chopped-up pipe tobacco, or even cigarette butts in boiling water. Leave them 24 hours, then strain and dilute with 4 pints water to 1 pint tobacco extract. This can be used as is or ¼ ounce of soft soap per quart can be added for a more penetrating spray. Tobacco dust can also be shaken directly over the plants. Nicotine fumigation is effective at getting into all the nooks and crannies of the greenhouse where pests lurk unseen waiting to reinfest the plant after you have cleaned it up. Don't use nicotine or any other tobacco products in a greenhouse with tomatoes, peppers, aubergines, petunias, or other solanaceous plants.

■ *Turpentine. See Rubbing alcohol*

■ *Water.*
A good, hard jet of plain water will remove a proportion of the insects on a plant, will remove dust and dirt that has accumulated on its leaves and seems to have a stimulating overall effect. Hosing the undersides of leaves is especially important since insects congregate there. Cover the soil and turn the plant upside down for a better aim. Rainwater is better than tap water both for watering and making sprays. Some plants resent the residues from hard water, but many more resent water-softening chemicals. ■

APPENDIX

GREENHOUSE AND COMPONENT SUPPLIERS

The following list is by no means complete, but we have included as many as we know of the major manufacturers of greenhouses, components, and auxiliary equipment that may be necessary for putting together a sunspace. Many of the manufacturers supply only the region in which they are located; others have franchise dealers throughout the continental United States and Canada. Contact them for details on your local supplier. A more comprehensive description of the major manufacturers, with photographs of the products, is published annually in *Greenhouses for Living* by the Greenhouses for Living Information Center at 359 Fifth Avenue, Suite 6124, New York 10001. Please note that some manufacturers have been around for a century or more, but the majority are relatively recently formed companies. Our information is correct to the best of our knowledge at the time of publication.

■ *The National Greenhouse Manufacturers Association (NGMA)* is a trade organization for producers, suppliers, and distributors of residential and commercial greenhouses and related products. It publishes standards on such matters as design loadings for greenhouse structures, ventilating and cooling, and the energy transmission of glazing materials. Information on the association and its members is available from:

NGMA,
P.O. Box 567,
Pana, Illinois 62557.
Telephone: (217) 562-2644.

PREFABRICATED ALUMINUM SUNSPACES

These are manufacturers of aluminum-framed greenhouses. Nearly all manufacturers now produce a curved-eave model, and many produce straight eave designs as well. With aluminum sunspaces it is worth looking for a glazing bar that has a 100 percent thermal break (i.e., there is no direct metal connection between the outer aluminum coverstrip and inner aluminum bar, the connecting members usually being plastic). It is also worth making sure that the glazing bars themselves are of a sturdy construction and have a good quality anodized finish. Most manufacturers offer a range of colored, anodized or baked-enamel finishes for low maintenance. Check the quality of the double-glazed units available. Most manufacturers also provide a wide variety of other products such as blinds for thermal and solar control, louvers, and fans for ventilation.

The name in parentheses is the tradename of the product in those cases where it is distinctly different from the manufacturer's name.

■ *Advance Energy Technologies (Zeroenergy System)*
P.O. Box 387
Clifton Park, NY 12065
(800) 351-1155; in NY
(800) 342-9830

■ *American Solar Systems, Ltd. (Sola-Room)*
13201 Hancock Dr.
Taylor, MI 48180
(313) 374-5300; (800) 628-2828

■ *Atria, Inc. (Solar Environment)*
10301 North Enterprise
P.O. Box 47
Mequon, WI 53092
(414) 242-2000

■ *Better Products, Inc.*
P.O. Box 1052
Alamosa, CO 81101
(303) 589-3032

■ *Commonwealth Solaroom-Greenhouse Corporation*
Rte 6, Box 302
Warrenton, VA 22186
(703) 349-1900

■ *California Solarium Products, Inc.*
5403 Ayon Avenue
Irwindale, CA. 91706
(818) 969-6767; (800) 344-7285

■ *English Greenhouse Products Corporation (Florex, Everlite, Excalibur)*
1501 Admiral Wilson Blvd.
Camden, NJ 08109
(609) 966-6161; (800) 223-0867

■ *Florian Greenhouse, Inc. (Sierra Room)*
64 Airport Road
West Milford, NJ 07480
(201) 728-7800; (800) 356-7426

■ *Four Seasons Solar Products Corp.*
5005 Veterans Memorial Highway
Holbrook, Farmingdale, NY 11741
(516) 563-4000

■ *Gammans Industries Inc.*
P.O. Box 1181
Newnan, GA 30264
(404) 253-8692

■ *Habitek, Inc. (Solarium One, Solarium Two)*
102 Queens Dr.
King of Prussia, PA 19406
(215) 962-0240

■ *Janco Greenhouses*
J.A. Nearing Co.
9390 Davis Ave., Dept. GF-E
Laurel, MD 20707
(301) 498-5700

■ *Lord and Burnham (Sol-Air-lum) Division of Lord and Burnham Corp.*
P.O. Box 255
2 Main St.
Irvington, NY 10533
(914) 591-8800

■ *National Greenhouse Co.*
P.O. Box 100
400 E. Main St.
Pana, IL 62557
(217) 562-9333; (800) 826-9314

■ *Paeco Industries Inc.*
(Sol-Area Sunroom)
P.O. Box 968
1 Executive Drive
Tom's River, NJ 08753
(201) 747-6184; (800) 631-2161

■ *Pella Rolscreen Company*
102 Main Street
Pella, IA 50219
(515) 628-1000.

■ *Serres Solarium Ltd.*
1195 Rue Principale
Granby, Quebec J2G 868 Canada
(514) 378-3211; (800) 363-7075

■ *Solar Components Corporation*
(Kalwall, Kalcurve, Sunlite)
88 Pine Street
Manchester, NH 03103
(603) 668-8186; (800) 258-3072

■ *Solar Resources Inc.*
(Solar Room)
P.O. Box 1848
Taos, NM 87571
(505) 758-9344

■ *Solarium Systems Inc.*
5340 Shoreline Blvd.
Mound, MN 55364
(612) 472-5556

■ *Solite Solar Systems*
1145 Bronx River Ave.
Bronx, NY 10472
(212) 842-4441

■ *The Sun Company*
14217 NE 200th St.
Woodinville, WA 98072
(206) 487-3834

■ *Sun Room Designs*
Corner of Depot and First St.
Youngwood, PA 15697
(412) 925-1100; (800) 621-1110

■ *Sun System Solar Greenhouses*
60 Vanderbilt Motor Parkway
Commack, NY 11725
(516) 543-7600.

■ *Sunbilt Solar Products Inc.*
109 180th Street
Jamaica, NY 11433
(718) 297-6040

■ *Sunglo Solar Greenhouses*
4441 26th Avenue West
Seattle, WA 98199
(206) 284-8900; (800) 647-0606

■ *Sunplace Inc.*
P.O. Box 236, Dept. DL-1
Hinesburg, VT 05461
(802) 482-2163

■ *Texas Greenhouse Company*
2779 St. Louis Avenue
Fort Worth, TX 76110
(817) 926-5447

■ *21st Century Limited*
(Skytech Systems)
P.O. Box 763
Bloomsburg, PA 17815
(717) 389-1111

■ *Vegetable Factory Inc.*
(Sun-Porch)
P.O. Box 2235
New York, NY 10163
(212) 867-0110; (800) 221-2550

PREFABRICATED TIMBER SUNSPACES

The following manufacturers produce wooden greenhouses and sunspaces either to a traditional design or using curved, laminated timber beams spanning both the front wall and the roof. Look for high quality glazing and glazing systems; it is more difficult to get a tightly sealed and weatherproof glazed skin with timber than with aluminum. It is also important to make sure that all timber is kiln-dried to avoid shrinkage and the possibility of sap exuding from it under greenhouse conditions. Many manufacturers use cedar or hardwood in place of redwood to produce greater durability and a better finish.

■ *Brady and Sun, Inc.*
97 Webster Street
Worcester, MA 01603
(617) 755-9580; (800) 722-1900

■ *Brother Sun Glass and Window Center*
2907 Agua Fria
Santa Fe, NM 87501
(505) 471-5157

■ *Classic Solar Design Inc.*
(Classic Solar Sunroom, Classic Solar Atrium)
200-7 East Second St.
Huntington Station, NY 11746
(516) 385-9475

■ *Contemporary Structures Inc.*
1102 Center Street
Ludlow, MA 01056
(413) 583-8300

■ *Creative Structures Inc.*
RD1, Box 173
Walnut Lane
Quakertown, PA 18951
(215) 538-2426

■ *Evergreen Systems USA, Inc.*
P.O. Box 128
Highway 26
Burnett, WI 53922
(414) 689-2471

■ *Freedom Sunspace*
RD 5, Box 172
Freehold, NJ 07728
(201) 577-8142

■ *Green Mountain Homes, Inc.*
RFD 1, Waterman Rd.
Royalton, VT 05068
(802) 763-8384

■ *Habitat Solar Rooms*
123 Elm Street
South Deerfield, MA 01373
(413) 665-4006; (800) 992-0121

■ *LRC Products*
(Sun Shed Leisure Room)
P.O. Box 706
Warsaw, IN 46580
(219) 267-6561

■ *Lindal Cedar Homes, Inc.*
P.O. Box 24426
Seattle, WA 98124
(206) 725-0900

■ *Machin Designs (USA) Inc.*
557 Danbury Rd.
Wilton, CT 06897
(203) 834-9566

■ *Northern Sun Inc.*
P.O. Box 3516
Redmond, WA 98073
(206) 885-1700

■ *Pacific Coast Greenhouse Mfg. Co.*
8360 Industrial Avenue
Cotati, CA 94928
(707) 795-2164

■ *Santa Barbara Greenhouses*
1115 Avenue Acaso, Suite J
Camarillo, CA 93010
(805) 482-3765

■ *Solar Additions, Inc.*
(Nature's Arch)
P.O. Box 241
Greenwich, NY 12834
(518) 692-9673; (800) 833-2300

■ *Sturdi-Built Greenhouse Mfg. Co.*
11304 SW Boones Ferry Road
Portland, OR 97219
(503) 244-4100

■ *The Sun Company*
14217 NE 200th Street
Woodinville, WA 98072
(206) 487-3834

■ *Sun Room Company*
P.O. Box 301
2761 Creek Hill Road
Leola, PA 17540
(717) 656-8018; (717) 656-9391

■ *Sunworks Greenhouses*
3060 S. Twenty-fourth St.
Kansas City, KA 66106
(913) 362-8724

■ *21st Century Ltd.*
(Skytech Systems)
P.O. Box 763
Bloomsburg, PA 17815
(717) 389-1111

■ *Westview Products, Inc.*
12775 Westview Drive
Dallas, OR 97338
(503) 623-5174

GLAZING SYSTEMS, PANELS, ETC.

The following manufacturers produce components that are useful in the design and construction of sunspaces. Some of them also produce complete kit-built units.

■ *Abundant Energy Inc.*
P.O. Box 307
Pine Island, NY 10969
(914) 258-4022

Seal-Safe extruded aluminum glazing system for use on timber glazing bars.

■ *Brother Sun Glass and Window Center*
2907 Agua Fria
Santa Fe, NM 87501
(505) 471-5157

■ *Fox Plastics Corporation*
(Foxlite)
8300 Dayton Road
Fairborn, OH 45324
(513) 864-1966; (800) 233-3699

Manufactures triple-glazed dome skylights.

■ *Pella/Rolscreen Company*
102 Main Street
Pella, IA 50219
(515) 628-1000

High quality windows, doors, and roof-glazing systems incorporating fine venetian blinds.

■ *Skymaster Skylights*
413 Virginia Drive
Orlando, FL 32803
(305) 898-2881

Manufactures double-glazed skylights and rooflights

■ *Solar Components Corporation*
88 Pine Street
Manchester, NH 03105
(603) 668-8186

Kalwall twin-wall fiberglass panels and Kalcurve solariums; also manufactures Sunlite Greenhouses and fiberglass water storage containers.

■ *Vegetable Factory Inc.*
P.O. Box 2235
New York, NY 10163
(212) 867-0110; (800) 221-2550

Offers a range of fiberglass or acrylic glazing panels.

■ *Velux-America Inc.*
P.O. Box 3208
Greenwood, SC 29648
(803) 223-3149

A complete range of rooflights with different types of glazing, blinds, remote controls, etc.

■ *Ventarama Skylight Corp.*
140 Cantiague Rock Road
Hicksville, NY 11801
(516) 931-0202; (800) 237-8096

Manufactures double-glazed rooflights and skylights.

GLASS MANUFACTURERS

Glass manufacturers will supply glass direct or, more usually, through a network of dealers who also produce sealed double-glazed units. Contact the manufacturer for names and addresses of local dealers and fabricators. Major manufacturers other than those listed below include Corning Glass Works, Ford Glass Division, General Glass International Corp., Libby-Owens-Ford, and PPG Industries.

■ *AFG Industries, Inc.*
P.O. Box 929
Kingsport, TN 37662
(615) 229-7200; (800) 251-0441

Manufactures Solatex low-iron glass and Comfort-E hard-coat low-E glass.

■ *SNE Corporation (Crestline, Vetter)*
P.O. Box 1007
Wausau, WI 54401
(715) 845-1161

Imports Enerpane gas-filled, soft-coat low-E, double-glazed units from Switzerland.

■ *Sentinel Agencies Inc.*
P.O. Box 905
Miami, FL 33137
(305) 573-7600

Imports Glaverbel hard-coat low-E glass from Belgium.

LOW-EMISSIVITY PLASTIC FILMS

The 3-M Company also manufactures a low-E film.

■ *Southwall Technologies*
1029 Corporation Way
Palo Alto, CA 94303
(415) 962-9111

Manufactures Heat Mirror low-E film.

ACRYLIC AND POLYCARBONATE SHEET

Major manufacturers other than those listed below include DuPont, General Electric, and Rohm and Haas.

■ *CYRO Industries*
155 Tice Blvd
Woodcliff Lake, NJ 07675
(201) 930-0100

Exolite double-skin panels and Cyroflex twin-wall polycarbonate.

MOVABLE INSULATION SYSTEMS

■ *Appropriate Technology Corporation*
7 Technology Drive
P.O. Box 975
Brattleboro, VT 05301
(802) 257-4500

Manufactures Window Quilt roller blinds.

■ *Dirt Road Co.*
R.D. 1, Box 260
Waitsfield, VT 05673
(802) 496-2373

Manufactures insulating window shades.

■ *Hunter Douglas Inc. (Duette Window Fashions)*
601 Alter St.
Broomfield, CO 80020

Manufactures a pleated shade.

■ *Boston Shutter and Door*
P.O. Box 888
Island Mill
Keene, NH 03431
(603) 352-2726

Manufactures Boston Shutter (formerly Insulshutter) and Boston Louver (formerly Insul-Louver) timber-faced insulating shutters for windows and rooflights.

■ *Zomeworks Corporation*
P.O. Box 25805
Albuquerque, NM 87125
(505) 242-5354

Manufactures magnetic clips for do-it-yourself foam shutters, plus Skylid insulating louvers, Beadwall movable insulation systems, and Big Fin solar water heaters.

SOLAR SHADING SYSTEMS

The following manufacturers produce internal and external solar shading devices.

■ *Nicolon Corporation (Solar Guard, Solar Screen) Baycor Division*
3150 Holcomb Bridge Road
Suite 300 Norcross, GA 30071
(404) 447-6272

■ *Shading Systems Incorporated*
P.O. Box 5697
Clark, NJ 07066
(201) 686-4466

The following manufacturers produce track-mounted shading and insulating systems primarily for commercial greenhouses:

■ *Automatic Devices Co.*
2121 South Twelfth Street
Allentown, PA 18103
(215) 797-6000

■ *Sarlon Industries Inc.*
775 NW 71st Street
Miami, FL 33150
(305) 836-0530

THERMAL STORAGE

Major manufacturers of thermal storage units in addition to those listed below include Dow Chemical.

■ *One Design Inc.*
Mountain Falls Route
Winchester, VA 22601
(703) 877-2172

Manufactures containers for water storage within studwalls.

■ *Solar Components Corporation (Kalwall)*
88 Pine St.
Manchester, NH 03105
(603) 668-8186

Manufactures fiberglass tubes for vertical water storage, plus phase-change materials encapsulated in fiberglass solar pods for installation in studwalls.

HEAT PISTON VENT OPENERS

■ *Dalen Products Inc. (SolarVent)*
11110 Gilbert Drive
Knoxville, TN 37932
(615) 966-3256

Manufactures automatic, solar-operated greenhouse or cold-frame ventilator.

■ *Heat Motors Inc.*
635 West Grandview Avenue
Sierra Madre, CA 91024
(818) 355-6919

■ *Thermofor Vent Openers*
Bramen Co.
P.O. Box 70
Salem, MA 01970
(617) 745-7765

SUNSPACE FANS

■ *Ventaxia Inc.*
P.O. Box 2204
4F Henshaw Street
Woburn, MA 01801
(617) 935-4735

■ *Weather Energy Systems Inc.*
P.O. Box 459
Kendrick Road
West Wareham, MA 02576
(617) 295-8103

Fans and motorized vent openers are also available through many of the following greenhouse suppliers.

GENERAL GREENHOUSE SUPPLIES AND EQUIPMENT

■ *Charley's Greenhouse Supply*
1569 Memorial Highway
Mt. Vernon, WA 98273
(206) 428-2626

■ *Domestic Grower's Supply*
P.O. Box 809
Cave Junction, OR 97523
(503) 592-3615

■ *E.C. Geiger*
Box 285
Harleysville, PA 19438
(215) 256-6511; (800) 443-4437

■ *Friends of the Sun*
Putney Rd.
Brattleboro, VT 05301
(802) 254-4208

■ *Gardener's Supply Company*
128 Intervale Rd.
Burlington, VT 05401
(802) 863-4535

■ *George Ball Inc. Greenhouse Supplies*
P.O. Box 335
West Chicago, IL 60185
(312) 231-3500

■ *Indoor Gardening Supplies*
P.O. Box 40567H
Detroit, MI 48240
(313) 277-1960

■ *Mellinger's, Inc.*
2310 West South Range Rd.
North Lima, OH 44452
(216) 549-9861

■ *Necessary Trading Co.*
P.O. Box 305
Main St.
Newcastle, VA 24127
(703) 864-5103

■ *Solar Components Corporation*
88 Pine St.
Manchester, NH 03103
(603) 668-8186; (800) 258-3072

■ *Stuppy Greenhouse Manufacturing, Inc.*
P.O. Box 12456
No. Kansas City, MO 64116
(816) 842-6796

BENEFICIAL INSECTS

■ *Abbott Laboratories*
14th and Sheridan Roads
North Chicago, IL 60064
(312) 937-6100; (800) 323-9100

Bacillus thuringiensis

■ *Natural Pest Controls*
8864 Little Creek Dr.
Orangevale, CA 95662
(916) 726-0855

Predator mites, scale parasites, green lacewings, cryptolameus (mealybug predator), ladybugs, praying mantis

■ *Organic Control, Inc.*
P.O. Box 78999
Los Angeles, CA 90019
(213) 937-7444

Bacillus thuringiensis

■ *Rincon Vitova*
P.O. Box 95
Oakview, CA 93022
(805) 643-5407

Green lacewings, ladybugs, predator mites, encarsia formosa, cryptolameus (mealybug predator)

SUGGESTED READING

Brookes, John. *The Indoor Garden Book.* London: Dorling Kindersley, 1986. A masterly guide to the use of plants, including cut and dried flower arrangements as well as houseplants, as decorative features in the home; beautifully illustrated.

Clegg, Peter, and Derry Watkins. *The Complete Greenhouse Book.* Pownal, VT: Garden Way Publishing, 1978.

Fichter, George. *Insect Pests: A Guide to More Than 350 Pests of Home, Garden, Field, and Forest.* New York: Western Publishing Co., 1966. Good pictorial guide to pest identification.

Foster, Catherine O. *The Organic Gardener.* New York: Alfred A. Knopf, Inc., 1972.

Gloag, John. *Victorian Comfort: A Social History of Design from 1830-1900.* New York: David and Charles, 1980. Victorian values and mores as reflected in the architecture of the time.

Greenhouses for Living. New York: The Greenhouse for Living Information Center. Contains a national directory of sunspace builders and dealers. This annual guide comparing over 100 prefabricated sunspaces may be obtained from the publisher at 350 Fifth Ave., Suite 6124, New York, NY 10001 (telephone: 212-967-8382).

Hill, Lewis. *Secrets of Plant Propagation.* Pownal, VT: Garden Way Publishing, 1985.

Hix, John. *The Glass House.* Cambridge, MA: MIT Press, 1974. A complete history of the artificial climates people have devised to protect their plants, from the Greeks through the Victorians to present-day agribusinesses and even science fiction visions of the future.

Hussey, N.W., and Nigel Eric Anthony Scopes, eds. *Biological Pest Control: The Glasshouse Experience.* Poole, Dorset, England: Blandford Press, 1985. An up-to-date and unbiased assessment of organic methods of controlling greenhouse pests. Excellent background information on the lifecycles of individual pests, plus detailed information on what conditions foster success and what sprays can be used at what stages without harming particular predators.

Jacobs, Betty E. *Growing and Using Herbs Successfully.* Pownal, VT: Garden Way Publishing, 1981.

Jones, Robert, and Robert McFarland. *The Sunspace Primer; Guide for Solar Heating.* New York: Van Nostrand Reinhold Co., 1984. Accurate and detailed information on all aspects of passive solar heating.

Klein, Miriam. "Biological Management of Passive Solar Greenhouses." Butte, MT: National Center for Alternative Technology. An annotated bibliography and resource list, available from NCAT, P.O. Box 3838, Butte, MT 59701.

Koppelkamm, Stefan. *Glasshouses and Wintergardens of the Nineteenth Century.* New York: Rizzoli International Publications, 1984. A history of the Victorian love affair with cast iron and glass; mostly public buildings.

Larson, Roy, editor. *Introduction to Floriculture.* New York: Academic, 1980. Each chapter is written by a different specialist and devoted to one particular plant or plant type. Although written for commercial flower growers, much is adaptable to the home greenhouse.

Mastalerz, John. *The Greenhouse Environment.* New York: John Wiley and Sons, 1977. A textbook for greenhouse managers that incorporates the latest research in order to develop a full understanding of all aspects of plant growth.

Mazria, Edward. *The Passive Solar Energy Book.* Emmaus, PA: Rodale Press, 1979. Good on overhangs, reflectors, and heat storage.

Moore, Charles W., Gerald Allen, and Donlyn Lyndon. *The Place of Houses.* New York: Holt, Rinehart and Winston, 1979. Helpful guide to principles of house design decisions, though not specifically sunspace design.

Olgyay, Victor V. *Design with Climate.* Princeton: Princeton University Press, 1963. Basic book on energy-efficient house design.

Philbrick, John, and Helen Philbrick. *The Bug Book.* Pownal, VT: Garden Way Publishing, 1974.

Reader's Digest Editors. *Success with Houseplants.* Pleasantville, NY: Random House, 1979. Thorough and accurate guide to the needs of almost all the ornamental plants grown indoors; no food crops.

Reader's Digest Encyclopaedia of Garden Plants and Flowers. London: Reader's Digest Association Ltd., 1971. How to grow and propagate every conceivable garden plant, including many grown under glass; good for plant identification. This English book will need some adaptation for local climatic conditions in the United States.

Riotte, Louise. *Roses Love Garlic: Secrets of Companion Planting with Flowers.* Pownal, VT: Garden Way Publishing, 1983.

———. *Carrots Love Tomatoes: Secrets of Companion Planting for Successful Gardening.* Pownal, VT: Garden Way Publishing, 1986.

Rodale, J.I., editor. *The Basic Book of Organic Gardening.* New York: Ballantine, 1981.

Sanders' Encyclopaedia of Gardening. 22nd ed. London: Collingridge Books and Hamlyn Publishing Group, 1971. Similar to the *Reader's Digest Encyclopaedia of Garden Plants and Flowers;* though less detailed, contains a wider range of plants.

Shapiro, Andrew. *The Homeowner's Complete Handbook for Add-on Solar Greenhouses and Sunspaces.* Emmaus, PA: Rodale Press, 1985. Detailed discussion of choosing solar greenhouse size, shape, and details to match the heat output to the needs of your house.

Smith Miranda. *Greenhouse Gardening.* Emmaus, PA: Rodale Press, 1985. Practical advice and background information on how plants grow and what they need.

Smith, Shane. *The Bountiful Solar Greenhouse.* Santa Fe, NM: John Muir Publications, 1982. Good on edible greenhouse crops.

Solar Age. Harrisville, NH. Monthly magazine for solar energy enthusiasts.

Solit, Karen, and Jim Solit. *Keep Your Gift Plants Thriving.* Pownal, VT: Garden Way Publishing, 1985.

Stewart, Annie, and Richard Sassaman, editors. *A Solar Greenhouse Guide for the Pacific Northwest.* Seattle, WA: Ecotope Group, 1979.

Taylor, Jasmine, editor. *Conservatories and Garden Rooms.* London: Macdonald and Co., 1985. More mouth-watering than practical, this lavishly illustrated collection emphasizes interior design.

Tressider, Jane, and Stafford Cliff. *Living Under Glass.* London: Thames and Hudson, 1986.

Westcott, Cynthia. *The Gardener's Bug Book.* New York: Doubleday and Co., Inc., 1973. A massive reference work identifying and combatting all insect pests.

Yanda, Bill and Rick Fisher. *The Food and Heat Producing Solar Greenhouse.* Rev. ed. Santa Fe: John Muir Publications, 1980. Classic description of how to build and run a very cheap, efficient solar greenhouse. ■

INDEX

(Numbers in boldface indicate illustrations)

E

F

G

H

I

J

K

L

M